MORPHS, MALLARDS & MONTAGES

MORPHS, MALLARDS & MONTAGES

COMPUTER-AIDED IMAGINATION

Andrew Glassner

A K Peters
Wellesley, Massachusetts

Editorial, Sales, and Customer Service Office

A K Peters, Ltd.
888 Worcester Street, Suite 230
Wellesley, MA 02482
www.akpeters.com

Library of Congress Cataloging-in-Publication Data

Glassner, Andrew S.
   Morphs, mallards, and montages : computer-aided imagination / Andrew Glassner.
      p. cm.
   Includes bibliographical references and index.
   ISBN 1-56881-231-0

    1. Computer graphics. I. Title.

T385.G583 2004
006.6–dc22

                                                     2004050378

Morphs, Mallards, and Montages
Designed by Darren Wotherspoon
Composed in New Century Schoolbook with display lines in Century Gothic
Printed and Manufactured by Replika Press, Haryana, India
Cover Design by Judith Arisman

Printed in India
08 07 06 05 04   10 9 8 7 6 5 4 3 2 1

To Eric Haines

Contents

Introduction

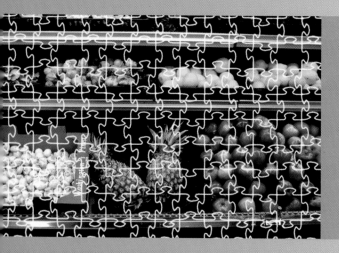

I love computer graphics, and I love to write.

Since 1996, I've been writing a regular column called *Andrew Glassner's Notebook* for the bimonthly magazine *IEEE Computer Graphics & Applications*. The chapters in this book are derived from those columns, but I've looked at each one with a fresh eye. I've restored material that had to be cut due to space limitations, fixed errors, and revised, expanded, corrected, and improved both the text and the figures.

This book is for everyone who's interested in computer graphics and how it can take us on exciting journeys powered by imagination and a love of discovery and invention.

THE JOY OF COMPUTER GRAPHICS

There's something wonderful about computer graphics. Ever since I first started working with computers, I've used them to make pictures of some sort.

I made my first images in the mid 1970s on a Teletype machine connected to a PDP-8/E minicomputer. The output media it offered were pretty limited: I could print out ASCII characters on a long scroll of paper, or punch out holes on a yellow strip of paper tape. Our technologies are much more advanced now, but the fun of making pictures with computers is undiminished.

One of the beauties of computer graphics is that we can build up our understanding and knowledge of something by experimenting with it.

Once we think we know something about a topic, we can write some code and make some pictures. The pictures themselves will tell us how well we understand what's going on. If we're trying to see where a leopard's spots come from, and we produce a flat field of grey, we probably need to think about things a little more.

Once we have a start on how something works, another beauty of graphics comes into play: we can change it! We can modify the code, play with the controls, and generally follow our intuition to develop new kinds of techniques for making images.

As in so many aspects of life, everything begins by asking the right question.

THE RIGHT QUESTION

In school we spend a lot of time thinking about good answers, but in creative pursuits it's often more important to ask good questions.

Suppose you've landed a job as a professor of computer science in a university, or you're a computer scientist in an industrial research lab. In most of these situations, part of your job is to figure out what you should do with your days. In other words, you need to come up with research topics. If you have students to advise, you may have to come up with topics for them as well. Research topics are basically questions.

Perhaps you're feeling really ambitious. You might ask this question to direct your work: "How do I build a time-travel machine?" Now I have to admit that I absolutely love this question; it's given rise to some great stories and films, and it actually has led to very interesting discoveries by theoretical physicists. But for most computer-based explorers, this isn't a very good question. It's too diffuse, and there's no clear way to start. How do you even begin to tackle a question like this? What do you need to know? What equipment do you have to acquire or build? Nobody has a clue. The question is too vague, and there's no answer in sight.

How do we find a better question? Many of the best research questions contain within themselves the seeds of their own answer (of course, this doesn't apply to the great existential questions like "What is the purpose of my life?").

To illustrate this, let's think about the perennial question, "What's for lunch?" There's not much we can do to actually answer this question without first getting a whole lot of additional information. The way it stands, it's not something we can answer very well.

Let's refine the question a bit. How about, "What can I make for lunch using what's in the kitchen right now?" Ah, much better. If your kitchen is anything like mine, this question immediately excludes meals like iguana cake, caviar fondue, or moose ravioli. But we still have too much ambiguity in this question to really give a good answer. Let's reduce the possibilities a little more, add some more context, and sharpen the question.

"What's the most nutritious sandwich I can make in 10 minutes using what's in the kitchen right now?" Now that's a good research question. Obviously the other questions were important in reaching this point, but this question finally gives us something we can directly go about answering. If you're strapped for time, you can give this question to someone else, and if they're competent, they can come up with a perfectly good answer. This question contains the seeds of its own answer, because the question itself tells us what information to gather and how to evaluate it. There's still significant work to be done, but the heart of the solution is right there in the question.

The chapters in this book are each the result of having followed chains of thought like this, refining a question from a vague musing like "What's for lunch?" to something specific enough that I could actually turn it into something real. The first inspiration, often borne of intuition, is clarified with context and particulars, often the result of applied analytic thought. While thinking about a topic, I frequently bounce back and forth between these logical and intuitive ways of thinking, which is a big part of the fun!

THE PROCESS

Of course, the creative process is anything but a clean, linear chain of events. The clearest indication of that is in the messy and often contradictory notes I make while working on a project, and in the nature of the code. When I write software for a project, of course I try to write the cleanest and most careful code I can. But that's only the start of the process, because it's by playing with that code that I start to really understand the problem I'm trying to address. I might even realize that I've been answering the wrong question, and then I gradually redirect things in a different direction.

So the software changes, accumulating late-night patches, stop-gap measures followed by temporary fixes, special-case handlers, and debugging statements, until ultimately the software looks like spaghetti. I'm so intimately familiar with the code that I know how to keep it from crashing (usually), but I would be horrified to let anyone else see what I've written. The software is my learning experience captured in code and often has as many dead ends and strange little pieces as the most fossil-rich valley found by any archaeologist.

The descriptions of the algorithms and techniques in this book are based on the best versions that I developed through this iterative development process. Usually I keep hacking away at something until I find a solution that I feel solves the problem nicely. It's hard to quantify this, but a good solution has a feeling of elegance and even inevitability: It's just so clear that it *feels* right. When I've found that answer, and it's embodied in the code and it works the way I expect, I know I've found the approach that I'll describe in the text. I usually leave the dead ends and false starts unmentioned. Like the pencil sketches that lie buried under layers of paint in an oil painting, they're necessary precursors, but it's the final result that gets shown.

I've developed these projects on a regular schedule. My column appeared every other month, so every eight weeks I had to have new text and figures ready for the publisher. If I needed to write (and debug!) software to make the figures and present the material, I had to make sure I started soon enough that I could make the deadline.

ABOUT THE BOOK

Nothing in this book assumes you have any particular hardware or software. Sometimes I'll mention the tools that I used, but I rarely talk about the mechanics of any particular product.

One place where I do go into mechanics is in the math. If you flip through this book, you may notice that most of the chapters have equations mixed in with the text. You don't need to read the math to understand the material, and you certainly don't need to pay it much attention the first time you read a chapter. When I read material with math in it, usually I simply skip over the equations on my first reading.

The math in this book serves the same function as the blueprints for a building. Think of the chapters as discussions of different buildings, each with pictures of their internal decoration and discussions of their designs. If you want to know how each building was constructed, or the details of some particular joint or fitting, the blueprints give you specific answers for those details. If you plan to construct the building yourself, you'll probably want to study those blueprints at some point, to make sure that your version will stand up. But when you're first reading about the building, studying the blueprints is overkill.

I've included the math so that you can reproduce everything I've done: it makes the presentation precise and avoids the ambiguity of words. If you don't care for that insider's detail, you can simply skip over the math without harm.

As I mentioned, nothing in this book requires you to have any particular software or hardware. But I believe that our work is influenced by our tools, so I'll take a moment here to share with you the tools that I used to develop this material.

Everything begins with an observation or an idea, and then pencil and paper. I doodle and make notes, think about connections and make drawings, and fill page after page of scrap paper. I usually fill up at least 20 or 30 pages of notes before I even begin to feel the shape of the column take form.

I work on a dual-processor Pentium computer running Windows XP. I write my text using Visual SlickEdit, in the vi emulation mode (I got used to the text editor vi while still an undergraduate, and the vi commands are burned deeply into my nervous system). I write the text as LaTeX, and I use the public-domain MiKTeX system to convert my plain text into PDF files.

I draw my line art with Adobe Illustrator, and my raster art with Adobe Photoshop and Corel Painter. To quickly sort through my pictures I use ACDSee.

For three-dimensional work, I use 3ds max by Discreet. Most of the rendered images in this book were created using the Brazil rendering system by Splutterfish. I used Poser by Curious Labs for human figures, which I import into max for rendering. I've used public-domain models and textures for some of the images.

To make most of the graphs and charts, I used Mathematica from Wolfram Research, which I also used to compute some of the data and to double-check my algebraic results.

I've written all the code here using Microsoft's development environments. The first few projects were written in C using Visual Studio, while the last few were in C# using Visual .NET.

ACKNOWLEDGEMENTS

I often draw on the help of my friends and colleagues as I work on these projects. They offer expertise, advice, support, feedback, and help, and I am very grateful to them all. In alphabetical order, thank you to Steve Blackmon, Eric Braun, Matt Conway, Becky Brendlin, Maarten van Dantzich, Lisa DeGisi, Steven Drucker, Bruce Glassner, Ned Greene, Eric Haines, Greg Hitchcock, Scott Kirvan, Tom McClure, Frieda Monroe, Paul Perrault, Tom Rieke, Claude Robillard, Sally Rosenthal, Christopher Rosenfelder, and Geraldine Wade.

Introduction

Thank you to Tammi Titsworth, my editor at CG&A who improves everything I write, and CG&A Editor-in-Chief John Dill for the freedom to choose my own topics and the pages in which to print them. Thank you to Alice and Klaus Peters, Darren Wotherspoon, and the rest of the crew at A K Peters for their help in putting this project together.

WRAPPING UP

Writing these columns has been an invigorating mixture of pleasingly hard work, original research, library reading, analytical thought, hands-off daydreaming, programming, writing, photography, and conversations.

I hope you enjoy reading them as much as I enjoyed creating them!

Andrew Glassner
Seattle, Washington

Interactive Pop-Up Card Design

1

I love pop-up cards. They're fun to make and receive, and it's a pleasure to watch three-dimensional shapes appear out of nowhere, jump up off the page, and reach for the sky. And as an output medium for three-dimensional computer graphics, they're just a perfect match.

I've made and sent out original pop-up cards each time I've moved to a new house over the last few years. Some of these cards are shown in Figure 1.1.

Anyone who sets out to create their own pop-up cards or books faces two tasks: design and construction. Pop-up design is difficult enough that the really good professionals in the field describe themselves as "paper engineers," and they deserve the title.

Creating a great pop-up presents both artistic and technical challenges. Once you have an idea in mind, you need to think about the best way to bring it about: each pop-up mechanism has its own pros and cons in terms of design time, rigidity, durability, complexity, and construction.

In my experience, coming up with a good idea is just the first step. Typically you want the pieces to unfold and stand upon the "stage" of the card in just the right way, and this is a delicate matter of just how the pieces are shaped and where they're glued down. If during the design stage you build a piece and it's not looking quite right, there's nothing to do except cut a new piece with a slightly different shape, glue it in, and see how that looks. This is a time-consuming process of trial and error. And when several pieces interact, each change to one

 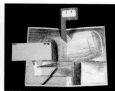 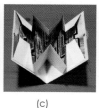  

(a)   (b)   (c)   (d)   (e)

Figure 1.1

Some of my own pop-up cards announcing recent changes of address. (a) The *blank*, or *mechanical*, for a multi-level card. The three V-folds represent mountains, and the curvy path that passes through them was the road I drove across the country. The "road" was pulled up into place by the motion of the V-folds. The final version of the card had artwork on all the pieces. (b) Opening this card causes the envelope to tilt out of the mailbox and the red flag to go up. (c) This is a "no-cut" pop-up that has just been opened. (d) The pop-up of (c) as it opens up. (e) The final version of (c), before the placement of the new contact information in the lower-right.

piece can have a ripple effect, requiring changes to the others. Each iteration of the process can easily take a quarter-hour or more for even simple cards.

Once the design looks right, you then have to make sure that the pieces of your card don't jam up during opening and closing. Getting all the pieces to move in the right ways and not get bent or scrunched against each other is a challenging task.

Once the card is successfully designed, then you have to actually make the thing. This involves cutting out the pieces, decorating them (or affixing decorations to them), gluing them in place, and including any other necessary mechanisms like grommets or string. Making one card is kind of fun, but making fifty quickly becomes tedious.

Each time I've designed and sent out one of my pop-up cards, I've wished I had some kind of tool to help me design the cards and some assistants to help construct them. I can't hire the assistants, but I decided to finally go ahead and make the tool in the form of a Pop-up Design Assistant. In this chapter I'll talk about the issues involved in designing and writing such a program.

My goal in creating my Assistant was not to create pop-up cards for viewing on the computer. That might be fun, but it seems to miss the point, which is the tactile pleasure in opening the card and the delight of feeling it open up. The idea is to make it easier to design wonderful cards that can then be constructed and shared in the real world.

A BIT OF HISTORY

Today we have a great variety of pop-up and moving books to enjoy. This wasn't always the case, of course. The history of pop-up books blends together commerce, innovation, book publishing, personal creativity, and even world events. Movable books were not originally meant for children. In fact, it wasn't until the 1700s that there was any serious trade in children's literature at all. Before that date, all books were for adults and usually serious in subject matter.

The first movable book seems to predate even traditional printed books. In Majorca, a Catalan mystic named Ramon Llull (1235–1316) drew a book that represented his mystical philosophy using a set of differently-sized revolving discs or *volvelles*. He divided up the world into several categories, and within each category he identified entities as either "superior" or "inferior." Some of Llull's categories included things and ideas, substances, adjectives and verbs, and knowledge and actions. He divided each disc up into sectors (like pie wedges) and assigned one theme to each sector. The discs were then cut out and stacked up, so that one needed only to turn the wheels to understand nature, and thus also predict the future.

Volvelles were particularly used for astrology. A Latin manuscript used volvelles to describe the motion of the planets over an almost 400-year period from 1428 to 1808. The first use of volvelles in a printed book was *The Calendarium* by Regiomontanus in 1474. This wasn't really a movable book in today's terms, because you had to cut the discs out and assemble them.

Movable discs were also used for mathematics. In 1551, Johannes Schoner, a Nurenberg professor, published a calculator in movable-disc form in *Opera Mathematica*.

Although the volvelle was popular, as early as the 1300s people were also using flap techniques for mechanical books. These were called *turn-up* or *lift-the-flap* books. They were used in many different fields, but perhaps nowhere as often as in anatomy, because one could simulate a dissection simply by raising up successive layers. One of the most famous examples of an anatomical movable book is Andreas Vesalius' *De humani corporis fabrica librorum epitome*, printed in Basel in 1543. The book presents the chest, abdomen, and viscera through seven highly-detailed, superimposed layers that were hinged at the neck.

All of these books were hand-made. Perhaps the first printed movable book was *Cosmographia Petri Apiani*, an astrological book published in 1564.

In the 1700s the economics of printing changed, and gave birth to a new class of literature: children's books. Most of these books told well-known children's stories and fables that presumably everyone already knew. The value of the books was that children could read them for themselves when their parents weren't there. Movable devices made them even more appealing.

In 1765, the London book publisher Robert Sayer created a series of children's books which he called *metamorphoses*. Sayer took a single large sheet and folded it to create four panels, each of which could be opened to reveal a different scene or bit of verse. Several of the books featured a character from Pantomime Theater known as

Harlequin, so the books also came to be known as *harlequinades*, as well as *turn-up* books.

In the 1860s, a London publisher named Dean and Sons became the first to devote themselves entirely to what was now called the field of children's *toy books*. They created books that were based on the popular *accordion*, or *peep-show* style. The idea was that many layers were stacked up one behind the other. The child opened the book by pulling the layers apart and setting them up on a table. The layers were connected by a ribbon that ran through each one and emerged from the rearmost layer. When the child pulled this ribbon, the structures in each layer were pulled out and into position. Then the child peered through a hole in the front cover to view the newly-created diorama. From the 1860s to about 1900, Dean and Sons produced about 50 toy books based on this principle. Dean and Sons also developed a crude technique for dissolving one picture to another using a low-resolution "Venetian blind" effect (or *jalousie*).

By this time high-quality toy books had become a luxury item for the children of rich Europeans and Americans. In 1891 a German publisher named Ernest Nister started designing new mechanical books in his Nuremberg studio and printing them in Bavaria where costs were low and quality was high. Nister refined the Venetian blind effect and extended it to a circular version that he used in a book called *Magic Windows*. Because he could afford to charge high prices, Nister was able to make very high-quality books and became the best-known publisher of them by the turn of the century. Another of Nister's innovations was that his books did not require a ribbon: the illustrations stood up automatically when the pages were turned.

Although Nister was the best-known publisher of movable books for children, a contemporary of his named Lothar Meggendorfer was setting a new standard for complexity and ingenuity. Meggendorfer was a mechanical wizard who created tiny metal rivets out of very tightly-wound thin copper wire. He embedded these rivets inside double-paned pages and connected them on the outside to colorful, die-cut figures. When a single tab was pulled, the figures moved in elaborate ways in many different directions at once. Some of the actions were even staged to occur in time-delayed sequences as the wire uncoiled from one rivet to the next. Meggendorfer's books were widely praised as much for their humorous visuals and verses as for their innovation and complexity. Even today, Meggendorfer's works are considered some of the finest movable books ever made. His book *The Circus* has been described as one of the most sought-after books of the nineteenth century. Between 1878 and 1910

Meggendorfer wrote and designed over 300 complex, funny, and innovative mechanical books.

World War I put an end to what is now considered the Golden Age of mechanical books.

After the war, movable books were revived by the British publisher Louis "The Wizard" Giraud. From 1929 to 1949 he produced 16 annual books named the *Daily Express Children's Annual*, as well as several books called the *Bookano Stories*. These were called *dimensional books* because they were mostly about depth and perspective, rather than moving parts. He also called them *living models* because they were designed to be viewed from several different directions, like today's books, rather than through a pinhole or from just one point.

Giraud's books delivered two other innovations. First, they were able to lift themselves up when the book was opened 180 degrees. Second, the action sometimes continued even after the book was open. For example, in one particularly clever construction the opening of the pages reveals a clown swinging on a trapeze. Even after the book is completely open, the clown continues to swing back and forth. Although uncredited, it appears that Theodore Brown, an inventor who also worked on motion pictures, was the paper engineer who worked these surprises.

In 1932 the term *pop-up* first appeared. The American publisher Blue Ribbon Publishing of New York created a line of illustrated Disney stories books created by the Ohio artist Harold Lentz, which they called *pop-up books*.

The economics of children's book publishing and mechanical book construction changed for the better in the 1960s. Julian Wehr created a series of movable books featuring colorful, articulated people that moved in response to pulling a tab. At the same time, Czechoslovakian artist Viotech Kubasta created dozens of popular pop-up books based on fairy tales.

Today, many English-language books are designed in Europe and America, but almost all printed and constructed in Columbia, Mexico, and Singapore, where the tedious and painstaking cutting and assembly steps are less expensive.

Publisher Waldo Hunt has estimated that, from 1850 to 1965, a total of less than ten million pop-up books were produced in the entire world. Today, up to 25 million mechanical books are published annually, with 200 to 300 new titles appearing in English every year. Many chain bookstores now have an entire section devoted to pop-up and movable children's books.

Pop-up and movable books have also become popular for adults again. Publishers are discovering that they're a great way to show complicated spatial relationships, as well as surprise, delight, and entertain adult readers.

The best way to learn about pop-up books is to study some great ones. The easiest way to do that is to observe the works of the masters: buy great pop-up books and carefully disassemble them, learning the techniques of the best paper engineers by reverse-engineering their constructions.

The books I like the best are generally for children, where the designers are able to really cut loose and blend their talent for manipulating paper with beautiful illustrations and reality-bending shapes (some great examples are listed in the Further Reading section).

There are a few good books available on designing pop-ups. There are easily dozens of techniques; I casually reviewed my own work and counted at least two dozen different kinds of mechanisms. That's a lot. The good news is that a most of these techniques are based on just a handful of basic ideas. Think of pop-ups like a guitar: there are only so many ways to pluck and strum the strings and rap on the body of the instrument, yet great guitarists are able to create a tremendous range of personally expressive and distinctive styles.

In this discussion, I'll limit my attention to cards that are based on stiff sheets of paper, so I'm ruling out bending and curling as deliberate design elements.

It's important to keep the complexity of the card under control. I know from personal experience that the complexity of a card has a huge impact on how long it takes to build. Remember that each cut and fold will have to be repeated for each card. Many cards have multiple pieces, so it's not unusual to spend an hour per card for even the simplest pop-ups. It's easy to design a card that would take an afternoon to build. If you're making only one or two (like a special birthday card), this can be a fun weekend or evening project, and the extra complexity can be fun for you and the receiver alike. If you're making lots of cards, then getting the most out of simple techniques becomes essential.

90-Degree Mechanisms

The *single-slit mechanism* is part of the class of *90-degree techniques*. That means that they are at their most effective when the card is open to a right angle. When the card is fully closed, of course, there's nothing to be seen, and when it's fully open, these mechanisms retreat into the plane of the card itself.

In the single-slit method, we fold the card and make a single cut. Typically we also make a single corresponding fold from the edge of

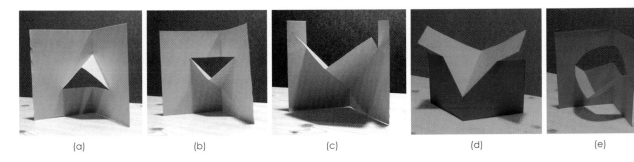

| (a) | (b) | (c) | (d) | (e) |

the cut to the central fold of the card. Then we open the card partly, push the cut-and-folded section forward until it snaps into the forward position, and we've created a pop-up!

Figure 1.2(a) shows a paper model of the most basic single-slit pop-up: the right-angle single slit with a fold to the crease. Basically all that's happening here is that segment of the card is bending away from the fold rather than along it.

Despite its simplicity, this mechanism contains most of what we need to know about the geometry of pop-up cards. It also has a lot of flexibility, as shown by Figures 1.2(b) through (d) (technically Figure 1.2(e) is a *double-slit* design, but the idea is the same).

Before we dig into the geometry, though, we should think about our options. I investigated two approaches to pop-up geometry: *constraint systems* and *explicit modeling*.

A constraint system is a general-purpose piece of computer code that's designed to find values for a set of variables, so that those values satisfy a certain list of requirements, or *constraints*. For example, we might require that variable A must always be larger than B, or that they are always equal, or that when compared to another variable C we always have $A + B > C$.

Constraint systems are wonderful, flexible tools for solving very complex problems. But they have three big drawbacks for this application. First, the programs themselves are typically large and complex, which makes them hard to write and debug. Second, constraint systems are notoriously sensitive to issues of numerical stability. Calculations must be carried out very precisely, with a lot of attention given to the principles of numerical computation, including precision and rounding errors. Constraint systems can "blow up" (or produce wildly incorrect answers) when these delicate issues are not fastidiously addressed. Even when the program itself is well designed, the inputs must obey the same standards. Constraint systems are very sensitive to seemingly small changes in the input. For example,

Figure 1.2

The simplest pop-up: the *single-slit* design. These are photographs of paper models. (a) The canonical single-slit. (b) A different view of (a). (c) A variant single-slit design. (d) Another variant single-slit design. (e) A double-slit design.

simply changing the order of the constraints can sometimes affect the solution that the system finds. Third, constraint systems can "lock up," or get stuck in local minima where there are no valid solutions. That is, the system finds itself unable to find a valid answer and just meanders, searching for alternatives. Some systems are able to break free of the region of bad answers and go hunting in a different and potentially more fruitful range of possible solutions, but this process can take a long time.

All of these issues can be addressed, of course, and robust constraint systems are used in many fields as a part of everyday work. But these problems seemed to me to make a constraint system an unlikely candidate for a small, interactive design program.

The alternative I followed was to write special-purpose code to explicitly calculate the geometry of the pop-up cards.

This approach has a few things going for it. First, the geometry is relatively straightforward (as we'll see below), so the code is easy to write and debug. Second, it's fast. Third, it's stable: the code doesn't go searching around for a good answer, but just calculates the proper answer right away, the first time. And finally, it's *invertible*, which means you can run it in reverse. It's easy to set up the card roughly the way you want it and then have the system compute the best valid geometry that will let you make that card.

One downside of writing the explicit geometry in the code is that it limits the designer to creating mechanisms that have already been prepared, so he or she cannot invent new mechanisms. I think this is a reasonable limitation, since there seem to be relatively few mechanisms in general use. If someone cooks up something surprisingly new, then it can be added to the library.

Let's look at the geometry behind creating a new single-slit pop-up.

Figure 1.3 shows the essential geometry behind all single-slit designs. We begin with a *card*, or *backing plane*. Point A is on the *central fold*, and points C and D lie at equal distances from the fold along a line perpendicular to it. The card is scored along the lines AD and AC, and cut along CD.

Before we make the cut, the line CD crosses the fold at point E. After the cut, I distinguish point E as that spot on the card where the cut crosses the fold, and point B as that point on the paper that is at the end of the folded segment. When the card is flat, points B and E are theoretically coincident (in practice, of course, B will be slightly closer to A). As the card folds, point B will move in a direction opposite to that of point E, and that's what make the pop-up pop.

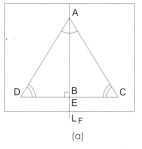

(a)

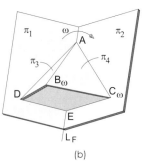

(b)

Figure 1.3

The basic geometry of the single-slit mechanism.

Let's label the right side of the card as plane π_2 and the left as π_1, as in Figure 1.3(b). I'll say that the angle formed between these two planes is ω, measured from π_1 to π_2 as in the figure. The fold line itself is called L_F. As the card is folded, triangle ABC rises up; I'll call this plane π_4. Similarly, triangle ABD is π_3.

To make things easier, I'll assume that the left half of the card (plane π_1) is held flat on the table, and the right plane (π_2) is opened up. This doesn't limit our generality in any way, but it makes it easier to label the points. Points A, D, and E are all constant in this setup, because they lie in the unmoving plane π_1. Points B and C do move. I'll label the position of these points for a given angle ω as B_ω and C_ω respectively, as in the figure. Specifically, B_π is the position of B when the card is fully open, and B_0 is the position of B when the card is fully closed. Our goal is to find the position of B_ω for an arbitrary value of ω.

Since L_F refers to line AE, I'll designate line AB_ω as L_ω, which I also call the *central pop-up crease*. The two edges AD and AC_ω I call the *induced creases*, since they appear as a result of the pop-up action.

This is a right-angle mechanism, because it's at its best when $\omega = \pi/2$. When $\omega = \pi$, then points B_ω and E are coincident, and there's nothing very interesting happening, and when $\omega = 0$, the card is closed.

FINDING B_ω

When the card is fully open, point B_π lies in the plane next to point E. As the card unfolds (that is, we lift up plane π_2 by rotating it around line L_F), point B_ω rises up.

In this situation, it's easy to observe that B_ω always travels in a circle with center at point A and radius AE, in the plane that lies between π_1 and π_2. But a more general solution will prove useful later when we consider more complex types of cards.

To find the location of B_ω for any value of ω, let's start with the things we know. We know the positions of points A, D, and E since they're fixed. We can easily find point C_ω since it's just point C rotated around line L_F by $-(\pi - \omega)$. We also know that because the card is stiff, the distances between points A, B_ω, C_ω, and D are all constant.

The key insight is to think of the construction in terms of spheres. Point B_ω always lies on the surface of a sphere with center D and radius $|DE|$, since that distance never changes and the line pivots around point D. Let's call that sphere S_D. Similarly, B_ω lies on sphere S_A with center A and radius AE. Point B_ω also lies on sphere S_C with center C_ω and radius $|DE|$ (since $|C_\omega E| = |DE|$).

Since point B_ω lies on the surface of three different spheres, if we could find all the points of intersection of these three spheres, we'd know that B_ω was one of those points.

Three different intersecting spheres that aren't degenerate (that is, they don't have a radius of zero, and none of them is identical with the others) intersect in exactly two points. Of course, one or more of the spheres could fail to intersect with the others, but in our case we know they do, since we're working from a physical construction. If our three spheres S_A, S_D, and S_C, didn't intersect, then our card has come apart!

I don't know of a standard solution for the problem of finding the intersection of three spheres, but I cooked up one that is simple, stable, and easy to implement. Let's look at it here.

To begin with, remember that the implicit formula for a sphere with center C and radius r says that all points P on the sphere evaluate to 0:

$$(P_x - C_x)^2 + (P_y - C_y)^2 + (P_z - C_z)^2 - r^2 = 0.$$

So when we plug in B_ω for P into each of the three sphere equations, it will come out to zero for all of them.

Now imagine a plane through the centers of our three spheres, as shown in Figure 1.4. I'll call this π_S. Symmetry tells us that the points of intersection of the three spheres lie on a line that is perpendicular to π_S, as shown in the Figure. The point of intersection of that line with π_S is marked with a dot.

The three spheres turn into circles in the plane π_S. When we plug the marked point into those three circle equations, it will have the same value with respect to them all (note that the value won't be zero, since the point doesn't lie on the circles themselves).

Let's pick any two of these two circles and call them U and V:

$$U(x, y) = (P_x - U_x)^2 + (P_y - U_y)^2 - r_U{}^2,$$
$$V(x, y) = (P_x - V_x)^2 + (P_y - V_y)^2 - r_V{}^2.$$

Now let's look at the structure of all points P that have the same value with respect to these two circles. That is, we want to find all points where $U(P) = V(P)$, or equivalently, $U(P) - V(P) = 0$. I'll write this difference of two circles, expand their definitions, and collect like terms:

$$
\begin{aligned}
0 &= U(x, y) - V(x, y) \\
&= (x - U_x)^2 + (y - U_y)^2 + U_r{}^2 - [(x - V_x)^2 + (y - V_y)^2 + V_r{}^2] \\
&= x^2 - 2U_x x + U_x{}^2 + y^2 - 2U_y y + U_y{}^2 + U_r{}^2 \\
&\quad - x^2 + 2V_x x - V_x{}^2 - y^2 + 2V_y y - V_y{}^2 - V_r{}^2 \\
&= 2x(V_x - U_x) + 2y(V_y - U_y) + U(0, 0) - V(0, 0) \\
&= Ax + By + C.
\end{aligned}
$$

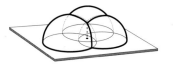

Figure 1.4

Three mutually intersecting spheres. The plane π_S joins their centers. The two points of intersection of the three spheres line on the dashed line that is perpendicular to the plane.

Recalling that $Ax + By + C = 0$ is the equation of a line, we've just discovered that all points (x, y) which have the same value with respect to both circles lie on a straight line! This line is called the *radical axis*.

Now let's look back at our three-circle problem, where I'll add in circle W. Figure 1.5(a) shows these three circles in the general case, where they have different radii and intersect. Circles U and V meet in two points, which I've labeled P_{UV} and Q_{UV}. Since both of these points have the value 0 with respect to both circle equations, they must lie on the radical axis of those two circles. In other words, to find the radical axis for circles U and V we need only find their points of intersection P_{UV} and Q_{UV}. I'll call this line L_{UV}.

Similarly, I've labeled points P_{UW} and Q_{UW} at the intersections of circles U and W, and done the same thing for circles V and W. These two pairs of points respectively define the radical axes L_{UW} and L_{VW}.

Now, since the circles intersect, certainly L_{UV} and L_{UW} must meet; we'll call that point M. Since M is on the radical axis between U and V, $U(M) = V(M)$. And since M is on the radical axis between U and W, $U(M) = W(M)$. Thus $V(M) = W(M)$, which means that M also lies on the radical axis L_{VW}.

This little bit of reasoning proves that if three circles are mutually intersecting, then their radical axes intersect at the unique point M.

We're halfway home now. Our next step is to locate point M, given the three spheres.

I do this by creating a plane for each pair of spheres. The plane contains the radical axis and is perpendicular to the plane that joins their centers. So for example the plane for spheres U and V contains line L_{UV} and comes out of the page in Figure 1.5.

To find this plane, take a look at the geometry in Figure 1.5(b). In this figure, we are given the centers of circles C_1 and C_2, their radii r_1 and r_2, and the distance $d = C_1 - C_2$. Of course, this is all the same information as the center, radii, and distances of the spheres. We want to find the point J.

From triangle PJC_1 we see that $a = r_1 \cos \alpha$. To find $\cos \alpha$ we can use the Law of Cosines with C_1PC_2 to find

$$\cos \alpha = (d^2 + r_1{}^2 - r_2{}^2)/(2r_1\, d),$$

so

$$a = r_1 \cos \alpha$$
$$= (d^2 + r_1{}^2 - r_2{}^2)/(2d).$$

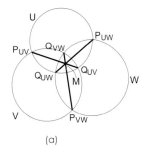

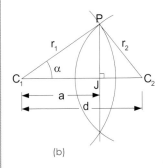

(a)

(b)

Figure 1.5

The geometry for finding the point of mutual intersection of three spheres. (a) Intersecting the three radical axes. (b) Finding the radical axis through points P and J for the two circles with centers C_1 and C_2, radii r_1 and r_2 and distance $d = |C_1 - C_2|$.

So using these usings for a and d, we can find

$$J = C_1 + (C_2 - C_1)(a/d)$$
$$= C_1 + (C_2 - C_1)((d^2 + r_1^2 - r_2^2)/(2d^2)).$$

Our plane passes through J with a normal parallel to $C_2 - C_1$. Intersecting any two of these planes gives us the dashed line of Figure 1.4.

With this line in hand, we need only intersect it with any of the spheres to find the two points of intersection, one above and one below the plane π_S. Which point do we want? Refer to Figure 1.3. We want the point that is on the same side of plane π_S as point C_ω, which we know.

And that point, finally, is B_ω! This was a long road, but most of it was just to set up the situation and figure out what the geometry of the situation looked like. Now that we have the solution, the code itself is pretty short, as we'll see later on.

If the circles of Figure 1.5 do not mutually intersect, then the radical axes are parallel, and there is no point of intersection. But this case never holds in our situation. The most extreme case is when the card is fully open or closed, and the circles are tangent; they never fully separate.

INTERACTIVE MATH

Now that we can find B_ω, we can draw the card for any given value of the opening fold angle ω. Just find the point C_ω; then intersect the spheres, and draw the polygons.

Suppose that we don't like the way that the card looks. Then we can simply grab B_ω and move it around interactively. There is only one geometric limit the system needs to enforce on the user: point B_ω must lie on the plane that is halfway between π_1 and π_2 at any stage of folding. We don't even require that the corresponding point E be on the card itself. There's no reason not to allow the person using the program to create a card that pokes up from the bottom, or down from the top, as shown in Figure 1.2.

Finding B_ω is the heart of my Pop-up Design Assistant. Figure 1.6 shows the results of using my program to recreate the paper models of Figure 1.2.

ASYMMETRIC SLITS

An important variant of the single slit is the *asymmetric slit*. Here the fold does not follow the crease of the backing card, but is at an angle to it. This variation gives the designer some more freedom to create slanted and forced-perspective effects.

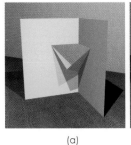 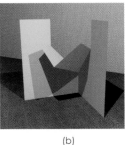   

(a)　　　　　　　(b)　　　　　　　(c)　　　　　　　(d)　　　　　　　(e)

Figure 1.7 shows the essential geometry; Figure 1.7(a) is the open card, and Figure 1.7(b) shows it in closed position. In Figure 1.7(a), the central pop-up crease AB_π forms an angle β to the support crease AE. Although in action the card looks generally like Figure 1.2(b), the central pop-up crease is rotated, creating an asymmetrical pair of triangles on each side. In Figure 1.7(a), we are free to choose A, D, and C_π; we want to find B_π that allows the card to fold flat. In terms of angles, we have ψ, γ, and δ and wish to find α.

In Figure 1.7, we can see that as the card folds, point B_π comes up out of the plane and eventually comes down to rest at B_0. This causes triangle $\triangle ADB_\pi$ to become reflected, since B_ω pulls it around AD. Triangle $\triangle AB_\pi C_\pi$ is pulled along by the motion of B_ω and comes to rest at $\triangle AB_0C_0$ in an orientation equal to a rotation of γ around A. Because EC_π is perpendicular to the folding axis AE, point C_π moves to C_0 along line DE; this means that triangle $\triangle AC_0E$ is similar to triangle $\triangle AC_\pi E$.

To find α, we begin with $\triangle B_0DC_0$ in Figures 1.7(b) and (c), giving $2\psi + (\pi - 2\delta) + (\pi - 2\phi) = \pi$, or $\phi = \psi - \delta + (\pi/2)$.

From $\triangle ADB_\pi$ in Figure 1.5(a), write $\alpha + \psi + \pi - \phi = \pi$. With the value for ϕ found above, this becomes $\alpha = (\pi/2) - \delta$. From $\triangle AEC_\pi$ we find that $\delta = (\pi/2) - \gamma$. Combining these last two results, we find our goal: $\alpha = (\pi/2) - ((\pi/2) - \gamma) = \gamma$.

This long road ends with a simple conclusion: to construct an asymmetric slit pop-up that folds flat, place B_π in Figure 1.7(a) so that $\alpha = \gamma$.

Figure 1.6

The paper models of Figure 1.2 modeled by my Pop-up Design Assistant.

Figure 1.7

The geometry of the asymmetric single-slit.

V-Fold Mechanisms

The *V-fold* mechanism creates a pair of free-standing slanted planes when the card is opened, as shown in Figure 1.1. The V-fold is one of the hardest pieces to design using paper and scissors, since one indirectly controls how much the plane leans back by changing the angle at the base of the piece when it is cut out; this angle is the V at the bottom of Figure 1.8(a).

Figure 1.8

V-fold mechanisms. (a) The basic V-fold. (b) How it sits on the card. (c) A second-generation V-fold.

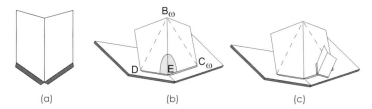

(a)　　　　　(b)　　　　　(c)

Because a V-fold is a separate piece attached to the backing card, it can rise out of the card plane when the card is fully open, unlike the single-slit. Thus the geometry of the V-fold is based on that of the single slit but allows more flexibility in its design. Though B_ω still locates the central crease, there may be no paper at that point in space. For example, the apex of the fold (point E in Figure 1.8) need not be included; the shaded "tunnel" region in Figure 1.8(b) can even be cut out of the card. Figure 1.8 also shows the small flaps which are scored, bent back, and then glued to the support planes.

Since V-folds don't cut into the page, they may be placed on any crease, which is then treated just like the card's crease for that mechanism. Figure 1.8(c) shows a cascaded pair of V-folds. The larger one uses the card fold as its support crease and creates EC_ω as one of its side pop-up creases. The smaller V-fold uses EC_ω as its support crease. So opening the card pops up the big V-fold, which then drives the smaller one to pop up as well.

The tabs of a V-fold must be carefully glued in the right places, or the card may not open or close fully.

Depending on the placement of the V-fold on the support planes, it can be designed to fold either towards or away from the reader. When the planes of the V-fold become parallel to the support planes, all the folding lines become parallel to one another. This configuration is sometimes called a *floating layer*.

Figure 1.9(a) shows a computer-rendered V-fold. In Figure 1.9(b) I show a second-generation V-fold rising up from the crease between the first V-fold and the card. Higher generations of V-folds work just like their parents, though they require a bit of care in programming to keep track of all the points during the opening and closing of the card.

Happily, the single-slit and V-fold mechanisms are also among the most general of all techniques used in pop-ups; many of the other constructions are combinations of these mechanisms or variations on their geometry.

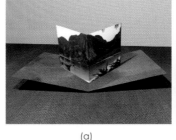 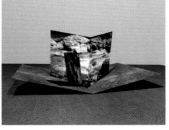

(a)   (b)

Figure 1.9

Computer-rendered V-folds. (a) A single fold sitting atop a backing card. (b) A second generation, or cascaded, V-fold in the process of opening.

There are of course a variety of pop-up mechanisms that aren't captured by those ideas. Most of those are straightforward to design and create with special-purpose code and don't present the sort of design challenges that the slit and V-fold designs do. We'll see some of them later on.

BUILDING AN ASSISTANT

In this section I'll describe how I put together my Pop-up Design Assistant.

The heart of any program lies in its data structures. For my Assistant, the most important data structure is the *riser*. A riser contains the information needed to position all the points of a single-slit or V-fold element.

The first job of the riser is to help us identify points A, D, and C_ω as in Figure 1.3. I represent each point with three pieces of information: a pair of co-ordinates, a pointer to another riser, and a flag. To position a point, I retrieve the pointed-to riser, and select either the left or right side as specified by the flag. I then use the central fold and the bottom edge as two vectors that span a plane, scale those vectors by the co-ordinate values, and add those results together to find the position of the sought-after point. Figure 1.10 shows the idea.

This recursion of risers pointing to risers ends with a special riser that is marked as the *card*.

I maintain all of the risers in a list. I take it easy and simply add new risers to the end of this list as they're created (and of course I remove them when the designer decides to eliminate one).

To position the risers, I simply start at the beginning of the list and look for a riser that can be positioned; that is, the risers it depends on have both already been positioned, and it has not already been positioned itself. If I find such a riser, I compute its points and mark it as positioned. When I reach the end of the list, if I've positioned any riser on that pass, I go back to the start and go through the list again.

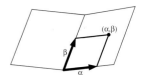

Figure 1.10

To find a point on a riser, I use the coordinates (α, β) associated with that riser to scale the central fold and one of the lower edges respectively. The point is the sum of these two scaled vectors.

When I pass through the list but nothing gets positioned, that should have handled everything. I scan the list once more as a check and look for unpositioned risers; if I find any, I report an error.

On the first pass through the list, none of risers can be positioned except for the card itself. Special-purpose code handles the card, since it doesn't depend on any other risers. I mark it as positioned and then continue running through the list. Since the risers are strictly hierarchical, this algorithm should always produce a completely-positioned card.

The two coordinates associated with each point describe the scale factors on the edges of the riser the point depends on. One of those edges is always the central edge of the riser. The other is the left or right bottom edge, as selected by the left/right flag.

The entire card must be repositioned every time the designer changes the opening angle, which is typically a frequent operation. If efficiency is an issue, one could preprocess the list and build a tree structure that can later be traversed in a single pass. I found that repeatedly running through the list of a dozen or so risers was no problem for my 800 MHz Pentium III PC to handle in real time.

GEOMETRY FOR ALL

Earlier I described my algorithm for finding B_ω as the intersection of three spheres. Here are the details behind the heart of the routine.

Suppose we have three spheres, S_1, S_2, and S_3, which have radii r_1, r_2 and r_3. The radii needn't be different, but they generally will be. Figure 1.11 shows three such spheres, and the plane that contains their centers. I've also marked in black one of their points of intersection; there's another point symmetrically placed on the other side of the plane.

We'll work with these spheres in pairs. It doesn't matter where we start, so let's pick S_1 and S_2 first. When two spheres intersect, the points in common form a circle. Our first goal is to find the plane that contains that circle, shown in Figure 1.12.

We saw in Figure 1.5 how to find the point J on the line that contains the two sphere centers. Our plane passes through J with a normal parallel to $C_2 - C_1$, shown in Figure 1.13. Let's call this plane π_{12}. I package this up in a routine that takes as input two spheres and returns their plane of intersection.

We can repeat this for the other two pairs of spheres, creating planes π_{23} and π_{13}. The three planes together are shown in Figure 1.14.

Now I intersect any two of these planes to find the line they have in common, illustrated in Figure 1.15. For numerical stability I

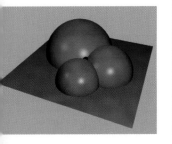

Figure 1.11

Three spheres that meet in a single point.

use a robust technique published by Jim Blinn. This algorithm takes as input two planes represented with homogeneous coordinates and returns their line of intersection, if there is one (if the planes are parallel, they don't intersect and there is no common line).

Since Blinn's paper presents the theory, I'll just summarize the necessary equations here. The input to the algorithm is two planes, which I'll call P and Q. Plane P has a normal given by (P_x, P_y, P_z) and an offset P_d; plane Q is similar. The output is a line defined by a point B and a direction vector $\mathbf{V}$. The first step is to compute six handy terms, p through u:

$$p = P_z Q_d - P_d Q_z,$$
$$q = P_y Q_d - P_d Q_y,$$
$$r = P_y Q_z - P_z Q_y,$$
$$s = P_x Q_d - P_d Q_x,$$
$$t = P_x Q_z - P_z Q_x,$$
$$u = P_x Q_y - P_y Q_x.$$

These tell us all we need to find the direction vector $\mathbf{V}$:

$$\mathbf{V} = (r, -t, u).$$

I then normalize $\mathbf{V}$ (that is, I scale it so that it has a length of 1.0). Now we can find the base point B. We have three cases which handle any degeneracies and special cases:

$$\text{if } r \neq 0 \text{ then } B = (0, p/r, -q/r)$$
$$\text{else} \quad \text{if } t \neq 0 \text{ then } B = (p/t, 0, -s/t)$$
$$\text{else} \quad \text{if } u \neq 0 \text{ then } B = (q/u, -s/u, 0)$$
$$\text{else} \quad \text{error: planes are parallel.}$$

Now we have the line in a convenient parametric form: $L = B + t\mathbf{V}$, where the real number t sweeps us along all the points on the line L

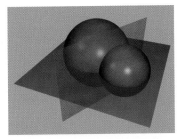

Figure 1.12

The points common to two intersecting spheres lie in a plane that is perpendicular to the line that joins their centers.

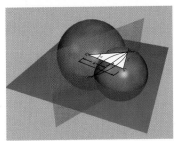

Figure 1.13

The geometry of Figure 1.12. We are given the centers C_1 and C_2, the radii r_1 and r_2, and the distance d, and use this information to find point J which is contained in the plane.

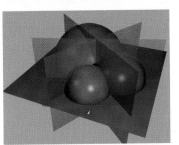

Figure 1.14

The three intersection planes created by the three spheres.

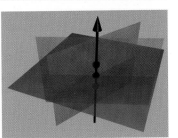

Figure 1.15

Intersecting two planes gives us a line.

with direction **V** and passing through point B. In Figure 1.15 the point B appears on the line where it pierces the plane.

Now that we have a sphere and a parametric line, we can use standard ray-tracing techniques to intersect that line with any of the three spheres. I use a library function that takes a line and a sphere and returns the two points of intersection. I won't give the details of that calculation here, as they're available in every book on ray-tracing (see the Further Reading section). For numerical stability, I use the sphere with the largest radius (if more than one sphere has the largest radius, I use one of them at random).

Figure 1.16

In this application, each pair of planes results in the same line.

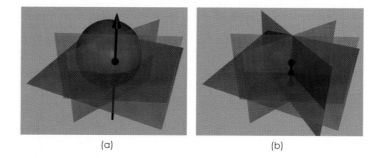

(a)   (b)

The result is a pair of points, as shown in Figure 1.16. Which one do we want? That's up to whether the card designer wants the pop-up to rise up out of the center of the card or fall back behind it. This choice is made at design time, of course, and is stored with the riser. I use the normal of the riser that is referenced by point D to categorize the two points: each point will be either on the positive or negative side of that riser. The designer's choice is stored in a flag associated with the riser. The most common case is where the pop-up rises up from the card.

This line/sphere intersection point is of course shared by all three spheres, since it is their point of common contact; Figure 1.17 shows the line and spheres.

Figure 1.17

(a) The common line of intersection of two planes and its intersections with the largest sphere. (b) The point is common to all three spheres.

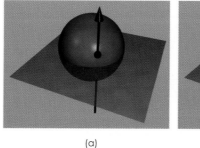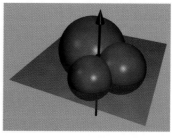

(a)   (b)

Another useful library routine is one that rotates a point around a given line by a given angle. This is useful when we want to position points on risers as they are moving around a fold axis. Suppose that we have a point P and a line given by the two points A and B, and we want to find point Q, the result of rotating P around line (A, B) by an angle θ.

You can write some very efficient code to do this if you need it a lot. Here's a solution that uses only common vector operations that should be available in almost any 3D library. Figure 1.18 shows the basic setup.

We first find the point M which is the point on line (A, B) which is closest to P. I find the vectors $\mathbf{C}$ and $\mathbf{D}$:

$$\mathbf{C} = B - A,$$

$$\mathbf{D} = P - A.$$

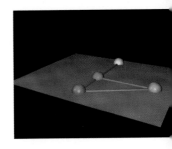

Figure 1.18

Rotating a point around a line. The line AB is shown by point A in orange and point B in yellow. The point to be rotated, Point P is in cyan off to one side. The point M in green is the point on AB that is closest to P.

Writing $\hat{\mathbf{C}}$ for the normalized version of $\mathbf{C}$, we find M by simply scaling $\hat{\mathbf{C}}$ by the length of the projection of $\mathbf{D}$ onto $\mathbf{C}$,

$$M = A + \hat{\mathbf{C}} \, (\hat{\mathbf{C}} \cdot \mathbf{D})$$

where I'm using the dot product between $\hat{\mathbf{C}}$ and $\mathbf{D}$. Figure 1.18 shows point M in green.

Now I make two vectors $\mathbf{V}$ and $\mathbf{H}$ that span the plane that includes this line and point:

$$\mathbf{H} = P - M$$
$$\mathbf{V} = \mathbf{H} \times \mathbf{C}$$

where $\times$ is the cross product. I also find the distance r from P to M:

$$r = |P - M|.$$

Figure 1.19 shows the vector $\mathbf{H}$ in red and $\mathbf{V}$ in purple.

The new point Q is now easy to find. Essentially we rotate the point P in a circle spanned by the normalized $\mathbf{H}$ and $\mathbf{V}$ vectors, and then recenter it to point M:

$$Q = M + r\hat{\mathbf{H}} \cos \theta + r\hat{\mathbf{V}} \sin \theta$$

Figure 1.20 shows this circle and the position of the new point Q.

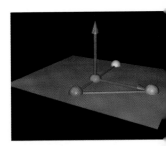

Figure 1.19

The H vector is in red, and the V vector is in purple.

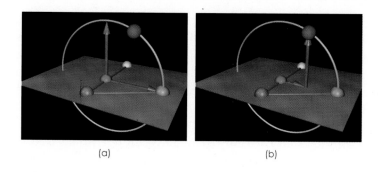

Figure 1.20

(a) The plane of rotation is formed by the H and V vectors. The yellow ring shows the circle in this plane with center M and radius |MP|. The new point, Q, shown in red, lies on this circle. (b) We find Q as a sum of scaled versions of the H and V vectors.

(a)   (b)

GENERATIONS

The technique of determining a pop-up's points with respect to its base risers makes it easy to provide designers with a technique known as *generations*. Basically that just means cascading a series of mechanisms one after the other. In terms of single-slit and V-fold mechanisms, it usually means placing a new mechanism on the card so that it is not powered by the central card fold, but rather by the induced creases of an earlier riser. So as the riser pops up, it's like a little card that is closing, and the fold of that little card drives another pop-up. Figure 1.21 shows the basic idea schematically.

Figure 1.21

The basic idea of creating generations by using one V-fold as part of the base for another.

The Design Assistant I described in the last section handles this mechanism naturally, since it just involves placing the points of one riser with respect to an earlier one. Figure 1.22 shows an example of a card with multiple-generation V-folds. Note that it's hard to make more than a few generations of V-folds on top of each other. This is because each V-fold sits at an angle a little closer to the viewer than the one it's based on. This means that eventually we'll run out of nice angles for viewing. But more importantly, each generation reduces the angle of the crease that the V-fold sits upon. When a V-fold sits on an open card, the two sides are flat. As the sides come together at a smaller angle, as they do on higher-generation V-folds, it gets more difficult to both design and construct the card so it both works properly and looks good.

Figure 1.22

A pop-up card based on generations of V-folds. The yellow flowers are on a third-generation riser.

Though the V-fold and the single slit provide the basic geometry for a wide variety of pop-up designs, I've included several other mechanisms in my Design Assistant. The books in the Further Reading section provide more details on these mechanisms. I won't describe the geometry of these mechanisms because they're all either variations on what we've already seen, or else they're pretty straightforward on their own.

For simplicity I'll discuss these mechanisms with respect to the main card. Of course, they can all be built with respect to any two risers, and built up in generations style one upon the other.

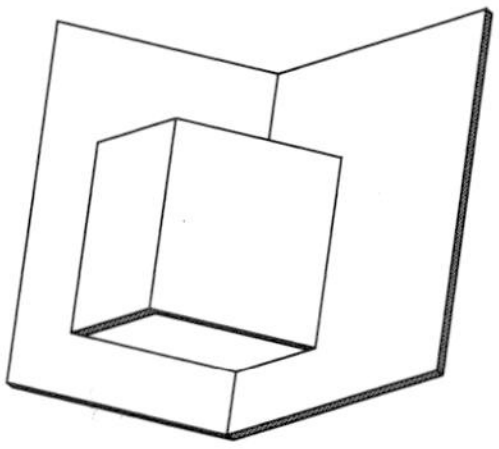

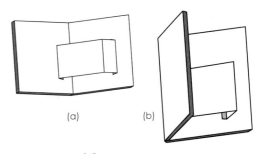

Figure 1.23

A schematic for a double-slit mechanism.

The *double slit*, shown in Figure 1.23, is a minor variation on the single-slit design. Though I've shown it with cuts that are straight, perpendicular to the fold, and symmetrical about the fold, none of these need to hold true: the cuts can be of any shape.

Let's next look at the *strap*, illustrated in Figure 1.24. The strap lets us do two things at once: displace the central fold to the left or right, and reverse the direction of the fold. In the figure I've used the strap to move the fold to the right, and though the sides of the card form a valley with respect to the card's central fold, the sides of the strap form a mountain. The geometry of the strap is easy to implement, since it always forms a parallelogram with the card.

(a) (b)

Figure 1.24

A schematic for the strap mechanism.

Figure 1.25 shows a card built on a strap and two V-folds. The two icebergs are standard V-folds that rise off the sides of the card. The ship is a V-fold that sits on one end of a strap that straddles the central fold. Thus when the card is opened, that end of the strap flattens out, and the ship pops up behind the iceberg. Because the card isn't fully opened in this image, you can see the strap to the left of the ship where it hasn't quite flattened out yet.

Figure 1.25

A greeting card that uses V-folds and a strap. The icebergs are V-folds. The ship is also a V-fold, based on one edge of a strap (you can see the strap to the left of the ship since the card is still slightly open).

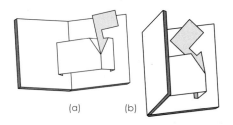

Figure 1.26

A schematic for a moving-arm mechanism, created by merging a strap with a single-slit. This is the schematic for Figure 1.1(b).

(a)   (b)

You can combine the strap with the single-slit to create the *moving arm* or *pivot* mechanism, shown in Figure 1.26 (this is a schematic of the card in Figure 1.1). The single-slit may be a little hard to see; think of the top of the strap as the slit. Many of the most surprising pop-up effects can be achieved through this kind of simple combination of basic mechanisms.

Figure 1.27

A greeting card that uses the moving-arm.

Figure 1.27 shows a New Year's card made with a moving arm. The dragon pivots out of the card counterclockwise.

You can create a layer that is parallel to the card, but sitting above it, using a technique called the *floating layer*, shown in Figure 1.28. The floating layer is held up by supports at the two sides, which are generally of the same height and placed an equal distance from the center fold. For stability, one often includes a support piece in the middle, as shown in the figure.

Figure 1.28

A schematic for a floating-layer mechanism.

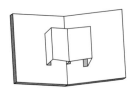

By changing the heights of the three supports, you can change the slope of the two sides of the floating layer from flat to inclined in either dimension. At the extremes, you can shrink the side supports to create a mountain or tent, or shrink the support in the middle to make a valley. The floating layer idea is versatile, and you can use it to make complex figures like boxes and even cylinders.

Figure 1.29

An invitation card that uses a floating layer for the table. The chairs are V-folds.

Figure 1.29 uses the floating-layer technique for the dinner table. The two chairs are built out of V-folds.

So far we've looked at pop-up mechanisms that work themselves. That is, all the reader has to do is open the book or card, and the paper does its thing. There are a few popular mechanisms that allow the reader to take a more active role.

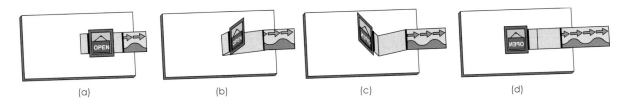

(a) (b) (c) (d)

One such device is known as the *pull-tab*, or *pull-up plane*, and it too has a variety of implementations. Figure 1.30 shows one of the basic versions. In this mechanism, the page is actually made up of two sheets that sandwich the mechanism between them. I've drawn these obscured parts in gray.

It's convenient to think of three parts to the pull tab, but they're all made out of one piece of paper. There's the tab itself, which sticks out from the page through a slot cut in the upper sheet. Then there's the visible flap, which also sticks up through a slot. Finally there's the bit underneath, which is a single rectangle of paper with a fold in it.

As the tab is pulled, the segment underneath tries to straighten out and bulges downward. It tries to pull the visible flap into the space between the paper, but this flap is taller than the slot. Thus the part underneath causes the flap to pivot around the slot. When the tab has been pulled out all the way, the flap has flipped over and now lies flush against the page in the other direction, revealing the back of the flap and whatever was on the page underneath it.

You can get this effect for free if you use a complete collision-detection or constraint system, as I discussed earlier. But the mechanism is so simple that a very little bit of special-purpose code to flip the flap around the slot can do the job quickly and accurately.

The pull-tab is a nice way to create a card within a card. Really ambitious designers can include V-folds and other mechanisms inside this little mini-card, but one must be careful not to get carried away. The risk is that people (both adults and children) often quite understandably think that if pulling the tab opens the mechanism, then pushing the tab should close it. This sometimes works in simple cases, but if there's much happening inside, then the flap under the card often buckles, and then the mechanism never again works as it should. Sometimes designers reinforce the hidden flap with additional layers of paper or thicker board to prevent this problem.

Another popular technique is based on the idea of a *wheel*. The wheel has four parts, as shown in Figure 1.31. In Figure 1.31(a) I show the front of the card. The notch on the left gives the reader access to the edge of the wheel, and the holes in the card let what's printed on the

Figure 1.30

A schematic for the pull-tab mechanism.

Figure 1.31

The parts for a wheel mechanism. (a) The front card with a notch to allow the reader access to the wheel's edge, and holes through which to see the wheel itself. (b) The wheel. (c) The nut. (d) The "butterfly" hub. (e) The completed card as seen from the front.

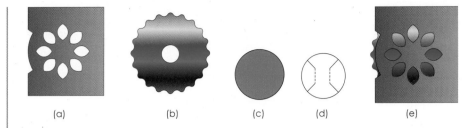

(a)   (b)   (c)   (d)   (e)

wheel itself show through. These holes can be of any shape and number as long as the card still holds together. A second card of the same size and shape (except without the holes) is usually made for the back.

Figure 1.31(b) shows the wheel itself, which has a rippled edge so that the reader can easily spin it. The two small parts in Figure 1.31(c) and Figure 1.31(d) form the hub and nut, which I'll show in more detail in a moment. The final card as seen from the front is in Figure 1.31(e); the wheel shows through the holes, and the reader can spin the wheel from the side.

The hub is easy to make (once *you* know the secret!). To make the center of the wheel, we need one piece I call the "butterfly," as in Figure 1.31(c), and one "nut" in Figure 1.31(d). The assembly process is shown in Figure 1.32. Flip the top sheet over and glue two wings of the butterfly to the back of the front card. The red dots in Figure 1.32(a) show where the glue goes to fix the butterfly to the back of the card. Then we fold up the wings of the butterfly and pass them through the hole in the center of the wheel. Next, straighten out the butterfly flaps, and glue the top of each one to the "nut" that goes on the top of the stack; the red dots in Figure 1.32(c) show where to apply glue. The final assembly is shown in Figure 1.32(d). Notice that nothing gets glued to the wheel itself! That's the reason it rotates freely. Cut the wings so that the cuts in the center are just a little bit smaller than the disk cut out of the center of the wheel. You'll need to curl up the flaps when you thread them, but they will hold the wheel securely once the nut is in place. When the whole sandwich is complete, you can

Figure 1.32

Constructing a wheel. (a) First glue two wings of the butterfly to the back of the front card. (b) Thread the other wings through the wheel. (c) Glue the top of the wings to the nut. (d) The completed sandwich seen from the back.

(a)   (b)   (c)   (d)

glue the front and back of the card together around their rim; make sure to leave enough room for the wheel to spin freely.

Figure 1.33 shows a birthday card based on the wheel. The spokes on the unicycle turn when the wheel spins. As the wheel turns the rider rocks back and forth, as shown in the Figure. To make the rider rock, I perched the unicyclist on an arm that passes through a slot in the front of the card, as shown schematically in Figure 1.34. Inside the card, I attached a larger disk behind the wheel with the spokes printed on it, and then placed another hub on the outside of that disk. Thus as the main wheel goes around, the smaller hub on its edge goes with it. The rider is pulled up and down with the motion of the wheel and pivots when the wheel extends to the left or right of the slot.

(a)

(b)

Figure 1.33

A birthday card based on a wheel mechanism. The rider sits on an extension that is affixed to the wheel. (a) The card at one position of the wheel. (b) When the wheel is turned, the spokes turn (they are visible through the holes in the front of the card), and the rider rocks back and forth.

STAYING IN BOUNDS

When the card is folded flat, we usually don't want any of the pieces to stick out beyond the cover. I check for this condition by setting the folding angle ω to 0, and then calculating the position of every point in the card. I check to make sure that each of these points lies within the region defined by the outermost card. If any points are outside this region, they'll stick out when the card is closed. I mark them with a bright color so that the designer can fix the problem.

Note that the shape of the outside card doesn't have to be rectangular. That's by far the most common shape for self-contained cards, but there's no reason not to use a card cut into an ellipse or any other shape.

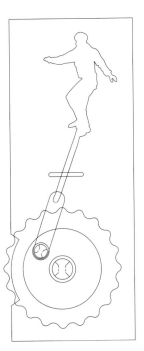

Figure 1.34

A schematic for the cam mechanism of Figure 1.33. The rider sits on a piece that rotates around a point on the wheel, through the use of another "butterfly" hub and nut at that point.

Interactive
Pop-Up
Card Design

COLLISIONS

One of the hardest problems to solve when manually designing a card is detecting and resolving collisions. When you have several mechanisms all moving at the same time, in different places and at different speeds, it's all too easy to end up with the pieces banging into each other. This is bad enough when the card is opening, but it makes it almost impossible to close the card again without damaging it.

I think the best way to handle collisions is to detect them and then let the designer figure out how to resolve them. One can certainly cook up all kinds of automatic schemes that move the points around algorithmically, and that will solve the technical side of the problem, but it may also change the aesthetics of the result. The point here is to make a designer's tool, not to find a result that makes the computer happy! So I prefer to let the designer know that there's a problem and apply a human touch to make things right.

A really careful, algorithmically complete job of collision detection would certainly work well. But it looked to me like it would be a complicated program: I'd have to figure out the motion paths for every point, edge, and plane, and then check them all against each other. It seemed easier to take a rough-and-ready approach inspired by the rendering technique of point sampling.

To search for collisions, I just simulate the opening of the card by stepping the fold angle ω from 0 to π. At each step, I completely position the card and then look for any edges that pass through any planes. If I find them, I flag them and continue. When I'm done, I highlight any offending edges with a bright color. If the designer clicks on any of those edges, a display shows all the angles where collisions occurred. The designer can then click to set the card to one of those angles, which will show the collision. The designer can then manually adjust the points to repair the collision, and can then go on to fix other problems or run the collision-detection routine again.

This scheme is fast and has always worked for me. It has the potential to fail when there's an intersection for a very brief period of time between two of the checked angles. The easiest way to reduce the risk of a collision falling between the cracks is to simply crank up the number of steps taken by ω. I use 250 steps by default, and I've never been surprised when building the card. I bet you could get away with 100 steps or even fewer, if the simulation time became too long.

Any collisions that sneak through this test are probably not worth worrying about, because they come and go so quickly that the inherent flexibility of the paper will probably allow it to bend a little and avoid actually intersecting. It is possible that some big collisions could sneak through, or two corners could just touch and lock up against each other, but I've never seen these things so far.

Printing It Out

As I said earlier, my reason for making my Pop-up Design Assistant isn't to create cards for viewing on the computer, but rather to create cards to print, cut out, build, and share. So printing out the designed card is important.

The first issue is making sure that the card can be easily and properly assembled. Gluing down the risers in the right position has always been tricky for me. It's important that each piece is just where it should be, so that the card will be flat when folded shut, the pieces will rise and stand up in the correct place and angle when the card is open, and we won't have any collisions along the way.

Before we figure out how to indicate how to glue the card together, we have to make sure that there's something to be glued down! So far all of my discussions have assumed that risers are infinitely thin and sit on the card, perched there as if by magic. The stiff paper I use for construction is thin enough that I don't have to explicitly model its thickness for most things. But somehow we do have to provide tabs for gluing pieces into place.

Figure 1.35 shows a typical V-fold riser and the two tabs that I automatically generate for gluing it down into place. Note that these glue tabs are little trapezoids, not rectangles: particularly at the center of a V-fold, rectangular tabs would overlap. This would create an ugly bump and also make the card a little harder to close.

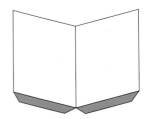

Figure 1.35

Creating little glue-down tabs for a V-fold.

To help me assemble cards, I have a switch to turn on the printing of *guide lines* on each riser that has another riser built upon it. This is just a colored line where the riser should be glued down. I then print the tabs with the same color. So anywhere I see a red line, for example, I know that a riser with a red-colored tab should be glued down on that line.

If you build a card, you'll quickly discover that the part of the tab that shows is the back of the page, which can look pretty bad if the color of the page doesn't blend in with the artwork. One solution is to actually cut a slit where the riser meets the card, and then slip the tab through the slit, gluing it to the underside of the card. This requires a really sharp crease to make sure the mechanisms can rise and fall properly.

A better approach would be to print the texture of the base riser on the tab of the riser that sits upon it, so that you can glue down the tab and the art is seamless. This requires a color printer that can print on both sides of the page with very good registration.

Interactive Pop-Up Card Design

Now that we know how to assemble the card, we need to get the pieces onto paper. Of course, we could be lazy and print one piece per page, but that would be wasteful. What we really want to do is to pack the pieces together into the smallest number of pages.

The best references I could find for this process were in the clothing manufacturing industry, where it's very important to try to conserve materials. Every bit of waste is expensive, so manufacturers work very hard to lay out the pieces as efficiently as possible, including rotating them and otherwise shuffling them around to get the densest packing. The Further Reading section identifies a good paper for getting into that literature.

Those algorithms can be complex. As always, I prefer simple solutions that get me 90% of the way there over complex solutions that get me to 100%. Achieving that last 10% often requires ten times more work! My simple technique is a greedy algorithm that packs the pieces in one at a time from largest to smallest.

I begin by creating a data structure called a *page*, which contains a list of *rectangles*. This list begins with a single rectangle that spans the page. I run through the list of pieces as a one-time preprocess and sort them by the size of their bounding rectangles. I start with the largest rectangle and work my way down to the smallest, placing them as I go and creating new pages when necessary.

To place a piece, I look at the first page and its list of available space (that is, the list of rectangles representing blank space on the page). I try to position the bounding rectangle of the piece on this page, trying it in both horizontal and vertical orientations. If there's a way to get the current piece's bounding rectangle onto the page, I place it in there as snugly as I can. I then use simple geometry to remove that rectangle from the page's available rectangle list; if the rectangle won't fit on this page, I repeat the process on the next page. If it doesn't fit on any existing pages, I create a new page. In this way I tend to make a bunch of pages that start out with just one or two big pieces and a lot of empty space, but then that space gets nibbled away by the smaller pieces as they arrive and are placed.

Figure 1.36 shows the result of this algorithm for the card design in Figure 1.25. Note that one of the icebergs, and the strap, were rotated 90 degrees to fit the page. Without this rotation, the pieces would have taken up two pages.

This algorithm isn't perfect by any means. There is some wastage, and the pieces could surely be packed more tightly. But I usually get pretty good density on the pages, and the algorithm has the benefits of being easy to program and fast to run.

(a)   (b)

Figure 1.36

The final cutout pages for Figure 1.25. I've turned on the optional heavy black outline for these pieces to help make them easier to cut out. (a) The base of the card. (b) The pieces to be cut out. Notice that the strap and one of the icebergs are rotated 90 degrees.

MOVING UP

There are lots of ways to extend my Pop-up Design Assistant. One thing I'd really like to try is to apply computer-vision segmentation techniques to photographs, automatically dividing them into several planes based on distance. For example, we could have a foreground, several middle grounds, and a background. The system could then take these segmented regions of the photo, place them on a series of V-folds that are spaced roughly as the objects in the scene are spaced, and create a three-dimensional version of a photograph, sort of like Figure 1.25. If a couple of versions of the photo are available, they could be used to fill in the holes in the background layers where the foreground information was cut out. Alternatively, one could fill in the holes using texture synthesis methods.

Another fun project would be to create pop-ups automatically from three-dimensional scene descriptions. There are many special-purpose tools up a pop-up designer's sleeve, from self-assembling tables and cubes to lattices and stacks. It would be very cool to be able to take a three-dimensional model—say of a car, or teapot, or flamingo—and automatically generate a pop-up version for three-dimensional, interactive, offline viewing. Even scientific visualizations could be done this way. The advantage is that the pieces can be made available on any image medium, from a printed journal to the web. Then someone just prints them out, assembles them, and enjoys the view.

It would be interesting to automatically incorporate forced-perspective illusions onto the planes to give the card an even richer illusion of depth.

I'd like to also add support for non-rigid constructions, curved folds, and pressure forces. For example, in Figure 1.1(a) I showed a moving card I designed where I made three V-folds with holes cut through them. As the card opened and the V-folds rose, they pulled up a floating layer that passed through them. There's no explicit mechanism here that causes this to happen; it's just that there's nowhere else for the layer that passes through the V-folds to go, so it must rise up with the V-folds themselves. There are many such possibilities, and it would be nice to provide them explicitly to the designer.

I'd like to flesh out my program with some of the other special-purpose pop-up mechanisms, such as pulleys, Venetian blinds, cylinders and cubes, and other uncommon but useful constructions.

Finally, I'd like to move my bundle up my design system into a plug-in for a commercial modeling package. That way people could use systems they're already familiar with, and use all the tools they already know for modeling, texturing, lighting, rendering, and so on.

I think that these are all rich research topics full of juicy pieces of geometry, optimization, segmentation, and interface design.

FURTHER READING

There are a few books on paper engineering that should be in the library of anyone who's thinking of getting involved in the field. A terrific listing of all the essential mechanisms, complete with working examples, is given in *The Elements of Pop-Up* by David A. Carter and James Diaz (Simon Schuster, 1999). Another book offers fewer mechanisms, but gives more detail on each one, including some preprinted pages for you to cut out and fold up; this book is *Paper Engineering* by Mark Hiner (Tarquin Publications, 1985). Another great survey of the essentials, with dozens of suggested projects, is provided in *The Pop-Up Book* by Paul Jackson (Henry Holt, 1993).

Everyone has their favorite pop-up books. Like any other kind of books, what delights one person can leave another bored. But here are some pop-up books that I believe most people will find entertaining, or at least very interesting. These are by no means exhaustive lists, nor do they include all my favorites; that would take pages. Rather, they're just good jumping-off places into the literature.

For children, I recommend *Robot* by Jan Pienkowski, paper engineering by James Roger Diaz, Tor Lokvig, and Marcin Stajewski; *Haunted House* by Jan Pienkowski, paper engineering by Tor Lokvig; *Alice's Adventures in Wonderland* by Lewis Carroll, illustrated by Jenny Thorne, paper engineering by James Roger Diaz; and *Monster Island*, illustrated by Ron Van der Meer, paper engineering by Tor Lokvig and John Strejan. Some people do both the illustrations and paper engineering for their books. Some great examples include *Sam's Pizza* by David Pelham, *The Movable Mother Goose* by Robert Sabuda, *Bed Bugs: A Pop-Up Bedtime Book* by David A. Carter, and *Chuck Murphy's One to Ten Pop-Up Surprises!* by Chuck Murphy.

Robert Sabuda, one of the most respected paper engineers working today, has created an international online gallery of great pop-up work from all over the world. You can browse the gallery at http://robertsabuda.com/intgallery_files/.

A couple of recent pop-ups for adults include *The Human Body* by Jonathan Miller and David Pelham, and *The Pop-Up Book of Phobias*, illustrated by Balvis Rubess, paper engineering by Matthew Reinhart.

Three library web sites were invaluable to me in compiling my history of pop-up books. *Moving Tales: Paper Engineering and Children's Pop-Up Books* is a record of the Foyer exhibit in the State Library of Victoria in 1995: http://www.vicnet.net.au/vicnet/book/popups/popup.html A short but very readable account appears in the Rutgers University web site *A Concise History of Pop-Up and Movable Books* by Ann Montanaro: http://www.libraries.rutgers.edu/rulib/spcol/montanar/p-intro.htm The University of North Texas has two great sites that contain a ton of information. But even better, they contain many photographs of mechanical books through history. They show animated versions of the books being worked, and even provide videos of some books being opened. They appear at *Pop-Up and Movable Books: A Tour Through Their History*: http://www.library.unt.edu/rarebooks/exhibits/popup2/default.htm and *The Great Menagerie: The Wonderful World of Pop-Up and Movable Books, 1911–1996* : http://www.library.unt.edu/rarebooks/exhibits/popup/main.htm.

If you're keen to look more closely at constraint systems, a good place to get started is the book *Solving Geometric Constraint Systems* by Glenn A. Kramer (MIT Press, 1992).

You can find out a lot more about the radical axis and other aspects of circular geometry in the excellent book *Geometry: A Comprehensive Course*, by Dan Pedoe (Dover Publications, 1970).

Some of the material in this chapter was carried out while I worked at Microsoft Research. That work appears in my technical report, *Interactive Pop-Up Card Design* (Microsoft Research Technical Report MSR-TR-98-03, January 1998 http://research.microsoft.com/scripts/pubs/view.asp?TR_ID=MSR-TR-98-03), and is covered by Patent 6,311,142.

I'm not the first person to have his hand at bringing together computers and pop-ups. You can read about a rather different approach in the article "Mathematical Modelling and Simulation of Pop-Up Books" by Y. T. Lee, B. Tor, and E. L. Soo (Computers Graphics, 20(1), 1996, pgs. 21–31). Another article on paper manipulation that is relevant to pop-up techniques is "Bending and Creasing Virtual Paper" by Yannick L. Kergosien, Hironoba Gotoda, and Tosiyasu L. Kunii (*IEEE Computer Graphics & Applications*, Volume 14, January 1994, pgs. 40–48). A great reference on paper and its geometric properties is "Curvature and Creases: A Primer on Paper" by David A. Huffman (*IEEE Transactions on Computing*, Volume C-25, Number 10, October 1976, pgs. 1010–1019).

The solution I presented for finding the line of intersection formed by two planes was published by Jim Blinn in his classic paper "A Homogeneous Formulation for Lines in 3-Space" in *Computer Graphics* (Proceedings of SIGGRAPH 77, 11 (2), pp. 237–241).

A good place to start to learn about packing algorithms in the textiles industry is "Placement and Compaction of Nonconvex Polygons for Clothing Manufacture" by V. Milenkovic, K. Daniels, and Z. Li (*Proceedings 4th Canadian Conference on Computational Geometry*, pages 236–243, 1992).

For information on ray tracing, and how to find the intersection of lines with a variety of geometric objects including spheres, you can look at *An Introduction to Ray Tracing* by Glassner et al. (Academic Press, 1989) or the more recent *Realistic Ray Tracing* by Peter Shirley (A K Peters, 2000).

Picking up the Pieces

2

Secrets are sensitive things. The more people you tell, the less your secret is secure. So usually we try to control the spread of secrets as much as possible.

In Chapter 10 of *Andrew Glassner's Other Notebook*, I discussed a radically new way to keep secrets using the techniques of quantum cryptography. Though it's a fascinating theory, we don't have products yet that actually implement those principles, so in the meantime we have to manage with more traditional techniques.

Of all the ways to share a secret, perhaps the most dangerous is to write it down on paper in plain language. That has the advantages of permanence and some reduction in the need to repeat yourself verbally, but it runs a big risk: anyone who can get hold of the paper can read your secret, even years later. If you think someone is going to see your document and use it against you, you've got to destroy the paper before they get to it.

But then you have another problem, which is how to best destroy the paper. If the secret is important enough that you need to protect it, probably the best course is to burn the page, and then if you're really worried, scatter the ashes. If for some reason you can't burn it, you could try instead ripping it up into tiny pieces. But that doesn't seem very secure.

In recent years, manufacturers have started to offer devices known as "document shredders." A review of a few big office-supply stores reveals that there are two major categories of these machines: *strip-*

cutters and *cross-cutters* (also known as *confetti-cutters*). Both of these look like tall garbage cans with a mechanical unit on the top into which you feed sheets of paper.

The strip-cutters slice pages into parallel strips, usually ranging from 0.25 to 0.125 inches wide. Since the pages are usually fed in short side first, an American legal-sized page results in 34 to 68 strips, each 11 inches long. The cross-cutters add another step by cutting each of these strips into shorter segments, typically between 1.25 and 1.5 inches long.

Using one of these shredding machines seems to me like using a simple lock on a door. A simple lock keeps out the casual passer-by who might just happen to wander in, but it won't keep out an even slightly motivated intruder. If the protected material is important enough to warrant a lock, shouldn't it be a good lock? Similarly, if some documents are sensitive enough that they shouldn't be read, shouldn't they be made unreadable? Making them merely inconvenient to read seems like pretty flimsy protection.

Suppose that a big company (let's call it, say, Enron) has suddenly become the focus of intense public and legal scrutiny, and people in that company feel the need to destroy some of their documents as quickly as possible. So they run them through their strip-cut shredders, and then give the strips to their employees to use as disposable packing material. The employees later give that material to the court to be used as evidence. Are the secrets that were printed on those documents safe?

It seemed unlikely to me that those strips couldn't be reassembled. So I thought I'd see what might be involved in putting strip-cut documents back together again.

The tools that solve this problem can also address a more general and interesting problem: given a collection of arbitrarily-sized pieces with images upon them, and some expectation that they fit together to make one or more larger images, can you assemble the pieces into these larger images? In the case of shredded documents, the pieces are vertical strips of paper containing pages of text. Other applications include repairing a broken object that has shattered or assembling a jigsaw puzzle. Let's see how we might go about solving the text reconstruction problem.

Getting Started

It's hard to assemble a lot of pieces at once, so I decided to put the pieces together two at a time. In other words, I'll "grow" the reconstruction by first combining two pieces that belong together, and then combining two more, and so on.

There are two questions to ask any time you test objects pair-wise like this. First, do I have two objects that are likely to be matches? Second, do they indeed match? The first question is important for reasons of efficiency, while the second is necessary to get a good assembly.

To get a handle on typical numbers, suppose you're recovering a bag of slice-cut documents. Each 8.5 inch wide page will have been sliced into 68 strips, each 0.125 inches. In practice, the left and right margins of each page are generally about 1.25 inches. If we eliminate these all-white strips, then we have 6 inches of printed width, or 480 strips per page. So if someone shredded 200 pages, there would be about 96,000 strips, which often all go into a single bag below the shredder and get thrown away en masse. In contrast, jigsaw puzzles that are sold in the stores seem to max out at about 1000 pieces.

So if we were to compare every jigsaw piece to every other piece (and remembering that each piece generally has four sides), that's $4N^2$ tests, which for $N = 1000$ is about 4 million tests. The strip-cut shredder problem has only two sides per strip, so we'd require $2N^2$ tests, which for $N = 96,000$ strips is somewhat more than eighteen billion. That's going to be a tough order, even on supercomputers. Hence, the efficiency question is important, so that we're not wasting time comparing pieces that have no chance of matching.

A good matching test is important to make sure that pieces are correctly combined. It needs to be efficient, of course, since this is where the program will spend most of its time. It also needs to look for a good match, but be tolerant of near-matches. When a razor slices a page, or a jigsaw or other cutter makes puzzle pieces, the material directly under the blade is naturally lost, so the remaining two sides will not fit perfectly. Furthermore, borders and edges are common features, and they might happen to align with the piece edges. This is often the case for text. Consider a letter like a capital I, or lower-case L. These both have most of their information in a vertical line, aligned to the long side of the page. If the shredding machine cuts just to the left of one of these letters, there will be nothing shared between the two strips over this border. In fact, much printed text is this way: two strips that started out adjacent have frequent regions where corresponding regions of the two strips are opposite in color: one edge is black and the other is white. Thus our matching test needs to be able to pick up on what similarities are available, and not overly-penalize mismatches. These are contradictory desires, of course, which is what makes matching functions so interesting!

For simplicity, in the following discussions I'll stick to the document reconstruction problem where the pieces are strips. Later on we'll see that the ideas easily generalize to jigsaw and other types of shapes.

(a) (b) (c) (d)

Figure 2.1

Test images for the "thin" figure set. (a) Gas station (Fremont, Seattle). (b) Turtle lamp (Los Angeles). (c) Saturn V liftoff (NASA). (d) Mayan pillar (San Diego).

TEST DATA

Although my original inspiration was to reassemble text documents, I quickly found that visually checking the reconstructions was tedious, and it was hard to spot where a misplaced strip ought to have gone.

To make things easier, I used two sets of public-domain images to develop my reconstruction software. Figure 2.1 shows what I call the "thin" set, made of four images each about two-thirds as wide as they are tall. Figure 2.2 shows the "wide" set, where each image is about twice as wide as the thin images.

(a) (b) (c) (d)

Figure 2.2

Test images for the "wide" figure set. (a) Earth (NASA). (b) Gazebo (Woodland Park Zoo, Seattle). (c) Music Room (Fremont, Seattle). (d) Fourth of July (Gasworks Park, Seattle).

I'll use these images for the following discussions.

GOT A MATCH?

To judge the quality of the fit between two strips, I run them through a *fitness function* to compute a *score*. I decided to code things so that the score indicates the degree of mismatch. Thus the higher the score, the worse the match between the pieces. So the ideal matching function would evaluate to 0 for two strips that were supposed to be adjacent, and to infinity for all other pairs.

The principle at work here is *coherence*. In this context, coherence says that we're betting that any given column of pixels in an image is going to be a lot like the columns immediately to its left and right. After all, if the images were random noise (that is, just black and white dots with no features), then matching up strips would be hopeless, since statistically no pair of strips would be any better than any other pair.

The most obvious place to start is just to compare the RGB values of adjacent pixels over the edge and add them up. If we have two pixels P_0 and P_1 with colors (r_0, g_0, b_0) and (r_1, g_1, b_1), then we can find their simple difference, which I'll call D_0, by just summing up the absolute values of their differences:

$$D_0 = \Delta r + \Delta g + \Delta b,$$

where

$$\Delta r = |r_0 - r_1|, \quad \Delta g = |g_0 - g_1|, \quad \Delta b = |b_0 - b_1|.$$

Let's see how well this metric works out. I'll take the four thin images in Figure 2.1, cut them into 40 strips each, and randomly scramble them up. Now let's try to find the piece that best fits the right-hand side of the leftmost strip from the Mayan pillar. By looking through the scrambled pieces, I found that the leftmost strip of this image was assigned strip number 69, and that the strip that was originally to its right became strip 27. So I'll place each strip to the right of strip 69, compute its score using D_0, above, and see if strip 27 has the lowest score.

Figure 2.3

Looking for strip 27 using metric D_0. (a) The scores using D_0. (b) The inverse of part a. The ratio of the spike to the minimum value is about 16.

Figure 2.3(a) shows the result. The scores range from a low of 15,366 for strip 27, to a high score of 248,939. Number 27 does seem to stand out, but perhaps we can improve the data. In Figure 2.3(b) I've plotted the inverse of Figure 2.3(a) (that is, each value x is replaced by $1/x$). This looks great, and strip 27 sure stands out, so we're off to a good start. The ratio between the highest value in the inverse plot to the lowest value is about 16; let's see if we can improve that.

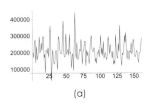

(a)

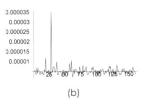

(b)

Consider the real world for a moment. Paper has variations, and scanners are noisy. We'd like to avoid penalizing little imperfections caused by dust and scratches and printing technology, where one dot might be just slightly darker or lighter than another. So I'll add another step to the test function: a *threshold*. If the difference between two color values is less than the threshold T, I'll set it to zero:

$$\Delta r^T = \begin{cases} if\ \Delta r < T_r, & 0 \\ else, & \Delta r. \end{cases}$$

and similarly for Δg^T and Δb^T. The result is a new, thresholded metric D_1:

$$D_1 = \Delta r^T + \Delta g^T + \Delta b^T.$$

Figure 2.4(a) shows the result. The scores range from a low of 8,601 for strip 27, to a high score of 192,532. Figure 2.4(b) shows the inverse function. Here I used the same value of 10 for the three thresholds T_r, T_g, and T_b. The noise seems to have settled down a little in the inverse plot, which makes the spike at 27 even easier to find. The ratio between that highest spike to the smallest value in the plot is about 28, which is a nice improvement.

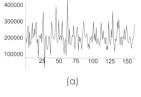
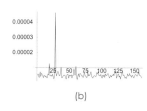

(a)   (b)

Figure 2.4

Looking for strip 27 using metric D_1. (a) The scores using D_1. (b) The inverse of part (a). The ratio of the spike to the minimum value is about 28.

So far I've been treating the three color components equally. In the case of a black-and-white document, like type on paper, that's pretty reasonable. But when it comes to images, we know that we're more sensitive to some colors than others. This perceptual quirk won't generally help us put together photographs of the real world, but I think it might help us with rendered creations like paintings, and even computer graphics. My hypothesis is that since artists are using the same visual system as their audience, they tend to create works that are tailored to that system. For example, we're more sensitive to variations in greens than in blues, so there might be more information packed into the green part of a painting than the blue parts.

I encoded this observation into a metric D_2 that weights the three color components individually. Including the thresholded colors as before, metric D_2 is given by

$$D_2 = w_r\,\Delta r^T + w_g\,\Delta g^T + w_b\,\Delta b^T,$$

where I used weights from the standard luminance function:

$$w_r = 0.3, \quad w_g = 0.59, \quad w_b = 0.11.$$

Figure 2.5(a) shows the result. The scores range from a low of 2,892 for strip 27, to a high score of 81,266. Figure 2.5(b) shows the inverse function. This modification hasn't made a big change in this data, but we've had a slight improvement on the ratio to about 29. In my experience this weighting of the colors can lead to a bit of an improvement for color images.

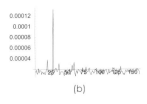

(a)

(b)

Figure 2.5

Looking for strip 27 using metric D_2. (a) The scores using D_2. (b) The inverse of part (a). The ratio of the spike to the minimum value is about 29.

Remember that our goal is to make the spike for slice 27 as unambiguous as possible. A useful way to crank up differences in data is to exponentiate them. This leads to a third metric, D_3:

$$D_3 = (w_r \, \Delta r^T)^{n_r} + (w_g \, \Delta g^T)^{n_g} + (w_b \, \Delta b^T)^{n_b}$$

Figure 2.6(a) shows the results when I used the same value of 2 for all three exponents: $n_r = n_g = n_b = 2$. The scores range from a low of 76,761 for strip 27, to a high score of about 9 million. Figure 2.6(b) shows the inverse function. The spike now is just about impossible to miss; the ratio of the spike's value to the minimum value in the plot is about 127.

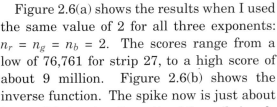
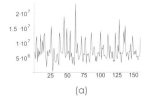

(a)

(b)

Figure 2.6

Looking for strip 27 using metric D_3. (a) The scores using D_3. (b) The inverse of part (a). The ratio of the spike to the minimum value is about 127.

Experiments with text and color images have led me to settle on D_3 for my testing function. On each run, though, I have the opportunity to tweak all the variables, weights, thresholds, and exponents, in order to accommodate the peculiarities of different printers, scanners, paper types, etc.

So that we can see how this metric performs on a larger problem, Figure 2.7(a) shows the scores resulting from slicing all four images into ten strips each, and then comparing every pair. Figure 2.7(b) contains the inverse plot, which shows the spikes pretty well. Those spikes are where the metric says the two pieces match up well. In Figure 2.7(c) I processed the inverse data so that any values below a threshold set

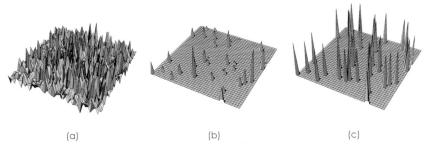

(a)   (b)   (c)

Figure 2.7

Comparing the four thin images after being cut into 10 strips each, using metric D_3. (a) The output of the metric. (b) The inverse of part (a). (c) A thresholded version of (b).

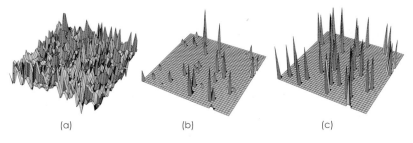

(a)   (b)   (c)

Figure 2.8

Comparing the four wide images after being cut into 10 strips each, using metric D_3. (a) The output of the metric. (b) The inverse of part (a). (c) A thresholded version of (b).

halfway between the average and the largest value are set to zero, and the others are set to one. This basically pushes all the noise to zero and leaves just the spikes.

Figure 2.8 shows the same data for the wide data set. Some of the spikes are in the same place as in Figure 2.7 because I used the same random number seed for shuffling the strips in both figures.

If we could afford to run this metric on all the objects in the database, it suggests an easy way to get a good initial match: just compute all the pairings, and then threshold the result until just the right number of matches remain. For example, when we have four images of ten strips each, there are 36 good pairings to be found. We need only 36 rather than 40 because four of these pairs just connect up the edges of unconnected pages, and since their order doesn't matter, we don't have to worry about them.

Just thresholding the pairing data and connecting up the strips wouldn't always solve the problem perfectly, because that process ignores some important issues. For example, we have to make sure that no strip is a neighbor to itself, and that we don't accidentally make cycles of strips. I'll talk about these issues some more below.

AN ORDERLY DEVELOPMENT

Let's suppose that we had access to the entire grid of all pairings, like that of Figures 2.7 and 2.8. How might we use this data to assemble the pieces?

In this section I'll describe my first approach to assembly, which ended up not working out very well. I'll describe it here for two reasons. First, we hardly ever talk about our unsuccessful ideas in print. Most research papers state the problem they want to solve, and then present the solution that worked. That's just fine, and how it ought to be. But where do we document the dead ends? We all go through them, and yet we never talk about them. Every now and then I like to talk about the approaches that didn't work, both for their own sake, and because they're instructive. And that's the second reason for talking about the methods that didn't work out so well: we often learn more from our failures than from our successes. It was by trying to solve this problem in a reasonable way that didn't work out in the long run that I came to understand the problem well enough to cook up a better solution

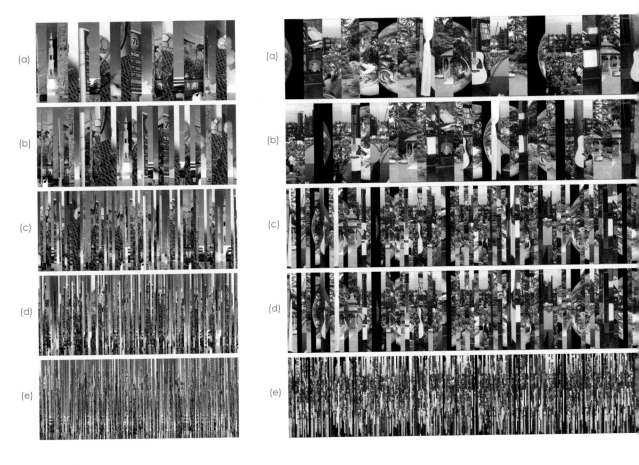

that does work. So let's dig in to a sensible reassembly strategy that manages to do a good, but not great, job.

Let's begin by looking at the input. Figure 2.9 shows the thin image set after it has been sliced into several different numbers of strips. Note that there's no obvious correlation between the strips, just as though they'd been fished out of wastebasket and scanned in randomly. One thing that we do know is which way is up (I'll talk about handling unknown orientation later on). Figure 2.10 shows the wide data set, in the same initial condition.

Let's pick one strip at random, and then try to build to its right using a greedy technique. So if we have a given strip, we'll consult the database of scores, find the strip that is most suited to be the right-hand neighbor of this strip, and place that down. Then we'll get the best right neighbor for that strip, and so on, working our way from left to right, until we've finally placed them all.

Figure 2.9 (top Left)

The unorganized strips associated with the thin data set. (a) 5 strips per image. (b) 10 strips per image. (c) 20 strips per image. (d) 40 strips per image. (e) 80 strips per image.

Figure 2.10 (top right)

The unorganized strips associated with the wide data set. (a) 5 strips per image. (b) 10 strips per image. (c) 20 strips per image. (d) 40 strips per image. (e) 80 strips per image.

Picking up
the Pieces

(top left) Figure 2.11

The result of starting with a random strip and building to the right for the thin data set. (a) 5 strips per image. (b) 10 strips per image. (c) 20 strips per image. (d) 40 strips per image. (e) 80 strips per image.

(top right) Figure 2.12

The result of starting with a random strip and building to the right for the wide data set. (a) 5 strips per image. (b) 10 strips per image. (c) 20 strips per image. (d) 40 strips per image. (e) 80 strips per image.

Figure 2.11 shows the result for several different numbers of strips in the thin data set, and Figure 2.12 shows the results for the wide data set. The good news is that we've reduced the chaos of unrelated strips into a few large chunks (and some smaller ones). But the images aren't quite assembled the way we'd like. Curiously, the number of strips involved changes the result, but not the general feel of the errors. What went wrong?

As long as we're working our way to the right in a given image, generally the pieces go together well. But then when we hit the right edge of the picture, the best remaining strip to its right is essentially a random choice. From that point on we continue to the right again, until we either hit the right side of the image, or need a strip that's already been used. Then we start again. Thus we end up getting chunks of images that get smaller and smaller as we work to the right.

Let's see what happens if we start off with a better choice. Before we put down the very first piece, we'll look through all the strips and find the one that has the worst match on its left side. The idea is that

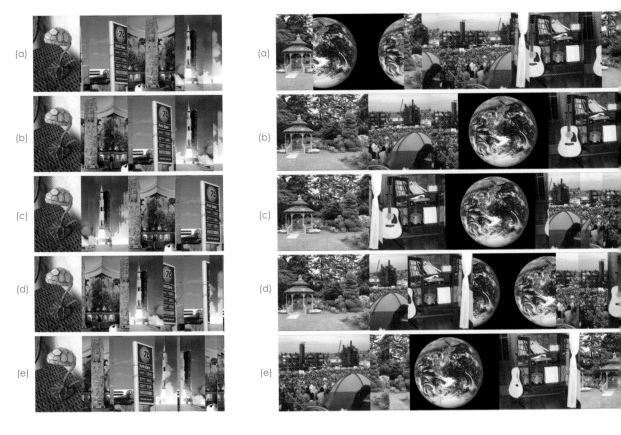

whatever strip has no good left neighbors is probably the left edge of an image.

Figure 2.13 shows the result of this change for the thin test cases. This is encouraging, but still not quite right. Figure 2.14 show the result for the wide test cases. We still sometimes start at the wrong place, because the piece with the worst left neighbor, as determined by the scoring function D_3, isn't always at the left edge of the image. Sometimes there's another strip somewhere in the database whose right edge just happens to match the left edge of an image pretty well, so the piece we end up with isn't really what we wanted.

As I thought about it more, I realized that this left-to-right growing approach could be endlessly tweaked, but was probably doomed in the long run. One big problem of course is that it requires access to all the pairing data, which for a large data set will be prohibitive. But the essential problem is that as we march along, looking for the best match to a given piece, we may end up selecting a piece that has a really terrific match somewhere else, and then that piece is over. For

Figure 2.13 (top left)

The result of starting with the strip with the worst left neighbor and then building to the right for the thin data set. (a) 5 strips per image. (b) 10 strips per image. (c) 20 strips per image. (d) 40 strips per image. (e) 80 strips per image.

Figure 2.14 (top right)

The result of starting with the strip with the worst left neighbor and then building to the right for the wide data set. (a) 5 strips per image. (b) 10 strips per image. (c) 20 strips per image. (d) 40 strips per image. (e) 80 strips per image.

example, suppose that by coincidence some strip in the middle of the Earth image nicely matched a strip in the middle of the gazebo image. When we place the Earth strip down in the middle of the gazebo image, we've just ruined our chance to get either of those images right.

Faced with these difficulties, I decided to shift gears and try a clustering approach.

CLUSTERING

My clustering algorithm was inspired by the observation at the end of the last section. Suppose we have four pieces, which I'll call A, B, C, and D, and when correctly assembled they'd be in the order $ABCD$. Now suppose that the match between C and D is excellent, but the match between A and B isn't as good. When we've placed A, we look through the remaining pieces. It can happen that we find that piece D is the best match for the right hand side of A. But "best" in this case might mean nothing more than "least-worst." Of course, the computer has no way of knowing that, so it picks D and places it next to A. The shame here is that this now removes the possibility of ever getting the CD pairing, which had a very low score.

This of course is a common problem with all greedy algorithms and philosophies: by doing what's most expeditious at the moment, one can eliminate the opportunity to do something better later on.

So instead, let's take a *clustering* approach. Here's the basic idea behind clustering: if C and D have a really low score, let's put them together first. Then we'll deal with the rest of the pieces.

So assuming again for the moment that we have access to the entire database of scores for every pair of pieces, we could first put together the two pieces with the lowest score, then the next two, and the next two, and so on, until every piece has been placed.

This algorithm works beautifully once you take care of an important gotcha: you can't make cycles. I'll reuse our $ABCD$ example from before, but to make the discussion clearer, I'll indicate each pairing with subscripts. Thus we have one score for when the right side of A abuts the left side of B, which I'll write $A_R B_L$, and another score for when the right side of B abuts the left side of A, which I'll write $B_R A_L$. Suppose that the four lowest scores in the database are, in ascending order, $B_R D_L$, $D_R A_L$, $A_R B_L$. This would create the cyclic sequence BDA where the right side of A is linked to the left side of B. Where is C to go? It's left out in the cold.

Even worse, if we're not careful we might find that a single strip best matches itself; for example, $A_R A_L$ might have a really low score if A is

Figure 2.15

The result of the clustering algorithm for the thin database.

just a solid color. Obviously we can handle that as a special case, but if we prevent cycles of any size from forming, then single-piece cycles are prevented as well.

I prevent the formation of cycles with a brute-force technique. Whenever I want to add a piece to either end of a cluster, I check the other end of the cluster to see if that piece is already there. If so, I skip adding that one in and move on to the next-best pairing. The only exception to this rule is when all the pieces have been placed; then the very last one will necessarily make a single big cycle that contains the whole database.

So to recap, I search the database for the lowest-scored pair and put those two pieces together. Then I search for the next lowest pair, and assemble those, and so on, until all the pieces have been placed. Along the way, I make sure that I don't create any cycles except when placing the very last piece.

Figure 2.16

The result of the clustering algorithm for the wide database.

This algorithm works great. Figure 2.15 shows the result for the thin data set, and Figure 2.16 shows the wide data set. Since the whole reconstruction creates a cycle, it doesn't matter which piece you choose as the "leftmost" one when printing them out; in effect, the printout is a tube. But because it's nicer to start on a boundary, I search the entire chain, after it's been completely assembled, for the worst score between two neighboring pieces, on the assumption that that spot is likely to be a border. When I create the output image, I use the strip to the right of that border as my starting point.

SORTING IT ALL OUT

The data sets in the last examples had at most a few hundred strips. Suppose that we had a few thousand strips, or even a couple of orders of magnitude more. As I discussed earlier, computing and storing all the pairwise scores demands resources proportional to the square of the number of pieces, and that's a number that grows very quickly.

To work with large data sets, I scanned in some PDF pages of text for a set of columns I wrote in 2001 on quantum computing. I didn't use the published pages with the figures on them because I wanted to simulate the kind of text-only documents people shred in offices. There were 51 pages in all, with text in the middle six inches of the page, giving me 306 horizontal inches of text. Cutting those pages into 0.125 inch wide strips gave me 2,480 strips to reassemble, which I call the QC data set (for Quantum Cryptography, the subject matter of the shredded text). Figure 2.17 shows a piece of this data set in its original, random order.

All the pairwise scores for this data set would mean creating and storing just under six million scores. The amount of time it takes to compute D_3 for any given pair of strips depends of course on the size of the strips and the speed of the processor, but when you get into these large numbers, all sorts of practical issues like paging, which didn't matter much before, can become significant. Though one can imagine handling six million scores, if I had just 250 pages to reassemble, that would be 144 million scores, and things would be getting pretty well out of hand by that point.

Figure 2.17

Some of the 24,480 strips making up the text-only QC data set.

My approach was to sort the pieces that had a reasonable likelihood of belonging together into smaller bins. Then I could apply the clustering algorithm of the last section just to the contents of the bins. For example, using just ten bins for the QC data set results in about 244 strips per bin, which is even smaller than the image-based data sets I used above (when each image was cut into 80 strips, there were 320 strips to be assembled). Those data sets assembled in about a second on my little home PC using entirely unoptimized code. If I had 250 pages (or about 12,000 strips), then using 60 bins would let us assemble the entire database in about a minute.

Note that when a piece goes into a bin, we indicate whether it's the left or right edge of the piece that has landed it there. A piece might appear in more than one bin if its left side matches one group and its right side another. Keeping this detail in mind, I'll just speak of strips and bins from here on.

The trick to this approach is to make sure that we get the right pieces into the bins. This is a question of heuristics, or approaches that seem to make sense but may not have a deep theoretical foundation. Basically I just thought about what tests might be good at picking up features between strips and tried them out.

I experimented with several different sorting heuristics, using both the QC data set, and the thin and wide image data sets.

My first, and simplest, approach was to simply average together all the colors along the side of the strip and then take the luminance of that color. I set up as many bins as I wanted, each holding a range of luminances from 0 to 1. Since many of the text pieces were near mid-gray in average intensity, I used pretty big bins for the brightest and darkest ends, and smaller ones in the middle. For example, one bin might hold all sides with luminances in the range (0.0, 0.15), while one closer to the middle of the range might hold the range (0.45, 0.46). I call this sorter L, for luminance.

That test works very well, but the middle bins fill up very fast, and sometimes near neighbors fall into different bins. That meant that pieces that ought to match never got the chance to see each other. So I opened up the range of each bin so that they overlap. For example, the first two bins might now cover (0.0, 0.2) and (0.1, 0.3) while a couple of bins near the middle could hold (0.445, 0.465) and (0.455, 0.475). A factor f that the user can set determines how much the bins overlap. I call this overlapping luminance sorter L_f.

The sorters L and L_f group text-based pages based on the density of black ink to white paper, but they don't take into account how the patterns fall on the page.

I implemented a run-length metric that tries to get at some of this information. I start at the top of the page and count the lengths of continuous sequences of the same color. For full-color images such as those in my data sets above, this isn't a very useful metric, but it's well suited to text. I save the length and color of the longest run, and the arithmetic average of all the runs. I used these values in different ways to create a few different sorters. One useful value comes from multiplying the longest-run color by its length, taking its luminance, and dividing by the average run-length. As before, I have a variety of overlapping bins for the result; I call this overlapping run-length sorter R_f. In another sorter I use just the luminance of the color in the longest run, giving me sorter S_f.

These sorters all have different strengths, and I'm sure one could cook up any number of additional sorters which are sensitive to different aspects of the data that one might be interested in.

In practice, I use them all. So each strip gets run through each sorter and placed into a bin from that sorter. Then I score all the strips in each bin for all the sorters.

With that data in hand, I assemble the clusters by looking first for the lowest-scored pair among all the pairs in all the bins, and then the next lowest-scored pair, and so on. That way if one of the sorters misses out on connecting two pieces that really belong together, one of the other sorters has a chance to catch it.

Between these two metrics, and the clustering step, the two image sets assembled perfectly, and the QC data set went together almost perfectly; out of 2480 strips, only 15 strips weren't properly matched up on one side or the other. Figure 2.18 shows a piece of the results; the complete output just looks like a bunch of pages of text side-by-side, as it should.

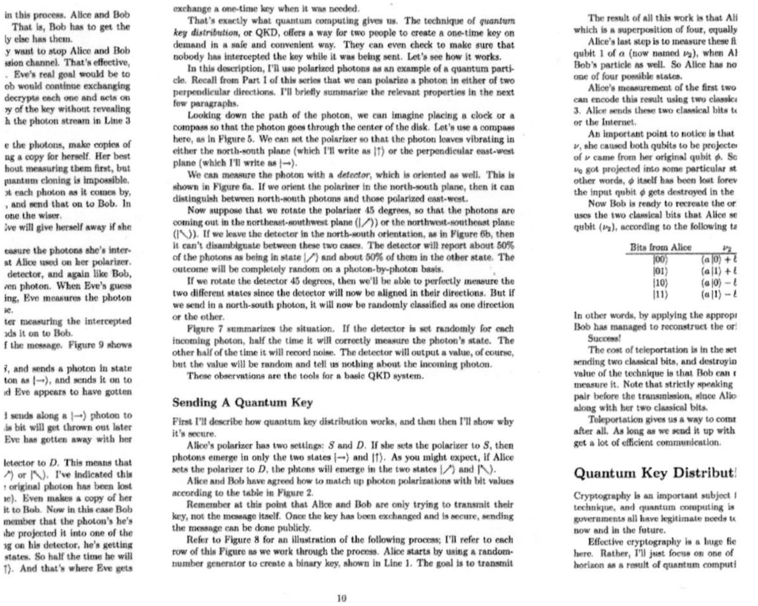

Figure 2.18

Results of running the multiple-bin sorters on the QC data set, followed by clustering.

(Figure content — reassembled text strips:)

in this process. Alice and Bob
That is, Bob has to get the
ly else has them.
y want to stop Alice and Bob
ssion channel. That's effective.
. Eve's real goal would be to
ob would continue exchanging
decrypts each one and acts on
y of the key without revealing
h the photon stream in Line 3

e the photons, make copies of
ng a copy for herself. Her best
hout measuring them first, but
quantum cloning is impossible.
t each photon as it comes by,
, and send that on to Bob. In
one the wiser.
ive will give herself away if she

easure the photons she's inter-
st Alice used on her polarizer.
detector, and again like Bob,
en photon. When Eve's measuring, Eve measures the photon
ie.
ter measuring the intercepted
ds it on to Bob.
f the message. Figure 9 shows

i, and sends a photon in state
ton as $|\rightarrow\rangle$, and sends it on to
d Eve appears to have gotten

l sends along a $|\rightarrow\rangle$ photon to
is bit will get thrown out later
Eve has gotten away with her

letector to D. This means that
$\nearrow\rangle$ or $|\searrow\rangle$. I've indicated this
: original photon has been lost
se). Even makes a copy of her
it to Bob. Now in this case Bob
member that the photon's he's
he projected it into one of the
ig on his detector, he's getting
states. So half the time he will
$\uparrow\rangle$. And that's where Eve gets

---

exchange a one-time key when it was needed.

That's exactly what quantum computing gives us. The technique of *quantum key distribution*, or QKD, offers a way for two people to create a one-time key on demand in a safe and convenient way. They can even check to make sure that nobody has intercepted the key while it was being sent. Let's see how it works.

In this description, I'll use polarized photons as an example of a quantum parti-cle. Recall from Part 1 of this series that we can polarize a photon in either of two perpendicular directions. I'll briefly summarize the relevant properties in the next few paragraphs.

Looking down the path of the photon, we can imagine placing a clock or a compass so that the photon goes through the center of the disk. Let's use a compass here, as in Figure 5. We can set the polarizer so that the photon leaves vibrating in either the north-south plane (which I'll write as $|\uparrow\rangle$) or the perpendicular east-west plane (which I'll write as $|\rightarrow\rangle$).

We can measure the photon with a *detector*, which is oriented as well. This is shown in Figure 6a. If we orient the polarizer in the north-south plane, then it can distinguish between north-south photons and those polarized east-west.

Now suppose that we rotate the polarizer 45 degrees, so that the photons are coming out in the northeast-southwest plane ($|\nearrow\rangle$) or the northwest-southeast plane ($|\nwarrow\rangle$). If we leave the detector in the north-south orientation, as in Figure 6b, then it can't disambiguate between these two cases. The detector will report about 50% of the photons as being in state $|\nearrow\rangle$ and about 50% of them in the other state. The outcome will be completely random on a photon-by-photon basis.

If we rotate the detector 45 degrees, then we'll be able to perfectly measure the two different states since the detector will now be aligned with their directions. But if we send in a north-south photon, it will now be randomly classified as one direction or the other.

Figure 7 summarizes the situation. If the detector is set randomly for each incoming photon, half the time it will correctly measure the photon's state. The other half of the time it will record noise. The detector will output a value, of course, but the value will be random and tell us nothing about the incoming photon.

These observations are the tools for a basic QKD system.

Sending A Quantum Key

First I'll describe how quantum key distribution works, and then then I'll show why it's secure.

Alice's polarizer has two settings: S and D. If she sets the polarizer to S, then photons emerge in only the two states $|\rightarrow\rangle$ and $|\uparrow\rangle$. As you might expect, if Alice sets the polarizer to D, the photons will emerge in the two states $|\nearrow\rangle$ and $|\searrow\rangle$.

Alice and Bob have agreed how to match up photon polarizations with bit values according to the table in Figure 2.

Remember at this point that Alice and Bob are only trying to transmit their key, not the message itself. Once the key has been exchanged and is secure, sending the message can be done publicly.

Refer to Figure 8 for an illustration of the following process; I'll refer to each row of this Figure as we work through the process. Alice starts by using a random-number generator to create a binary key, shown in Line 1. The goal is to transmit

10

The result of all this work is that Ali which is a superposition of four, equally

Alice's last step is to measure these fi qubit 1 of α (now named ν_2), when Al Bob's particle as well. So Alice has no one of four possible states.

Alice's measurement of the first two can encode this result using two classica 3. Alice sends these two classical bits to or the Internet.

An important point to notice is that ν, she caused both qubits to be projecte of ν came from her original qubit α. So ν_2 got projected into some particular st other words, ϕ itself has been lost forev the input qubit ϕ gets destroyed in the Now Bob is ready to recreate the ori uses the two classical bits that Alice se qubit (ν_2), according to the following ta

Bits from Alice	ν_2
$|00\rangle$	$(a|0\rangle + b$
$|01\rangle$	$(a|1\rangle + b$
$|10\rangle$	$(a|0\rangle - b$
$|11\rangle$	$(a|1\rangle - b$

In other words, by applying the appropr Bob has managed to reconstruct the ori Success!

The cost of teleportation is in the set sending two classical bits, and destroyin value of the technique is that Bob can r measure it. Note that strictly speaking pair before the transmission, since Alic along with her two classical bits.

Teleportation gives us a way to comr after all. As long as we send it up with get a lot of efficient communication.

Quantum Key Distributi

Cryptography is an important subject i technique, and quantum computing is governments all have legitimate needs to now and in the future.

Effective cryptography is a huge fie here. Rather, I'll just focus on one of horizon as a result of quantum computi

---

HEURISTICS

There are a few other heuristics that could be added to this system. For example, we might know that we were scanning in pages of text on standard American-sized letter paper. Printers generally need at least a half-inch of margin on both sides of the text. If we found that we were making a cluster that was more than about 7.5 inches wide, we could suspect an error and try to find a place to split it apart.

We could also try to detect, and weight, specific image features. For example, many office memos, particularly involving numbers, have horizontal rules and borders. We could look for such features and give them weight in the sorting step.

I mentioned earlier that I assumed that all the strips were scanned in so that they're in the proper orientation. In the case of text, we could precede the matching process with a step of optical character recognition on the strip in both its original orientation, and after rotating it 180 degrees. The OCR process tries to recognize letters and is likely to find much better matches in one orientation rather than the other.

In the case of images, the problem is a little harder. I haven't implemented it, but I think that you could get pretty far by scoring all the strips in both orientations, and then using whichever orientation produced lower scores overall.

CROSSCUTS AND JIGSAW PUZZLES

So far I've only spoken about strips, but the general approach works for more irregularly-shaped pieces.

As I mentioned above, some shredding machines cut the strips into smaller pieces. At first, this may seem to be a straightforward problem: just build a few more tables, and match all four sides of the rectangular strips, rather than just the left and right sides.

There is a problem, though, which comes from the fact that there's a lot of white space on a page of text. The top and bottom of many of these crosscut strips will be white (since that edge will fall between lines of text). Since these edges are all completely white, they will have near-perfect scores of zero (or almost zero). Of course, we can't just line up these pieces vertically!

My approach is to look for edges that are all the same color, within some threshold. If an edge is a single color (or colors very close to a single color), then it simply does not take part in the matching process. That edge is essentially ignored and doesn't influence the scoring, sorting, or clustering processes.

Using just this simple test, I matched my QC data using strip lengths of 1.25 inches (each 11-inch strip was cut into 8 pieces of 1.25 inches each and one piece of 1.5 inches), resulting in 22,032 pieces. I applied the sorting and clustering techniques above and got very good, but not perfect, results. I think a better sorting metric would go a long way here.

The sorting technique is amenable to multiresolution methods, where you try to match things up quickly at a coarse level, and then apply a more expensive test to refine the collection, and then an even more expensive test, and so on, until you finally apply the most complete and accurate test only to a very few candidates with a high likelihood of matching. One could certainly use a sequence of sorting steps, where the first few are very crude and fast and only become more accurate (and slower) as the number of elements in the ever-smaller bins becomes tractable.

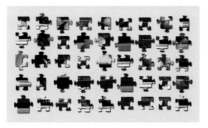

A fun application of this technique is to solve jigsaw puzzles. To test this out, I took a photograph and drew jigsaw-shaped pieces on it in Photoshop. I then wrote a program that broke the pieces apart and scattered them. Figure 2.19 shows some of the pieces.

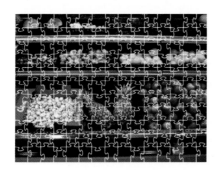

To reconstruct the image, I simply used my assembly algorithm. I replaced the idea of a strip's "side" with the color values running around the perimeter of one side of the piece. This 165-piece puzzle, shown in Figure 2.20, assembled perfectly in just a few seconds. This really surprised me, since I was kind of looking forward to writing some code to account for the shape information of the pieces. Finding a nice characterization of the shapes so that one could match them up quickly on a purely geometric basis would be an interesting project.

PUTTING THE PIECES TOGETHER

In this discussion I've overlooked a few practical problems. When reconstructing a document, sometimes strips will be missing. Happily, the clustering algorithm doesn't care about that and will just match up pieces as well as possible. Missing cross-cut pieces are more troublesome and will result in irregularly-shaped chunks of the original images.

I've also assumed that the pieces fit together without gaps or overlaps. If a vase shatters on the floor, you often get a lot of tiny little pieces and some dust. The big shards will fit together pretty well, but the joins will be imperfect due to the lost material. I haven't thought about how to account for that lost material in a good way.

If you are putting a vase back together again, one thing that helps is the fact that the vase has some thickness: the shapes go together not just based on a two-dimensional outline, like a jigsaw puzzle piece, but also in terms of how the edges are scalloped and shaped.

The researchers at Brown University's SHAPE Lab have been studying exactly this question. Working as digital archaeologists, they're developing ways to assemble the fragments of ancient, broken works. Their home page at http://www.lems.brown.edu/vision/extra/ SHAPE/ provides a wealth of information. You can also dig into their many publications, and learn a lot more about this three-dimensional reconstruction work at http://www.lems.brown.edu/vision/people/ leymarie/Refs/Archa/Sherds.html.

Duck!

3

When ducks swim on a smooth deep lake, they create a V-shaped ripple of waves behind them. Boats and ships do the same thing, as shown in Figure 3.1, as do human swimmers.

Figure 3.1

The wake created by a moving boat.

I saw a duck swimming across a glass-smooth pond a few weeks ago, and I wondered what it might be like if I could choreograph a flock of trained ducks to swim as I wanted. Could the ducks be induced to make interesting patterns out of their overlapping wakes?

Since I probably couldn't get real ducks to obey my instructions, I decided to build a flock of virtual ducks and experiment with them. The only problem with this scheme was that it required first finding a way to compute the wake that a duck creates behind it as it swims.

Writing an accurate, general-purpose, fluid-flow simulator is a difficult job. Happily, finding the wake created by any object moving with constant speed in deep water is much easier.

Finding a duck's wake is of course just a special case of the more general problem of the modeling and simulation of water. Computing water flow is nothing new in either engineering or computer graphics. There have been thousands of papers and hundreds of books written on the simulation of water, many of which are intricately detailed.

Water is very special stuff and has some surprising properties. Hydraulics engineers describe water as a "non-viscous incompressible fluid that moves under the influence of gravity." The important word for us in this definition is "incompressible."

Air, on the other hand, is compressible: if you walk into a sealed room, then your body will displace the air that used to be where your body is. That air mixes with the other air in the room, creating a slightly higher air pressure on your skin. You can even compress a lot of air into a small space and store it efficiently, which is why underwater divers are able to get so much time out of a single tank of air.

But water is not compressible. If you try to walk into a closed room full of water, you won't get in the door: there's nowhere for the water to go when your body tries to push it out of the way.

This principle is illustrated by a famous (and probably apocryphal) story of the Greek philosopher Archimedes of Syracuse (who lived around 240 B.C.). The story begins with the King coming to Archimedes with a problem. The King had purchased a new crown of solid gold, but the King was suspicious and thought that perhaps the artisans who made the crown had cheated, and simply melted a layer of gold leaf over a core of some cheaper metal. He asked Archimedes to determine if the crown really was solid gold, but with the condition that Archimedes not damage or alter the crown in any way.

This seemed an impossible problem. Then one day Archimedes climbed into a bathtub, causing the water to slosh over the sides. According to legend, Archimedes suddenly saw how to solve his problem and ran naked down the street shouting "Eureka!"

The insight that Archimedes had was that the volume of water that had spilled over side of the tub was exactly equal to the volume of his immersed body. In other words, because water can't be compressed, the volume of water displaced by an object is equal to the volume of that object. So Archimedes dunked the crown into a tub of water and measured how much water spilled out. Then he weighed the crown, and divided the weight by the volume to get the average density of the crown. It turned out to be the density of gold, so it meant that unless the artisans had found a way to make another metal with the same density as gold (which nobody knew how to do), then the crown was indeed made of solid gold after all.

Drawing our inspiration from this legend, let's push around the water that is displaced by a swimming duck and create the wave pattern that flows out behind it.

KELVIN WAVES

To find a duck's wake, I'll make an important simplifying assumption: the duck is in a body of water that is infinitely deep. This means that no waves bounce off the bottom and come back up, and it also means that we don't have to worry about where the water goes when we push it downward: it just goes down, pushing down all the water below it as well. In real life, of course, eventually that downward-moving water will hit the bottom and then move to the sides.

With this assumption, it's possible to start with a few basic equations of fluid motion and related boundary conditions, and find an explicit formula for the shape of the wave propagating behind the duck.

I won't provide this derivation here, because it's complicated and not very revealing. You can find the details in Chapter 2 of *Water Waves and Ship Hydrodynamics: An Introduction* by R. Timman, A. J. Hermans, and G. C. Hsiao (Delft University Press, 1985).

The bottom line is that we can find the wave by tracing out a parametric curve, which I'll call $K(\psi, u)$. The curve K is given by two expressions, which give us its x and y components. K is defined by two parameters. The first, ψ, is called the *phase* of the wave. Basically this is a shape control that accommodates the fact that the wave gets larger as time goes on. The second parameter, u, sweeps out the curve for a given value of ψ. Here's the definition of K:

$$K_x(u) = (-\psi/4)(5\cos u - \cos 3u),$$
$$K_y(u) = (-\psi/4)(\sin u - \sin 3u),$$

where $-\pi/2 \leq u \leq \pi/2$.

K is sometimes called a *phase wave*. It's also called a *Kelvin wave* after the physicist Lord Kelvin (William Thomson), who was the first to study this phenomenon mathematically. You can think of ψ as simply a measure of how long the wave has been expanding.

Figure 3.2(a) shows this curve for $\psi = 1$ behind a duck swimming from left to right. In Figure 3.2(b) I've overlapped several plots of K for different values of ψ.

Notice that the waves all lie in a cone behind the duck. For some applications it's useful to know the angle of this cone, since everything outside of the cone is guaranteed to be unaffected by this particular

Figure 3.2

(a) A Kelvin wave for $\psi = 1$.
(b) Kelvin waves for $0 \leq \psi \leq 1$ superimposed.

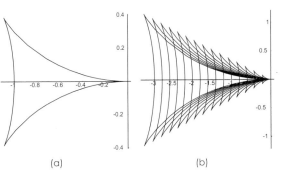

(a)　　　　　(b)

Figure 3.3

Finding the angle α that points to the cusp of a Kelvin wave.

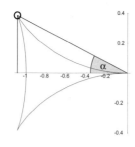

duck. The half-angle at the tip of this cone is called the *Kelvin angle*, labeled α in Figure 3.3. To find the Kelvin angle, we can determine the locations of the two points, or *cusps*, of the phase wave.

These cusps appear where the derivatives of K_x and K_y are both simultaneously zero with respect to the variable u. These derivatives are

$$dK_x/du = (-\psi/4)(-5\sin u + 3\sin(3u)) \text{ and}$$
$$dK_y/du = (-\psi/4)(\cos u + 3\cos(3u))$$

Figure 3.4

Plots of the derivatives of a Kelvin wave. dx/du is in red, dy/du is in green. The Kelvin angle is where these are both zero simultaneously.

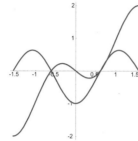

and are plotted in Figure 3.4. It's easy to confirm that these functions are both zero at $u = \cos^{-1}(\sqrt{2/3})$. If we plug this value for u into the curve K above, we get a point at about $(-1.088, -.385)$, as shown in Figure 3.3. The angle between the X axis and the line from the origin to this point can be found from this triangle to be about 19.5 degrees.

I've plotted $K_x(1, u)$ and $K_y(1, u)$ in Figure 3.5(a), and I've marked the locations of $u = 19.5$ degrees and $u = -19.5$ degrees in Figure 3.5(b). Reassuringly, both graphs are flat at those points.

Figure 3.5

(a) The Kelvin functions $x(u)$ (red) and $y(u)$ (green) for $-\pi/2 \le u \le \pi/2$. (b) The Kelvin angle is where these functions have zero slope.

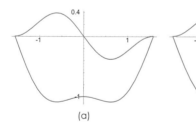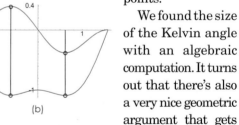

(a) (b)

We found the size of the Kelvin angle with an algebraic computation. It turns out that there's also a very nice geometric argument that gets us to the same result. I like geometric approaches in general for their intuitive appeal, but this one also helps us understand something about water waves in the process.

To start with an analogy, think of an airplane flying left to right with constant velocity v, as illustrated in Figure 3.6(a). We'll just look at a two-dimensional, simplified version of the complex three-dimensional waves created by the airplane.

Imagine that as the plane flies, at every point it creates a whole bunch of circular waves of different frequencies, all radiating away at once. These are drawn as circles in Figure 3.6(a). An interesting property of sound waves in air is that they all travel at the same speed: the speed of sound does not depend on wavelength. So although the plane makes disturbances of many different frequencies, they all radiate away from the point at the same speed.

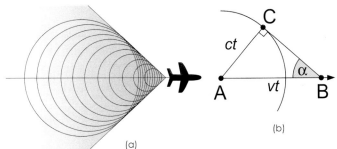

In Figure 3.6(a) the airplane is going at supersonic speed. That means that the plane is moving faster than the waves are expanding. What's the angle of the cone that contains these waves? Looking closely at Figure 3.6(a), we can see that all the circles are tangent to the cone that contains them. So in Figure 3.6(b) I've picked any circle. The circle was created when the plane was at point A, but the plane is now at point B. If the plane is flying with velocity v and it took t seconds to get from A to B, the distance $|AB| = vt$. If we write c for the speed of sound, then the radius of the circle is ct. Let's call the point of tangency C. Now we have a right triangle ACB where $|AB| = vt$, and $|AC| = ct$, and we want to find angle α at point B. Since $\sin\alpha = |AC|/|AB| = ct/vt$, then $\alpha = \sin^{-1}(c/v)$.

Now let's return to the water and more duck-like speeds. The situation will turn out to be somewhat different than the airplane because water waves of different wavelengths travel at different speeds.

Figure 3.6

(a) Forming a supersonic boom. Each of the circles is an expanding pulse of air from a point on the plane's path. (b) Finding the angle at the apex of the cone of part (a).

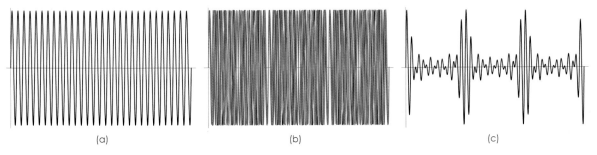

(a) (b) (c)

Thinking now of a duck traveling from A to B, at each point in its journey the duck creates a whole bunch of different waves at slightly different wavelengths. When many different waves of almost the same wavelength combine with each other, the result is that they tend to cancel out in some places and reinforce in other places. Figure 3.7 shows this phenomenon for six sine waves of only slightly different frequencies. In Figure 3.7(a) I show a sine wave from 0 to 60π. In Figure 3.7(b) I've plotted that wave as well as five more of just slightly higher frequencies, and it looks like a mess. In Figure 3.7(c) I've added

Figure 3.7

Several sine waves of almost the same frequency add up to make clear packets. (a) $\sin(x)$ for $0 \leq x \leq 60\pi$. (b) Sine waves from $\sin(x)$ to $\sin(1.5x)$ in steps of 0.1x. (c) $\sin(x) + \sin(1.1x) + \sin(1.2x) + \sin(1.3x) + \sin(1.4x) + \sin(1.5x)$.

59

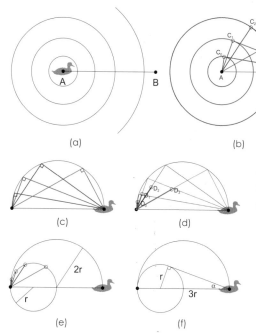

(a)

(b)

(c)

(d)

(e)

(f)

Figure 3.8

A geometric construction for the Kelvin angle. (a) A few different waves radiated from point A. (b) The angle each forms at point B, with a point of tangency given by a point C_i. (c) The points of (b) lie on a semicircle. (d) The waves from A move at the group velocity, which is half of the phase velocity, so they only get halfway, to points marked D_i. (e) The points D_i lie on a semicircle. (f) Finding the angle of the semicircle in (e).

up the six waves from Figure 3.7(b), and a surprising structure emerges. We say that the waves have combined to create a series of *packets*.

This is what happens to the water waves created by our duck. At each point the duck creates a variety of waves of slightly different wavelengths, but rather than disturbing all the water uniformly, they create easily-discerned packets, as in Figure 3.7. If you watch a fine-grain water wave start behind a duck, you can see it quickly move out until it reaches an existing packet, where it combines with the packet for a while, and then emerges from the other side to dissipate in the open water.

How fast does the packet move? We say that the individual waves move at a speed given by the *phase velocity*. But the packet moves at the *group velocity*, which in deep water is exactly half the phase velocity.

As a very rough analogy, think of a highway where an accident has recently been cleared. There's still a big clump of slowly-moving cars near the scene of where the problem had been. Fast-moving cars arrive at the tail of the pack and are forced to slow down, while cars near the front of the bunch are able to get back up to speed and drive away. Thus there's a big, slowly-moving clump of cars traveling up the highway, constantly being refreshed with new cars and losing old cars. The membership of cars in the blob is constantly changing, and the cluster moves more slowly than any of its components, but if you were watching it from a helicopter you'd have no trouble spotting and watching it.

Let's see how we can use this information to find the Kelvin angle. In Figure 3.8(a) I've drawn a number of circular waves as radiated from point A (the duck is now at point B). If we imagine that each one of these waves defines a cone behind B, then we can draw a line from B tangent to each circle, creating a point C_i for each wavelength of wave, as in Figure 3.8(b). In the figure I've shown four different waves, and thus there are four different tangency points. In reality, there's a smooth distribution of these waves from short to long.

Because every line from B to one of A's circles is always tangent to the circle at the corresponding point C_i, the angle formed at each of these points C_i is always a right angle. You may remember the geometric fact that all right triangles built above a common hypotenuse end up with their third vertex on a shared circle that uses that hypotenuse as a diameter. Figure 3.8(c) illustrates this point.

These points C_i are the points that enclose the individual waves. But remember that these waves combine to form a packet, as in Figure 3.7. So what we really want to find is the cone that encloses the packet, not the individual wave crests. Remember from above that the group velocity in deep water is exactly one half of the phase velocity. Since every line AC_i gives us the distance to a wave crest, if we mark a point halfway between A and C_i we've found the location of the packet. These points are marked in Figure 3.8(d) as D_i. So now our goal is to find the cone from B that encloses all the points D_i.

If you enjoy geometry problems, you might want to stop reading here and work out the shape formed by the points D_i.

The answer is shown in Figure 3.8(e): it's a new circle that has a radius of $|AB|/4$, and is located 1/4 of the way from A to B. All of the wave packets generated at point A live inside this circle. Thus to find the angle of the wake behind the duck when it's at B we need only draw a line from B that is tangent to this circle and read off the angle at B. Figure 3.8 (f) shows the setup. If we write $r = |AB|/4$, then $\alpha = \sin(r/3r) = \sin(1/3)$. If we evaulate $\alpha = \sin^{-1}(1/3)$, we get a Kelvin angle of about 19.5 degrees, just as we found before.

It's always a good day when we can reach the same result by two entirely different approaches!

To summarize these results, all the Kelvin waves created by any object moving with constant speed in deep water lie within a cone with a half-angle given by the Kelvin angle of about 19.5 degrees.

WAKE UP!

Now that we know how to create Kelvin waves $K(t)$, the only question left is how to use them to make a trail behind a swimming duck.

The easiest way is to simply let them grow as the duck moves. But as we can see from Figure 3.2, just superimposing the waves on each other will eventually lead to a black blob, which of course is not what we see in nature.

What we want to do is have the waves go up and down, as they do in the real world. You must remember this: as time goes by, any given Kelvin wave undergoes three changes.

First, it gets larger. This is automatically handled by the phase variable ψ. If we plot $K(t\psi, u)$ where t is time, then the wave naturally grows with t. Second, the wave goes up and down, or oscillates. We can model that easily by setting the amplitude of the wave A to $A = \cos(ct)$, where c is the speed of the Kelvin wave.

Figure 3.9

(a) The height field for a series of Kelvin waves, where the amplitude varies with the sine of the phase. (b) Adding damping to part (a).

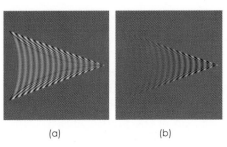

(a)   (b)

If we draw a great many waves with these first two rules and let them accumulate, the result is Figure 3.9(a), where I've drawn the waves for a duck swimming left-to-right.

In this and all similar figures in this chapter, the waves are represented as a height plot. We're looking straight down on the water. White points are closest to us (that is, they correspond to crests) and black points are farthest (corresponding to valleys). Neutral gray is undisturbed water level.

The third change to Kelvin waves as they expand is that they lose energy. That is, the amplitude diminishes with time. I use an exponential function to control this, setting $A = Ae^{-(bt)^2}$ for a user-defined constant b. The result of incorporating this third component gives us the wake of Figure 3.9(b).

To create Figure 3.9(b), I first created in memory a grid of floating-point values and initialized them all to 0. This is the sampled wave pattern into which all the Kelvin waves will be added; let's call it W.

Now I start at point B (I found it easier to move from the end to the start), and I draw a Kelvin wave with a phase of $\psi = 0$ and amplitude of $A = 1$. Using the equations K_x and K_y above, I step u in many small pieces from $-\pi/2$ to $\pi/2$. The number of steps is user-controlled; a smaller number results in coarser patterns but faster running time. Typically I'd use a small number of steps for u while working on my patterns, and then crank it up high for the final images. For each value of u I get a floating-point location (x, y). I then find the nearest pixel in W to that point and add to it the amplitude A.

When I've finished the u sweep, I then take a small step backwards on the path towards A, creating a new point P. As with the control of u, the number of steps taken from B to A is user-defined. Again, more steps result in smoother images. The first thing I do is calculate the length of the path from P to B. If AB is a straight line, this is just the distance $|PB|$. But if the duck is swimming on a curved path, I need to find the distance covered by the duck along the path from P to B. Sometimes I can find this analytically: I have special-purpose code for simple paths like straight lines and circular arcs. For more general curves, I have to compute an approximate arc-length by taking many little steps along the path from P to B and adding up all the little straight lines. Of course, this is the reason that I work backwards:

each time I compute a new point P, I don't need to compute the entire distance $|PB|$, but just the shorter distance to the previous point P, and then add that to the previous distance.

Given a point P and its distance along the path to B, I use the duck's speed to find the time t it took the duck to reach B from P. Using this value of t, I calculate the phase ψ, and the amplitude A. Then I walk though the values of u again, finding points along the way, and adding in the value A to those points. Then I take another step towards A and repeat the process.

When I'm done with all the paths for all the ducks in the scene, I scan the grid W and scale all of the values within it to the range $[0,1]$. Then I multiply each pixel by 255 and write it out as a gray-scale image.

To make the images in this figure I used a grid that was 512-by-512 elements large. If we call this grid 512 units on a side, I plotted from 50 to 100 values of ψ for every unit of length of the path on the grid. I typically took 500 to 1000 steps in u to generate the wave for each value of ψ.

This is a pretty good rough-and-ready simulation, but it has one big problem: as we walk along K in equal steps of u, the points we generate are not themselves equally-spaced along the curve. Figure 3.10 shows 100 points created by chopping the u interval $[-\pi/2, \pi/2]$ into 100 equal steps and then plotting the resulting points. Obviously, they tend to bunch up near the cusps.

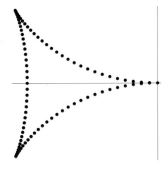

Figure 3.10

The range $-\pi/2 \leq u \leq \pi/2$ cut into 100 equally-spaced points and plugged into K. Note that the points are not equally-spaced along the path of K.

This can create some unpleasant artifacts at the edges of the duck's path. The value of plotting a great many K waves is that they all add up to make a smooth field. But if there are pixels that only get written to once or twice, they don't have a chance to combine with the other waves. If these pixels happen to have a large amplitude, when I search the image for the largest and smallest values prior the scaling step mentioned above, these can stand out. The result is that most of the wake is neutral gray, with a smattering of white and black pixels along the edges.

To solve this I precede the scaling step with a smoothing step. First I create a copy of W in a new grid called $W2$. Then I look through all the pixels in W that have been written to and compare each pixel's value to the average of its four immediate neighbors. If the difference between the pixel and its neighbors is above a threshold, then I replace that

Figure 3.11

A synthetic image using the wake pattern of Figure 3.2(b).

pixel's value in $W2$ with the average of its four neighbors in W. When I'm done with this pass, I copy $W2$ back to W and throw $W2$ away. Now that the numerical rogues have been tamed, I scale the data and write it out as a grayscale file, as before.

Figure 3.11 shows a duck on rather calm water. The wake pattern behind the duck is Figure 3.9(b). The only "real" thing in this image is the photo of the shoreline in the background of that I took of Green Lake in Seattle; everything else is synthetic.

Figure 3.12

(a) A wave pattern for a duck swimming on a twisty path. The heights are exaggerated for legibility. (b) A wave pattern for a duck swimming on a twisty path. (c) The path highlighted in red. (d) A synthetic image using the wave pattern of part (b).

THROWING A CURVE

I've described how I plot a path from A to B, but what if the path is not a straight line? I specify a duck's overall journey by stitching together a series of short paths. My palette of available paths contains line segments, circular arcs, spirals, Bézier curves , and cubic splines.

We saw an example of a straight line wake in Figure 3.9(b). The pattern due to a cubic spline is shown in Figure 3.12(a), where I've exaggerated the heights of the waves so you can see the beautiful

(a)   (b)   (c)

patterns. A proper result is in Figure 3.12(b). The path taken by the slowly-swimming duck is highlighted in red in Figure 3.12(c). Here I've kept the damping factor to a low value so that you can see the interesting shapes created by the Kelvin waves. Notice that the waves at the back are huge compared to those in the front, due to the additional amount of time they've had to spread out. Figure 3.12(d) shows this pattern in three dimensions behind our swimming duck.

(d)

Another spline is shown in grayscale in Figure 3.13(a), and in three dimensions in Figure 3.13(b). I've turned the damping back on here so that the oldest waves have just about (but not quite) died out.

The only trick to stitching together these different segments is to make sure that the phase at the end of one segment of the path matches the phase at the start of the next. By working backwards along the segments, this is easy to manage. The phase ψ just keeps growing with your accumulating, approximate arc length and everything goes together smoothly.

WATER BALLET

Now that we can create a wake pattern, let's put several swimmers together and see how the patterns interact.

Boat Trip

It appears the local radio-controlled model galleon club has been practicing their close-formation steering skills. Figure 3.14(a) shows the wake pattern created by six galleons that are traveling in alternating directions. They're trying to steer a straight course, but the wind is pushing them around a little. Figure 3.14(b) shows the wake in three dimensions.

Since these pilots are so good, they decided to try another go at closer quarters. In Figure 3.15(a) we can see the waves created when the ships sail much closer to one another: the wake patterns combine in beautiful ways. Figure 3.15(b) shows the result out on the water.

Rubber Duckies Unite

Everyone loves a rubber ducky in the bathtub. But it turns out that rubber duckies are very social creatures and enjoy one another's company. In fact, rubber ducks like to swim in the same sort of V-shaped formations as other ducks.

In Figure 3.16(a) we can see the wake pattern created by a phalanx of seven rubber ducks swimming along in a V. Each duck is swimming outside of the Kelvin wave created by the duck ahead of it, so it's easy to see the starting point of each duck's wake. Figure 3.16(b) shows the

(a)   (b)

Figure 3.13

(a) A wave pattern for a duck swimming on a twisty path. (b) A synthetic image using the wave pattern of part (a).

(a)   (b)

Figure 3.14

(a) A wave pattern for six boats on roughly parallel paths. (b) A synthetic image using the wave pattern of part (a).

(a)   (b)

Figure 3.15

(a) A wave pattern for six boats on roughly parallel paths. (b) A synthetic image using the wave pattern of part (a).

Figure 3.16

(a) A wave pattern for a V-shaped phalanx of seven ducks. Each is swimming outside of the wake of the duck in front. (b) A synthetic image using the wave pattern of part (a).

(a)   (b)

Figure 3.17

(a) A wave pattern for a V-shaped phalanx of seven ducks. Each is swimming just on the border of the wake of the duck in front. (b) A synthetic image using the wave pattern of part (a).

(a)   (b)

Figure 3.18

(a) A wave pattern for a V-shaped phalanx of seven ducks. Each is swimming inside the border of the wake of the duck in front. (b) A synthetic image using the wave pattern of part (a).

(a)   (b)

Figure 3.19

(a) A wave pattern for five submarines chasing each other in a circle. Each one is pretty far behind the one in front of it. (b) A synthetic image using the wave pattern of part (a).

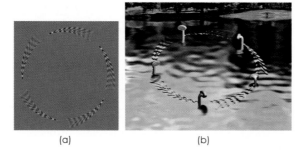

(a)   (b)

results as they swim together, creating the wake in Figure 3.16(a).

After a while the ducks moved into closer formation. Each duck swam right on the border of the Kelvin wave created by the lead duck. Since all Kelvin waves share the same angle, the waves created by these ducks shared the same outer border. Figure 3.17(a) shows wake pattern, and Figure 3.17(b) shows how it looks out on the lake.

Then the ducks moved closer in. When each duck started to swim within the Kelvin wave of the duck ahead, they created the wake pattern of Figure 3.18(a). Out on the water, this shows up as Figure 3.18(b).

Up Periscope

The recruiting poster exhorted young men to join the submariners and sail the seven underwater seas. What they didn't realize was that they would have to go on extensive training exercises out at the lake.

Their first exercise involved chasing each other in a circle. Figure 3.19(a) shows the wake pattern created by the periscopes of five subs following each other. You can see that they just recently brought their periscopes up. Figure 3.19(b) shows this training exercise in progress.

After some time elapsed, the subs continued to chase each other, and the wake patterns spread out more. You can see the wake pattern in Figure 3.20 (a), and the churning waves created by the subs in Figure 3.20(b).

(a) (b)

Figure 3.20

(a) A wave pattern for five submarines chasing each other in a circle. They've swum further than in Figure 3.19 and each one is now in the wake of the one in front. (b) A synthetic image using the wave pattern of part (a).

Mad Boaters

I was thinking about the Kelvin angle of about 19.5 degrees. Since the Kelvin angle is only half of the complete angle at the tip of the cone (as shown in Figure 3.3), then the cone itself has an angle of about 39 degrees. This rattled around in my head for a while until I realized it was pretty close to 36 degrees.

Why is that special? The angles at the tips of a five-pointed star are 36 degrees. I've never seen it reported before, but it seemed to me you could make a pretty cool star with Kelvin waves.

To check it out, I got five toy speedboats and sent them hurtling towards each other. The wake pattern during their initial

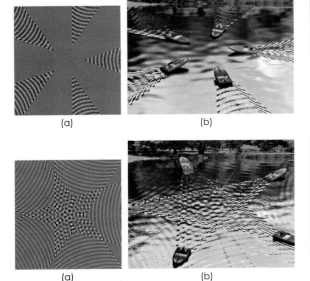

(a) (b)

(a) (b)

Figure 3.21

(a) Five speedboats heading toward a common point. (b) A synthetic image using the wave pattern of part (a).

Figure 3.22

(a) Five speedboats that have passed through a common point. The geometry of Kelvin waves creates a near-perfect five-pointed star behind them. (b) A synthetic image using the wake pattern of part (a).

approach is shown in Figure 3.21(a), and the rendered three-dimensional image out on the water is shown in Figure 3.21(b).

The boats raced towards one another at a very high but constant speed. A massive collision was inevitable. But when I opened my eyes again, *mirabile dictu*, somehow they had managed to pass through a center point and out the other side unscathed! Figure 3.22(a) shows the wake pattern, and Figure 3.22(b) shows how the lake appears. I really like this star!

Duck!

Figure 3.23

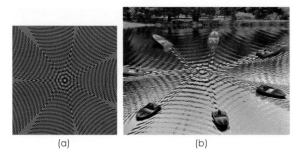

(a)   (b)

Even though the angles are no longer magical, I created some other stars as well. One of the prettiest was a seven-pointed star. The seven-star wake is shown in Figure 3.23(a), and the three-dimensional version is in Figure 3.23(b).

RETURNING TO SHORE

One of the great pleasures of computer graphics is that we can play around with the world in ways that are difficult, expensive, or just plain impractical in real life. I don't know if there are professional rubber duck wranglers out there, but even if there are, I doubt they're able to get ducks to swim in precision patterns. And certainly we can't get speedboats to pass through each other simultaneously without damage!

Yet we can do all of this with computer graphics. To me, the results are worth the effort, both for understanding nature and for the sheer fun of playing around with making interesting patterns. Remember, don't listen to them when they tell you to be quiet and not to make waves!

Getting the Picture

4

Most of the time we work hard to create images that are sharp and clear. After all, we work hard to make our pictures, so we want them to communicate our message as clearly and unambiguously as possible.

Pictures meant for utilitarian purposes should be as simple and direct as they can be. For example, if you need to change a part deep inside a photocopier, you want the repair diagram to be as uncluttered and comprehensible as possible. A verbal equivalent of these images is the fire-escape instruction card on the inside of hotel-room doors: "Turn right, go to the end of the hall, feel the door, and if it's not hot, enter and descend rapidly."

Then there are pictures that have a more human purpose, perhaps to help tell a story. The intention here is to not just convey information, but also to share a sense of mood and feeling. A verbal equivalent to these pictures is a prose narrative: "Baron Phelps slowly opened the safe, praying that the beads of nervous sweat on his forehead weren't visible to the man with the gun."

Then there are pictures that are almost all mood. These are abstract or impressionistic types of images. A verbal equivalent is a poem: "Chased by the angry sun / Choking on endless sand / Crawling, crawling / The air like water."

We've seen computer graphics used for all of these purposes in recent years, and the styles continue to proliferate. From an early focus on a kind of photo-realism, the kinds of pictures we create with computer have evolved to a wide variety of styles, some of which seem to look like traditional media.

Creating images that are imprecise replicas of another image is both useful and fun.

The technique of *successive approximation* helps us see a rough version of a picture quickly, with details filling in as time goes on. Many rendering systems first create and display a low-resolution version of the image, and then add in details as time goes on. If the user doesn't like the way the picture is shaping up, he or she can stop the program and fix things before trying again. This process leads to faster turnaround time than waiting for the complete final image to render before seeing anything at all.

Figure 4.1

Four images demonstrating the "windowshade" effect as a browser loads an image in progressive-GIF format. The scene is a boat dock at the Port of Edmonds, in Washington State.

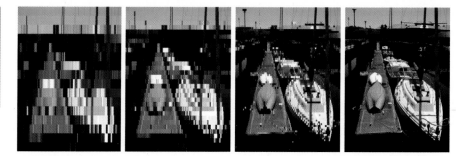

Successive approximation is also useful when we want to transmit models or images over low-bandwidth connections. Most browsers are able to show GIF images by first drawing only a small number of scanlines, replicating each line downward until the next piece of data. New lines fit in between the old ones, slowly building up the image, as in Figure 4.1. Some programs that display three-dimensional models use a similar technique, transmitting a low-resolution version of the model so that the person on the other end has something to look at quickly, and then sending more detail as time goes on.

There are lots of interesting ways to make approximate images. In this chapter, I'll look at some ways to create approximate images using relaxation and optimization techniques.

IT'S KIND OF RIGHT

There are two general techniques for making approximate images: transformations and algorithms.

"Transformations" take an image into another representation, operate upon it there, and then turn it back into an image. The most popular transformations for this sort of thing are Fourier and wavelet analysis. Using Fourier methods we can, for example, take a picture, lop off the high frequencies, and then recreate a new image from what's left. The result is an image that, loosely speaking, looks blurrier than the original. Wavelet transforms are similar. When the higher-order wavelets are removed, the reconstructed image tends to look a little blocky, like an image that has gone through strong JPEG compression.

Algorithmic techniques encompass just about everything else. Perhaps the most popular forms of creating approximate images algorithmically are *blur* and *pixelation*.

(a)   (b)   (c)

Figure 4.2

Blurring and pixelation. (a) A street scene in Edmonds, Washington. (b) A blurred version. (c) A pixelated version.

Blur is pretty simple: just take an image and smooth it out. Every image-processing program has some form of blur filter built into it. Figure 4.2(a) shows an image, and Figure 4.2(b) shows a blurry version. Pixelation involves creating a grid of large blocks over the image and filling in each block with the average color of the image beneath it, as in Figure 4.2(c). This technique is used all the time in television and video to obscure details such as faces and license plate numbers.

There are many other ways to create approximate images. Most image-editing programs contain a wealth of built-in filters to apply special effects to images, and there are several companies that sell packages of additional filters as plug-ins. Some of these filters are very simple and run with a single touch of a button, while others are complex, with many user-interface controls.

An interesting approach to creating an approximate image was presented in a 1990 paper by Paul Haeberli (see the Further Reading section for details). Among other approaches, he mentioned the use of "relaxation" to create an image and showed two example images. Although that paper doesn't talk about how the pictures were made, relaxation is a pretty well-known method for optimization in general, so it's not too hard to guess at what he was up to. In the next section I'll talk about writing a simple optimizer and then present the results of using that system with a variety of geometric elements to make approximate images.

Depending on the complexity of the problem you want to solve, and the sophistication of your means of solution, writing an optimization program can mean a few hours of low-stress programming or become a life's work. Of course, for this chapter I'll take the former approach. In particular, I'll look at what's sometimes called a *random-walk relaxation* routine.

The general idea behind this kind of program is that we have two basic creatures: a piece of data called a *candidate*, and a routine that evaluates a *fitness function*. The fitness function looks at the candidate and assigns it a numerical *score*. Typically a fitness function will assign a higher score to a better candidate than to a lesser one. Thus we want to maximize the score for maximum fitness.

If instead a better candidate gets a lower score, the fitness function is sometimes called a *penalty function*, since we want to minimize the penalty.

In this chapter, our candidates will be collections of geometric objects that we'll distribute over the original picture to create a new image. The fitness function will measure the total error in color space (more details below). Since we want this error to be as small as possible, this is technically a penalty function.

The process will be to generate an initial candidate, which I'll call the *best candidate*, and score it. Then I'll generate another candidate by randomly *perturbing* the best candidate, which just means changing it in some way. If the new candidate has a worse score than its predecessor, we throw it away. If its score is better, then it becomes the new best candidate. Then we perturb and score again, and again, and again. There are many tests for determining when to stop this loop, which I'll discuss a little later.

Since I wanted to try out a bunch of different geometries, each with its own descriptions and parameters, I thought it would be easiest to write a general-purpose routine to control the optimizing process.

One Step at a Time

This project is a natural for class-oriented programming languages like C#, though using function pointers it's easy to write it up in other languages as well. For the little fragments of pseudo-code in this article, I'll use traditional C-style notation.

Each type of candidate is implemented by exposing four functions to the system. For simplicity's sake I'll abstract them here by ignoring the important but cumbersome details of book-keeping, memory management, error-checking, and so on. Of course in any real system you'll need to manage those issues, but they're not central to the ideas of the algorithm.

- **Candidate init()** Called before the optimizer runs, this sets up any required storage, and generates and returns the first candidate.

- **Candidate perturb(Candidate c)** Perturb the input and return the perturbed version.

- **double score(Candidate c)** Compute the penalty score for this candidate.

- **save(Candidate c)** Save the image specified by this candidate.

Figure 4.3

Pseudo-code for the basic perturbation routine.

The basic loop of the perturbation algorithm is shown in Figure 4.3. I'll assume that we've already initialized the geometry (giving us the original best candidate) and have scored it (giving us the original best score). The basic idea is that the routine is handed pointers to the current best score and the best candidate, and a structure with the procedures for the current type of geometry. On line 3 we perturb the input candidate to create a new candidate, and on line 4

```
1.   Candidate PerturbStep(double *bestScore,
         Candidate bestC, Procs procs)
2.   {
3.       Candidate newC  =  procs->perturb(bestC);
4.       double newScore  =  procs->score(newC);
5.       if (newScore < *bestScore)  {
6.       procs->save(newC);
7.       bestC  =  newC;
8.       *bestScore  =  newScore;
9.       }
10.      return(bestC);
11.  }
```

we get its score. If the score is better than the best score we have so far, then we save the new candidate, put its score into the pointer for the score, and reassign the candidate pointer to the new structure. Then we return the candidate pointer. If the new version wasn't any better than what we had before, that pointer and the score will be unchanged; otherwise they'll both have the new values.

When I save a candidate, I simply write out the image file that it describes.

The procedures that get called aren't hard-wired into the loop, but get looked up on the fly through pointers in the structure that holds them. That makes it easy to write up and plug in new types of candidates: just fill up the structure and the program runs as before, except it calls the new routines.

Note that in C a procedure can only return one value, and this routine might need to change two things: the score and the pointer to the best candidate. To manage that in this pseudo-code, I passed in the current score as a pointer, so that the routine could change its value. In real code you'd want a more elegant solution.

Scoring

Coming up with a score is the job of the fitness function. For this project I started with a very simple function that took two inputs: the candidate image (which I'll call the *cImage*) and the reference image (which I'll call the *rImage*). The *cImage* is the rendered image produced by the geometry in the candidate, and the *rImage* is the original picture that we're trying to approximate.

My first metric was simply to run through all the pixels and compute the squared difference in each color component. If Δr is the difference between the red values in the two pictures, then the error at each pixel is $E_p = \Delta r^2 + \Delta g^2 + \Delta b^2$. The total error is just the result of summing up this measure for all pixels in the image. I square the values so that they'll always be positive, and so that big differences will count for a lot more than smaller differences.

This metric worked pretty well at capturing big blocks of color, but it was awful at finding the edges. It also doesn't allow any way for the image creator to influence the process. I decided to add a simple "importance" measure to the error metric. When you start the program, you have the option of supplying an "importance" image, *iImage*, of the same size as *rImage*. You can also supply an overall scale factor s, which applies to the entire importance image. Writing I for the value of *iImage* at a specific pixel (scaled to the range [0, 1]), the importance-weighted error is $E_i = sIE_p$. In words, this means that pixels that have been painted white (or assigned a high importance) contribute more to the final score. Typically I painted white around important edges and places where I felt details were important. Figure 4.4 shows an image with its hand-drawn importance image.

If you don't want to exercise personal control over the algorithm but would like to encourage it to preserve regions of high contrast, you could write a program to find edges in the original image and create an importance image where pixels near edges are shaded from black to white proportionally to the strength of their edge.

In addition to the importance-weighted color differences, I've included two more measures in my scoring function. The first is an *overlap penalty*. I count how many times a given pixel is written to over the course of rendering the image: let's call this value c. If $c > 1$,

(a)

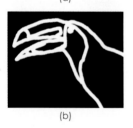

(b)

Figure 4.4

(a) An image of an toucan. Photograph by the U.S. Fish and Wildlife Service / photo by Mike Lockart. (b) The hand-drawn importance image. White means most important; black means least.

I multiply the excess by an overlap penalty value P_o and add that in to the total error; that is, I add in a value $(c - 1)P_o$, where P_o is a constant for the whole image. The larger the overlap value, the more the pieces will be penalized for landing on top of each other. Similarly, I include a *gap penalty*. If a given pixel has a count value $c = 0$, then I add to the score the value of a gap penalty value P_g, which again is constant for the whole image. The idea here is to try to get all the pixels to be covered by at least one object, so that most of the background is covered up.

Perturbing

The perturbation routine for each type of geometry is different. For example, circles change their center and radius, boxes change their length and angle, and so on. But there are a few things that are common to all the perturbation routines.

Each candidate is a list of geometric objects: dots, boxes, etc. The rendering algorithm draws these in order into a blank image, so that in effect they're rendered back-to-front (this is called a *painter's algorithm*).

When a perturbation routine is called, it first throws a random number, and if that number is above a threshold, the routine *swaps* a random pair of objects and returns. So none of the shapes change, but their order in the drawing process is altered. I set the swap probability and leave it unchanged throughout the entire run; generally I put the threshold at around .9 or .95, so pieces get swapped about one out of every 10 or 20 calls to the routine.

If there's no swap, the routine picks a piece and changes it. Because I don't want to pick pieces in the same order every time, when the perturb routine is called for the first time, I create a *permutation array* (let's call it P). P is an array of integers that has as many entries as there are pieces of geometry (let's call that number L), which I initialize so that $P_i = i$. Then I run through the array and for each element, I choose another element and swap them. That means that every element will get swapped at least once, and probably some will get swapped many times. The result is that the array still holds the numbers 0 through $L - 1$, but in scrambled order.

I then set a counter (which is persistent to the routine) to 0. The first time I enter the perturb routine, I choose the element from the list that corresponds to the value of P_0. The next time it's P_1, then P_2, and so on. I just keep bumping the counter each time. When the counter hits L, I rebuild the array and start the counter again at 0. This way the pieces get modified in a random order, but no pieces get skipped.

Now that we've selected a piece of geometry to modify, we need to decide what to do with it.

Each piece of geometry has its own data: a circle has a center and radius, a triangle has three points, and so on. We usually want these values to vary a lot in the beginning steps of the simulation, so that objects can try out many different places to land and see how well they contribute there. As the simulation continues, the changes get smaller and smaller as pieces jostle into their best settings.

I manage this change of scale with a simple linear transition. I set a scale factor for the start of the simulation, and one for the end. Since I know how many steps I'm going to take before I begin, I just interpolate based on the current step to come up with a current scaling factor. For example, I might say that the radius of a circle can change by up to ±40 pixels at the start of the run, but only up to ±5 pixels by the end.

In a more sophisticated technique, you might want to run the simulator until the changes become very small and save the result. Then reset the change factor to its maximum value and try again. This way the system can explore a variety of different starting conditions and follow each one to its best conclusion.

Toucan Play That Game

Let's look at a bunch of different geometric objects applied to an image of a toucan. This is a good test image because it has just a few regions of consistent color, a few details, and sharp, high-contrast edges. The original is shown in Figure 4.4(a), and its importance image is shown in Figure 4.4(b).

In each of the following techniques, I create an image from a candidate by starting off with a solid field that is set to the average color of the entire original image and then adding regions of constant color to it.

In each method except for the first two, the images were made with 144 geometric elements and 25,000 steps of relaxation (of course, not every step of relaxation was accepted by the optimizer as an improvement). The original formation was a 12-by-12 regular grid of elements of identical shape and size.

Scaled Boxes

I'll start off with two approximations that aren't really generated by relaxation, but they give us a nice starting point. In the first, I'll try to pack the image with big boxes and then fit ever-smaller boxes into the gaps.

Suppose that in the original picture you try to find the best location to place a box of a given side length. That is, you center the box on every pixel of the image and determine first of all whether or not it overlaps any other boxes. If it doesn't, then compute the error you'd have if you replaced all the pixels under the box by their average color. Repeat this for every possible location.

When you're done, you'll either have found that you can't place the box anywhere, or you'll have the location of the box that introduces the least error.

If you did find a spot for the box, add it to the list of boxes, creating the newly "perturbed" candidate, and return it. If you couldn't place the box, decrease the length of the side by a given fraction and start again. Repeat the process until the side of the box falls below some minimum size.

Figure 4.5 shows the result. In this example, the boxes started with a side length of 1/10 the length of the smaller dimension of the image, and continued until they were ten pixels on a side. My system was able to squeeze in 102 boxes until they got too small.

Scaled Dots

The approximation of scaled boxes in Figure 4.5 isn't much to write home about. But what if we replace the boxes with dots? Then the size of the box is replaced by the radius of the dot. Figure 4.6 shows the result, using the same sizes for the radius as for the boxes in the previous figure. The system stopped when it had packed in 144 dots, because all of the other simulations use 144 elements, and I didn't want this one using more.

This image also isn't that much to cheer about. Let's see if we can improve things by introducing relaxation into the process.

Relaxed Scaled Dots

As with all the examples to follow, I'll begin with 144 elements laid out on a regular grid, as in Figure 4.7(a).

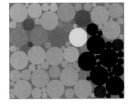

Figure 4.5

The 102 boxes produced by the scaling-box algorithm for the toucan image.

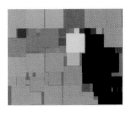

Figure 4.6

The 144 dots produced by the scaling-dot algorithm for the toucan image.

Figure 4.7

For each image, the first number refers to how many steps had been taken by the algorithm to produce that picture. The second number identifies how many times a new candidate had replaced an old one since the start of the run. (a) The original 12-by-12 grid of dots. (b) 6,000 / 485 (c) 12,000 / 680 (d) 18,000 / 834 (e) 25,000 / 1,093 (f–j) Parts (a–e) with outlines.

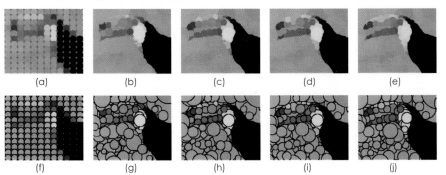

(a)　　　(b)　　　(c)　　　(d)　　　(e)

(f)　　　(g)　　　(h)　　　(i)　　　(j)

Since we're using dots, each element is described by three numbers: one each for the x and y coordinates of the center, and one for the radius. Each step of the perturbation either swapped two dots, or changed the center and radius of one of them.

The rest of Figure 4.7 shows the original dots, and the results after 6,000, 12,000, 18,000, and 25,000 steps respectively. By the last image, the system had accepted a new candidate 1,093 times. So that you can better see the way the dots are stacked, I've also provided a version of each figure where the dots are outlined.

Figure 4.8

Using relaxed half-dots to approximate the toucan. (a) The original 12-by-12 grid of half-dots. (b) 6,000 / 670 (c) 12,000 / 844 (d) 18,000 /1,026 (e) 25,000 / 1,242 (f–j) Parts (a–e) with outlines.

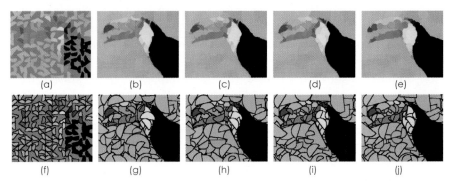

(a) (b) (c) (d) (e)

(f) (g) (h) (i) (j)

Half Dots

Dots look pretty good. What if we instead used half-dots? These have a center and radius but also have a fourth number that defines an angle that describes a diameter through the dot. Only those pixels on the positive side of that angle get drawn.

Figure 4.8 shows the results; after 25,000 steps, there had been 1,242 steps of improvement. Note that the little pointy bits of the half-dots are useful for filling in crevices.

Boxes

Let's use boxes as our geometric elements. An easy way to define a box is with five numbers that specify its center, width, height, and an angle

Figure 4.9

Using boxes to approximate the toucan. (a) The original 12-by-12 grid. (b) 6,000 / 228 (c) 12,000 / 318 (d) 18,000 / 435 (e) 25,000 / 602 (f–j) Parts (a–e) with outlines.

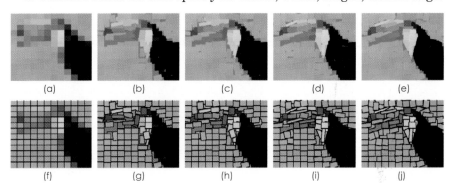

(a) (b) (c) (d) (e)

(f) (g) (h) (i) (j)

of rotation about its center. Whenever it's time to perturb a box, all of these parameters get tweaked.

Figure 4.9 shows the results. After 25,000 steps, there were 602 steps of improvement.

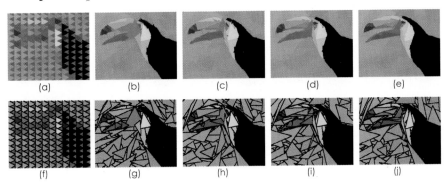

Figure 4.10

Using triangles to approximate the toucan. (a) The original 12-by-12 grid of triangles. (b) 6,000 / 635 (c) 12,000 / 882 (d) 18,000 / 1,079 (e) 25,000 / 1412 (f–j) Parts (a–e) with outlines.

Triangles

It's a small step from boxes to triangles. A triangle is made up of six numbers, corresponding to the locations of each of its three vertices.

Figure 4.10(a) shows the results. After 25,000 steps, there had been 1,412 steps of improvement.

Mesh

Rather than letting the triangles roam free, let's tie them down to a mesh, like that of Figure 4.11(a). The relaxer will then just move around the inner vertices of the mesh (the vertices on the border will remain fixed). My perturbation procedure starts with a hexagon made of the points nearest neighbors, as shown in Figure 4.11(b). To move a vertex, I randomly select an adjacent pair of these neighbors, which

Figure 4.11

Geometry for the mesh. (a) The basic mesh. (b) Each vertex can move within the hexagon formed by its six closest neighbors. (c) A triangle formed by the vertex and two adjacent neighbors. (d) Finding a point in that triangle. (e) Moving the vertex to that point.

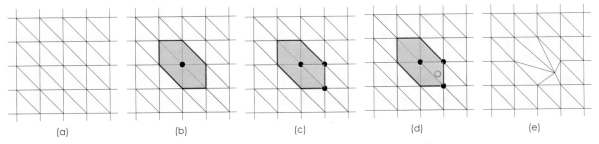

gives us a triangle as in Figure 4.11(c). I pick a random point in the triangle, as in Figure 4.11(d), and move the vertex to that point, Figure 4.11(e). I try to pick a point that's not too close to the edges so that the triangles don't get too long and skinny right away. Writing $?(a,b)$ for a random number in the range (a,b), I compute three numbers

Figure 4.12

Using the mesh to approx-
imate the toucan. (a) The
original 12-by-12 grid of
boxes. (b) 6,000 / 374
(c) 12,000 / 486 (d) 18,000
/ 571 (e) 25,000 / 616
(f–j) Parts (a–e) with outlines.
(c–d).

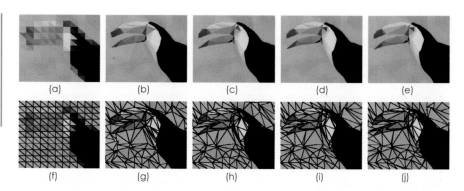

(a)   (b)   (c)   (d)   (e)

(f)   (g)   (h)   (i)   (j)

$a_0 = ?(.2, .7), a_1 = ?(.1, 1 - a_0)$, and $a_2 = 1 - (a_0 + a_1)$. I then randomly apply these weights to the three vertices of the triangle to get the new point. Because the weights are all positive and they sum to 1, the new point is guaranteed to lie inside the triangle.

Although the way the points are combined to create triangles (that is, the topology of the mesh) doesn't change over the course of the simulation, it can flop over on itself. In other words, some triangles can land on top of others. The overlap penalty helps prevent this from happening too much.

Figure 4.12 shows the results after 25,000 steps and 616 updates.

Voronoi Cells

A *Voronoi diagram* is made of a set of convex regions called *cells*. Each cell contains a single input point within it, and the region encloses all the points that are closer to that input point than to any other.

You can use that description to write a brute-force Voronoi renderer that fills each cell with the average color of the original pixels under it, using a list of N two-dimensional input points to define the cells. Let's do it in two passes.

Before we start, though, we'll create an auxiliary grayscale image called V, where each pixel is initially set to –1. What we want to do is to fill each pixel of V with a number from 0 to $N - 1$, indicating which input point it is closest to.

We'll also create two one-dimensional arrays. First, we'll make an array C of N colors and set each to $(0, 0, 0)$. We'll also create a counting array K of N integers, which we'll set to 0.

For the first pass, we'll visit each pixel (x, y) in the original image, compute its Euclidean distance to each of the input points, and find the closest one (note that since we're only comparing distances, we can work squared distances and save ourselves an expensive square root). Let's call the nearest input point v. We'll set the corresponding cell of

V to v. We'll also add that pixel's color from the original image into C_v, and increment K_v by one.

When we're done with the first pass, each element C_v contains the sum of the colors of all the pixels that are closer to input point v than to any other, and K_v tells us how many of them there are. We'll divide each color C_v by K_v to get C'_v, the average color of the pixels in that cell.

Now comes the second pass, which is easy. We scan through V, get the index v, and into the corresponding pixel in the output image we place the color C'_v.

This algorithm works, but the first pass is slow. It also doesn't scale well: if there are N input points, then every pixel has to compute the distance to all N points. If we double the input points to $2N$, it will take twice as long. The easy way to speed things up is to actually compute the Voronoi diagram using an efficient algorithm. To get going, I recommend using one of the implementations available for free on the web (see the Further Reading section).

Figure 4.13 shows the results. After 25,000 steps, there had been 769 improved images.

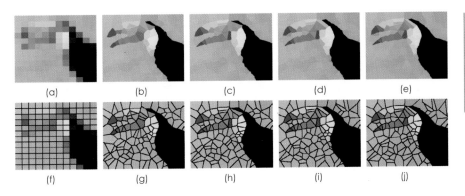

(a)   (b)   (c)   (d)   (e)

(f)   (g)   (h)   (i)   (j)

Figure 4.13

Using a Voronoi diagram to approximate the toucan. (a) The original 12-by-12 grid of cells. (b) 6000 / 369 (c) 12000 / 505 (d) 18000 / 599 (e) 25000 / 769 (f–j) Parts (a–e) with outlines.

Measure for Measure

Let's take a look at the performance of these different filters. In Figure 4.14 I show numerical data gathered from the runs that produced the images above.

To make the error plots, I drew a line of constant error from each iteration where a new image was produced to the right, until I reached the next iteration with a new error value. This is sometimes called a *sample and hold* type of plot.

The update plots are meant to try to capture the relative frequency with which new candidates are accepted. For each point on the plot, I looked throughout a window of 100 steps centered at the point in question and counted up how many times a new candidate was

Getting the Picture

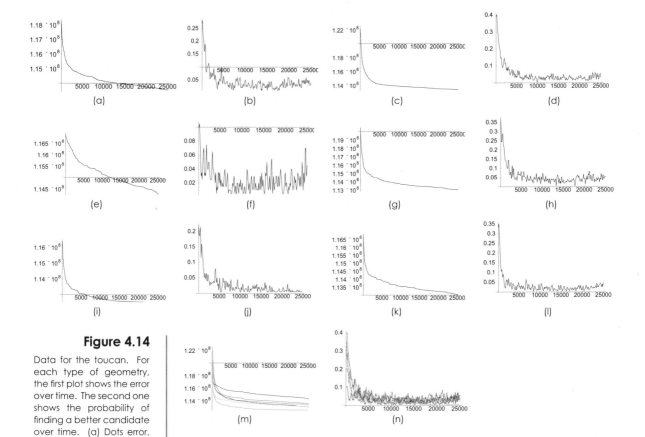

Figure 4.14

Data for the toucan. For each type of geometry, the first plot shows the error over time. The second one shows the probability of finding a better candidate over time. (a) Dots error. (b) Dots probability. (c) Half-dots error. (d) Half-dots probability. (e) Boxes error. (f) Boxes probability. (g) Triangles error. (h) Triangles probability. (i) Mesh error. (j) Mesh probability. (k) Voronoi error. (l) Voronoi probability. (m) Combined error plots, all scaled to the same range. Dots are in red, half-dots are green, boxes are blue, triangles are violet, the mesh is dark cyan, and Voronoi cells are pale red. (n) Combined update plots, using the same color scheme.

accepted. Then I divided that count by 100. That gives us a rough measure of the probability that a new candidate will be accepted as the simulation chugs along.

Figures 4.14(m) and (n) show these results superimposed. The point isn't to actually read off the data, but just to see how the different algorithms line up. Surprisingly, though the mesh is the most constrained geometry of them all, it seems to do the best job at minimizing the error.

Of course, we don't want to go too far in using these error values to measure the quality of the results; after all, if we wanted an error of zero, we could have it just by using the original image and spare ourselves all this effort! The real test comes from how the images look; the error is just to get a feel for how the algorithms proceed with their work.

I've run these eight algorithms on a few other images to show you how they look.

Figure 4.15 shows an image featuring a prominent Black-Eyed Susan, Figure 4.16 shows the results for a pair of puffins sitting on a shoreside rock, Figure 4.17 applies the filters to a hummingbird feeding at a yellow flower, and Figure 4.18 shows what happens to an image of a child's soft toy train.

Because of their low-res nature, these filters work best on images with large regions of similar color, where what really matters are the shapes and colors, and not the fine details. Running these filters on an image of a zebra is likely to replace its

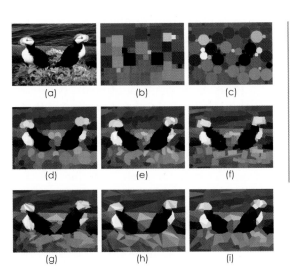

Figure 4.15

Applying the filters to a picture of a Black-Eyed Susan (Photograph by the U.S. Fish and Wildlife Service). The number in parentheses reflects how many times over the run of 25,000 iterations the perturbation was an improvement and became the new best image. (a) The original image. (b) Scaleboxes (98) (c) Scaledots (144) (d) Dots (1005) (e) Half-dots (1128) (f) Boxes (749) (g) Triangles (1219) (h) Mesh (560) (i) Voronoi (540)

Figure 4.16

Applying the filters to an image of two puffins sitting on a rock (Photograph by the U.S. Fish and Wildlife Service / photo by Richard Baetsen). (a) The original image. (b) Scaleboxes (66) (c) Scaledots (91) (d) Dots (917) (e) Half-dots (1100) (f) Boxes (810) (g) Triangles (1265) (h) Mesh (475) (i) Voronoi (575)

beautiful black-and-white stripes with a gray mush. Of course, if you like those stripes, then there are other ways to keep them while compressing the image. My goal here wasn't compression of the original image, but nice, low-fidelity approximations that look interesting.

DISCUSSION

The filters presented here aren't fast. On the other hand, I paid no attention to efficiency when I wrote the programs and ran them in debug mode; just a little profiling and tuning would doubtlessly improve

Figure 4.17

Applying the filters to an image of a Rufous Hummingbird (Photograph by the U.S. Fish and Wildlife Service / photo by Dean E. Biggins). (a) The original image. (b) Scaleboxes (73) (c) Scaledots (80) (d) Dots (942) (e) Half-dots (1226) (f) Boxes (732) (g) Triangles (1348) (h) Mesh (114) (i) Voronoi (593)

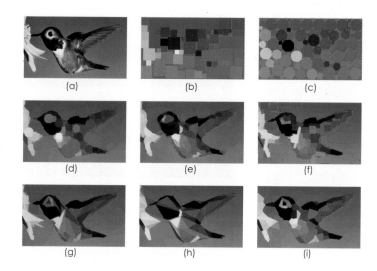

performance by a lot. On images of about 300 by 200 pixels, my 1.7 GHz home PC can deliver about two or three iterations per second for most of these filters. Making the 40 examples for this chapter took about 120 hours of steady computing. Though these filters are impractical for routine use today, I don't think that would be hard to change.

First of all, one could write better code and then compile it with optimizations. Second, I started each run by placing my geometry in a regular grid. Putting the elements down in a distribution that even roughly corresponds to the importance diagram would probably give the program an enormous head start. Third, I evaluate each image from scratch for each iteration. Since only one or two geometric

Figure 4.18

Applying the filters to an image of a child's toy train. (a) The original image. (b) Scaleboxes (66) (c) Scaledots (84) (d) Dots (1039) (e) Half-dots (1218) (f) Boxes (808) (g) Triangles (1335) (h) Mesh (69) (i) Voronoi(757)

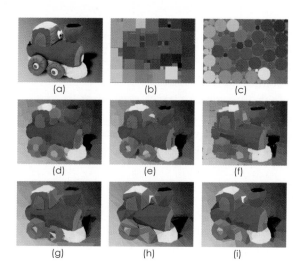

elements change per iteration, one could find the bounding boxes for those elements and just redraw the pixels in those boxes, which would mean only revisiting the geometric objects that fall into those boxes. Fourth, when I perturb my objects, I do so randomly. Again, using information from the importance diagram could go a long way towards getting them into good configurations quickly, rather than waiting for them to try many alternatives before lucking into a good spot. Fifth, one could use an estimate of the gradient of the error to nudge pieces in the direction where they'll do the most good. And finally, computers are of course getting faster all the time, so what's prohibitively slow today will certainly be very fast in the future. With enough speed, it would be fun to have a slider that set the number of steps to take or the number of improvements desired. Then by moving the slider back and forth, you can see the image interactively at different qualities of approximation and pick the one you like the best.

If you run one of these filters on one frame from an animation, and then run it again on the next frame, the geometry will probably pop around quite a bit. This look of a "boiling" image is sometimes desirable, but usually not. It can generally be avoided by using the final candidate for one frame as the starting candidate for the next, as in the technique in "Painterly Rendering for Animation" (see the Further Reading section). As long as the two images are somewhat similar (that is, they have some *image coherency*), the geometry shouldn't move too much to accommodate the changes.

Of course, one could actually make sure of this by using ideas from image processing and optical flow to deliberately move the geometry along paths (smooth or ragged, as desired) from one frame to the next.

As with any program that takes a long time to run, it's a good idea to save periodic checks as you go, in case the program needs to be stopped or the computer crashes. The easiest checkpoint for these filters is simply a list of the current geometric elements and the current iteration number. The program just takes the input as the best candidate and continues until the desired number of steps have been carried out. Using the final checkpoint of one frame of an animation as the starting state of the next one is an easy way to reduce the "boiling" effect I mentioned above.

It's also fun to take one set of geometry and apply it to another picture. Sometimes you get an interesting merge where you can discern the first picture from the shape of the pieces, but it seems to be hiding among the colors that come from the second picture. This effect is particularly noticeable in animation when your eyes have a few frames to catch and track the contours.

I ran each filter in this chapter on each image for 25,000 iterations. The number 25,000 was arbitrary: it just seemed like the simulations were settling down around there in my tests. It would be much better to instead use an automatic error-based stopping condition. A simple but effective condition is simply to stop when the score for an image (that is, it total error) is below some numerical threshold.

This is easy, but it has the problem that it can be hard to know what threshold to pick. After all, these images are approximations and will always have some error.

A better solution is to try to detect when the optimization has "flattened out." In other words, you try to detect when the error appears to have stopped improving for a long period of time. An easy implementation of this process uses two numbers. The first is a window width W, and the second is an error change threshold C. We apply the test every W iterations, find the difference between the score now and the score W iterations ago, and divide that difference by the score at the end of the window. This gives us a measure of the relative improvement over the last W iterations. If it's less than the threshold C, we stop.

When C is "small," the algorithm will continue to run even when the improvements are small in value. So you want C to be small enough to let the algorithm find a nice solution, but not so small that you wait endlessly while imperceptible changes accumulate. By the same token, the window W needs to be large enough that you don't stop when you've simply hit an unlucky sequence of perturbations. My rule of thumb is to set W to about $4N$, where there are N elements in the approximation. Then I set C automatically: I find the improvement for the first window of W elements, and I set C to $1/100$ of that value. It's not a perfect condition, but it's usually pretty close, and if I need more iterations I can just read the output file where the program stopped and start the system going again.

As with any stopping criteria, you'd probably also want to set a large upper limit on the number of steps so the program doesn't run forever.

FURTHER READING

The original inspiration for this chapter came from a couple of pictures at the end of the paper "Paint By Numbers: Abstract Image Representations," by Paul E. Haeberli (*Computer Graphics (Proceedings of SIGGRAPH 90)*, 24 (4), pp. 207–214, 1990). Those figures show a picture of a man sitting in a chair approximated by relaxed boxes, and a woman standing up approximated by a relaxed Voronoi diagram.

Adobe's *Photoshop* has a built-in filter called *Crystallize* which appears to build a Voronoi diagram, and then colors each cell with the average color under the cell. The filter doesn't seem to make any use of image information to place the points, and some cells have curiously soft or blurry boundaries.

One of the first papers to present a nice way to get non-photorealistic filters to work across animated sequences is "Painterly Rendering for Animation," by Barbara J. Meier (*Computer Graphics (Proceedings of SIGGRAPH 96)*, 30(4), pp. 477–484, 1996).

Many excellent filters exist for both still and moving images. Some filters use image-processing techniques to track the changes between frames and minimize the boiling effect when the geometry maneuvers to accommodate the new image. For example, some of the filters created by RE:Vision Effects for the film *What Dreams May Come* work this way. You can see them on their website at http://www.revisionfx.com.

Writing an efficient and stable program to compute Voronoi diagrams is no picnic. Rather than starting from scratch, I recommend building on C language source code written by Steve Fortune of Bell Labs, which he has made available at http://cm.bell-labs.com/who/sjf/. You can also find code for computing Voronoi diagrams and many other algorithms at the Computational Geometry Algorithms Library (CGAL) at http://www.cgal.org/.

Aaron Hertzmann has studied ways to use relaxation techniques to create images and video. His approach is to define an energy function over the image, and then he relaxes the painting so that he minimizes the total energy. You can find details of his algorithms and copies of his publications at http://mrl.nyu.edu/publications/painterly-relaxation/.

Digital
Weaving

5

Woven cloth is so common these days that many of us take it for granted. But even a moment's examination of an everyday cloth like denim reveals some beautiful patterns.

Weavers create cloth on a mechanical device called a *loom*. In terms of their complexity, looms are similar to old sailing ships: the basic ideas are pretty simple, but the actual implementation can be very complex.

One reason for this complexity is the quest for simple creature comforts: weavers often spend many continuous hours working at a loom, so a lot of effort has gone into the creation of comfortable and labor-saving mechanisms to make the job as pleasant as possible. So although you can build a simple loom with almost no moving parts, most modern looms are formidable machines.

In this chapter I'll describe enough of the basics of weaving so that we can write a loom simulator. Of course, nothing can beat actually going out and creating real, woven fabrics. My goal isn't to replace weaving, but to use the ideas of weaving to create software tools for making patterns.

People have already brought together computers and weaving in different ways. In the Further Reading section, I've identified several commercial programs on today's market that that are designed to help weavers. They are often complex and reward advanced knowledge of the craft of weaving. There's also a very interesting weaving language built into the art program *Painter*, which I'll talk about later. In fact, my wish for an interactive editor for that language was the original inspiration for this chapter.

Let's start with the basics of weaving.

The First Thread

A loom is typically a large wooden device with lots and lots of moving parts. In this section, I'll simplify and abstract the structure of a loom so that we can ultimately capture its essence in a computer program.

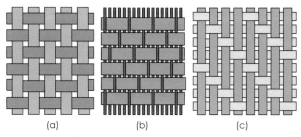

Treadles

Shafts

I'll speak of "threads" and "fabrics" in this discussion, though modern looms can weave all sorts of things, from thick, fuzzy yarns to thin, wide ribbons of satin and everything in between.

At its heart, a loom is a machine designed to interleave two sets of perpendicular threads. In one common format, one set of threads extends directly away from your body, and the others run left-to-right.

Figure 5.1 shows a simplified loom. The red fibers that go out away from us are called the *warp threads*, and they are fed from mechanical devices called *shafts*. The blue horizontal fibers are called the *weft threads* and are fed from devices called *treadles*.

Figure 5.1

A schematic version of a simple loom. The *shafts* along the bottom deliver the red, vertical *warp* threads. The *treadles* on the right deliver the blue, horizontal *weft* threads.

There is a substantial body of language associated with weaving, but I won't go any further into that lingo here. Check the Further Reading section for glossaries and introductions.

Setting up a loom is not unlike writing a program, and indeed some people cite the task of setting up a Jacquard loom as the birth of programming. Jacquard looms were able to produce extremely intricate designs by reading weaving instructions from a deck of punched cards, which embodied the weaver's design. Simply by loading up the loom with a different type of thread, the loom could produce many very different fabrics from the same basic pattern.

There are three fundamental types of basic weaves, which give rise to endless variations and combinations.

Figure 5.2

(a) A plain weave. (b) A satin weave. (c) A twill weave.

The most common is the *plain weave*, illustrated in Figure 5.2(a). In this pattern, each weft thread goes over and under each warp thread, in perfect alternation. Plain weaves are often used for clothing. An interesting variation is oxford cloth, which is often used for work shirts. Here each weft thread is actually doubled up, so although the

(a)   (b)   (c)

pattern is still square, there's double-frequency in the weft direction. This technique produces a durable yet attractive finish. You may also recognize the plain weave as the central element, or *plait*, of a classic Celtic knotwork panel, as I discussed in Chapter 3 of *Andrew Glassner's Other Notebook*.

Another common pattern is the *satin weave*. In this style, the weft threads pass over several warp threads before they pass under one, as shown in Figure 5.2(b). The interlaces are staggered so that no two overlaps are adjacent to each other. Typically the warp threads are thin and strong, and the weft threads are wide, smooth, shiny, and very closely packed. This gives the fabric a smooth and luxurious look and feel.

The third common pattern is the *twill* weave, shown in Figure 5.2(c). Twills are like satins, but differ in three respects: they often don't exaggerate the difference between wide and narrow threads like a satin, threads don't usually pass over as many threads before they pass under again, and sometimes the warp threads pass over several weft threads as well. Twills are easy to spot because of their distinctive diagonal component. As opposed to a satin weave, where the interlaces are not adjacent, in most twills each thread starts one step to the left or right of the one above it, creating the diagonal. Perhaps the most common twill used today is denim: if you look closely at your favorite blue jeans, you'll see the diagonals formed by the blue and white threads.

Now that we have some basics under our belts, let's look at how to describe a weave.

A ROUGH DRAFT

The basic pen-and-paper schematic for setting up a loom is called a *draft*. A draft has three parts: the setup of the warp threads, the setup of the weft threads, and something called the *tie-up*, which we'll get to in a moment.

The ability to read a draft is essential to understanding existing patterns and creating new ones. Happily, it's a pretty straightforward process.

A basic draft is no more than four simple black-and-white grids. This technique was originally developed for hand-drawing and hand-copying drafts since it's easy and fast to draw. It's also great for black-and-white photocopying. Although color and computer tools are both becoming more common, the black-and-white draft remains popular for many weavers.

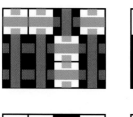

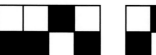

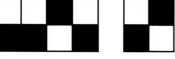

Figure 5.3

A simple draft. The threads superimposed on the cells in the upper-left part of the figure are not part of the draft. They're to help show the idea that the color of each cell in that part of the draft specifies which thread is on top.

Although a black-and-white draft is very convenient for doodling out a new design, I found that originally learning to read drafts in this form was a little difficult. Since I have the luxury of using color in this book, I'll augment the traditional black and white drafts with a colored and threaded version that I hope will make the pattern easier to visualize. I'll use greenish threads for the warp and ochre for the weft.

Take a look at Figure 5.3, which shows a very simple draft. The draft has four sections, each one a small grid separated from the others with a bit of white space.

In the lower left is the definition of the warp threading, in the upper right is the definition of the weft treadling, and in the lower right is the tie-up. These three grids describe how to set up the loom to weave fabric. The grid in the upper left shows the fabric that results from the other three grids. In this picture of the fabric, a black cell means that the warp thread is on top, while a white cell means that the weft is on top (look at the colored fabric to help make this clearer).

The layout of these four grids is by no means standardized. Sometimes you see the warp threads at the top rather than the bottom, or the weft threads on the left rather than the right, or both. The layout I'm using here is reasonably common. It's not too hard to convert a draft in any format into this one; after a little experience, you'll be able to do it by eye.

I'll now focus on the three lower-right grids and show how they specify the fabric in the upper left.

Let's look first at the warp pattern in the bottom left. It states that our fabric will be only four threads wide. Actually, it states that the *pattern* is only four threads wide; we can repeat this pattern over and over horizontally if we want to make a wider fabric, simply by repeating copies to the left as many times as we need.

The black cells in this grid tell us when to place the warp thread over the weft thread. In this draft, there are two rows to the threading pattern, so there are two ways to weave the weft threads into the warp threads. If we choose to use the pattern on the bottom row, then the weft threads are instructed to go under all but the second warp thread from the right. If we choose the upper pattern, then the weft threads go over all the warps threads except the second one from the right.

Which of these two patterns do we use for any given weft thread? The answer starts in the upper right of the draft, where the weft pattern is given. We can see that only three weft threads are defined, so we're going to create a tiny bit of fabric only four threads wide by three high (again, we can repeat this three-thread pattern over and over if we want to create a taller piece of fabric).

Let's weave our fabric from the bottom up, so we'll start at the bottommost line of the fabric (that is, the lowest row of the upper-left grid). Suppose we want to determine the color of the third cell from the right on the bottom row, marked in red in Figure 5.4.

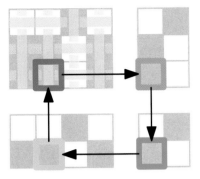

Figure 5.4

Colors indicating special cells from Figure 5.3. We want to fill in the red cell, so we look right to the weft pattern and find its one black entry marked in green. We look down to the tie-up from that cell to find the black cell marked blue, and left from that cell to the entry in the warp pattern below our red cell, marked in yellow. Since the yellow cell has a black interior, the red cell is marked black as well.

We look to the right of this cell to find the row of the weft pattern that corresponds to the row the cell is in. We're looking for a black cell (each row in the weft must have exactly one black cell). In this case, the cell in the leftmost column is filled in (I've marked that cell green in Figure 5.4). That tells us that this thread will be woven according to the instructions in the leftmost column of the tie-up.

I promised we'd talk about the tie-up, and the time has finally arrived. The job of the tie-up is to tell us which of the warp rows to use when we weave a given weft thread. The tie-up is the grid in the bottom right. In this example, it's very simple: it has two columns (because the weft treadling has two columns) and two rows (because the warp threading has two rows).

Because the row we used from the weft treadling has a black cell in its left column, we're instructed to look for black cells in the left column of the tie-up. In that column, there's only one black cell, which I've marked in blue in Figure 5.4.

Now that we've found a black cell in that column of the tie-up, we look left to the corresponding row of the warp pattern and look for the entry that is below the cell we started with. I've marked this warp cell in yellow in Figure 5.4. If that cell is black, then the warp thread in the red cell is on top; otherwise the weft thread is on top.

We fill in the entire fabric grid in this way, putting in a black cell everywhere a warp thread goes over a weft thread.

That's all there is to it! To recap, to determine which thread should be on top in a given cell, go right to the weft pattern, find the column with the black cell, go down to that column of the tie-up, find the row with the black cell, go left to that row of the warp pattern, and find the entry below the original cell. If that entry is black, the warp's on top; otherwise the weft is on top.

This is almost complete, but I've left something out. I promise I'll fix it up in a moment. But for now, look through the rest of Figure 5.3,

Figure 5.5

A taller version of Figure 5.3 with a different weft pattern.

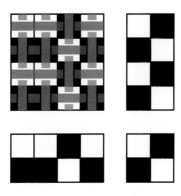

follow the description above, and see if the resulting fabric pattern in the upper left makes sense to you.

For another mental workout, take a look at Figure 5.5: it shows the same warp and tie-up, but with a different weft pattern.

You can see how these three grids interact in Figure 5.6. Figure 5.6(a) shows a weaving that's six threads wide by three high. In Figure 5.6(b) I've changed only the weft pattern, and in Figure 5.6(c) I've put the weft pattern back but changed the tie-up.

Figure 5.6

(a) A draft. (b) Varying the weft pattern. (c) Varying the tie-up.

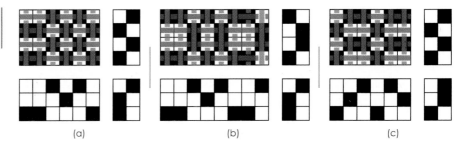

(a)   (b)   (c)

Now let's make that fix I promised. I said that each row of the weft pattern must have exactly one black cell, and that's true. Each column of the warp pattern must also have exactly one black cell. But, and this is the big one, the tie-up can be pretty much any combination of black-and-white cells that you care to create. Most importantly, each column can have any number of black cells, from none at all to a solid vertical column of them.

What does it mean if a column of the tie-up has more than two black cells? It tells us to use *both* indicated rows of the warp pattern. If *either* row has a black cell, then that cell of the fabric is black as well.

Figure 5.7

Three warp patterns can create four different rows of overlapping patterns, thanks to the tie-up.

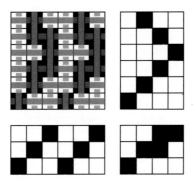

Look at Figure 5.7 to see an example of this. In Figure 5.8 I've followed one cell from the fabric, using the same coloring scheme as in Figure 5.4. Starting with the red cell, we move right to the corresponding row of the weft pattern, where we find the green cell. Moving down to the tie-up, we find two black cells, both marked in blue. Thus we look left for each one to find the warp entries in both rows under the fabric's cell; I've marked these in yellow. In this case, the upper cell is black and the middle cell is white; since at least one of them is black, the corresponding cell of the fabric is black.

The big advantage here is that the tie-up essentially lets us combine rows of the warp pattern without making the pattern bigger. In this figure, we have four different patterns (counting from the top, row 0, rows 0 and 1 together, row 1, and row 2). We could have made the warp grid taller by one and made a new row just for the combination of rows 0 and 1, but this form is more compact.

We can put this all together in Figure 5.9, which uses all of the ideas we've seen so far. In Figure 5.10 I've made a larger piece of fabric simply by repeating the sequences of the draft.

Sometimes the drafts you see in books or online are given in a numerical form rather than picture form. It's not too hard to turn one into the other, as long as you remember where the origin for each pattern is located.

Although this numbering style also varies, the most common style that I've seen is shown in Figure 5.11. The origin for each pattern is at the corner that they all share. The first coordinate counts vertically (up or down) from that point, and the second counts horizontally (left or right). Of course, this is a bit strange to get used to at first, but it becomes natural very quickly. Getting used to counting this way makes it easier to read the many drafts published on the web and in books, since no matter where

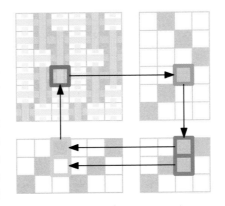

Figure 5.8

Finding the color of a cell using the draft of Figure 5.7 and the coloring scheme of Figure 5.4. To fill in the red cell, we go right to find the green cell, and down to the two blue cells. We go left from each of those to the yellow cells; since at least one of them is black, the red cell is colored black.

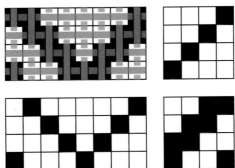

Figure 5.9

A small but practical draft.

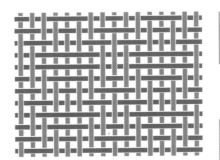

Figure 5.10

A pattern made by repeating the sequences of Figure 5.9.

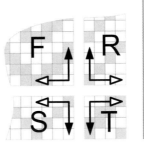

Figure 5.11

Note that each grid uses a different coordinate system. In all cases, the first coordinate named is the vertical one, marked with a black arrowhead, and the second is horizontal, marked with a white arrowhead. The region marked F is the fabric, S marks the shafts (describing the warp threads), R marks the treadles (for the weft threads), and T identifies the tie-up.

one puts the pieces of the diagram, you always count outwards from the shared corner, vertically and then horizontally.

Of course, some authors defy convention and count from the outside in, or horizontally first and then vertically. Generally it's worth a moment's thought to visualize where the origin is located before typing in a numerical draft that you get from someone else.

The Weaving Equation

Given the regularity of weaving and how the three grids (for warp, weft, and tie-up) look like matrices, I wondered if I could express the fabric grid mathematically.

It's actually pretty easy. Figure 5.11 shows how I'll label the matrices and their coordinate systems.

The biggest problem is finding names for things, since the words *warp*, *weft*, and *weaving* all start with the letter W! So I'll use the letter F for fabric to refer to the woven result, S for the shafts that control the warp threads, and R for the treadles that control the weft threads. That lets me use T for the tie-up matrix.

We know which two threads intersect at any given cell $F_{y,x}$, so our goal is only to determine which one is on top. I'll say that a value of 1 in the matrix F means that the vertical warp fiber is on top; otherwise it's the weft. I'll start by initializing all the elements of the matrix F to zero.

There are two important numbers associated with each of the patterns: the number of threads, and the length of the repeat. For example, we might have a pattern like that in Figure 5.10. From its draft in Figure 5.9, we can see that there are four warp threads, and the pattern repeats every eight units. Similarly, there are four weft threads, and they repeat every four units.

For the shaft pattern S, I'll write s for the number of threads, $\bar{s}$ for the length of the repeating sequence, and r and $\bar{r}$ for the threading. So in Figure 5.10, as in Figure 5.9, we have $s = 4$, $\bar{s} = 8$, $r = 4$, and $\bar{r} = 4$.

We'll index F by the values (y,x), measured from the lower right of F. Our first step is to find out which row of the treadling sequence R is called for. Since the weft sequence has $\bar{r}$ elements, we want row $y' = y \bmod \bar{r}$ (recall that $a \bmod b$ gives us the remainder of dividing a by b).

Now that we have the row, we look through it for the location of the one black cell; this is the one containing the value 1. Let's say that's at position c, so that $R_{y,c} = R_{y',c} = 1$, and all other $R_{y,j} = 0$ for $j \neq c$.

This tells us that we want to look at column c of the tie-up. There might be several 1s in this column, so we need to look at each one in turn. So we'll consider elements $T_{k,c}$ for $k = [0, \bar{s} - 1]$.

For each element in column k of T, we look at the corresponding warp thread pattern in S that's below x. Just as y might have been beyond the repeat length of the weft pattern, so might x, so we need to find $x' = x \bmod \bar{s}$, which is the index of x inside the warp pattern.

So now we look at $S_{k,x'}$. If that's a 1, then the warp thread should be on top, and we add 1 to $F_{y,x}$. We then step to the next value of k and then check the matrix S again, and so on, until we've taken care of all the rows.

The process matches the four arrows shown in Figures 5.4 and 5.5.

That's all there is to it! There's one little gotcha: each time we find a row that contributed to F, we added in 1. That means that some elements of F could have values as high as s. This isn't really a problem: we'll just say that a value of $F_{y,x} = 0$ means that the weft thread is on top, and any other value places the warp thread on top.

We can summarize the whole job with a few equations. First we get the values of x' and y', corresponding to the respective entries of x and y in the basic patterns:

$$x' = x \bmod \bar{s}$$
$$y' = y \bmod \bar{r}.$$

And now we just run through the algorithm I described above:

$$F_{y,x} = \sum_{c=0}^{t-1} \sum_{k=0}^{s-1} R_{y',c}\, T_{k,c}\, S_{k,x'}$$

I call this the *weaving equation*. It nicely packages up the algorithm that a simple loom is implicitly using when it weaves a piece of cloth. Unlike some mathematical expressions of physical procedures, the process of evaluating the equation very closely matches the real-world process. If you follow through the summation signs, you'll see that the equation is basically a mathematical mirror of the prose description of weaving that I gave above.

If you're familiar with Boolean logic, then you may have already noted that the weaving equation is expressed as a sum of products. Digital engineers will recognize this as a standard form of logical expression. Computing simplified versions of sum-of-product expressions is possible using a graphical technique called *Karnaugh maps* (which I'll discuss in Chapter 7), though the sheer number of terms in the weaving equation would make for a huge diagram.

But the digital perspective has value anyway: it gives us a way to write the weaving equation in a much simpler form. Think of the weft matrix R as an array $\hat{R}$ of decimal numbers. Index i in this array tells us the position of the single black cell in row i of R. Let's use the draft of Figure 5.7 as an example. In this draft, $\hat{R} = (0, 1, 2, 3, 2, 1)$ (of course, we're counting upward from the bottom of R, and assigning numbers left to right). Now let's think of the columns of the tie-up matrix as an array $\hat{T}$ of binary numbers. Taking each column from top to bottom, and reading the columns from left to right, the tie-up in Figure 5.7 gives us $\hat{T} = (001, 010, 110, 100)$. Finally, we'll think of the columns of the warp matrix S also in binary. Reading them top to bottom, right to left, we get the array $\hat{S} = (100, 010, 001, 100, 010, 001)$.

Now we can write the weaving equation more compactly. For a given cell $F_{y,x}$, we find the appropriate column of the tie-up to consult from $\hat{R}_{y'}$ (where I'm again using y' as defined before). Looking up that column in the array of binary numbers formed by the columns, the chosen column of the tie-up is just $\hat{T}_{\hat{R}y'}$. We find the proper column from S as $\hat{S}_{x'}$. Now we'll compute the logical AND (written &) of these two binary numbers. If any of the 1s in one number lines up with any of the 1s in the other, the result of the AND will be non-zero.

Summarizing this symbolically, the simplified form of the weaving equation is just:

$$F_{y,x} = \hat{T}_{\hat{R}\,y'} \ \& \ \hat{S}_{x'}$$

I like this result, because we've done away with both summations and gotten rid of a lot of overhead computation. We just look up a couple of numbers, compute their logical AND, and write that result into the fabric.

To see this equation in action, let's use it to evaluate the cell highlighted in Figure 5.8. We want $F_{3,2}$. We'll first note that the draft has a three-unit pattern for the warp, and a six-unit pattern for the weft. Thus, $y' = 2 \bmod 6 = 2$, and $x' = 3 \bmod 3 = 0$. So $\hat{R}_{y'} = \hat{R}_2 = 2$, and this sends us to $\hat{T}_2 = 110$. We also have $\hat{S}_{x'} = \hat{S}_0 = 100$. Computing the logical AND of these two bit patterns gives us 110 & 100 = 100. This is the value for $F_{y,x}$, and since it's non-zero, we know that the warp is on top in that cell, as it's marked in the figure.

DECORATED DRAFTS

Now that we've got the basics of drafts in hand, we can decorate them to create even more interesting patterns.

The basic idea behind decorated drafts is to add thread information to the basic pattern. Threads have many properties: color, shininess, fuzziness, thickness, and so on. I decided to implement three of the more geometric of these qualities: color, thickness, and spacing.

To add color, we just name a color for each thread of the warp and weft. It's tempting to actually color in the cells in the warp and weft grids with the color of that thread, but that can make the draft harder to read (a light-yellow thread is almost impossible to make out against a white background). So weavers typically add an extra row (or column) outside of the draft that indicates the color for each thread, as in Figure 5.12(a).

Figure 5.12

Adding color information to a draft. (a) The original weaving, using a single color each for the warp and weft. Both warp and weft patterns repeat every eight units. (b) The color patterns are each two threads long. (c) The weft color pattern has five entries, and the warp has three.

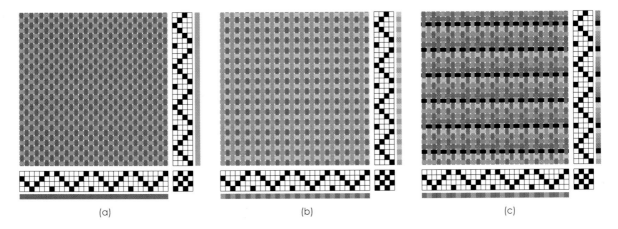

(a) (b) (c)

In Figure 5.12(a) I've assigned a single color to all of the warp threads and a different color to all of the weft threads. In Figure 5.12(b) I've given each of these groups a repeating pair of colors. In Figure 5.12(c) I've assigned three colors to the warp pattern, and five to the weft.

Adding thickness follows the same approach. To specify thickness I describe the width of a thread with an integer representing a percentage from 0 to 100, where 0 means it's invisibly thin, and 100 means it's as wide as the default cell size (of course, you could use actual widths like millimeters or inches here instead). As with colors, you can give a single number for all the threads in the weft and warp, as in Figure 5.13(a), or give a list for each, as in Figure 5.13(b). As with colors, these lists get reused when we reach the end. To save space, I've left off the drafts from this figure and the next two, since they're identical to that of Figure 5.12.

Figure 5.13

Adding thickness information to the draft of Figure 5.12(a). (a) The thickness patterns have the same length as the warp and weft patterns. (b) The thickness patterns have different lengths.

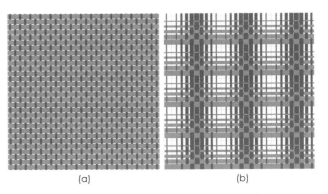

(a) (b)

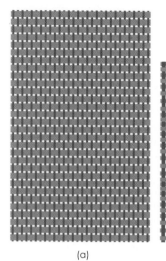

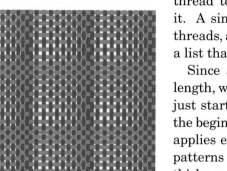

(a)   (b)

Figure 5.14

Adding spacing information to the draft of Figure 5.12(a). (a) The spacing patterns are constant for the warp and weft. (b) The spacing patterns have different lengths.

Figure 5.15

The draft of Figure 5.12(a), augmented with changes in color, spacing, and thickness.

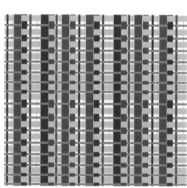

We can also control how much spacing appears between the threads. I use a number from 0 to 1, which gives a fraction of the width of the thread to appear as white space around it. A single number can apply to all the threads, as in Figure 5.14(a), or we can use a list that repeats, as in Figure 5.14(b).

Since any of these lists can have any length, when we reach the end of a list, we just start reading values over again from the beginning. This recycling of list values applies equally well to the warp and weft patterns themselves, as well as the colors, thickness, and spacing information.

Figure 5.15 shows an example of a weaving that uses variation in color, spacing, and thickness.

So now our basic repeating unit of fabric can be pretty big. Recall that the warp pattern repeats every $\bar{s}$ threads, so a simple fabric would repeat horizontally every $\bar{s}$ threads as well. But if the warp's color pattern has a entries, and the thickness pattern has b entries, and the spacing pattern has c entries, then the horizontal width of the repeating unit of fabric will be the least common multiple of all four numbers. If the numbers are relatively prime, then even if they're all small, the repeat can be large indeed. For example, if $\bar{s} = 7$, $a = 3$, $b = 4$, and $c = 5$, then the fabric will have a horizontal repeat of 420 threads! This is great news for those times when we want to generate big chunks of non-repeating texture. But remember that a lot of the appeal of many woven fabrics is precisely in their repeating nature, so you'd want to keep these two opposing desires balanced.

EXAMPLES

Let's look at some examples of weaving based on these ideas.

I'll begin with a screenshot of my weaving design environment: Figure 5.16 shows the two main windows of my program in action (we'll see more complex screenshots later on).

In the following examples, I've included the draft when I thought it was large enough to be both legible and interesting to look at. In some of the larger weavings, the full draft would be so small compared to the fabric that it would be illegible if we printed it here.

Figure 5.17 shows a simple two-color twill. Note the diagonal pattern characteristic of twills.

The *huck* pattern is a sort of fuzzy square. Figure 5.18 shows a checkerboard pattern composed on a variation of hucks. Figure 5.19 shows a large unit based on a huck. This draft uses eight threads in both the warp and weft, with a 30-unit repeating pattern. Figure 5.20 shows how it looks woven into a larger fabric. Figure 5.21 shows another variation on the huck, here used to make a blended sort of design.

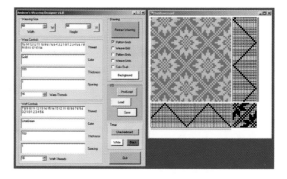

Figure 5.16

A screenshot of my digital loom.

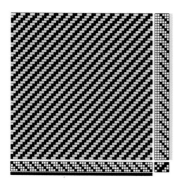

Figure 5.17

A simple two-color twill.

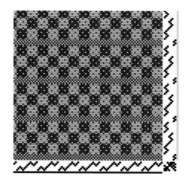

Figure 5.18

A two-color checkerboard pattern.

Figure 5.19

A unit for a weaving based on the huck pattern (draft from http://www.allfiberarts. com/library/gallery/blma- babyhuck.htm).

Figure 5.20

Several units of Figure 5.19 woven together.

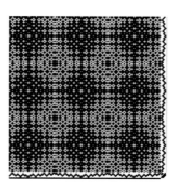

Figure 5.21

A two-color design based on a huck pattern.

Figure 5.22

An eight-pointed star design (draft from http://www.allfiberarts.com/library/bldraft/blstars.htm).

Figure 5.23

A simple but attractive "Norse Star" pattern (draft fromhttp://www.geocities.com/EnchantedForest/1154/rweave.html).

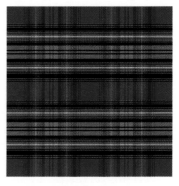

Figure 5.24

A colorful plaid based on the Arran tartan (adapted from draft TS204 at http://www.scottish-tartans-society.org).

Figure 5.25

A colorful plaid based on the Ainslee tartan (adapted from draft TS2673 at http://www.scottish-tartans-society.org).

Figure 5.26

A colorful plaid based on the Air Force regimental tartan (adapted from draft TS2123 at http://www.scottish-tartans-society.org).

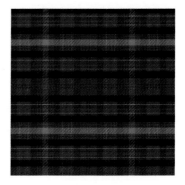

Figure 5.27

An original plaid.

Geometrics are fun weaving projects. Figure 5.22 shows one way to make eight-pointed stars. Figure 5.23 shows a simple but attractive form of alternating diamonds.

Plaids are of course one of the most popular forms of woven fabrics. Figures 5.24, 5.25, 5.26, and 5.27 show four different plaids.

Seemingly simple units can lead to surprising results. Figure 5.28 shows a single unit known as a "cat's paw." When we put a bunch of them together, as in Figure 5.29, we get a beautiful figure known as a "snail's trail."

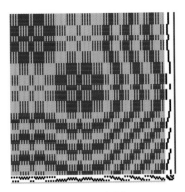

Figure 5.28

A single unit of a "cat's paw" design (draft from *The Key to Weaving*).

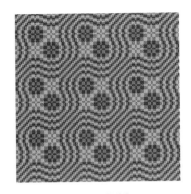

Figure 5.29

Many copies of Figure 5.28 make a pattern known as a "Snail's Trail."

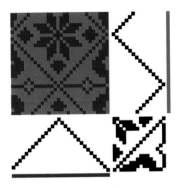

Figure 5.30

A single unit of a draft (draft adapted from *16 Harness Patterns*).

Figure 5.31

Many copies of Figure 5.30 woven together.

Figure 5.32

A minor change to the tie-up of Figure 5.30.

Figure 5.33

A bold geometric pattern (draft adapted from *16 Harness Patterns*).

To show just how much the tie-up affects a design, the next few figures all use the very same patterns in the warp and weft, and vary only in their tie-ups. Figure 5.30 shows a close-up of a single unit of patterns, and Figure 5.31 shows several of them repeated.

Figures 5.32, 5.33, and 5.34 show three more figures woven from the same warp and weft pattern as Figure 5.31. I've included the drafts here so that you can confirm that only the tie-up has changed.

I'll wrap up these examples with some nicely complex pieces of fabric. Figure 5.35 is a tablecloth pattern I designed. Using the same colors,

Digital Weaving

Figure 5.34

Sunflowers on a grassy field (draft adapted from *16 Harness Patterns*).

Figure 5.35

An original tablecloth design in red and coral.

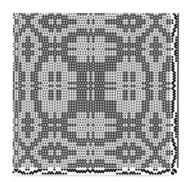

Figure 5.36

A single unit of the "Lover's Knot" pattern (draft from *The Key to Weaving*).

Figure 5.37

A larger fabric woven from Figure 5.36.

Figure 5.36 shows a single unit of the "lover's knot" pattern. Figure 5.37 shows that pattern repeated several times to make a piece of fabric.

DEDUCING THE DRAFT

So far I've talked about an approach based entirely on weaving new patterns from a given draft. It's natural to wonder if we can go the other way: given a piece of fabric, can we deduce the draft? In other words, can we invert the weaving equation?

The answer is yes, we can. The process is a deductive one, because we're not creating any new information. All the information we need to find the draft is already contained in the weaving. In other words, the piece of fabric and the draft are two representations of the same thing, and we can turn either into the other. To use the terminology of the weaving equation, in previous sections we were given the warp and weft patterns S and R and the tie-up T, and from them computed the fabric F. The deduction algorithm runs this the other way around: it takes the fabric overlapping matrix F as input, and finds $S, R,$ and T.

In this discussion, I'll ignore color, thickness, and spacing, since these can all be read off of the original fabric by eye. My goal is just to find the three binary matrices that determine the overlapping structure of the threads.

Note that determining F from a real, physical sample can be tricky: you need to look at the fabric closely and determine for every overlap which thread is on top. For closely-woven fabrics with fine threads, this process can require magnifying lenses, a steady hand, and a lot of patience. But in the end, you'll have a matrix that represents one complete unit of the repeating pattern that makes up the overall cloth.

Once we have F, we can use a nice algorithm for finding the other matrices, developed by Ralph Griswold (see the Further Reading section for a reference). It's surprisingly easy.

In early drafts of this material, I presented the deduction algorithm in pseudo-code as Griswold did, but then I decided that this was, after all, computer graphics, and it would be fun to instead find a visual presentation. After playing with it for a while, I found a satisfyingly graphical way to show what happens. Though I'll describe the process verbally as well, the next few figures are probably worth a few thousand words!

I'll begin by creating two "helper" data structures, which I'll call L_C and L_R. These will contain lists of columns and rows from F, and both begin empty.

To build L_C, I'll scan through the fabric F and look at each column. If the pattern for that column isn't yet in the collection L_C, I'll add it in. Then I'll do the same thing for L_R by scanning through the rows, adding in any row that's not yet in the list.

When the process is finished, L_C has one copy of each unique column in F, and L_R has one copy of each unique row in F. Figure 5.38(a) shows an example of this. Note that it ultimately doesn't matter in which order the rows and columns are added. If we scan the fabric's rows and columns in a different order, the arrangement of 1s in the three matrices would move around, but they would still generate the same fabric. In other words, there is more than one set of S, R, and T matrices that create a given F matrix. You might find it interesting to think about the relationships between these equivalent representations, but I won't go into it any further here.

When this scanning step is finished, L_C contains one copy of each unique column in F, and L_R contains one copy of each unique row. Let's use the notation $|L_C|$ to refer to the number of entries in L_C, and similarly $|L_R|$ is the number of unique rows in L_R.

Figure 5.38

Getting ready to deduce a draft from a fabric. (a) Given the fabric F, we create L_R, a collection of all the unique rows, shown in gold, and L_C, a collection of all the unique columns, shown in blue. (b) To make the process easier, I've created a blank draft around the fabric, and moved the two collections from step (a) around the draft. The heavy black lines around two edges of each collection show how I've rotated them.

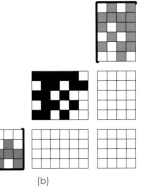

(a)   (b)

We can now create and initialize our three matrices. Starting with the weft pattern R, we note that it's as high as the height of F and $|L_R|$ wide. Similarly, S is as wide as F, and $|L_C|$ rows high. Finally, the tie-up matrix T is $|L_C|$ rows high by $|L_R|$ columns wide. I'll initialize all the elements of all three matrices to zero. Take a look at Figure 5.38(b) to confirm that these numbers all line up this way. I've positioned the two collections just outside of a blank draft. Note that I've rotated them from how they were drawn in Figure 5.38(a); this is just for convenience when following the graphical exposition to come.

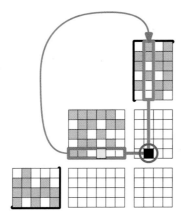

With that preparation finished, it's time to populate the matrices with 1s where they're needed. Because of all this preparation, the job itself is pretty easy.

Essentially we scan the matrix F one cell at a time, looking for black cells (that is, elements with the value 1). Each time we find one, we execute the same procedure. To illustrate the process, let's follow what happens to a black cell in the bottom row of F, third from the right: $F_{0,2}$. I've marked this cell in yellow in Figure 5.39.

The first thing we do is look up the row containing this cell in the collection of rows, L_R. I've marked the fabric row containing our yellow cell in red, and the corresponding row in the collection in blue. As we can see from the figure, it's row number 1 from the collection that we've matched. The intersection of the these two rectangles is a cell in the weft pattern R, and we set that to black, as in the Figure. In symbols, $R_{0,1} \leftarrow 1$.

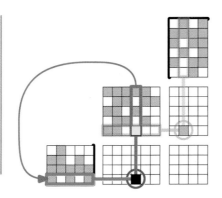

Now we look up the column containing this cell, marked in red in Figure 5.40, and find its entry in the collection of columns L_C. From the figure we can see that this is column number 3, again marked in blue. This time the intersection of the red and blue rectangles identifies a cell in the warp pattern S, so we set that to black as well: $S_{3,2} \leftarrow 1$.

Now for the tie-up. We found entries for row 3 and column 1 from the sets L_C and L_R, so we set the corresponding cell from the tie-up to black as well: $T_{3,1} \leftarrow 1$, as in Figure 5.41.

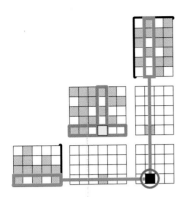

Figure 5.41

Step 3 of the deduction algorithm. The intersection of the row and column found in the first two steps identifies a cell in the tie-up T, which is then set to 1.

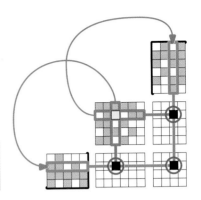

Figure 5.42

Processing of another black cell from F, again marked in yellow.

That's it for this cell from F. Now we march along for another black cell and handle it the same way. Figure 5.42 shows the process for another black cell from F. We repeat this process until we've run it for every black cell in F. When we've done that, the matrices are fully populated and we're done.

The draft that results from this deduction process is shown in Figure 5.43.

This algorithm is a natural for languages that support associative arrays, since then you can look up a row or column just by using it directly as an index, rather than searching through a list.

My description of the deduction algorithm was optimized for simplicity and an appealing visual presentation, rather than efficiency. But given the speed of today's computers, and the fact that even mechanized drafts are rarely larger than a few hundred cells on a side, even this algorithm effectively runs instantaneously.

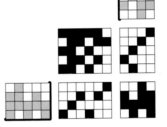

Figure 5.43

The completed draft resulting from the deduction algorithm.

WEAVING LANGUAGE

The art program *Painter* contains a very interesting weaving language. The basic ideas are terrific and allow you to create great-looking patterns.

The *Painter* weaving language has no name that I know of, so here I'll call it PWL. Although this language is innovative and powerful, using it is a bit tricky. The interface is buried deep inside the program, you have to hunt online for the documentation, and it has a lot of idiosyncracies and unexpected limitations. On the other hand, it's inside the *Painter* program, which means you can use it as another art

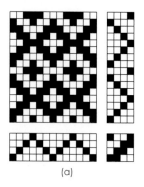

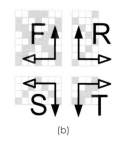

(b)

(a)

Figure 5.44

Setting up for AWL. (a) A simple draft. (b) As usual, the matrices are indexed as labeled, first in the black direction, then the white.

T	1 0 0 1 0 0 1 1 0 1 1 0 1 1 0 0
S	3 2 2 0 0 1 3 3 0 1 2 3 2
R	0 1 2 1 0 3 2 3 0 0 2 2 3 3 1 3

Figure 5.45

Specifying the different matrices with lists.

tool along with all the other tools in the system. In the Further Reading section I've provided a pointer to a document I wrote to help people use this great resource.

For my digital loom, I designed and implemented a variation on PWL. I added a bunch of new commands, changed the syntax a bit, and generalized it in several directions. Because it wouldn't be fair to the *Painter* folks to change their system and still use their name (they might not like the changes I've made), I've christened my variant Andrew's Weaving Language, or AWL. From now on I'll just stick to AWL, but be aware that it's just an extension of the *Painter* language.

The purpose of AWL is to create a sequence of numbers that can go into the S, R, and T matrices. Recall that each column of S can have only a single 1, and each row of R has the same restriction. So we can specify each of these matrices with just a list of integers. Figure 5.44 recaps our indexing convention: we count S down and to the left, and R up and to the right. Each list entry for R is in the range $[0, |L_R| - 1]$, and each entry for S is a number in the range $[0, |L_S| - 1]$. Figure 5.45 shows an example of how to specify each of these matrices with a list; the S and R matrices need only a single number per column and row respectively, while the T matrix has all of the 1s and 0s spelled out. For the tie-up, anything except a 0 is considered a 1.

I've implemented AWL as a *postfix* language, which uses a technique known as *stack* notation, or *reverse Polish notation* (this style was invented by Polish mathematician Jan Lukasiewicz (1878–1956)). In postfix notation, we write the *operands* first, and then the *operator*. So rather than writing 2+3, we'd write 2 3 +. Postfix is nice because we don't need parentheses. The expression 2+3*4 is ambiguous; if we multiply first we get 2+(3*4)=14, but if we add first we get (2+3)*4 = 20. Usually we use *precedence rules* to determine how to proceed. The convention is that multiplication has a higher priority than addition, so that expression would conventionally evaluate to 14. If we wanted to add first, we'd have to write (2+3)*4. Postfix gets around this problem. To add first, you could write 2 3 + 4 *, or even 4 2 3 + *.

These two forms are the same because the evaluation uses a *stack*. The standard metaphor for a stack is a pile of cafeteria trays: you remove them one at a time from the top, and new ones get added to the pile one at a time, also to the top. Each time we want to save a number, we push it onto the top of the stack. When an operator comes along, it pops its operands off the stack, computes with them, and then does a push to put the result back on. In a well-formed expression, when you reach the end, there's just one entry remaining in the stack, holding the final value of that computation. Probably the best-known and most widely-used postfix language today is PostScript, the language that's used by computers to communicate with printers and specify page layouts.

Postfix expressions are appealing from a programming point of view, because they're much easier to implement than more traditional *infix* expressions.

Getting Started

Before we get going, let's define a few terms. To make things easier for this discussion, I'll speak only about matrix S, which describes the warp threads and their associated treadles. Everything is the same for the weft and treadle matrix R, with just the obvious change to the matrix sizes. It also applies to the tie-up matrix T.

It's hard to present a language like this without it looking like just a big shopping list. But each command deserves a moment's explanation, and that inevitably turns into a big list. We can make that list as succinct as possible, though, by establishing some conventions first, and then using them to keep the discussion focused just on what each operator does.

The *domain* is a pair of numbers that specify a range of the available shafts. The domain is initialized to the range $[0, |L_S| - 1]$. Though I start at 0 for convenience, many weavers start counting at 1. The purpose of the domain is to allow us to conveniently create *runs*, or sequences of numbers that count up or down. A *complete run* cycles through the entire domain. For example, suppose that we've specified that we have seven treadles. Then a complete run might be 0 1 2 3 4 5 6. But we can start anywhere, so another complete run is 3 4 5 6 0 1 2. If we set the domain to the range $[2, 5]$, then a complete run might be 3 4 5 2.

As you've probably guessed, all numbers are adjusted to the domain using modulo arithmetic for the current domain when they're generated. So if we have seven treadles, no matter how we calculate them, the only numbers that actually come out at the end of the process are in the range $[0, 6]$. If we compute the sequence 4 5 6 7 8 9, then that would become 4 5 6 0 1 2.

The language has only three different elements: operators (which are identified by name, like reverse), and two different kinds of operands:

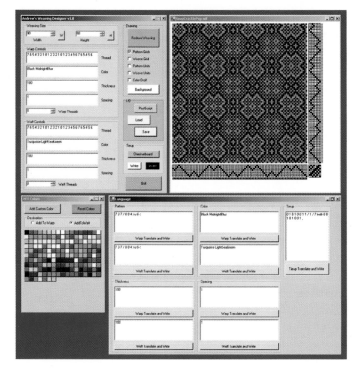

scalars (or individual numbers), and *sequences*, or lists of numbers.

To create a sequence, we can just list the numbers. Now suppose that we want to follow a sequence by another operand that is just a single number. For example, the `rotate` command takes a sequence and a number, and rotates the sequence that many steps. If the sequence is 1 2 3 4 and we want to rotate it two steps, if we had an infix language we could write 1 2 3 4 `rotate` 2. But in postfix we can't write 1 4 3 2 2 `rotate`, because the list 1 4 3 2 2 looks like a single big list. In this case we might be able to say that the last element on the list is the one we want, but many operators take two lists as input, so we need to distinguish where one ends and the next begins.

The trick is to use the `push` command after a list. That tells the system that all the numbers that have been given since the last operator are to be interpreted as a single operand, and get pushed on the stack that way. So we'd write 1 4 3 2 `push` 2 `rotate`. Note that we didn't need a `push` in front of `rotate`, since the command implicitly ends the operand that precedes it. Adding a `push` there wouldn't hurt, but it's not needed.

Figure 5.46 shows a screenshot of my digital loom in action, including the windows for entering the AWL expressions and choosing colors. We type in an AWL expression into the *Warp pattern* window in the AWL form and press the associated button. The expression is evaluated, and the resulting sequence is then copied into the warp pattern field in the weaving form. We can also of course type an expression into any of the other AWL fields, and they get copied into the weaving form, so we can use AWL to specify not just the S, R, and T matrices, but the spacing, thickness, and color patterns for the threads.

Finally, I'd like to cover an idea called *reshaping*. Some operators take two lists and combine them in a way that only makes sense if both lists have the same length. For example, the operator `interleave` creates a new list by folding together two others. If the first operand is 1 2 3 and the second is 7 8 9, we'd write this as 1 2 3 `push` 7 8 9 `interleave`. The similar expression 2 3 `push` 3 4 5 `interleave` wouldn't make sense, since the first operand 2 3 has length 2, while the second operand 3 4 5 has length 3. This kind of thing comes up a lot, and in many cases the right thing to do is to simply repeat the shorter operand until it's as long as the longer one. So in this case, we'd just repeat the operand 2 3 to create 2 3 2. This process is called *reshaping*. It doesn't matter which operand is longer: the shorter one just gets repeated until it's long enough. If they're both the same size, nothing happens to either. Many of the operators automatically perform a reshaping step before they go to work. This means that our earlier expression 2 3 push 3 4 5 interleave would be evaluated as though it was 2 3 2 push 3 4 5 interleave.

There's no provision for turning reshaping off, since if the operands were of different sizes and we didn't reshape them, it would raise an error.

Most operators take one or more elements off of the stack, process them, and then push a result back on the top. If the operand is a sequence, I'll write it as **A** or **B**. If it's a single number, I'll write that as c or d. Individual elements of sequence **A** are written $\mathbf{A}_i$. So $\mathbf{A}_0$ is the first number. I'll write $\mathbf{A}_L$ to represent the last number in the sequence, and $|\mathbf{A}|$ to refer to the length of **A**. So if **A** is 1 3 5 7, then $\mathbf{A}_0 = 1$, $\mathbf{A}_L = 7$, and $|\mathbf{A}| = 4$.

Operands are popped off the stack in the reverse order from the definition of the operator. For example, suppose we define an operator named combine as **A B** combine. If we enter an expression 1 2 push 3 4 5 combine, then we first pop 3 4 5 and it becomes **B**, and then we pop 1 2, which is treated as **A**.

In all of the following examples, the domain is [0, 7]. Many commands have symbolic shortcuts, which are given in parentheses right after the command itself. Note that the shortcuts all contain symbols, so that they don't eat up any more words. Since we can use AWL to create color expressions that use color names, any word used by an AWL command becomes unavailable as the name of a color. Many of the shortcuts are similar to those in PWL, but there are a few changes and lots of additions.

Basic Operators

There are a few operators that I think of as "basic," because they're pretty straightforward.

A d extend (+) :
If $|\mathbf{A}| > d$, truncate **A** to d elements. If $|\mathbf{A}| < d$, repeat **A** as needed until there are at least d elements, and then truncate that result after d elements.

```
1 2 3 4 5 push 3 extend = 1 2 3
    1 2 push 3 extend = 1 2 1
```

A *d* repeat (*) :
Repeat **A** a total of *d* times.

```
1 2 3 push 3 repeat = 1 2 3 1 2 3 1 2 3
```

A reverse (@) :
Reverse the order of the elements of **A**.

```
1 3 5 7 reverse = 7 5 3 1
```

A *d* rotateR (>>) *and* **A** *d* rotateL (<<) :
Rotate the elements of **A** to the right (or left) by *d* steps.

```
1 2 3 4 5 push 2 rotater = 4 5 1 2 3
```

A *c* nth :
Build the new sequence from element 0 of **A**, then skip $c - 1$ elements, take the next, skip another $c - 1$, take the next, and so on.

```
1 2 3 4 5 6 7 push 2 nth = 1 4 7
```

A palindrome (|) :
The output is **A** followed by the reverse of **A**, except that the first and last elements of **A** are not included in the reversed version. We don't repeat the first and last elements because we want to avoid flat spots both when making the new sequence and if we repeat palindromes. For example, if we didn't do this, then 1 2 3 palindrome 2 repeat would be 1 2 3 3 2 1 1 2 3 3 2 1 rather than 1 2 3 2 1 2 3 2, which is almost always more appropriate for creating weaving drafts.

```
1 2 3 4 5 palindrome = 1 2 3 4 5 4 3 2
```

UP AND DOWN

These operators are used to create runs, or ascending and descending integers within the current domain. Many drafts consist of these runs, so it's useful to have a bunch of convenient ways to specify them.

A B down (>) *and* **A B** up (<) :
For down, the result is **A**, followed by a run descending from the last
element of **A** to the first of **B**.

    1 5 3 push 6 3 down = 1 5 3 2 1 0 7 6 3

The command up is the same, but the run ascends.

A B c downloop (>l) *and* **A B** c uploop (<l) :
downloop is like down, but inserts c complete runs in addition to the
single descending run.

    1 2 3 push 6 3 push 1 downloop = 1 2 3 2 1 0 7 6 5
    4 3 2 1 0 7 6 3

The command uploop is the same, but each run ascends.

A B downup (>u) *and* **A B** updown (<d) :
Reshape the inputs. For downup, take the first element of **A** and
insert a descending run to the first element of **B**. Now ascend to the
second element of **A**, descend to the second element of **B**, and so on.

    1 2 3 push 6 7 downup = 1 0 7 6 7 0 1 2 1 0 7 0 1
    3 2 1 0 7 6

The command updown is the same, but the alternation begins with
an ascending run.

A B c downuploop (>ul) *and* **A B** c updownloop (<dl) :
downuploop is like *downup*, but inserts c complete runs in each
inserted sequence.

    1 push 5 push 2 downuploop = 1 0 7 6 5 4 3 2 1 0 7
    6 5 4 3 2 1 0 7 6 5

The command updownloop is the same, but the alternation begins
with an ascending run.

A B ramp (-)
This creates a run from A_L to B_0, but it does so entirely within the
domain. So if $A_L < B_0$, it creates an ascending run, otherwise a
descending one.

    2 push 5 ramp = 2 3 4 5
    7 push 5 ramp = 7 6 5

A B *c* ramploop (-1)
   Like ramp, but like uploop or downloop it includes *c* full runs.

ADVANCED OPERATIONS

The previous commands were all designed to do basic operations on sequences or to create simple runs. This next batch of commands lets us make more complex patterns.

A binary0 *and* **A** binary1 :
   Treat **A** as the length of alternating sequences of 0s and 1s. binary0 starts with 0, while binary1 starts with 1. This is a convenience command mostly useful for specifying tie-ups.

   3 1 4 2 2 binary0 = 0 0 0 1 0 0 0 0 1 1 0 0

A B block (#) :
   Reshape the inputs. Each entry A_i is repeated B_i times.

   3 4 5 1 2 push 2 3 block = 3 3 4 4 4 5 5 1 1 1 2 2

A B blockpal (#p) :
   blockpal is like a block, but it first processes its inputs by making a palindrome of them, treating the inputs as *pairs*. So in the following example, the pair 1   2 is considered the first element, so it's not repeated at the end, and the pair 2   2 is the last element, so it's not repeated in the middle.

   1 3 2 push 2 4 2 blockpal = 1 1 3 3 3 3 2 2 3 3 3 3

name c d eis :
   The value of *name* is a string, typically a single letter followed by digits. It specifies an index number in the *Encyclopedia of Integer Sequences*, which is a massive reference work containing thousands of interesting integer sequences (see the Further Reading section for more information). From that named sequence, we skip *c* entries, and then extract the next *d* values.

A B growblock (=) :
   First, reshape the inputs. Each element A_i is followed by a ramp to B_0 (recall that the ramp goes up or down, as needed, to stay within the run). At the end of the run, a palindrome of the first *i* elements of **B** is inserted, and then a run to A_{i+1} is made.
   This diagram shows the result for input sequences with three elements each. The right arrow → stands for a ramp.

$$\mathbf{A}_0 \to \mathbf{B}_0 \to \mathbf{A}_1 \to \mathbf{B}_0\ \mathbf{B}_1\ \mathbf{B}_0 \to \mathbf{A}_2 \to \mathbf{B}_0\ \mathbf{B}_1\ \mathbf{B}_2\ \mathbf{B}_1\ \mathbf{B}_0$$

```
0 1 2 push 4 5 6 growblock = 0 1 2 3 4 3 2 1 2 3 4
5 4 3 2 3 4 5 6 5 4
```

growblock was inspired by an analysis of shadow weaves by Ralph Griswold in one of his monographs (see the Further Reading section).

A iblock (i#) *and* **A** iblockpal (i#p):
Like block, but the values are interleaved in one operand. Thus element $\mathbf{A}_0$ is repeated $\mathbf{A}_1$ times, element $\mathbf{A}_2$ is repeated $\mathbf{A}_3$ times, and so on.
iblockpal is like blockpal, building palindromes from its input pairs, except that they're taken in interleaved fashion.

A B interleave (%):
Reshape the inputs. Then create a new string by taking each element of **A** and then **B** in turn.

```
1 2 3 4 push 9 7 5 interleave = 1 9 2 7 3 5 4 9
```

A B permute:
First, repeat **A** until its length is an integer multiple of the length of **B**. That is, create a new vector **A**′ by choosing the smallest r such that $r|\mathbf{A}|\,/\,|\mathbf{B}|$ is an integer.
Now create a new vector **B**′ by repeating **B** so that it is the same length as **A**′, but with a twist. Add 0 to the first repeat of **B**, and $|\mathbf{B}|$ to the second, $2|\mathbf{B}|$ to the third, and so on. For example, if **A** = 1 2 3 4 and **B** = 3 1 2, then we choose $r = 3$ and create

```
A' = 1 2 3 4 1 2 3 4 1 2 3 4
B' = 3 1 2 (3+(3 1 2)) (6+(3 1 2)) (9+(3 1 2))
   = 3 1 2 6 4 5 9 7 6 12 10 11
```

The output is then found by using each element of **B**′ as the index from **A**′. That is,

$$\mathbf{A}'_{\mathbf{B}'_0},\ \mathbf{A}'_{\mathbf{B}'_1},\ \mathbf{A}'_{\mathbf{B}'_2},\ \dots\ \mathbf{A}'_{\mathbf{B}'_p},$$

where p is the length of either of the new vectors. The entries of **B**′ are taken modulo p.

117

```
1 2 3 4 5 6 push 1 0 permute = 2 1 4 3 6 5
3 4 5 push 2 1 permute = 5 4 4 3 3 5
```

A B pbox :

This is a convenience for the following operation, where $|\mathbf{A}|$ is the length of $\mathbf{A}$:

A B $|\mathbf{A}|$ extend permute

A B tartan *and* **A B** tartanpal :

These are a small variation on the iblock and iblockpal commands. Some tartan descriptions double the thread count for each entry, and AWL expects single counts. So after reshaping, each $\mathbf{A}_i$ is repeated $\mathbf{B}_i/2$ times.

A B template (:) :

Replace each entry in **A** with a little pattern based on the elements of **B**. Weavers call this process *sub-articulation*.

First, create a new vector **C** with the same length as **B** (that is, $|\mathbf{C}| = |\mathbf{B}|$) and initialize **C** to all 0s. Now compute $\mathbf{C}_i = \mathbf{B}_i - \mathbf{B}_0$ for all $i = [1, |\mathbf{B}|]$. Thus the first element of **C** is 0, and all other elements are the signed distance of each $\mathbf{B}_i$ from $\mathbf{B}_0$. So if **B** = 6 7 5, then **C** = 0 1 -1, and if **B** = 3 4 5 1 2, then **C** = 0 1 2 -2 -1. The output is computed by replacing each element $\mathbf{A}_i$ with the new $|\mathbf{C}|$-length vector $\mathbf{A}_i + \mathbf{C} - 1$.

```
0 1 2 3 push 2 template = 1 2 3 4
0 3 6 push 2 3 1 template = 1 2 0 4 5 3 7 0 5
```

A *c* *d* twillr (t>>) *and* **A** *c* *d* twillll (t<<) :

Make *c* repeats of **A**, each time rotating it to the right (or left) one more time than before.

```
1 2 3 4 push 3 push 1 twillr = 1 2 3 4 4 1 2 3 3 4 1 2
```

UTILITIES

This last batch of commands is for utility, stack management, and book-keeping functions.

clear : Erase the entire stack.

concat (,) : Take the top two elements from the stack, create a new sequence by placing the second after the first, and push that result back on the stack.

`dup` : Get the top item on the stack and push a new copy of it onto the stack.

`pop` : Discard the top element of the stack.

`push` (`/`) : Take everything up to now and treat it as a single element of the stack.

c d `domain` : Set the limits on the domain to [*c,d*].

`swap` : Swap the top two entries on the stack.

`len` : Find the length of the top element on the stack and push that value.

`vmax` *and* `vmin` : Push the value of the largest (or smallest) element in the sequence on top of the stack.

A summary of all of these commands appears in Figure 5.47.

THE TIE-UP

The tie-up is a matrix of 1s and 0s. When applying the result of an AWL expression to a tie-up, the language treats anything that's not a 0 as a 1. The output is automatically extended as necessary to make it the correct size. Elements are applied to the tie-up using the indexing of Figure 5.44.

SOME EXAMPLES

Even short AWL expressions can easily produce very long, impenetrable sequences of digits. The ability of AWL to symbolically represent such lists with a few meaningful commands is one of its biggest advantages.

But that also poses a challenge for demonstration, since examples of expressions easily expand into giant strings of numbers. So Figures 5.48 through 5.50 provide some short examples. In those figures, I assume that the domain is set to [0, 7].

Command	S	R	Summary
A d extend	+		repeat or clip **A** to d elements
A d repeat	*		repeat **A** a total of d times
A reverse	@		reverse the elements of **A**
A d rotatel	<<		rotate **A** left by d steps
A d rotater	>>		rotate **A** right by d steps
A d nth			take every d'th element of **A**
A palindrome	|		**A** followed by a near-reversal
A B down	>		**A**, descending run from A_L to B_0, **B**
A B c downloop	>l		like down but include c runs as well
A B downup	>u	√	alternating down and up runs
A B c downuploop	>ul	√	like downup but include c runs as well
A B up	<		**A**, ascending run from A_L to B_0, **B**
A B c uploop	<l		like up but include c runs as well
A B updown	<d	√	alternating up and down runs
A B c updownloop	<dl	√	like updown but include c runs as well
A B ramp	-		go up or down as needed to stay in domain
A B c ramploop	-l		like ramp but include c runs as well
A binary1			treat **A** as lengths of alternating 1 s and 0 s
A binary0			treat **A** as lengths of alternating 0 s and 1 s
A B block	#	√	each A_i is repeated B_i times
A B blockpal	#p	√	block with an internal palindrome
name c d eis			extract d elements, starting at c, from EIS *name*
A B growblock	=	√	interleave **A** with growing palindromes of **B**
A iblock	i#	√	like block but the inputs are interleaved in **A**
A iblockpal	i#p	√	iblock with internal palindrome
A B interleave	%	√	take alternating elements of **A** and **B**
A B permute			use elements of **B** to index **A**
A B pbox			shortcut for **A B** |**A**| extend permute
A tartan		√	like iblock but repeats are $B_i/2$
A tartanpal		√	tartan with internal palindrome
A c d twillr	t>>		make c repeats of **A** rotating each by d more
A c d twilll	t<<		like twillr but rotate left
A B template	:		create a sub-articulation using **B** as a template
clear			erase the stack
concat	,		concatanate the top two stack elements
dup			pop the top of stack and push it back twice
pop			discard top of stack
push	/		consider all since last command a single sequence
c d domain			set the domain to $[c, d]$
swap			exchange top two stack elements
len			push length of list on top of stack
vmax			push largest element in sequence on top of stack
vmin			push smallest element in sequence on top of stack

Figure 5.47

Summary of AWL commands; see the text for details. The S column provides the symbolic shortcut, if available. If the R column is checked, the command reshapes its inputs.

Operation	Top of Stack	2nd Item in Stack
1 push 4 up	1 2 3 4	
palindrome	1 2 3 4 3 2	
2 push 7 up	2 3 4 5 6 7	1 2 3 4 3 2
interleave	2 1 3 2 4 3 5 4 5 3 7 2	
2 rotate	7 2 2 1 3 2 4 3 5 4 5 3	

Figure 5.48

The left column is the command that's just been processed, the column to its right is the top of the stack, and to its right is the second item in the stack. Evaluating the expression
```
1 push 4 up palindrome
2 push 7 up interleave
2 rotate
```

Operation	Top of Stack
2 3 push	2 3
3 2 block	2 2 2 3 3
4 5 3 template	5 6 4 5 6 4 5 6 4 6 7 5 6 7 5

Figure 5.49

Evaluating the expression
```
2 3 push 3 2 block 4 5
3 template
```

Operation	Top of Stack
1 3 push 6 2 updown	1 2 3 4 5 6 5 4 3 4 5 6 7 0 1 2
2 nth	1 4 5 4 7 2
reverse	2 7 4 5 4 1

Figure 5.50

Evaluating the expression
```
1 3 push 6 2 updown 2
nth reverse
```

Languages like AWL abound in idioms, or little constructions that seem to recur frequently. Let's look at one. Suppose we want to create a sequence which uses alternating members of **A** and **B**, giving us A_0 B_1 A_2 B_3 .... The general approach would be like this:

```
A 1 nth B 1 rotateL 1 nth interleave
```

Figure 5.51 shows this in action.

Using the domain command, you can change the domain as often as you like during an expression. So for example, in this expression

```
0 / 7 domain 4 / 2 up 1 / 5 domain 4 / 2 up concat
```

(where I've used the shortcut / for push), the domain is first set to [0, 7], and then an upward sequence 4 5 6 7 0 1 is generated. Then the domain is set to [1, 5] and the same run is specified, but this time the domain limits it, and we get 4 5 1 2.

Figure 5.51

How to create a simple sequence that uses alternating values from two others. We follow the expression `0 1 2 3 push 1 nth A B C D push 1 rotateL 1 nth interleave`

Operation	Top of Stack	2nd item in stack
`0 1 2 3 push`	`0 1 2 3`	
`1 nth`	`0 2`	
`A B C D push`	`A B C D`	`0 2`
`1 rotateL`	`B C D A`	`0 2`
`1 nth`	`B D`	`0 2`
`interleave`	`0 B 2 D`	

Sometimes there are several good ways to write a sequence. In the following discussion, I'll use AWL's symbolic shortcuts names for simplicity; recall that push is /, repeat is *, concat is ,, block is #, interleave is %, and template is :. Let's look at several ways to write the following:

> 7 6 7 6 7 6 7 6 5 4 5 4 5 4 5 4 3 2 3 2 3 2 3 2

One way to do this is to note that we have four repeats of the sequence 7 6, then four of 5 4 and four of 3 2, so we might write

> 7 6 / 4 * 5 4 / 4 * , 3 2 / 4 * ,

We might instead notice that this is four 7s interleaved with four 6s, and the other pairs follow the same pattern, leading us to write:

> 7 5 3 / 4 # 6 4 2 / 4 # %

We could also treat each eight-element chunk as a sub-articulation on the starting values:

> 7 5 3 / 8 7 8 7 8 7 8 7 :

where I used the wraparound feature of modulo arithmetic to get the effect we're looking for. We could further encode that pattern of 8s and 7s:

> 7 5 3 / 8 7 / 4 * :

All five of these expressions, from the explicit list of numbers to this most compact result, evaluate to the same thing. They're just different ways of looking at and expressing how we see the structure of the patterns. This example was not exhaustive by any means; there are lots of other ways to write this pattern.

Playing around with pattern languages is great fun. For example, suppose you had a sequence 1 2 3, and you wanted to make a new sequence that had each element repeated four times. How would you do it? Remembering that the `block` operator reshapes its inputs, we only need to say `1 2 3 / 4 #` and we're done. There are lots and lots of cool tricks like this.

I think it would be fascinating to write a program that tried to intelligently discover the shortest expression to represent a given pattern. The results might be impossibly cryptic, but they could also give us some new ideas for how to look at sequences.

COLORS, SPACING, AND THICKNESS

Earlier I talked about how we can specify each thread's thickness with a number between 0 and 100. I also talked about spacing as a number from 0 to 1, but we could just as easily use the range 0 to 100, and divide by 100 internally.

Thus all the language elements discussed above can be typed into the spacing or thickness fields just as easily as they can be typed into the warp and weft pattern fields.

Color is a slightly different issue. All of the examples in the last section were in terms of integer sequences. And for some operators, like `up`, that's the only kind of argument that makes sense. But other operators don't care what their operands look like. For example, `interleave` just takes out elements from one input sequence and then the other. Those input sequences can be integers, of course, but they could be anything. In particular, they can be text strings.

In my system, I provide access to colors by name. You can use any of the 140 built-in colors in the .NET environment, any of the roughly 40 colors commonly used in Scottish tartans, or any custom colors you create and name yourself.

Thus you can type in something like `Blue Gold Red reverse` and get back the list in opposite order, or something more ambitious like `Blue Gold Red push 2 3 2 block`.

If you type in non-numerical data into any of the fields except for the color field, the system will raise an error.

WEAVINGS

Of course, the whole reason for creating these interesting patterns is to use them to create attractive weavings.

Figures 5.52 through 5.71 show a variety of different weavings, along with the AWL expressions for the tie-up, warp, and weft. Many beautiful patterns come from very simple specifications. Sometimes the expressions are bulky, but they're still a lot shorter than simply listing all the numbers for a given matrix.

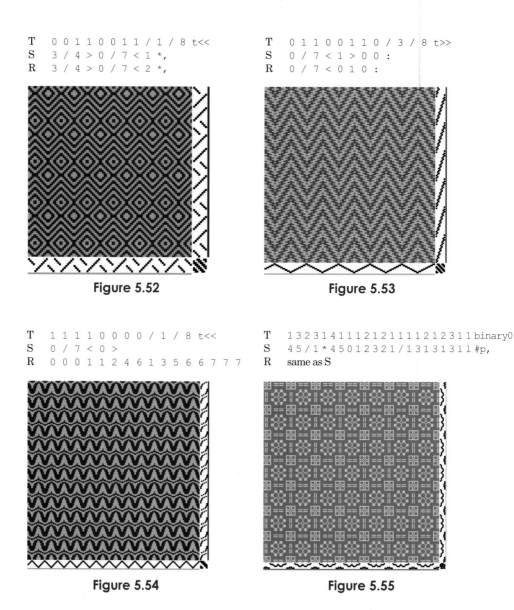

```
T   0 0 1 1 0 0 1 1 / 1 / 8 t<<
S   3 / 4 > 0 / 7 < 1 *,
R   3 / 4 > 0 / 7 < 2 *,
```

Figure 5.52

```
T   0 1 1 0 0 1 1 0 / 3 / 8 t>>
S   0 / 7 < 1 > 0 0 :
R   0 / 7 < 0 1 0 :
```

Figure 5.53

```
T   1 1 1 1 0 0 0 0 / 1 / 8 t<<
S   0 / 7 < 0 >
R   0 0 0 1 1 2 4 6 1 3 5 6 6 7 7
```

Figure 5.54

```
T   1 3 2 3 1 4 1 1 1 2 1 2 1 1 1 1 2 1 2 3 1 1 binary0
S   4 5 / 1 * 4 5 0 1 2 3 2 1 / 1 3 1 3 1 3 1 1 #p,
R   same as S
```

Figure 5.55

I came up with the AWL expressions for these drafts by looking at the matrices and hunting for patterns, and then trying to find succinct ways to express them. It's a lot of fun!

One of the most interesting things is that even though there are a lot of patterns to be discovered in weaving drafts, they don't always become shorter when we try to express them in AWL. Particularly when a sequence is on the order of 20 or 30 characters, sometimes just naming the elements is the most efficient way to go.

```
T   1 0 0 0 1 0 0 1 / 1 / 8 t>>
S   0 / 7 < 0 / 7 - 1 2 / 7 + :, |
R   same as S
```

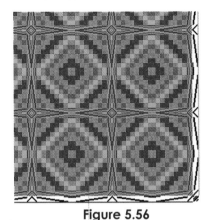

Figure 5.56

```
T   2 3 7 2 2 1 3 3 1 1 4 6 4 1 1 2 4 1 2 3 6 2 3 binary1
S   0 / 7 < 1 2 1 : |
R   0 / 7 < 0 1 0 : |
```

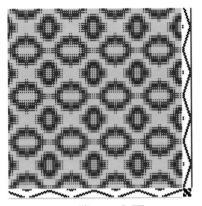

Figure 5.57

```
T   1 0 0 0 0 1 0 1 / 1 / 8 t<<
S   2 4 3 / 6 5 6 >u 7 / 0 >, |
R   same as S
```

Figure 5.58

```
T   1 1 1 0 0 1 1 0 / 1 / 8 t>>
S   0 / 5 < | 7 5 3 / 8 7 / 4 * :, 1, 0 1 / 4 * 2 3,, |
R   same as S
```

Figure 5.59

The real beauty of having a symbolic language is that it makes it very easy to try experiments. Once you have a pattern you like, you can easily explore variations. How about a sub-articulation here? Or a palindrome there? It's a lot of fun to start with something pretty and play with it for a while to come up with something else that you like as much.

Experimenting in a digital loom is a lot faster than doing it in real life, or even with paper and pencil. Just type in the expression, push the button, and see the result.

Figure 5.60

A variation on Figure 5.59. Only the tie-up has changed.

Figure 5.61

A "shadow weave." Both sets of threads alternate black and white, the warp starting with black and the weft starting with white.

S   0 / 6 - 1 / 7 - = |
R   0 / 6 - 0 / 6 - = |

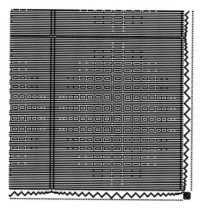

Figure 5.62

A variation on Figure 5.61. The tie-up is unchanged.

T   0 0 0 0 1 1 1 1 / 1 / 8 t<<
S   0 / 7 - 1 1 2 3 6 5 3 2 # 0 4 :
R   0 / 7 - 1 1 1 1 2 3 4 3 # 0 4 :

Figure 5.63

Another shadow weave.

Once you've created a draft you like, you can then take it to your real loom and produce a textile which is both functional and beautiful.

```
T    2 2 2 2 2 1 3 1 1 binary0 2 2 2 2 1 3 1 3
     binary1, 2 *
S    0 / 7 - 2 * | 1 2 3 4 5 6 7 8 / 1 2 2 2 4 5 6 8 # | 1, #1 1,
R    0 / 7 - 2 * | 1 2 3 4 5 6 7 8 / 1 2 3 4 5 7 8 # | 1, #1 1,
```

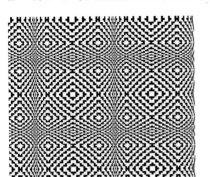

Figure 5.64

```
T    1 0 0 0 1 1 1 0 / 1 / 8 t<<
S    0 / 7 - 2 * / 1 1 2 1 2 2 3 2 3 3 4
     3 4 4 4 5 4 5 5 5 5 5 6 5 6 6 6 6 | #
R    same as S
```

Figure 5.65

A variation on Figure 5.64.

```
T    1 0 0 0 1 1 1 0 / 1 / 8 t>>
S    0 1 2 3 | 3 * 1 2 3 4 5 6 5 4 3 2 1 : 3 2 1 2 3 :
R    7 6 5 4 | 3 * 8 7 6 5 4 3 4 5 6 7 8 : 1 2 3 2 1 :
```

Figure 5.66

Sub-articulation can be
used to make large and
subtle patterns.

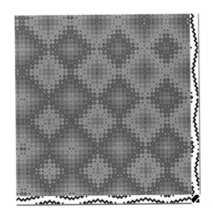

Figure 5.67

Detail of Figure 5.66.

```
T    1 1 1 0 0 1 1 0 / 1 / 8 t≪
S    0 1 2 3 | 3 * 1 2 3 4 5 | 1 , : 3 2 1 2 3 :
R    7 6 5 4 | 3 * 2 3 4 5 4 3 2 : 1 2 3 2 1 :
```

Figure 5.68

Another use of multiple sub-articulations.

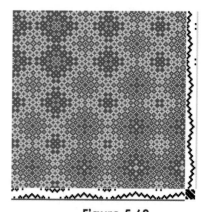

Figure 5.69

Detail of Figure 5.68.

```
T    3 2 3 3 2 2 1 1 1 2 1 2 1 4 1 1 4 1 1 binary1
S    4 5 0 1 2 3 2 1 / 1 3 2 3 1 3 1 1 #p
R    same as S
```

```
T    0 1 0 1 0 0 1 1 / 1 / 7 t≫ 0 0 1 0 1 0 0 1 ,
S    7 3 7 / 0 0 4 ≻u 6 <
R    7 3 7 / 0 0 4 ≻u 6 <
```

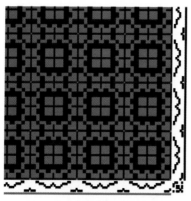

Figure 5.70

Figure 5.71

TARTANS

Recall from Figure 5.2 that a *twill* is a distinctive type of pattern, formed by a tie-up that creates a diagonal design. Perhaps the best-known twill fabric today is denim, but close behind that is the Scottish *tartan*. Tartans are the familiar colored plaids that have traditionally adorned kilts and other formal Scottish clothing.

Tartans always use the same pattern of colors in the warp and the weft; weavers say that such a pattern is "tromp as writ." The result is that tartans are made up of intersecting stripes of different widths and colors. As Figure 5.72 shows, when two stripes of different colors overlap, we get a blended color that mixes equal amounts of each one. When two stripes of the same color overlap, we get a solid rectangle of that color.

Figure 5.72

In a twill, when two stripes of different colors overlap, we see an equal mix of their colors. When the two stripes have the same color, we see a solid block of that color.

The color pattern that describes a particular tartan is called its *sett*.

Tartans have a long and fascinating history. The earliest known woven plaid fabric was found buried in the ground near Falkirk, in what is now Scotland. The fabric was buried in a pot along with 1,900 silver Roman coins. Its checked pattern is made of two colors of undyed wool: dark brown and light brownish green, the natural colors of the Soay sheep that are native to that region of Scotland. This fabric may have been woven as early as the year 300.

Such natural colors were the most common for early fabrics, since they could be used immediately after shearing. Black and white sheep were plentiful, so these colors appeared frequently as well. A black and white pattern with squares of equal size, as shown in Figure 5.73, is called the *Shepherd's Plaid*.

Figure 5.73

The black-and-white Shepherd's Plaid.

These basic, naturally-occurring colors were the only ones used for a long time. Eventually people started to create other colors of wool by dyeing the material before weaving with it. The original dyes came from local, natural plant matter such leaves, berries, and tree bark. After enough of these materials were collected, they were boiled in water to cause the colors to bleed, and then the wool was added to absorb the released colors now floating in the solution.

Bright colors were the hardest to obtain and transfer to the wool. Red could be extracted from *cochineal*, a substance made by grinding up dried insect bodies. Another source of red came from lichens. To dye wool red with these plants, a vat would be filled with clear, wet wool, lichen, and stale urine. The vat would be kept warm for at least a month, and longer if a deeper color was desired.

Natural dyes had some drawbacks. They were expensive and difficult to collect and store, and the color of the wool was unpredictable from one batch to the next. Natural dyes were seasonal, and many would not keep well. So if you wanted a dye extracted from a particular type of organic matter that wouldn't preserve, you had to collect all you could, and then dye as much wool as you could manage. That stockpile would then have to last the source materials became available again.

This whole process started to change in 1856 when H. H. Perkins created *aniline*, the first artificial dye. This oil-based dye had a violet color and was a quick success. Other artificial dyes followed soon after. These offered weavers a much broader palette of colors to work from, and the opportunity to design with colors that were brighter than those that could be extracted from boiled plant matter.

Until this arrival of artificial dyes, weavers were only able to work with the colors that were locally available. This meant that weavers in different regions favored different colors, depending on how easy they were to collect. Around 1695, a doctor named Martin Martin wrote a book called *A Description of the Western Isles of Scotland*. In that book, he claimed that he could tell where a Scotsman was from by the colors in his clothing. Just as Shaw's imaginary Professor Henry Higgins could tell, many decades later, where an Englishman had grown up just by listening to him speak, so too could Martin tell where someone lived simply by the colors they wore. Martin suggested that this ability to locate someone by the color of his clothes was commonplace at the time. There seemed to be no particular pride associated with these colors and patterns; they were just considered a natural part of living in that region of the country.

Through time, the wearing of colored plaids became an established part of Scottish culture.

All this changed when war broke out in 1689 between the Roman Catholic Scots, who supported the exiled Stuart dynasty, and the Protestants and Presbyterians that controlled England, Ireland, and Scotland. The third of these wars, called the Third Jacobite Rebellion, ended in 1746 in victory for the Protestants.

The winners of this third war wanted to crush the Scottish rebellion once and for all. They drew a line across Scotland, separating it into the Gaelic Highlands to the north and the Scots Lowlands in the south. The inhabitants of the Scots Lowlands were perceived by the Protestants to be supporters of the crown and less dangerous then their neighbors to the north. To suppress revolutionaries in the Gaelic Highlands in the north, in 1746 Parliament passed the Disarming Act. Among other requirements, this act demanded that most Highlanders take an oath against wearing tartan (the Gentry, sons of Gentry, women, and men serving as soldiers in the Highland Regiments were exempted from the act). Taking the oath meant swearing "never to use tartan plaid, or any part of the Highland Garb." Persons refusing to take the oath were treated just like those who violated it: they were arrested or killed. The act was enforced for 36 years, which effectively ended the popular wearing of tartan in the north of Scotland.

Soon after the act took effect on August 1, 1747, a weaver named William Wilson started a business in a town called Bannockburn, just south of the Highland boundary. Since he was exempt from the Disarming Act by virtue of geography, Wilson took advantage of this opportunity and became the only weaver of tartans in the country. He produced a wide variety of setts, many of his own design. His company, William Wilson and Sons, initially identified their many tartans simply by number. But late in the eighteenth century they started naming their designs after towns, families, and districts. Wilson's choice of names may have been influenced by who wore (or used to wear) different patterns, but it seems likely that many tartans were simply given geographical or clan names based on marketing considerations, or even simply at random. Although these names were arbitrary, by the time the Disarming Act was finally rescinded, Wilson's catalog had become a *de facto* standard, and his names were the ones that stuck.

When the act was lifted, some people went back to wearing the tartans they had worn almost four decades earlier. But many people in the north hadn't ever worn a local tartan and simply started wearing designs that they found appealing. Although there was a renewed feeling that tartans were uniquely Scottish, the relationship between particular patterns and locales was all but nonexistent by this point.

Things changed in 1822, when Sir Walter Scott arranged for George IV to visit Edinburgh. This was a big event, being the first visit to Scotland by a King in 150 years. To make the event as sensational and special as possible, Scott asked the chiefs of all the Scottish clans to wear the "traditional clothes" of their clans. Scott encouraged the chiefs to identify and then officially validate, or register, the tartan of their clan.

This was a confusing request, because people at this point didn't feel any particular ownership of a particular tartan. But this procedure, which appears to have been invented by Scott, suddenly implied that every self-respecting clan must have an official tartan, and what's more, they needed to register it officially or risk having it claimed by some other clan. Thus was born the idea that some tartans "belonged" to some regions or families.

In response to Scott's call, many clans sought to identify and validate "their" tartan. These patterns were identified in two principal ways. One was simple popularity: if a particular pattern seemed to be most liked or popular among the people of a particular group, they then tried to claim it. The other approach was to look at Wilson's catalog and claim any tartans named for their clan or locale. The fact that these names were essentially arbitrary got lost in the competitive rush to register and validate tartans.

Once this process had concluded, the idea of a "clan tartan" had taken hold. The idea has endured, and now many families closely identify themselves with a particular sett. The formalities for wearing setts differ from one group to another. Some groups feel very protective of their pattern and consider it very bad taste for anyone else to wear it at any time, for any reason. Other groups are more liberal and don't mind if outsiders wear their sett.

Today there are thousands of different setts regularly produced by weavers both inside and outside of Scotland. The cloth is used both casually and for ceremonial clothing, kilts, and other formal wear. Since some clans and families are protective of their registered tartans, there arose a need for some shared patterns that people could wear when they acted as a group. For example, if a traditional marching band got together and everyone wore their own family's sett, it could look like a crazy mishmash of patterns. To help unify groups that don't have their own tartan, three setts (Hunting Stewart, Caledonia, and Black Watch) have been generally accepted as universal tartans that may be worn by one and all.

Figure 5.74

The Hunting Stewart tartan. The AWL expression for this sett is B 9 G 4 B 9 K 3 B 3 K 8 G 27 R 4 G 27 K 8 G 5 K 13 G 4 K 13 G 5 K 8 G 27 Y 4 G 27 K 8 B 3 K 3 tartan.

The Hunting Stewart pattern, shown in Figure 5.74, has been around since the early 1800s. The name is something of a mystery: it's not a pattern ever associated with the Stewart family, nor one that was used while hunting. The Caledonia sett, shown in Figure 5.75, probably dates back to about 1800, and the Black Watch (or Government) sett, shown in Figure 5.76, has been worn by members of the British Army since the 1740s.

Tartan colors are generally drawn from a palette of a couple of dozen colors, with custom colors occasionally included for specific setts. Most

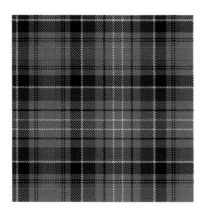

Figure 5.75

The Caledonia tartan. The AWL expression for this sett is R 42 A 18 K 4 A 4 K 4 A 18 K 36 Y 6 G 42 R 26 K 6 R 26 W 4 R 26 tartan.

Figure 5.76

The Black Watch tartan. The AWL expression for this sett is B 22 K 2 B 2 K 2 B 2 K 16 G 16 K 2 G 16 K 16 B 16 K 2 B 2 tartan.

colors are referred to with labels that consist of just a few letters. I'm not aware of any standardized RGB list of these colors, so I examined and measured several hundred tartans and compared their actual colors against their labels. There is some variation, of course, but the colors are pretty consistent across different manufacturers and sources. The tartan colors are summarized in Figure 5.77. Note that white and black in particular are not at the limits of the RGB range; this is because natural wools have a more limited color gamut than the phosphors we find on most cathode ray tubes (CRTs).

BUILDING A DIGITAL LOOM

I built my digital loom using C#, a new programming language from Microsoft. For many years I've been happily programming in good, old-fashioned, vanilla C. When C++ first came out, I spent some time learning it. I built a few projects with the language, but I never liked it very much. After trying to force myself to appreciate C++, I eventually decided it just wasn't for me, and I went back to C.

Friends have told me that even with this experience, I'd enjoy trying out C#. So I decided to use my digital loom as an immigration project into the C# language and its associated .NET environment for writing Windows code. I was surprised by how easy and fun it was to write my program in this system, and in the course of this one project I've become a C# convert.

Let's look at the digital loom from the outside in, starting with the user interface. Figure 5.78 shows a screenshot of the digital loom in action, with all the windows visible. This figure includes a graphical editor window in the lower left that I didn't include in previous screenshots.

Figure 5.77

RGB values for tartan colors, identified by their traditional initials and a more informative label.

Initial	R	G	B	Name
A	60	132	172	Aqua
B	44	58	132	Blue
DB	12	10	76	Dark Blue
LB	124	130	196	Light Blue
MB	20	26	68	Dark Blue
NB	4	2	36	Navy Blue
RB	4	2	100	Royal Blue
C	148	2	36	Dark Pink
VLC	220	170	172	Pink
DG	4	50	20	Dark Green
FG	68	106	84	Blue-Green
G	4	82	36	Green
LG	44	154	20	Light Green
MG	4	58	20	Darker Green
K	20	18	20	Black
M	116	26	52	Magenta
DN	76	74	76	Dark Gray
LN	188	186	188	Light Gray
N	124	122	124	Mid Gray
DO	220	90	4	Dark Orange
LO	236	114	60	Light Orange
O	252	74	4	Orange
P	116	2	116	Purple
DR	204	2	4	Dark Red
LR	204	42	44	Light Red
R	204	2	4	Red
WR	100	2	44	Dark Magenta
S	228	86	4	Sandy Yellow
DT	68	18	4	Dark Tan
LPT	204	150	100	Lightish Tan
LT	148	102	52	Light Tan
RT	244	90	44	Reddish-Tan
T	84	62	20	Tan
MU	204	122	20	Orange-ish
W	228	226	228	White
DY	148	122	4	Dark Yellow
LY	244	218	4	Light yellow
Y	236	194	4	Yellow

I built this because I thought it might be fun to create AWL expressions by drawing them, rather than typing them in.

The main control form in the upper center and the woven fabric output in the upper right were the only two windows I had for quite a while. The weaving display shows the warp and weft patterns and the tie-up using traditional black-and-white matrices, and thread colors drawn outside them. This is mostly a read-only display, but you can flip bits in the tie-up by clicking on them.

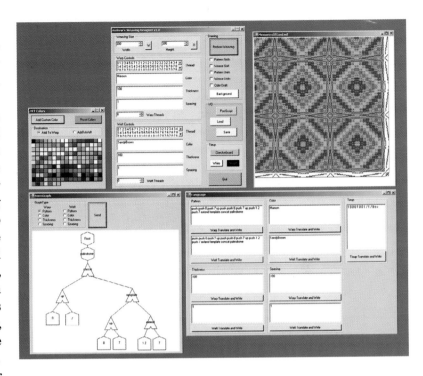

Figure 5.78

A screen shot of my digital loom. In the upper left is the window of color chips. Upper center is the main control panel, and the upper right window holds the woven fabric. In the lower left corner is my graphical AWL editor, and in the lower right is the AWL evaluation window.

The panel in the upper center of the figure holds most of the basic controls. In the upper left of this panel are counters to set the width and height of the displayed fabric in the weaving window. The other major controls are buttons to specify some details about the display itself, saving and loading weaving files in the WIF format (discussed later), and a button to save the weaving in PostScript.

Most of the left side of this panel is taken up by two sets of four text boxes. Each set (one for the warp threads, one for the weft) lets me enter expressions for the threading pattern, thread colors, thickness, and spacing. There's also a numeric box for identifying how many threads are to be used for that pattern.

Since I specify colors by name in the text fields (e.g., Black or Aqua), I provided a little color selector panel as well, shown in the upper left. It contains all the default colors in the .NET environment, as well as all the tartan colors named in Figure 5.77. You can also create your own colors and add them to the list. If you click on a color chip, its name is appended to the list of colors in either the warp or weft window, depending on which of the two radio buttons you've selected.

For a long time this was all I had. Then when I wrote my interpreter for AWL, I created the new form in the lower right. This has nine text boxes. The first eight correspond one-to-one to the text boxes in the main panel. The difference is that in the main panel you enter explicit numerical patterns for the warp and weft, whereas in the AWL windows you enter AWL expressions. By clicking the button beneath each box, the system translates the AWL into its resulting pattern and copies that into the corresponding box in the main form. That way you can see what your expression translates to, while the AWL is still there and editable. A ninth box on this form lets you enter an AWL expression for the tie-up.

I thought it might be fun to write a graphical editor for AWL expressions, and you can see that window in the lower left of the figure. As with most such editors, you can create and delete nodes, drag them around, change the wiring, and so on. Once you have a drawing you like, you identify which AWL expression window you want to send it to, and push the Send button to translate the drawing into AWL. If you like the expression you've created, then you press the button below that window as usual to evaluate it and pass it on to the main form. The graphical editor is kind of fun to play with, but I eventually found that I preferred to type and edit my AWL expressions directly. You can see in Figure 5.78 the result of the expression drawn in the graphical editor. The expression contains some redundant instances of the *push*

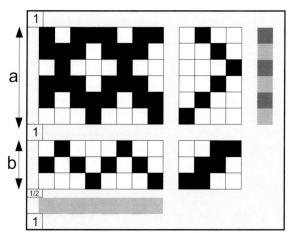

Figure 5.79

Counting up the number of cells required to draw the weaving window.

command, which doesn't hurt things (nothing happens if there's nothing new to push).

Let's move inside the code now. Programming this digital loom was straightforward, which was a good thing since I was learning a new language while I was at it. Of course, the structure of the final code reflects the fact that I learned as I went, but it works fine and the tasks are simple enough that everything happens effectively instantly, even with a naive and blunt programming style.

I'll discuss three bits of the program that were most interesting: drawing the fabric, reading and writing WIF files, and evaluating AWL expressions.

To draw the fabric, I start by finding the current size of the window (since you can grab it at a corner and make it bigger and smaller), and I compare this to the size of the fabric that I want to draw inside of it. As shown in Figure 5.79, suppose the weaving is to be *a* cells high, and there are *b* boxes necessary to hold the pattern along the bottom. I need to also include space equal to one box at the top for a border, one between the weaving and the pattern, and one more at the bottom for a border. I also use a half-cell of space between the weaving pattern and the thread colors, resulting in a height of $a + b + 3.5$ cells. I then use the same layout to find the number of cells that are required horizontally.

From this I can find the size of the largest-sized square that I can use for a cell that will still fit in the window. Even though the spacing specification for a given weaving can change the location and aspect ratio of the cells in the weaving itself, I treat everything as squares at this point.

Filling in the cells for the tie-up, the pattern grids, and the row or column of colors is straightforward. I just draw the grids and fill in the boxes where necessary, either with the thread color or black and white for the patterns and tie-up.

To draw the weaving itself, I proceed one cell at a time. First I use the spacing information to determine the location and size of the cell. Then I consult the thickness and color for the threads at this cell to find the two rectangles that fit into the cell. Finally, I consult the warp, weft, and tie-up patterns using my weaving equation to determine which rectangle is on top. I draw the two rectangles in the proper order, and then move on to the next cell.

The usual way to save weaving information is defined by the WIF (Weaving Information File) standard. Adhering to WIF means that my system can trade weaving files with the commercially available digital weaving systems, and I can also read the many WIF files available on the web.

WIF files are easy to write but can be tricky to read. The WIF standard allows you to write out sections, or blocks, of information in any order, so that sometimes information that you require in order to parse one part of the file doesn't appear until much later. And some sections don't need to exist at all.

There are two general approaches to handling this sort of thing.

The more efficient way is to first create a list of pointers into the file that indicate where every possible section starts. If you save these as integer offsets from the start of the file, you might initialize them all to -1. Then you read through the file, and each time you encounter the start of a new section you determine which field it is and set the corresponding pointer to the current position of file pointer into the file.

Once you've passed through the whole file this way, you go to another routine that sets everything to a default value and then looks at the pointers in a fixed order. You look for the section you want, and if it's there, you jump to it, read it in, and overwrite the default. Then you do the same thing for the next section and the next, until you've read in everything. Then you can evaluate all of this data to create the weaving specification.

The other way to go is simpler but slower. As before, you initialize all your data to defaults and in a fixed order for each section in the file, but you simply reread the file from the start each time you need a new section. This is slightly easier to write and debug. I wrote my first WIF reader this way, with the intention of turning it into the more efficient version once I got it working. But WIF files are typically pretty small, and I found that even this inefficient approach read in almost every WIF file essentially instantaneously, so I left it that way.

Parsing AWL expressions turned out to be very easy, largely because I defined AWL as a postfix language.

I simply split up the AWL expression into tokens separated by blank spaces, and read each token one at a time, with no lookahead. If the token is not a keyword (or a symbolic shortcut for one), it goes at the end of the list that's currently on the top of the stack. If the token is a keyword, then I pop the necessary arguments, process them, and push the result back on top. When I'm done parsing a valid expression, there's only thing on the top of the stack: a list of elements that's ready to be copied over into the main weaving window. You can get a copy of my AWL parser written in C# for free from my website.

FURTHER READING

Reading drafts was pretty mysterious to me for a while. Surprisingly, although there are many books and videos available on weaving, there's not much introductory material available on the web. I found a good introduction to drafts and weaving in *Designing and Drafting for Handweavers* by Berta Frey (Macmillan Company, 1958). An online glossary for basic terms can be found at http://people.montana.com/~elh/glossary.htm.

The deduction algorithm for finding the matrices from a weaving was originally presented in "From Drawdown to Draft—A Programmer's View," by Ralph E. Griswold, April 2000 (http://www.cs.arizona.edu/patterns/weaving/). In this article, Griswold provides fragments of source code in the Icon language. You can download Icon for free from http://www.cs.arizona.edu/icon/index.htm, and the complete program for the deduction algorithm from http://www.cs.arizona.edu/patterns/weaving/FA/index.html.

There are a variety of commercial and public-domain programs available to weavers. I haven't used any of these programs myself. Some of the better-known programs include Fiberworks (http://www.fiberworks-pcw.com), Patternland (http://www.mhsoft.com), Swiftweave (http://www.swiftweave.com), WeaveIt (http://www.weaveit.com),

WeaveMaker (http://www.weavemaker.com), and WeavePoint (http://www.weavepoint.com).

As a result of this commercial development, there's now a standard file format for descriptions of weavings. It's called WIF (the Weaving Information File), and it seems to be pretty stable (the most recent specification of it that I can find is dated 1997). You can read about the WIF format at http://www.mhsoft.com/wif/wif.html. It is a pretty straightforward format, so I decided to use it for my program. This also allowed me to read in weaving drafts that people have shared online in this format. I found that although writing WIF is a snap, implementing a WIF reader was harder than expected due to a bunch of important little issues. If you're going to write a program to read WIF files, download a bunch of the examples on the WIF information web page and use them for debugging.

You can find fun drafts for playing around with on http://www.wyellowstone.com/users/ww/weaving.htm and http://www.allfiberarts.com/cs/patternsdrafts.htm. There are many books full of great patterns. Two books that I found useful were *The New Key to Weaving* by Mary E. Black (McMillan Publishing, 1945), and *16 Harness Patterns* by Fred Pennington (Robin & Russ, 1943).

Weaving patterns are very similar to the patterns produced by Celtic knotwork. I discussed that topic in some detail in Chapter 3 of *Andrew Glassner's Other Notebook* (A K Peters, 2000).

A programming language that's well-suited to the deduction algorithm is perl, available for free from http://www.activestate.com.

The AWL language draws very strongly on two sources: the *Painter* weaving language and monographs by Ralph Griswold.

The painting program *Painter 8*, published by Corel (http://www.corel.com), has had a weaving language built into it for quite a while, and it allows you design your own weaves and then use them as patterns for filling. Their weaving language is a bit tricky to use. I've written a set of notes that you may find useful if you want to use their system. You can find them on my webpage at http://www.glassner.com.

The `growblock` operator is based on a discussion by Ralph Griswold in his paper, "Variations On A Shadow Weave," by Ralph E. Griswold, April 1999 (http://www.cs.arizona.edu/patterns/weaving/). The idea of using integer sequences was presented in "Drafting with Sequences," by Ralph E. Griswold, March 2002, and a number of other monographs that deal with specific sequences. Griswold's website contains a wealth of useful information, including scanned-in copies of long out-of-print but fascinating reference books.

Integer sequences for the `eis` command come from *The Encyclopedia of Integer Sequences* by Simon Plouffe and Neil J. A. Sloane (Academic Press, 1995). The contents of that book are available in a terrific online resource that allows you to look up sequences by name or even by the numbers in the sequence. Go to http://www.research.att.com/~njas/sequences to use this database of over 76,000 sequences. I've only provided a small handful of these directly in my code. An AWL interpreter connected to the net could do a real-time query to the online database to pick up any sequence named.

I got a lot of inspiration for weaving patterns from *A Weaver's Book of 8-Shaft Patterns*, edited by Carol Strickler (Interweave Press, 1991).

You can find thousands of traditional tartan plaids online. One good place to start is http://www.house-of-tartan.scotland.net, where you can search for tartans based on a sequence of colors, or their traditional associations with Scottish clans, districts, and regiments. You can find another list of tartans, complete with photos of woven examples, at http://www.shetlandpiper.com/tartan_finder. An extensive collection is available at http://www.scottish-tartans-society.org, where you can see a picture of each tartan, as well as the explicit color sequence for weaving it.

Image Search
and Replace

6

The world is imperfect. It's sad, but true: not everything in the world is exactly the way each of us wishes it would be. Perhaps this is a good thing, as improving the world gives us something to strive for. But philosophical consolation is a poor substitute for immediate and complete gratification.

One way to better the world is to edit it: we start with something that's close to what we want and then improve on it. Editing is a normal part of almost every creative process, whether we're starting with something made by someone else, or our own creation.

A common way to improve something by editing is to find a feature we don't like and replace it with something we prefer. Text editors universally provide this ability with some kind of *search and replace* command. So if you're reading a big document that discusses the adventures of a character named Fred, but you think it would be better if his name were David, you can simply tell the system to replace all occurrences, or *instances*, of Fred with David.

Most programs let you apply the change as a *global substitution*, automatically altering each instance of the *target* (here the name Fred) with the *replacement* (David). Usually you can also tell the system to preview each substitution for you before it's committed, so you can make sure nothing goes astray in the process. If you forego this manual confirmation step, the substitution process can go much faster, but you may end up (if your search is case-insensitive) with some character in your story inexplicably ordering pasta with aldavido sauce.

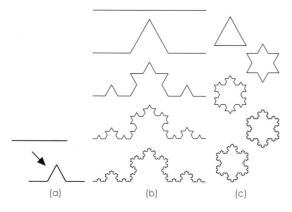

Figure 6.1

Creating one edge of a Koch snowflake. (a) The rule is that each straight line is replaced by a line of the same length, but with a point in the middle. (b) Applying that rule four times to a single straight line creates a crinkly shape. (c) Applying the rule to the three sides of a triangle makes a Koch snowflake.

Search and replace is too good an idea to limit it just to text. In 1988 David Kurlander and Eric Bier showed how to use this idea in line drawings (see the Further Reading section for more information on this and other references). As Figure 6.1 shows, this is a great way to build up a Koch snowflake: just replace each straight line with a new line with a point on it, and then do it again, and again. In this example, the program looks for straight lines at any position, angle, and length, and replaces them with the replacement pattern transformed so that the endpoints match up.

Here we can see the basic ideas behind all search and replace methods: *search* for the target, *remove* the target, and *insert* the replacement properly transformed to match the target.

Some interesting variations on this idea have appeared on television in recent years, particularly during sports broadcasts. It's now common for the advertising signs in a stadium to be replaced by the broadcasters with different signs, so the ads seen by the home viewer are not those seen by the fans at the game.

Other techniques are used to enhance the visual presentation of the game itself. For example, some systems augment the video image of the field in a football game with a synthetic yellow line that represents where the offensive team must advance the ball to secure a first down. The line is not painted on the ground itself, but is inserted electronically on top of the video signal somewhere between the camera and the transmitter. The illusion is convincing because the system is sophisticated enough to recognize when a player or official on the field has moved into a position where he would be blocking our view of the line, were it really there. When the line would be obscured in this way by a person on the field, the system suppresses drawing it into the image, so that it appears to be naturally obscured.

Note that this interesting system isn't actually a search and replace technique, since there's no searching or removal; the yellow line is just added to the video. The technique belongs to the field now called augmented reality.

In this chapter I'll talk about building a system that can let a user perform search and replace on raster images. The basic goal is simple to state: we provide a source picture, a target image, and a replacement image, and the system removes every instance of the target from the source and inserts in its place a copy of the replacement. Of course, an implementation is a little more complicated than that, so let's look a little closer.

THE BIG AND SMALL PICTURES

The search and replace algorithm starts with three pictures, as shown in Figure 6.2: the *source* picture S, the *target* picture T, and the *replacement* picture R.

Our goal is to find each instance of T in S, and replace it with R.

Because it's rare that the target and replacement images will be rectangular, both T and R can each have an associated *mask*, T_M and R_M respectively. These masks indicate the opacity of their corresponding pixels in T and R: a value of 0 (or black) means the pixel is transparent, while a value of 255 (or white) means the pixel is opaque. Intermediate shades of gray represent intermediate amounts of transparency. This lets us create a smooth edge around the parts of T and R so that the images aren't jagged.

To build my prototype, I started with a simple searching technique that just marches through the source picture one pixel at a time, looking for copies of the target. This will prove to be much too inefficient when we later start adding in other transformations like rotation, scaling, and color shifting. But for simplicity, right now I'll stick to simple, brute-force searching for copies of T that seem to be simply pasted right into the source picture without any geometrical or color changes. Later on I'll return to this step.

Using this automatic searching, we start by looking through the source image for *candidates*: these are regions of the source that might (or might not) be instances of the target. Unlike text processing, we often can't be sure exactly when we've found a match. Small variations in color or shape can make it hard for a computer to detect a match even when the general features seem to be in close agreement. So rather than make a final decision at this point, when we think we've found a region that could be a copy of the target, we call it a candidate and add it to a growing list of possibilities for later consideration.

Then we'll rank those candidates with some measure, so that the most-likely matches will bubble up to the top. A simple sum of absolute color differences on a pixel-by-pixel basis does a pretty good job of distinguishing the really close matches from the ones that are worse.

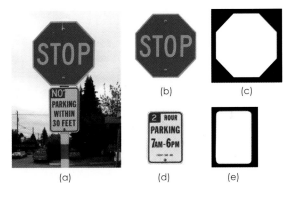

(a) (b) (c) (d) (e)

Figure 6.2

(a) The source image S.
(b) The target image T.
(c) The target mask T_M.
(d) The replacement image R.
(e) The replacement mask R_M.

Image Search and Relace

Figure 6.3

We'll then present each candidate to the user one by one, in its ranked order, the best ones first. If the user says that yes, this candidate should be replaced, we can't just drop the replacement over the source. Take a look a Figure 6.3. You can see that if we simply drop a copy of the replacement R over the target T, bits of the target will still be visible. What to do?

The answer comes from a new class of texture synthesis algorithms that has appeared in the last few years. These algorithms take some piece of *reference* texture, and are able to "grow" arbitrary amounts of that texture to fill any desired region. They can also blend that new texture into the boundaries of a region so that it smoothly blends into the parts of the image that already exist.

We can see this in action in Figure 6.4(a) and (b). The target mask T_M tells us which pixels need to be replaced. Now we can simply write the replacement pattern R on top of

(a)   (b)   (c)

Figure 6.4

(a) First we remove the source (I've marked the removed pixels in blue). (b) Then we fill in the source with synthetic texture. (c) Now the replacement can be simply dropped into the scene.

where T was, as in Figure 6.4(c), and all is well. The replacement mask R_M tells us which pixels to copy out of R and how strongly to blend them into S.

By default, the replacement is positioned over the target so that centers of both bounding boxes overlap. Of course, the user can change this default alignment on both images, and also on a per-substitution basis.

In summary, the basic algorithm goes like this:

1. **Search:** Look through S and find candidates, assigning each one a score based on the quality of the match.

2. **Offer:** Offer the user a chance to accept or reject the highest-ranked candidate (this step can be skipped if the user feels brave). Once the choice has been made, remove this candidate from the list. If the user decides that this candidate shouldn't be replaced, jump to step 5, else continue to step 3.

3. Erase: Remove this instance of T from the source image, and fill in the hole with synthetic texture.

4. Replace: Draw the replacement image R over the spot where the match was found.

5. Repeat: If there are candidates yet to be considered, return to step 2, else quit.

Let's look at the scoring and synthesis steps a little more closely.

Scoring

Probably the easiest way to determine if one picture is like another is to compute a penalty or difference score: simply add up the differences in the color values of the pixels, one by one. We find the absolute difference in each of the red, green, and blue components and add them together. Lower penalty scores indicate a better match.

There's a little gotcha with this technique: it has trouble if some of the target falls off the edge of the source, as in Figure 6.5. We might just ignore any pixels in T that fall outside of S, but then we'd only accumulate penalty scores for a smaller number of pixels, which would reduce the overall penalty and make this match look really good. In the extreme, there might be just one pixel of T that overlaps S, and if they happen to be the same color, then the penalty score would be 0, indicating a perfect match!

One way to fix up the score for partial overlaps is to divide the total penalty score by the number of pixels actually compared, creating an average per-pixel difference. But we'll want to still make sure that there are enough pixels compared so that we're considering a significant overlap. The easy way here is to simply set a user-adjustable threshold: for example, at least 40 percent of the pixels of T must overlap with S for us to even consider that position as a candidate. If the user sets this percentage to 100, only copies of T that are completely contained within S are candidates. Smaller values will catch instances of T that are partly over the edge, but will also start picking up more noise and bogus instances.

Figure 6.5

We have to be careful if we want to catch the upper copy of the sign, which is only partly visible.

Synthesizing

Once the user has accepted a candidate for T, we need to get rid of it. The first part is easy: we can just erase pixels in the source, modulated by the mask T_M, as in Figure 6.4(a). The second part requires filling those erased pixels in with something that looks good.

In the last few years we've seen a number of algorithms that can create arbitrary amounts of seamless, synthetic texture in an image, such as those presented by Heeger and Bergen, and Portilla and Simoncelli. These are sometimes called texture-expansion algorithms, since rather than creating texture from first principles, they start with a piece of reference image and then generate new texture that looks like the reference.

It's easy to get going with basic texture expansion algorithms, even if you don't want to write the code yourself. For example, free source code is available for a plug-in for the GIMP image editor, and the Image Doctor is available commercially for editors such as Photoshop. For my prototype, I wrote a simple texture generator based on the technique by Wei and Levoy along with a robust substitution method designed for masked images by Igehy and Pereira (see Further Reading section for references).

(a)   (b)   (c)   (d)

Figure 6.6

(a) The source picture. (b) I've manually identified the region I want to remove. (c) Filling in this region with synthetic texture based on the background trees doesn't look very good. (d) Basing the synthetic texture on the nearby water looks much better.

REFERENCE MATERIAL

Texture expansion algorithms create texture by generalizing from a reference sample. So where that sample comes from makes a big difference to the image. For example, in Figure 6.6(b) I've deleted a patch of water. In Figure 6.6(c) I've selected a reference from a patch of the background greenery, and as you can see the results are more surreal than realistic. By contrast, in Figure 6.6(d) I've told the system to create new texture based on some nearby water, which looks much better.

When we replace a candidate, where should we go looking for new texture?

There are a few answers, depending on how hard we want to work. I think the simplest answer is to look in the neighborhood of the pixels we're replacing. For example, if we draw a bounding box around the patch we're replacing and then expand it, then we can pull texture from the region between the two boxes.

This solution works pretty well in general, and it serves as a good starting point for many replacements, but it won't always work. So each time a user is shown a candidate for replacement, we also show the region from which reference texture will be drawn for that replacement. If the user doesn't like the choice of region, he or she can identify a new region somewhere else in the image.

Obviously this solution is not going to work all the time. One common problem is when there just isn't a big enough patch of "clean" texture available; for example, if we want to replace a sky full of hot-air balloons, there might not be much blue sky visible between them. So we can also let the user point the system to another image for reference. In this case, all of our balloons might get erased using reference texture taken from another picture of an empty blue sky.

Another problem with using nearby pixels arises when those pixels also contain pieces of other objects, including other copies of the target. For example, we might be trying to get rid of a computer mouse sitting on a wooden tabletop, so we hope to fill in the region under the mouse with wooden grain. But in the box around the mouse we might accidentally catch the corner of the keyboard, and then that little corner will be replicated as part of the texture. Choosing as a reference a piece of the table that's showing nothing but wood grain does the trick.

Figure 6.7

If we wanted to remove this truck, we'd have to generate texture for the upper part based on the greenery behind it, and texture for the lower part and shadow would have to come from the road surface.

A really troublesome situation can occur if we're replacing an object that straddles two types of background, as in Figure 6.7. In this example, the bottom half of the truck should be replaced with texture from the street, and the top half should be replaced with greenery from the street. Sometimes the texture generator can do pretty well with a situation like this, and sometimes it can't. For the times when automatic methods fail, it would be useful to have a manual tool so that the user can break up the region under the candidate and apply different textures to different regions.

MATCHMAKER, MATCHMAKER

So far I've limited the search to simple copies of the target image that haven't been changed in any way except for position. Let's see what happens when we relax that restriction.

The first things that we'll want to include are, of course, rotation and scaling. We should be able to match the target no matter what size it is, or how it's been rotated.

We do need to be careful that the target isn't too much smaller than its largest appearance in the source. If we have to scale up the target too much to test it against a region of the source, the target is going to get pretty blurry, and it might not match the source very well. By the same token, the source instances we're trying to find can't be too small: if a candidate is only a few pixels large in the source, then we're going to have a lot of trouble being sure it's a match.

We can include some other important geometric transformations as well. Perhaps the most important is perspective, since that's going to be present in almost any photograph we want to manipulate, and in most computer-generated images as well.

There are also some image-based transformations that will be important for us to include. Suppose that we're working with a source image that's a photograph taken on a hazy day: instances of the target that are far away will have less contrast than those that are closer, and their colors will be shifted a bit. Or suppose we have a picture of a bunch of cars parked outside, and we want to replace all of last year's models with shiny new ones. If some of those cars are partly or completely shadowed by clouds or buildings, then those regions of the cars will be darker than a uniformly-lit car. But of course it's perfectly obvious to us as human observers that they still should be replaced.

Shadows result from the absence of light, but we can also have problems if our images contain different kinds of light. Suppose that we're working with a clothing store that has invested heavily in lots of in-store signs, each of which carries a large and prominent copy of the store's logo. The owners are now considering changing their logo, and they want to see how the store will look when all the signs have the new logo on them. So they come to us with a photograph of the store that they've shot from the front door, and a picture of their new logo, and ask us to show them how the store would look if all the signs were updated.

A potential problem here is sheer variety of different lights that could influence the store photograph. There might be sunlight coming in through the big front windows, fluorescent bulbs illuminating most of the store, and halogen bulbs highlighting some the merchandise. Each of these lights has a different white point and a different illumination spectrum, which will affect the colors of the logos on the signs. The logo might be red-shifted in one place and blue-shifted in another, even if to the human eye all of the logos appear pretty much the same. To allow the computer to find these matches, we'd want our search to include accommodation for a range of tonal and color shifts.

There are other reasons to allow for tonal and color shifts. To just scratch the surface, we'd want to be able to match in the presence of color bleeding (as when a bright red carpet casts a red tint on objects near to it) and local discolorations (as when a shiny object has a highlight that's missing in the target image), and accommodate aging (when some dyes get old, they tend to fade, particularly those exposed to the sun). So it's important that we detect instances in the source that are close to, but not exactly the same, as the target.

Of course, loading in all of these geometric and color transformations makes the searching problem much more expensive. Just how much more expensive might come as a surprise.

BETTER SEARCH

We've got a lot of dimensions going on now. There's translation (two dimensions), rotation (one dimension), scaling (two dimensions) perspective (which we might model as one-point perspective characterized by amount, and the horizontal and vertical location of the vanishing point, for three dimensions), overall brightness (one dimension), and color shifting (which we could model as shifts in red, green, and blue, for three dimensions). That's twelve dimensions so far.

The brute-force way to do this search would be to make twelve nested loops. Let's get a rough handle on the numbers. Suppose we have a 512-by-512 source picture, color ranges from 0 to 255, and we want to consider 360 degrees of rotation, scaling from 0.5 to 1.5 in each direction (in 100 steps of 0.01), and brightness and perspective measures from 0 to 100. If we take eight steps between values for each measure along each range, then we'll have to make around 2.8×10^{39} tests. Let's assume we have a really fast computer and it can do 100 tests per second; this search would take around 1.5×10^{28} years. Astronomers are estimating the age of the universe at something around 12.5 billion years (give or take three billion). Taking the high-end estimate of 15.5 billion years, this says that our one little search would take about 9.6×10^{19} universe lifetimes to complete. Of course, we could complete this search in only 96 years using parallel computing if we could assign an equal-sized chunk of the search to each of about a billion billion different universes, but since we only have the one universe at the moment, that seems just a bit impractical. A billion billion computers running in parallel would also impose some difficulties; just logging in to each one would take quite a while. Of course, we could hand-optimize the code a bit, but to get this search to run in an hour would require speeding things up by a factor of 460 trillion trillion billion (or is that 460 billion trillion trillion?), which would require a *really* good programmer.

Okay, if brute-force at full resolution doesn't work, let's try working with a simpler problem. Probably the easiest way to get out of this computational nightmare is to chop down all of those numbers by big amounts.

We can make some progress computationally. Suppose that we're looking for red balloons against a blue sky. Then we don't need to take lots of steps when we're looking at regions with no red in them; in fact, we can skip such regions altogether.

One way to figure this kind of thing out is to simplify both the target and the source, and do a series of matching steps at different resolutions, using a *multiresolution* algorithm. We'd start with simple versions of both images, perhaps just by scaling them way down, and then search those much smaller images for matches with a somewhat looser tolerance. If we find a match, then we use that as the starting point for a more careful search at a slightly higher resolution, and so on, working our way up until we reach the original images at their original resolution.

There are other ways to reduce the size of the data describing the image but still capture some of its important features. Both Fourier analysis and wavelet decomposition are mathematical methods that let us compare images at a variety of ranges of scales.

But I think such a computational approach is coming at it all wrong, because we're using the computer to do something that people are extremely good at: pattern matching. If I'm looking at a picture and looking for a target image as complicated as the faces of a couple of friends, I can instantly spot them with no difficulty. Waiting for over a billion billion lifetimes of the universe to pass for the computer to come to the same conclusion using brute force seems like a poor use of resources.

So the better matching algorithm is human-driven. We can do extremely well with just one piece of human input: ask the user to tap once with his or her pen or mouse in roughly the center of each instance of the target in the source. Then we can carry out a much more efficient search using that as a starting point. Again, we can use multiresolution methods to start the search coarsely at first, and then refine our match with a series of ever-finer searches.

This is a huge step forward, but with a little more effort we can do even better. The user can provide a complete multidimensional starting point. To make a match, the user can drag a copy of the target over the source, drop it in about the right place, quickly scale and rotate it into position, and then optionally do a little color shifting if necessary to make it look like the source. The computer can then refine that guess with a fine-resolution search in the neighborhood of the initial input, tweaking each of the parameters for the best fit.

The big value here is that we actually know that there's a match to be found, so we're never wasting time in completely unproductive searches. And we can use a very simple and greedy maximum-descent algorithm, simply repeatedly looking for parameter tweaks that make the match better and accepting them, rather than looking all over each parameter's entire range for the best place to start looking.

This human-seeded approach works very well, and I've found that even with my unoptimized code I can zero in on a good match in just a minute or less, given a good starting hint. The user doesn't need to sit and wait for each refinement: he or she can give the machine a bunch of starting points and then go off to lunch or do other work, and let the machine crunch away at them.

You can also specify the quality of the match you require on each hint. For example, if you're replacing a logo on a department-store sign, it's probably important to have high-quality matches that are rotated and sized correctly. But if you're doing something more casual, like replacing round red balloons with long yellow ones, then you might be willing to accept a much cruder match; as long as the new balloon is roughly matching the old one, that's good enough. Such a match can of course be found much faster. In fact, you can lower the search quality to zero, which means that your hint is exactly the match.

While you're identifying candidates, you can also provide the region of the source image (or another image) that should be used as the reference texture for filling in the hole.

The human-driven version of the algorithm goes like this:

1. **Seed:** The user creates a list of seeds by dropping copies of the target on the source, applying geometric and color transformations as desired to make the instances match the source.

2. **Refine:** Tweak a seed provided by the user to get a match that's as good as the user has requested.

3. **Erase:** Remove this instance of T from the source image, and fill in the hole with synthetic texture.

4. **Replace:** Draw the replacement image R over the spot where the match was found.

5. **Repeat:** If there are seeds yet to be handled, return to Step 2, else quit.

(a)

Figure 6.8

(a) The original image of the trailer. (b) The orange cone target. (c) The detour sign replacement. (d) The cones erased. (e) The replaced final.

(b)

(c)

(a)

Figure 6.9

(a) The original candle display. (b) The candle target. (c) The panda head replacement. (d) Removal of the candles. (e) The final replacement

(b)

(c)

(d)

(d)

(e)

(e)

Some Examples

Let's look at a few examples.

In Figure 6.8 (a) I've taken a picture of a trailer with a few orange traffic cones around it. Let's isolate one of those cones, as in Figure 6.8 (b), and replace each instance of it with the detour sign of Figure 6.8 (c). You can see the result of the erasure in Figure 6.8(d). In general, this looks pretty good, but you can certainly see artifacts in the texture replacement if you look closely. This is largely due to the simplicity of my texture synthesis routine; a more sophisticated algorithm could probably have done a better job of filling in the holes. The detour signs are then scaled and placed at the appropriate locations, giving us the final result in Figure 6.8 (e).

In Figure 6.9 (a) I've started out with a candle display from a local store. I want to replace the medium-sized green candles of Figure 6.9 (b) with the soft panda heads of Figure 6.9 (c). You can see the result of the removal in of Figure 6.9 (d). This task has stressed out my texture synthesizer pretty badly, but most of this stuff will get covered up when we put the pandas in. The final image, Figure 6.9 (e), shows the new store display.

(a)   (b)

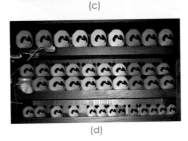

(c)

We can do a little better with this by adding the ability to handle color shifts. In Figure 6.10 (a) and Figure 6.10 (b) I've converted the green candle and the panda's head into black-and-white versions. The search algorithm looks for this black-and-white candle in a black-and-white version of the source. Now when I drop a panda on a candle, in addition to giving it a bit of differential scaling if required, I can also click on the color of the candle to apply a color shift to the inserted panda. I did this for all the candles that my system could match in the image; you'll notice there's one candle I just couldn't detect accurately due to the occluding leaf. The synthetic texture here leaves a lot to be desired, but again I think a more robust implementation could do a far better job. Even so, once the panda heads are in position, the whole thing certainly works well enough to let us see what the new display would look like. Figure 6.10 (c) shows our new line of colored, scented panda heads.

Finally, let's look at a three-dimensional rendered example. In Figure 6.11 (a) I've made a simple bedroom with a festive wallpaper pattern on the wall. Let's suppose we'd like to see what this looks like if we had fish instead of elephants. Of course, if we had the original three-dimensional scene around, we could just rerender it, but let's suppose that we don't have the three-dimensional model available. In Figure 6.11 (b) and Figure 6.11 (c), I've shown just the elephant and his mask. Note that the elephant isn't distorted by perspective or rotation, as he is in the wallpapered room. Since I still had the original elephant that I drew, I just grabbed that image and used it. It's possible with many modern image editing programs to correct for distortions like

Figure 6.10

(a) The black and white candle. (b) The black-and-white panda. (c) Removing all candles. (d) Pandas for sale!

Image Search and Relace

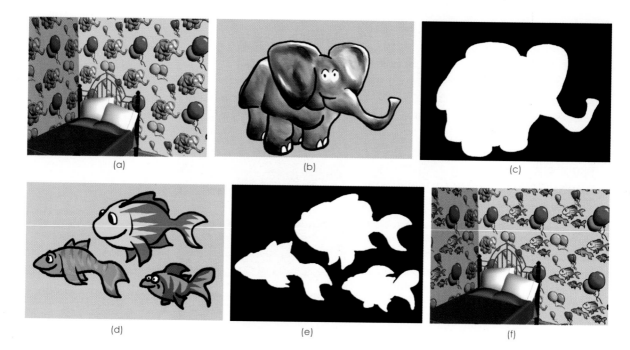

(a)   (b)   (c)

(d)   (e)   (f)

Figure 6.11

(a) A wallpapered room.
(b) Target elephant.
(c) Target elephant mask.
(d) Fish replacement.
(e) Fish replacement mask.
(f) The replaced final. Note
that the fish are darker on
the left wall, following the
overall darkness there. Note
that some of the elephants
were not replaced.

perspective, so even if I didn't have my original I could have gotten a pretty good target working from the image. Or I could have just used one of the elephants directly off the wallpaper with no correction; in that case I'd need to do a second search-and-replace to handle the elephants on the left wall, which are distorted somewhat differently. I drew the fish of Figure 6.11(d) to replace the elephant; their mask is in Figure 6.11(e). The final result is Figure 6.11(f).

There are a couple of things to note here. First, my input to the system was to drop the target elephant on each occurrence in the source, and then I manually gave the system a pretty good starting hint for the perspective distortion. Second, I wrote a special little routine that computed the average change in luminance over all the pixels that were being removed, and I applied that change to the replacements. Thus the fish on the left wall are a little darker than the fish on the right wall, as they should be to fit the overall tone. Third, the elephants near the top of the room were present enough that I could match to them, even though in some cases not much of the corresponding fish replacements showed up in the result.

Notice that some elephants didn't get matched. Three of these elephants are hiding behind the bed: one in the lower right, one above the bedspread on the left wall, and one behind the headboard. Two of the elephants cross over the corner of the room, so that their bodies are on the left but pieces of their trunks are on the right. These didn't get replaced because the fish would have to have the same visible bend in them to look good. Finally, I left unchanged the two elephants just to the right of the corner. That's because although the elephant doesn't straddle the corner, the fish would have (or rather, they should: in fact they wouldn't, and therefore it would look wrong).

Wrapping Up

One thing I'd like to add to this system is the ability to identify and replace obscured matches. For example, sometimes an instance is recognizable, even though it's partly hidden by some other object. Often even an obscured object is visible enough to be recognizable to the human eye, like the medium-sized candle at the far left of Figure 6.10. It would be nice to be able to capture the match, and then use the same occlusion on the replacement so that it's blocked the same way.

Shadows pose an interesting problem. Suppose that a shadow falls halfway across an instance of the target. We might be able to match this, but the algorithm I've presented doesn't replicate the shadow in the replacement. With a little more work, I think we could analyze each match to find how it deviates from the source, and then apply those deviations to the replacement. This way we'd maintain not only the original shadows in source, but also highlights, reflections, and other surface variations.

Taking a cue from some modern image-editing programs like *Painter* and *Photoshop*, it would be fun to have a variety of replacement images for each target. For example, we might have several images of the panda head in Figure 6.9, and each replacement uses one of those at random (or as chosen by the user), so that the pandas aren't all identical to one another (after all, pandas aren't that precise). And we needn't use just pandas; if we wanted to replace the candles with a variety of toys, we could fill the shelves with a collection of different toys simply by picking different replacement images for each candle.

I'm intrigued by just how much of a speedup I was able to get by moving the matching problem from the computer to the person. Of course, I would like an automatic program that I could just get started, ignore for a few minutes, and then return to to collect my completely processed image (as one does with slow *Photoshop* filters on big pictures, for instance). But I like the idea that a we're able to harness the amazing power of the human visual system and brain to make a staggeringly slow and complex process relatively fast and easy.

FURTHER READING

The idea of using search and replace in a graphical editor was first introduced in "Graphical Search and Replace" by David Kurlander and Eric Bier (*Proceedings of SIGGRAPH 88*, pp. 113–120).

When you watch football games on television, you can sometimes see a yellow line on the ground that indicates where the first down is located. The line really seems to be painted there: people can walk in front of it, the grass shows up under it, and it doesn't wiggle or move around on the screen as though it were an electronic effect. But the line is indeed an electronic effect, added into the video signal in real time. You can read about how this is done in "TV Football's MVP—Yellow First-Down Line" by Joe Flint (*The Wall Street Journal Online*, Jan 26, 2000). You can also visit the website of SportVision, the company that makes the system, at http://www.sportvision.com.

You can get up to speed on texture generation from photographs from a wide variety of recent papers. A good place to start is "Pyramid-Based Texture Analysis/Synthesis" by David J. Heeger and James R. Bergen (*Proceedings of SIGGRAPH 95*, pp. 229–238), and "A Parametric Texture Model Based on Joint Statistics of Complex Wavelet Coefficients" by Javier Portilla and Eero P. Simoncelli (*International Journal of Computer Vision*, 40(1), October 2000, pp. 49–70).

For the images in this chapter, I wrote my own texture generation algorithm, based on the ideas in two recent papers. "Fast Texture Synthesis using Tree-Structured Vector Quantization" by L. Wei and M. Levoy (*Proceedings of SIGGRAPH 2000*, pp. 479–488) gives the basic algorithm. To help make the synthetic texture blend better into the surrounding photograph, I used ideas from "Image Replacement Through Texture Synthesis" by Homan Igehy and Lucas Pereira (*Proceedings of the 1997 IEEE International Conference on Image Processing*, October 1997). You can also get a copy of this online at http://graphics.stanford.edu/papers/texture_replace/texture_replace.pdf.

If you don't want to write your own code, you can get a good head start with the source code written by Paul Harrison, designed as a plug-in for the GIMP image editor. He describes it in "A Non-hierarchical Procedure for Re-synthesis of Complex Textures" by Paul Harrison (*Proceedings of the 9th International Conference in Central Europe on Computer Graphics, Visualization and Computer Vision*, February 2001). You can download the code for free from http://www.csse.monash.edu.au/~pfh/resynthesizer/.

A commercial implementation of texture synthesis is available in the Image Doctor plug-in, published by Alien Skin Software. This can be used with *Photoshop*, *Painter*, and any other image editor that can use *Photoshop*-style plug-ins.

Venn
and
Now

"I know what you're thinking about," said Tweedledum, "but it isn't so, nohow."

"Contrariwise," continued Tweedledee, "if it was so, it might be; and if it were so, it would be; but as it isn't, it ain't. That's logic."

(from *Through the Looking-Glass* by Lewis Carroll, 1872)

Who knows what the truth really is? Not just temporary or relative truth, but eternal and universal truth? Truth with a capital T.

Nobody knows the Truth, of course. But that hasn't stopped people from looking. One of the results of that search has been systems of formal logic that try to turn the work of reasoning and arguing into mechanical processes, where errors of interpretation and execution can be detected and corrected. Formal logic can't tell us much about the human condition, but it is one useful tool for reasoning our way through the world.

One of the most famous visual tools for logic is the *Venn diagram*, which most frequently shows the relationship between three classes of objects by drawing three overlapping circles.

In this chapter I'll talk about Venn diagrams, how we can generalize them to more than three sets of objects, and some related tools for visual logic.

Logical Arguments

The goal of all the visual techniques I'll be discussing here is to help us decide a class of logical questions. To get the ball rolling, I'll start by defining some useful terms.

A *logical argument* is a sequence of *statements*. The last statement is called the *conclusion*; the others are called variously the *premises*, *hypotheses*, or *assumptions*. Each statement, including the conclusion, refers to the existence of one or more *classes* of *objects*. A logical argument is *valid* if the conclusion is always true when all of the assumptions are true. Any logical argument that is not valid is *invalid*.

Here's an example of a logical argument with two premises and a conclusion:

> **Premise 1:** It rains a lot in the Northwest.
> **Premise 2:** Seattle is in the Northwest.
> **Conclusion:** It rains a lot in Seattle.

In this case, the argument is valid. How about this one?

> **Premise 1:** Some dogs are known for their bark.
> **Premise 2:** Some trees are known for their bark.
> **Conclusion:** Some dogs are trees.

This argument is invalid for so many reasons!

Let's look first at the structure of valid statements, and then at how we use them in patterns to create arguments.

Statements typically refer to the world using a small vocabulary of common terms. The connective terms *and*, *or*, and *not* have their common interpretations.

The *if/then* construction is used to build a logical chain of true statements. For example, I might say, "If I am driving my car, then I am sitting down." Let's call this statement S. Since there are two conditions in an *if/then* construction, and each condition can be true or false, there are four possible combinations for the entire statement. Let's rephrase S abstractly as "If a then b." Let's now make four observations, one for each combination of true and false for a and b. We'll say that S is true or false depending on whether it matches our observation. Figure 7.1 shows the four choices and the results.

Most of these decisions are reasonable given how we normally use language. Cases 3 and 4 are perhaps unusual. The rule for interpreting an *if/then* statement is that if the first clause is not satisfied, then the

Case	*a*	*b*	Observation	Statement *S*
1	True	True	I'm driving my car, and I am sitting down.	True
2	True	False	I'm driving my car, and I am not sitting down.	False
3	False	True	I'm not driving my car, and I am sitting down.	True
4	False	False	I'm not driving my car, and I am not sitting down.	True

whole statement is true. The principle here is that if the first clause is not met, then the whole thing is irrelevant. Since the statement is irrelevant, it's certainly not false. And whatever isn't false, is true. So in any *if/then* statement, if the *if* clause is not satisfied, then the whole statement is taken to be true. For example, let's suppose that there are no talking dogs, so our first premise is, "There are no talking dogs." Then the statements, "All talking dogs enjoy Shakespeare," "Some talking dogs like to water-ski," and "No talking dogs enjoy sipping coffee in outdoor Parisian bistros" are all defined to be true, because the premise on which they are based is untrue. This can be a little strange when you first encounter it: basically if you start with something untrue, any derivative statements about that untruth are themselves true, because their underlying assumption is not. So "All talking dogs enjoy Shakespeare" is true.

One of the most common errors in logical reasoning is to get the chain of cause and effect wrong. The opposite of "If *a* then *b*" is *not* "If *a* is false, then *b* is false." Let's try that out with the language of our example *S*: "If I am not driving my car, then I am not sitting down." That's clearly not going to be true in general. In fact, I'm sitting down right now as I type these words, but I'm not in my car. The correct logical opposite is called the *contrapositive* and may be expressed, "If *b* is false, then *a* is false." Note that *b* comes first. In fact, this is exactly the same as the original statement *S*. The contrapositive of *S* is "If I am not sitting down, then I am not driving my car." Now that makes sense.

A phrasing more common to our everyday use of *if* and *then* is the *if and only if/then* statement. For example, "If, and only if, it's cold outside, then I'll turn on the heat." In this case, we know that if the heat is on, then it's necessarily cold outside, and vice-versa.

It's easy to mix up the rules for *if/then* and *if and only if/then*, but the rules of logic are careful about keeping them distinct.

It's also useful to be able to make statements about whole *classes* of variables.

The phrases *for any*, *for all*, and *for every* are synonyms that allow us to make a claim about every element in a class. For example, we could say "For all birds, birds have wings." Often *for all* statements are

Figure 7.1

Checking the validity of the statement "If I am driving my car (*a*), then I am sitting down (*b*)."

compressed a bit, as in "All birds have wing " We can also phrase this in an equivalent form that expresses the nonexistence of a class: "No birds are wingless. "

If we want to assert that there is at least one element of the class that has some property, we use phrases like *there exists*, *there is at least one*, and *there is an*. These are all synonyms that let us claim that at least one thing with this property exists. For example, we might say "There exists a bird that cannot fly." This does not mean that all birds cannot fly, or that there are even two. It just means that there is at least one.

The phrases *for all* (and its variants) and *there exists* (and its variants) are called *quantifiers*.

PROVE IT AIN'T SO

There are at least three generally useful tools for determining if an argument is valid or invalid.

First, one can simplify the statements using *tautologies*, or statements that are known to be true. Tautologies are useful because they typically express true statements in slightly different terms than those used in the original statements. A tautology adds no new information to an argument, but just helps us convert or simplify it.

The second tool for proving an argument is to search for a *contradiction*. Here we show that if we assume the premises are true, we reach a conclusion that is the opposite of the conclusion in the argument. Sometimes this can be done from within the argument itself, and sometimes we find it useful to apply tautologies to transform one or more of the statements into a more convenient form.

The third tool, and the one I'll focus on here, is to convert everything into symbols and then manipulate those symbols in a mechanical way, without concerning ourselves with what they stand for. In this symbolic form, we often use the following notation:

$\forall a$	For all a
$\exists a$	There exists an a
$a \wedge b, ab$	a and b
$a \vee b, a + b$	a or b
$\sim a, a'$	Not a
$a \rightarrow b$	If a then b

For example, ab means "a and b," or more completely, "both a and b are true." The expression ad' means "a and not-d," or "a is true and d is false."

Now that we know the forms of statements, let's look at what happens when we bring them together to form arguments. The first person to study such chains of symbolic statements was Aristotle (380–320 B.C.). He game the name *syllogisms* to patterns of arguments. Syllogisms are sets of *inference rules* that we apply to arguments to determine their validity, using a technique called *deductive reasoning*.

Aristotle's insight was that if we can convert our statements into symbolic form, then we can just apply standard patterns to those symbols. It's just like how symbols are used to solve word problems. For example, we might be asked, "Bob has three chickens and bought four more chickens. How many chickens does he have?" We convert this word problem into the symbolic expression $3 + 4 = ?$ and apply our rules of arithmetic to find the answer. Then we convert the symbolic result, 7, back into the vocabulary of the original problem, leading to our conclusion ("Bob has too many chickens!").

Here are four of Aristotle's patterns with examples: (recall that $a \rightarrow b$ means "If a then b"):

Modus Ponens (method of affirming):
>　(1) $a \rightarrow b$: If it's a folk song, it has just three chords.
>　(2) a: It's a folk song.

Therefore (3) b: It has just three chords.

Modus Tollens (method of denying):
>　(1) $a \rightarrow b$: If the shoe fits, I'll wear it.
>　(2) b': I'm not wearing the shoe.

Therefore (3) a': The shoe doesn't fit.

Disjunctive syllogism:
>　(1) $a \vee b$: My master plan is either brilliant or insane.
>　(2) a': My master plan is not brilliant.

Therefore (3) b: My master plan is insane.

Hypothetical syllogism:
>　(1) $a \rightarrow b$: If it's on the web, then it's true.
>　(2) $b \rightarrow c$: If it's true, then it's important.

Therefore (3) $a \rightarrow c$: If it's on the web, then it's important.

Venn and Now

There are three important "cons" that arise all the time when working with logical arguments.

We saw the *contradiction* above. It just means that we show that if we follow the premises, we can arrive at a conclusion that is incompatible with the stated conclusion. Proving this contradiction proves that the argument is invalid.

We also saw the *contrapositive*. Symbolically, if we are given a statement "If a then b" (or $a \rightarrow b$), then the contrapositive is "If b' then a'" (or $b' \rightarrow a'$). If we can prove the contrapositive of the conclusion, then we've also proven the conclusion itself.

The *converse* is an error of reasoning that goes like this:

(1) $a \rightarrow b$: If it's chocolate, it's delicious.

(2) b: It's delicious.

Therefore (3) a: It's chocolate (**invalid conclusion!**).

In other words, just because the conclusion of an *if/then* statement is true, that doesn't mean that the premise is true; the conclusion could be true for other reasons.

Whew. Now that we have all this terminology under our belts, let's look at representing logical arguments visually.

3-VENN DIAGRAMS

Figure 7.2 shows the famous *Venn diagram* for three classes of objects, sometimes called a *3-Venn diagram*. If we name these three classes a, b, and c, then we can label each of the regions of the diagram as in Figure 7.3.

Note that there are eight regions, corresponding to the eight possible combinations of these three classes. Suppose that we assign the three classes this way:

a things that are scary movie monsters,
b things that are unusually large,
c things that are airborne.

Figure 7.2

The three circles of the traditional three-element Venn diagram.

Figure 7.3

The Venn diagram of Figure 7.2 with labels for each region. The gray unlabelled region outside the circles represents elements that are not within any of the sets.

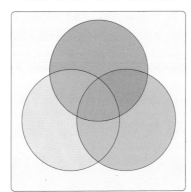

Then here are examples of the eight combinations. Remember that if a category is negated, that means the object does not have that trait.

Scary Movie Monsters	Unusually Large Things	Airborne Things	Example
a'	b'	c'	A puppy
a'	b'	c	A helium balloon
a'	b	c'	The pyramids
a'	b	c	A pterodactyl
a	b'	c'	The Blob
a	b'	c	Dracula
a	b	c'	Godzilla
a	b	c	Giant atomic grasshoppers

These are placed in the appropriate zones in Figure 7.4. Note that the white outer region contains all those things that do not belong within one or more circles.

This is an example of using Venn diagrams for *classifying*. Here we have three criteria, and we place objects in the diagram according to which of these criteria they satisfy. You can pick any three traits, plug them in for a, b, and c, and then populate all eight cells (don't forget the outer cell corresponding to a' b' c').

We can also use Venn diagrams to follow a chain of statements and see if they form a valid conclusion. For example, consider the following logical argument:

     (1) All winged monkeys have tails.
     (2) All doctors are tail-less.
Therefore (3) No winged monkeys are doctors.

Is this valid? The first thing we do is convert it into symbolic form.

a things that have tails;
b winged monkeys;
c doctors.

With these substitutions, we get

     (1) All b are a.
     (2) All c are a'.
Therefore (3) No b are c.

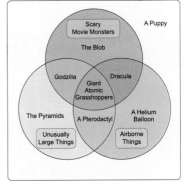

Figure 7.4

The Venn diagram of Figure 7.3 with examples placed in the cells. Here a = Scary Movie Monsters, b = Unusually Large Things, c = Airborne Things.

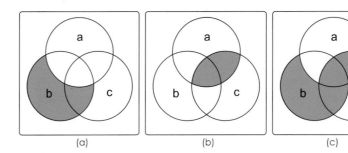

Figure 7.5

A worked-out syllogism with the three-circle Venn diagram. Regions marked in red are known to be empty. (a) Premise 1: "All b are a." (b) Premise 2: "All c are a'." (c) The conclusion: "No b are c."

Is this true? Figure 7.5 shows the steps, starting with a blank slate, indicating that we don't know if any of the cells are occupied. In Figure 7.5(a) I've marked in red the two cells $a'\,bc$ and $a'\,bc'$. This is because statement 1, "All b are a"; is equivalent to "No b are a'." Similarly, in Figure 7.5(b) I've marked in red cells abc and $a\,b'\,c$. I was able to mark these cells as empty by converting statement 2, "All c are a'" to the equivalent "No c are a." Figure 7.5(c) puts the diagrams together, and to confirm the third statement, we need only look to see if any b cells overlap with c. They don't, so the logical argument is true.

Let's look at a second example with four statements:

(1) Some children are intelligent.

(2) Some government officials are intelligent.

(3) No government officials are children.

Therefore (4) Some government officials are intelligent adults.

As before, first we convert this to symbols:

a children;
b government officials;
c intelligent people.

The symbolic form of the argument is:

(1) Some a are c.

(2) Some b are c.

(3) No b are a.

Therefore (4) Some b are ca'.

Figure 7.6(a) shows the first statement, "Some a are c." Note that I've marked in yellow the two cells ac and abc, and joined them with a

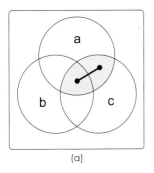 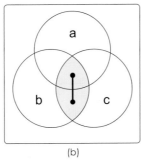 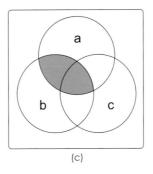 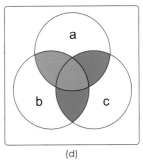

(a)　　　　　　　(b)　　　　　　　(c)　　　　　　　(d)

connective line. This means that we know that at least one of them is occupied, but not necessarily both. Similarly, Figure 7.6(b) marks the cells bc and abc the same way. Figure 7.6(c) resolves the issue for us by turning off cell abc. Figure 7.6(d) shows that both ac and bc must therefore be occupied, while abc is empty. Thus the conclusion that "Some b are ca'" is also true, because we have occupancy in cell bc but none in abc. The argument is valid!

Figure 7.6

A worked-out four-statement syllogism with the three-circle Venn diagram. (a) Premise 1: "Some a are c." (b) Premise 2: "Some b are c." (c) Premise 3: "No b are a." (d) The conclusion: "Some b are a'c."

HOW MUCH OF NOTHING DO YOU HAVE?

There's an interesting subtlety that we need to address before moving on.

The Venn diagrams we've seen above with three overlapping circles aren't the only way to draw such things. The idea is simply to graphically capture the relationships between collections of objects, with shared characteristics represented by overlapping sets. We'll find this more general approach useful for our discussion here.

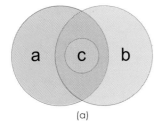 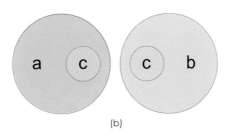

(a)　　　　　　　　　　(b)

Figure 7.7

Inconsistencies in Venn diagrams. (a) An incorrect diagram that might seem to result from "All c are a" and "All c are b." (b) A correct (but temporary) diagram.

Suppose that we have these two premises: "All c are a" and "All c are b." This seems to suggest a Venn diagram like Figure 7.7(a), where c is completely within a, and also within b. Two conclusions we can draw from this diagram are "Some b are a" and "Some a are b."

But that's not quite right. Suppose that no elements of the class c exist at all. Then the two premises are both trivially true; after all, if there are no elements c at all, then anything we assert about them can be true. But if that's the case, then the overlap implied by the figure is misleading. The overlap also implies that some things are both a and b but are not c, and we have no reason to make such an assertion.

To make this concrete, let's assign class a to *intelligent things*, class b to *scissors*, and c to *extraterrestrials*. Let's assume for the moment that no extraterrestrials exist. Then I can assert both "All extraterrestrials are intelligent things" and "All extraterrestrials are scissors." Remember that since we've assumed that there are no extraterrestrials, both of these statements are defined to be true according to the rules of the *if/then* statements that we saw earlier. From these premises we could then conclude that "Some scissors are intelligent things," which most people would agree is not true.

Lewis Carroll was aware of the subtleties that occur when things don't exist. Here's a scene from the Mad Hatter's tea party:

> "Take some more tea," the March Hare said to Alice, very earnestly.
> "I've had nothing yet," Alice replied in an offended tone, "so I can't take more."
> "You mean you can't take *less*," said the Hatter, "it's very easy to take *more* than nothing."

> (from *Alice's Adventures in Wonderland* by Lewis Carroll, 1865)

You can try to define your way around the problem of not knowing what to do with nothing, and Carroll did so in his books. He defined a proposition "Some a are b" to mean three things: "Some a exist," "Some b exist," and "Some a are b." This approach has its own drawbacks and has not been widely adopted.

One way to handle this situation is to use a diagram like Figure 7.7(b). Here we've reserved judgment about the overlap between a and b until we receive more information. This diagram can be as misleading as Figure 7.7(a), since it seems to imply "No a are b." We should treat this as a provisional, or working, diagram, pending more information that may yet bring regions a and b together.

Although explicitly handling the status of undefined things is important, it also makes everything a little more messy. In this chapter, I'm going to adopt Carroll's approach. If I make a statement like "Some apples are fruit," I'll mean it to imply that there do exist things that are apples, and things that are fruit.

4-VENN DIAGRAMS

What if we want to show examples of objects that share four traits? Or what if we want to prove the truth of a logical argument with four variables? The obvious answer is to use a *4-Venn diagram*, the generalization of the 3-Venn diagram.

A reasonable first step is shown in Figure 7.8, where I've taken four circles and overlapped them. Is this actually a 4-Venn diagram? One way to check quickly is to see if the diagram has the necessary number of cells. But how many cells should we have?

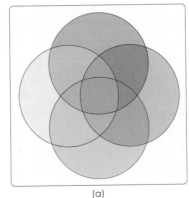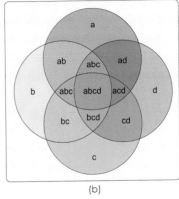

The easy way to answer is to think of each cell in a diagram with n traits as an n-bit binary number. For example, 0110 would indicate a cell where the second and third traits were included, but the first and fourth were not; that is, it's an overlap between just the second and third regions. For a diagram with n regions, we will have one cell for every binary combination from 0 to $2^n - 1$, or 2^n cells in all. When $n = 4$, we have should 16 cells. A quick check of Figure 7.8 turns up only 14.

What's wrong? We're missing two cells: ac and bd.

I monkeyed around with this diagram quite a bit, and I managed to get one of the missing cells represented. But I couldn't figure how to create a nice Venn diagram on the plane just by distorting the circles.

It's probably worth noting what "nice" means in this case. If you look at Figure 7.3, you can see a couple of characteristics I'd like to preserve. First, each cell, including the outermost cell, appears once and only once. Second, the cell shapes are simple; that is, they're not long, convoluted, snaky shapes that twist around. Finally, the cells are arranged in a way that matches a *gray code*. This is a way of counting in binary such that each number differs from the previous one in only one bit. For example, to count in a three-bit gray code, we'd write 000, 001, 011, 010, 110, 111, 101, 100. If you look at any two adjacent cells in Figure 7.3, you'll notice that they have this property, so when we cross a border, we gain or lose a single element: never more, never less. This creates a nice visual cohesion in the diagram, so that we can roam around it with our eyes and see gradual changes. It also tells us that objects that are next to each other in a classification diagram are similar, differing only in exactly one trait.

How might we capture these criteria in a four-element Venn diagram?

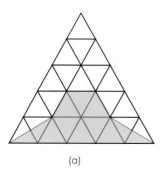

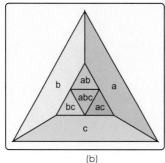

(a)

(b)

Figure 7.9

An alternative way to draw the three-element circle diagram of Figure 7.2.

(a)

(b)

Figure 7.10

An alternative way to draw the four-element circle diagram of Figure 7.8.

Figure 7.9 shows another way to construct the three-cell diagram, and Figure 7.10 shows the result of applying this approach to four cells. We're still missing two cells. The lesson I learned from this is that simply jiggling around the shapes of the cells isn't going to get us to a 4-Venn diagram; we need a new approach.

I've included some quotes from Lewis Carroll's books in this chapter. I used them not only because they're clever and illuminating, but because Carroll also worked on this problem of multicell diagrams. In his book *Symbolic Logic*, published in 1896, he presented what he called the *bilateral diagram* for solving logical arguments involving two variables. Naturally enough, the *trilateral diagram* was provided for arguments in three variables. Figure 7.11(a) shows a version of his diagram. Figure 7.11(b) marks the cells. Figure 7.12 shows the region associated with each variable. These diagrams often use lower-case letters starting with *a* to label the regions, so I'll switch over to that notation for the rest of this chapter.

Note that Carroll started with a different approach than that used in the Venn diagrams. Rather than drawing regions within an outer cell, he takes the whole world (the surrounding rectangle) and cuts it in half vertically and horizontally, creating four cells.

Let's work a syllogism with the trilateral diagram.

(1) No apples are dangerous.

(2) Some witches are dangerous.

(3) No bananas are safe.

Therefore (4) Some bananas are dangerous.

Making the symbolic substitutions

a witches;
b apples (*b'* = bananas);
c dangerous things (*c'* = safe things),

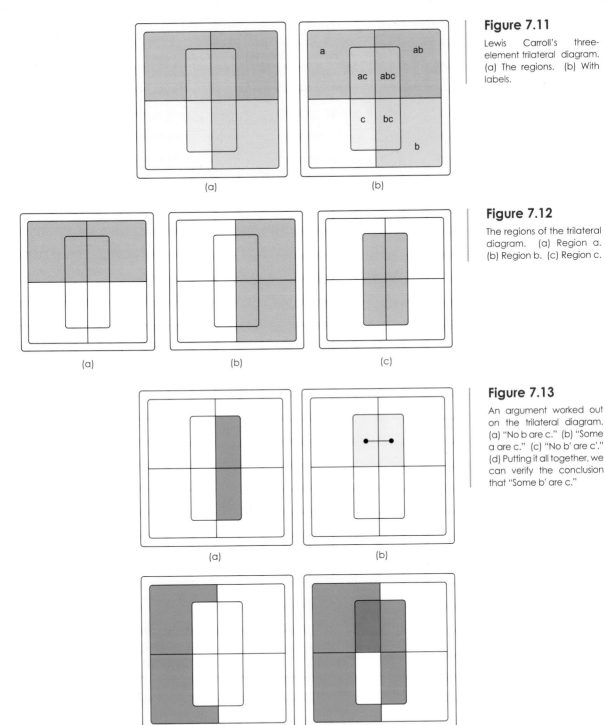

Figure 7.11

Lewis Carroll's three-element trilateral diagram. (a) The regions. (b) With labels.

Figure 7.12

The regions of the trilateral diagram. (a) Region a. (b) Region b. (c) Region c.

Figure 7.13

An argument worked out on the trilateral diagram. (a) "No b are c." (b) "Some a are c." (c) "No b' are c'." (d) Putting it all together, we can verify the conclusion that "Some b' are c."

Figure 7.14

Lewis Carroll's four-element quadrilateral diagram. (a) The regions. (b) With labels.

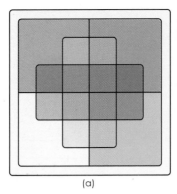 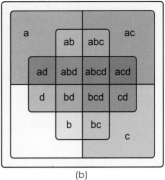

(a) (b)

we can write the argument symbolically as

(1) No *b* are *c*.

(2) Some *a* are *c*.

(3) No *b'* are *c'*.

Therefore (4) Some *b'* are *c*.

Figure 7.15

The Carroll diagrams for many elements. (a) Five elements. (b) Six elements. (c) Seven elements. (d) Eight elements.

Figure 7.13 works through this argument, and you can see from Figure 7.13(d) that the conclusion is true, so the argument is valid.

Carroll's next step was his *quadrilateral diagram*, shown in Figure 7.14. This is a very nice solution. To add a fourth class of objects, Carroll drew a new rectangle. Note that the new cell boundary passes through each of the existing cells once; we'll see that this is a general rule for adding new traits to an existing diagram.

FIVE AND MORE

We've successfully managed to create a diagram for four elements, so let's try for five!

You won't be surprised to learn that Carroll had a go at this problem; his solution is shown in Figure 7.15(a), where he just cut each cell in two with a diagonal line.

I found this a very disappointing result. It's not very nice to look at, but more importantly, it doesn't have the gray code property. To my mind, this makes it almost useless as a visual tool for anything but the most mechanical proof-checking. Carroll continued extending his diagrams in the most straightforward way, as shown in Figure 7.15(b) through (d).

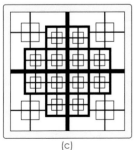

(a)

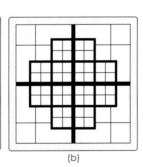

(b)

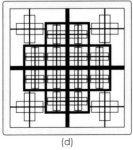

(c)

(d)

There's a nice solution right around the corner, though. I was looking at Carroll's quadrilateral diagram and wondered if I could cut through every cell with a single boundary, as he did to create to the quadrilateral diagram from the trilateral one.

After a little fooling around with pencil and paper, I came up with the solution of Figure 7.16. That seems to satisfy all of criteria, and it's not bad-looking at all. If you check, you'll see that all $2^5 = 32$ cells are present and appear only once, and that each cell boundary changes only one variable.

Well, that got me going. I had to try my hand at six variables, with the 64-cell result of Figure 7.17.

I invite you to cook up some logical arguments in five or six variables and have a go at proving a conclusion with these diagrams. It's kind of fun to first set up the argument symbolically (that is, "All *b* are *d*") and then after you have a bunch of statements, assign properties to them (e.g., *b* = *insects*, *c* = *carnival attractions*). As long as you create statements that originally make some degree of sense, you can discover some pretty goofy "truths" this way!

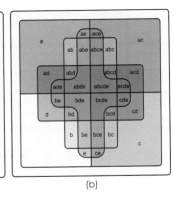

Figure 7.16

My five-element Venn diagram based on a square design. (a) The regions. (b) With labels.

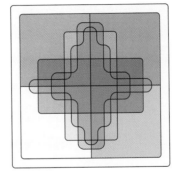

Figure 7.17

My six-element Venn diagram based on a square design.

OTHER SOLUTIONS

There are other ways to cook up interesting Venn diagrams.

Venn himself suggested a general construction technique based on his three-circle technique. Figure 7.18 shows the steps. We begin with the three circles in Figure 7.18(a) and add a fat half-circle in Figure 7.18(b). Recall that the general trick is to draw a line that crosses all the existing cells, so the simplest approach to extend this would be just to follow this fat half-circle, as in Figure 7.18(c). You can keep going to Figure 7.18(d) and beyond, as long as your patience holds and you can draw the tiny little lines between the curves! Figure 7.18(e) shows the construction without any fills, and Figure 7.18(f) shows the result if we tint each region in Figure 7.18.

Venn and Now

Figure 7.18

Venn's construction for increasing the number of elements beyond three, based on the original three-circle diagram. (a) Start with the traditional 3-Venn diagram. (b) Pick one of the circles, and draw a thick blob around part of the circle so that the blob passes through every region. (c) Draw another blob (a little thinner this time) around the last one. (d) And now another blob. (e) And yet another blob. (f) Here I've filled in each blob with a unique, transparent color. It would take enormous patience to try to actually work a logic problem with this diagram.

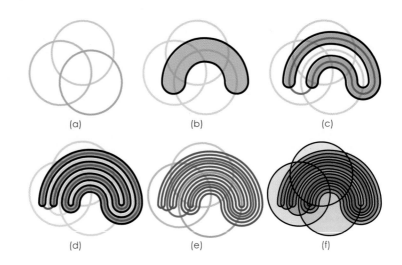

(a)   (b)   (c)

(d)   (e)   (f)

Figure 7.19

A three-dimensional version of Figure 7.18(f).

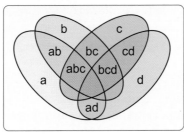

Figure 7.20

A four-element diagram made out of four congruent ellipses.

Figure 7.21

A five-element diagram made out of five congruent ellipses.

Figure 7.18(f) is hard to interpret. An extruded, three-dimensional view of is shown in Figure 7.19.

This isn't a terribly nice solution. Could there be other approaches which retain the nice circular forms of the simple 3-Venn diagram?

In Carroll's *Symbolic Logic*, he presents a four-ellipse solution by Venn, shown in Figure 7.20.

More recently, Branko Grünbaum found a lovely arrangement of ellipses for a five-element diagram, shown in Figure 7.21. This approach doesn't seem to generalize; I don't know of any Venn diagrams of six or more congruent ellipses.

Another approach was developed recently by Anthony Edwards. The first two steps are like those of Carroll's: take the plane and cut it in half vertically and then horizontally, as in Figure 7.22(a) and (b). But where Carroll places a square, Edwards places a circle, as in Figure 7.22(c). Now draw a big serpentine curve that cuts all the cells as in Figure 7.22(d). To keep going, draw ever-denser

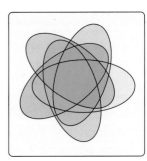

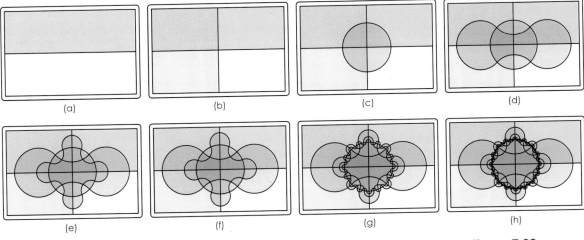

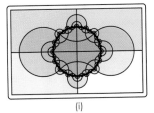

serpentine curves that follow the circle, as in Figure 7.22(e) through (i).

This diagram meets all of our desires for a "nice" diagram. It's easy to program up and extend to any number of terms. And unlike Carroll's diagrams, it continues to look good even for high numbers of terms.

Figure 7.22

Edward's development for a multi-element diagram. (a) The first variable splits the rectangular cell into a top and bottom. (b) Now split left and right. (c) Add a circle into the center, resulting in eight cells for three variables. (d) Add a two-lobed blob centered at the middle of the rectangle. (e) Add a four-lobed blob. (f) And an eight-lobed blob. (g) And a sixteen-lobed blob. (h) A thirty-two-lobed blob. (i) And finally a blob with sixty-four lobes, giving us a diagram for nine variables.

Let's take a look at proving a logical argument using a six-term Edwards diagram:

(1) No b' are d'

(2) No g are df'

(3) No d are f'

(4) Some b are ed

(5) No a' are dg

Therefore (6) No a' are b' cfg

Figure 7.23 plots this argument, and we can see that the result is true. I sure wouldn't want to have to work this one out in my head!

Once I had the Edwards diagram programmed up, I tried out a few variations. In Figure 7.24(a) I've pulled the big blobs in close to the main circle using circular arcs. I also gave it a shot using Bézier curves, as in Figure 7.24(b).

I also tried replacing the inner circle with a box. The results are shown in Figure 7.25, where I again used arcs and Bézier curves in parts (a) and (b). In Figure 7.25(c) I used straight lines to join up the regions; I like the looks of these diagrams a lot.

Figure 7.23

An argument plotted on Edwards' diagram. (a) No b' are d'. (b) No g are df'. (c) No d are f'. (d) Some b are ed. (e) No a' are dg. (f) The five statements taken together prove the conclusion "No a' are b' cfg."

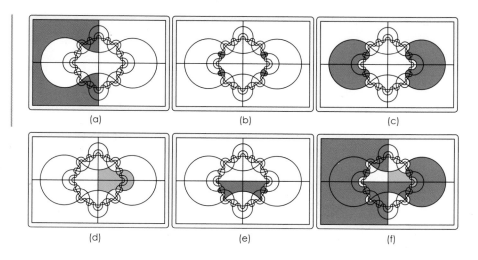

Figure 7.24

A variation on Edwards' development for a multi-element diagram. Here I've kept the circle for the third element, but wrapped the other curves more closely around it. (a) Using circular arcs. (b) Using Bézier curves.

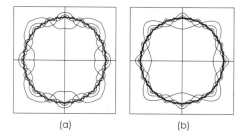

Figure 7.25

My variants on Edwards' development in Figure 7.22. I've taken the inner circle and replaced it with a square. (a) Using arcs for the curves. (b) Using Bézier curves. (c) Using straight lines.

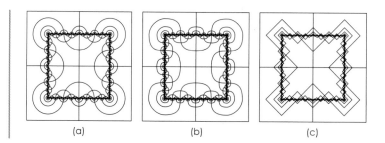

COUNTING CELLS

As I mentioned before, a diagram representing n classes of objects will contain 2^n cells. I call the number of elements in a cell that cell's *density*, so a cell with three items has a density of 3.

It's interesting to look at the patterns formed by the density of the cells for different diagrams. Figure 7.26 shows the density diagrams for the basic 3-Venn circular diagram, Carroll's three- and four-element diagrams, my five- and six-element diagrams, Edwards' eight-element diagram, and one of my variants.

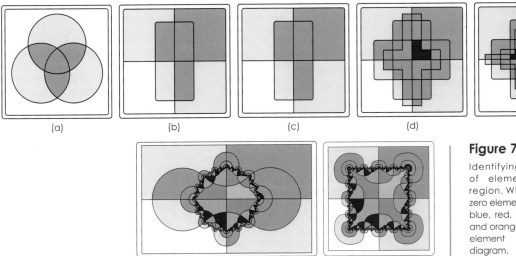

(a)   (b)   (c)   (d)   (e)

(f)   (g)

Figure 7.26

Identifying the number of elements in each region. White represents zero elements, then yellow, blue, red, green, maroon, and orange. (a) The three-element circular Venn diagram. (b) The three-element rectangular Venn diagram. (c) The four-element rectangular Venn diagram. (d) The five-element rectangular Venn diagram. (e) The six-element rectangular Venn diagram. (f) The eight-element Edwards diagram. (g) One of my variants on the eight-element Edwards diagram.

KARNAUGH MAPS

Related to Venn diagrams are a class of diagrams called *Karnaugh maps* (which I mentioned in Chapter 5). These are typically used by electrical engineers to simplify Boolean circuits. Simplifying a circuit really just means finding a terse representation for the truth states of the circuit, just as we try to verify a short statement of truth resulting from a logical argument.

Figure 7.27 shows the simplest Karnaugh map based on just two one-bit variables, a and b. The trick with Karnaugh maps is to try to find the biggest rectangles of 0s and 1s that you can. If Figure 7.27 tells us the output of a circuit $K_1(a, b)$, then it's easy to tell that $K_1(a, b) = a$. We hardly needed any fancy tools for this example, so let's get a little more complex.

Figure 7.27

A two-term Karnaugh map $K(a, b) = a$. (a) The map. (b) A rectangle of 1s.

Karnaugh maps have only two dimensions, so to represent three variables, we need to bundle them somehow. Typically we treat the first two as a pair and the third as a single free variable, as in Figure 7.28. Notice that I've laid out the possibilities for ab along the top line using a gray code, as we discussed before. As we'll see, this is critical to the technique.

In this figure it's easy again to spot the cluster of 1s, which I've circled in red. If Figure 7.28 represents a circuit $K_2(a, b, c)$, then

Venn and Now

Figure 7.28

A three-term Karnaugh map $K(a, b, c) = b$. (a) The map. (b) A square of 1s.

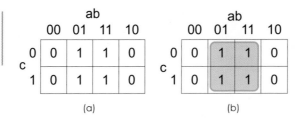

(a)

(b)

Figure 7.29

A four-term Karnaugh map $K(a, b, c, d) = c + abc + b'$. (a) The map. (b) A 2-by-4 rectangle, a 1-by-2 rectangle, and a 2-by-2 square of 1s. (c) Seeing the green square in part (b) by placing copies of the map side by side.

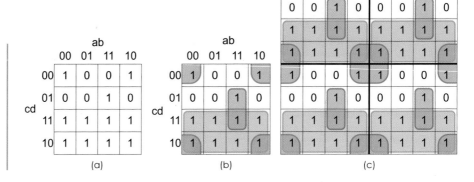

(a)

(b)

(c)

$K_2(a, b, c) = b$. In other words, inputs a and c are irrelevant, which we can tell just by looking at the diagram.

Now let's get interesting and look at a circuit with four variables. As before, I'll pair them up and lay them out in gray code order, as in Figure 7.29. I've decided to try to simplify this circuit by identifying rectangles of ones, and I've found three such rectangles in Figure 7.29(b). The blue and red rectangles are straightforward, but the four green regions don't look much like a single square. To see why they can be considered to be a square, take a look at Figure 7.29(c), where I've simply laid out multiple copies of the map side by side. The gray code layout makes this a valid approach, because even across map boundaries, we are only changing one bit. In other words, you can pick any 4-by-4 block out of Figure 7.29(c) and you're still working with the original problem.

In this example, the red rectangle corresponds to simply c, the blue one to abc, and the green one to b'. So if Figure 7.29(c) is circuit K_3, then $K_3(a, b, c, d) = c + abc + b'$ (remember that in this context, + means "or").

Another pair of four-term examples is worked in Figure 7.30. You can see that the larger the blocks, the simpler the resulting expression.

Figure 7.30

Two more four-term Karnaugh maps. (a) $K(a, b, c, d) = a'b'c' + a'c'd' + a'b'd' + ab'c' + ab'd'$. (b) $K(a, b, c, d) = (ab + bd + cd + bc)'$.

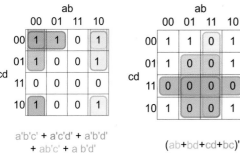

a'b'c' + a'c'd' + a'b'd'
+ ab'c' + a b'd'

(a)

(ab+bd+cd+bc)'

(b)

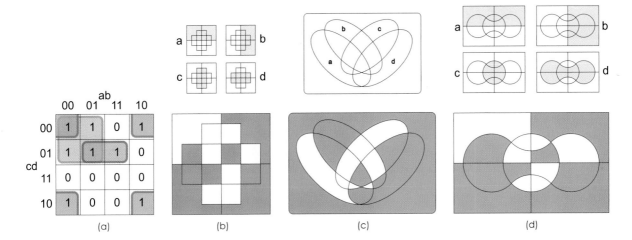

Figure 7.31

The same four-element data in four different visual representations. (a) A Karnaugh map. (b) Carroll's quadrilateral diagram. (c) Venn's four-ellipse diagram. (d) Edwards's four-element diagram.

The connection between Karnaugh maps and the logic diagrams we've been using so far is made explicit in Figure 7.31. Here I've plotted the same data in four different visual maps.

GEOMETRY

If you like geometry, you might want to sit down and figure out how to make an Edwards diagram like the one I show in Figure 7.22.

I only had an image to work from and originally assumed that the curves were just hand-drawn lobes that looked nice. But as I was drawing a version of this diagram by hand, it seemed to me that all the curves were crossing the inner circle perpendicularly to the circle itself. To check this hypothesis, I wrote a program to draw the curves in this way. The results look great, and it sure beats the heck out of drawing the image by hand.

It's actually not that tricky. Figure 7.32 shows the basic geometry. We start with a circle $\mathbf{C}_1$, with center C_1 and radius r_1, and two points on that circle, which I've labeled A and B. Our goal is to find circle $\mathbf{C}_2$,

Figure 7.32

The geometry for Edwards' construction of Figure 7.22. (a) The main circle C1 and the two points A and B that we're given, and the circle C2 that we want to find. (b) Some labels. Point M = (A + B)/2. (c) A triangle extracted from part (b). (d) Another triangle from part (b).

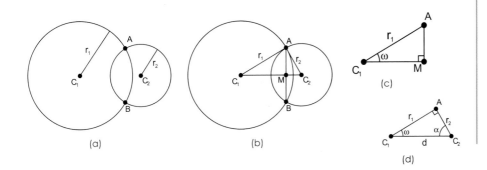

with center C_2 and radius r_2. Circle $\mathbf{C}_2$ crosses $\mathbf{C}_1$ at points A and B, and is perpendicular to $\mathbf{C}_2$ at each crossing.

Although the goals are different, the geometry here has a lot in common with the pop-up card geometry we saw in Chapter 1, Figure 1.5. I love how basic geometrical relationships like this keep cropping up in such different contexts.

To find $\mathbf{C}_2$, we can augment Figure 7.32(a) with some extra construction lines, as in Figure 7.32(b). Symmetry tells us that C_2 lies on a line that passes through C_1 and point M, the midpoint of segment AB. From this diagram we can extract the triangle in Figure 7.32(c). We want to find the angle ω, which is easy because we know the lengths of all three sides of the triangle:

$$\omega = \tan^{-1}\left(\frac{||A - M||}{||M - C_1||}\right)$$

From Figure 7.32(b) we can also extract the triangle in Figure 7.32(d). Note that $\alpha = (\pi/2) - \omega$. The Law of Sines is useful here; recall that it tells us that in any triangle, the ratio of the length of any leg to the sine of the angle opposite it is the same for all three legs. Using this, we can write

$$\frac{r_2}{\sin \omega} = \frac{r_1}{\sin \alpha} = \frac{d}{\sin(\pi/2)}$$

Since $\sin(\pi/2) = 1$, we have

$$d = \frac{r_1}{\sin \alpha} = \frac{r_1}{\sin((\pi/2) - \omega)}$$

Great! This gives us the distance d from C_1 to C_2. Now we just have to find the radius r_2, which also comes from the same Law of Sines relation above:

$$r_2 = d\sin \omega$$

To actually find the center C_2, we just find the vector from C_1 to M, normalize it to unit length, and then scale it up by the distance d:

$$C_2 = C_1 + d\frac{M - C_1}{||M - C_1||}$$

Now that we know $\mathbf{C}_2$, we can draw the Edwards diagram. We just choose alternating arcs (the one inside the circle and the one outside) as we work our way around the inner circle, stepping points A and B around the circle in lockstep.

You can generate as many generations of the Edwards diagram that you want by simply chopping the big circle into smaller and smaller pieces. I created all of the Edwards-style figures printed here with this algorithm.

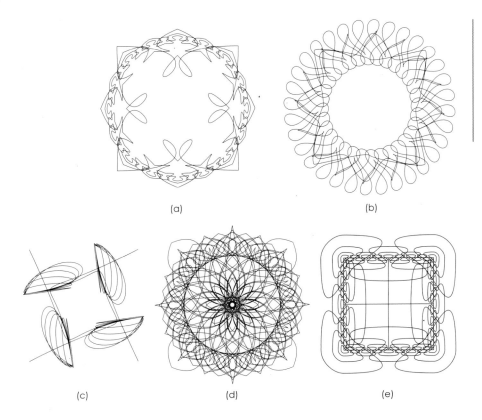

(a)　　　　　　　　　　　　(b)

(c)　　　　　　　(d)　　　　　　　(e)

Figure 7.33

Some out-takes. These pictures came up while I was debugging the program that drew Figure 7.22 through Figure 7.25. It's always surprising to me how simple changes in the code can produce such different results.

Bart Barenbrug suggested a nice geometric alternative for finding C_2 and r_2. Since C_2 lies on the line from C_1 through M, we can write $C_2 = C_1 + q(M - C_1)$. As before, $M = (A + B)/2$. We also note that because the circles are perpendicular at point A, the dot product of their radii will be zero: $(C_1 - A) \cdot (C_2 - A) = 0$. Plugging in the value of C_2 above into this equation, we get

$$(C_1 - A) \cdot (C_1 + q(M - C_1) - A) = 0.$$

If we expand this out and simplify for q, we get

$$q = \frac{(C_1 - A) \cdot (A - C_1)}{(C_1 - A) \cdot (M - C_1)}$$

We now plug this value of q into the formula for C_2, and then find $r_2 = |C_2 - A|$. Voila!

Debugging graphical programs like this can be as much fun as cooking them up. While I was getting a generalized version of this to work for Figures 22 through 25 I generated a whole lot of interesting "outtakes"; Figure 7.33 shows some of my favorites.

3D

Now that we've talked about creating Venn diagrams in the plane, how about going into three dimensions? Are there any interesting developments to be found by drawing our diagrams on the surface of three-dimensional objects such as spheres and donuts? Or how about creating bona-fide three-dimensional diagrams, say by replacing the circles of the classic 3-Venn diagram with spheres? I don't know the answers to these questions, but I bet it would be a lot of fun to explore them and find out.

FURTHER READING

One of my primary references for this material was the excellent paper, "A Survey of Venn Diagrams" by Frank Ruskey (*The Electronic Journal of Combinatorics*, February, 1997). Ruskey goes into much more detail on many of the topics I've covered here. It is also available online at http://www.combinatorics.org/Surveys/ds5/VennEJC.html.

The construction of Figure 7.22 due to Anthony Edwards appears in "Venn Diagrams for Many Sets" by Anthony W. F. Edwards (*New Scientist*, 7 January 1989, 51–56).

Karnaugh maps were first introduced in the classic paper "The Map Method for Synthesis of Combinational Logic Circuits" by Maurice Karnaugh, (*Transactions of the AIEE*. Part I, 72(9), 1953, 593–599).

Grünbaum's ellipses in Figure 7.21 were originally published in "Venn Diagrams and Independent Families of Sets" by Branko Grünbaum (*Mathematics Magazine*, 48, Jan–Feb 1975, 12–23).

Symbolic Logic by Lewis Carroll was originally published in 1896. It has been reprinted in a single volume called *Symbolic Logic and Game of Logic* (Dover Publications, New York, 1955). The second half of this book contains hundreds of syllogisms; the author intended to help readers develop fluency with the notions and the mechanics by presenting the working-out of syllogisms as a two-player competitive game.

My quotes from Lewis Carroll's books *Alice's Adventures in Wonderland* (1865) and *Through the Looking-Glass* (1872) came from the public-domain editions of these classics at Project Gutenberg: http://www.gutenberg.net.

DMorph

8

From Ovid to Kafka, the idea of metamorphosis has been a powerful literary metaphor. More recently, it has become a common but strong visual device.

Image metamorphosis became a sensation in 1992 when Pacific Data Images produced Michael Jackson's video "Black or White," which showed viewers a variety of people seamlessly changing from one into another. In almost no time at all, *morphing* was everywhere, from movies to television.

Image morphing is an artist-driven process. A creative human being looks at the images (or sequences) to be bridged, and determines a way to make the change that will be pleasing to the viewer and harmonious with the piece.

In this chapter I'll talk about a technique I've developed for automatically and smoothly turning one convex three-dimensional shape into another.

Like any automatic morph method, this technique should be viewed as a tool and not a self-guided process.

The critical reason for this is that a morph doesn't simply transform two images or shapes. Much more significantly, it says something about those shapes. If I turn a human face into another human face, I'm saying that these faces are essentially similar, and that only small changes are needed to turn one into another. Indeed, that was the whole message of "Black or White," and it is why the technique was so perfect for that subject.

Suppose that we want to turn a picture of a giraffe into a picture of a rhinoceros. Probably we'd turn the giraffe's body and feet into the rhino's body and feet, which implicitly tells the viewer that these are both quadrupeds. So we're saying something by our choice of what goes to what.

Now suppose we're working on a movie where the evil villain keeps a rattlesnake as a pet, and at one point we want to morph from the snake into the bad guy holding a gun. We could turn the snake's head into the man's head, and grow arms and feet from the rest of the snake's body. But we might want to emphasize the bad guy's nature by turning the snake's rattle into his head. Or we might choose to turn the snake's rattle into the gun, and grow the other body parts from the snake's body. These are all pretty cheesy transformations from a storytelling point of view, but each one says something different about the correspondence between the snake and the man and his weapon. There's no way a computer can choose among these for us; it's an artistic decision motivated by what we want the transformation to say.

FIGURING CHANGE

The problems of artistic choice in a transformation are no less important for shapes than they are for images.

The essential problem is that of *feature matching*, or determining which elements of one shape should correspond to elements of the other shape.

Automatic feature-matching tools can be used to get a good starting guess, subject to an ensuing adjustment by an artist. Alternatively, an artist can use a program to manually correspond features (e.g., by telling the computer that the front-left foot of a giraffe should turn into the front-left foot of a rhino). Then the computer can do its best to make the rest of the shape move in a reasonable way as the features move.

Let's look at how people have done things in two dimensions. Perhaps the simplest way to transform two polygonal shapes S_0 and S_1 is to require that they each have the same number of vertices, numbered clockwise, and identify the first vertex v_0 in each shape. Then to morph the shapes, we move v_0 from its position in S_0 to its position in S_1, and do the same with all the other vertices. The result is often acceptable as long as the two shapes are pretty simple, as in Figure 8.1.

Figure 8.1

A simple two-dimensional morph between two shapes with the same number of vertices.

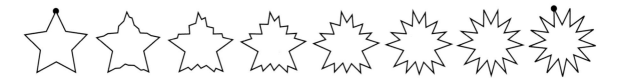

But requiring both shapes to have the same number of vertices is a tough constraint, often meaning we have to manually add or remove vertices to get the right number on each, which can be a lot of work for big shapes. An alternative is to compute the least common multiple of the number of vertices in each shape. For example, if S_0 has five vertices and S_1 has 13, then their least common multiple is 65. A system can run around each shape and automatically insert vertices between the existing ones to bring both up to 65. Typically it tries to spread them out as evenly as possible. A result of this process for two very similar figures is shown in Figure 8.2, and it looks pretty good.

Unfortunately, when the figures are dissimilar, the results are much more disappointing, as shown in Figure 8.3. The tangled knot that appears at the halfway point is a very common result of this technique.

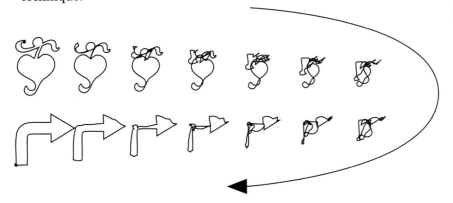

Figure 8.2

A morph where the system inserted new vertices into both shapes so they both had the same number of points.

Figure 8.3

Automatic morphs often get tangled up in the middle as vertices pass through each other en route to their destinations.

There are many more ways to look at this problem, both manually and automatically. For example, Tom Sederberg and colleagues took a sophisticated approach that involved blending the edge lengths and vertex angles of the two shapes being morphed.

The automatic morphing problem is tough because algorithmic solutions cannot substitute for artistic judgment, and manual solutions are very time-consuming and repetitive.

The three-dimensional morphing problem is just like the two-dimensional morphing problem, only a lot harder.

Many three-dimensional systems let us easily transform one shape into another as long as they both have the same number of vertices, arranged into the same number of faces. Such packages let animators create "morph targets" that can then be blended together. For example, we might carefully construct a three-dimensional model of someone's face. We could then painstakingly move the vertices of that face around until the person is smiling happily, and save that as the "smile" target. Similarly, we could make targets for "frown," "grin," "cry," and so on. Then if someone walks into a birthday party and cries with pleasure, we might tell the system to take the original, neutral face and add in 50% of the displacement to get to the "happy" face, and another 50% of the displacement to get to the "crying" face. Obviously for real performance the technique is much more subtle, but the basic idea stays the same.

This morph-target approach is very useful for lip-synching animated characters. The animator makes targets for the standard mouth positions (e.g., pursed lips for "o," and tongue between the teeth for "th"), and then dials in the appropriate target to match the words in the soundtrack.

Morph targets don't work very well when the models don't have the same topology (that is, the same numbers of vertices connected the same way into faces). Many systems don't support morphing at all when the topologies are different. Part of the problem is that there's just no clear way of making the shapes match up. In two dimensions, we could run around the perimeter of the shape and add new vertices as needed. But in three dimensions, choosing the locations of new vertices is much less well specified.

Even when the models have the same topologies, if the deformation from one morph target to the next is too extreme, the shape can crumple into itself just like the two-dimensional example of Figure 8.3.

There are lots of ways you can think of to fix this problem, and it's fun to dream up heuristics that work in one kind of special case or another. But nobody's yet found an automatic method that is both general and efficient enough to be widely adopted.

DMORPH

I wanted to find an automatic technique for morphing polygonal objects that wouldn't demand that the shapes have the same numbers of vertices and faces. Being automatic, it would be appropriate either for things that happen in the background, or as a starting point for manual tweaking.

The method, which I call *DMorph*, is robust and fast. It does have one important limitation, though: it only works for *convex* objects. Convex objects are those that have no holes or indentations. One way to test if an object is convex or not is to imagine moving around inside it with a piece of string. Pick any two points inside the object, and pull the string taut between them. If the string never goes outside of the shape for any pair of points, then it's convex (otherwise, we say it's non-convex, or *concave*). Convex objects can have flat sides, like a cube, or they can be curved, like a sphere. Convex objects include soccer balls, loaves of bread, and Egyptian pyramids. Objects like bagels, puppies, and chairs are concave.

Another way to think about convexity that will be helpful is to start with a convex blob (say a big sphere) and slice off a piece of it with a straight razor. As long as that's all you do, your object will still be convex after every slice.

Let's get a feeling for DMorph with a two-dimensional analogy: we'll turn a triangle into a rectangle. Note that these two shapes have different numbers of points and edges. This will be no problem for us.

Rather than represent the triangle as three vertices and the three edges that join them, I'll instead represent it as the intersection of three half-planes. Figure 8.4(a) shows the idea. We build three planes

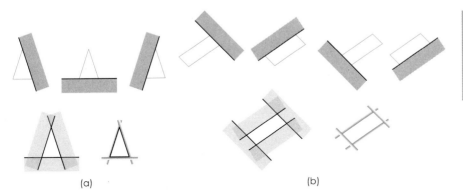

(a)   (b)

Figure 8.4

Defining convex objects as the intersection of planes. (a) A triangle made by three planes. (b) A rectangle made by four planes.

perpendicular to the plane of the paper, and each one cuts the paper into an "inside" in front of the plane, and an "outside" behind it. The triangle is simply that region of the paper that is inside all three planes. Figure 8.4(b) shows the same thing for our rectangle, which is defined by its own set of four planes.

We'll create our morphs by moving these planes around and finding the area inside them.

Figure 8.5

Moving the three planes of the triangle along their normals until they just enclose the rectangle. Parts (a) through (c) show each plane moving independently until it is just touching the outside of the rectangle. Part (d) shows the final position of the planes.

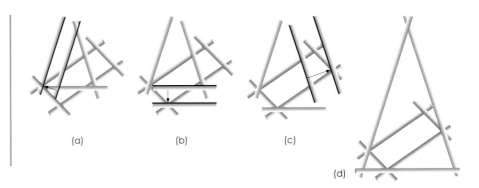

We begin by taking the four planes of the triangle and moving each one until it it hugs the rectangle as closely as possible, as in Figure 8.5. Although in the figure I've drawn the planes with line segments, in theory they go on forever in both directions. So all we need to do is move each plane forward (or backward) along its normal until it's got the rectangle sitting right on its positive side.

The result is in Figure 8.5(e). These are the ending positions for the three planes that define the triangle. Their starting positions are where they sit to define the triangle, that is, where they appear in Figure 8.5(a).

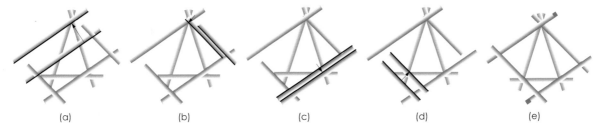

Figure 8.6

Moving the four planes of the rectangle along their normals until the just enclose the triangle. Parts (a) through (d) show each plane moving independently until it is just touching the outside of the triangle. Part (e) shows the final position of the planes. Note that the shape formed by these planes is not simply a scaled-up version of the original rectangle, which is long and skinny.

Now we do the same thing for the rectangle's planes. This time their positions in Figure 8.6(a) are their ending positions. We move each plane forward or backward until it abuts the triangle on its positive side, and that marks its starting position. The result is in Figure 8.6(e). Note that this isn't just a scaled version of the rectangle. Because each plane moves individually, the shape formed by the planes in these positions is only reminiscent of the original rectangle.

That's the entire setup. To create the morph, we simply move all seven planes in unison from their starting positions to their ending positions. The shape that's formed by their intersection at each step is the morph!

Figure 8.7 shows this process in action. The red planes came from the triangle, and the blue ones came from the rectangle. I've marked

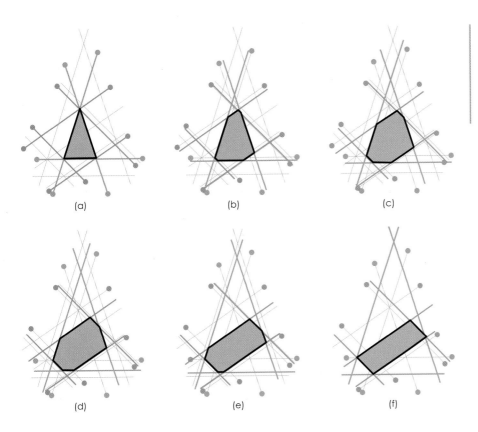

(a) (b) (c)

(d) (e) (f)

Figure 8.7

During the transformation we move each plane from its starting location to its ending location. The morph is that region of space on the positive side of all the planes.

the starting position of each plane with a pair of dots. You can see that at each step we just move each plane along its normal, and the shape that's formed inside them is the morph at that step.

Figure 8.8 shows the shapes from this process stacked up so that you can see how they change over time.

That's it! In three dimensions, it's precisely the same algorithm, except we use three-dimensional planes and three-dimensional vertices. Just treat each face of the starting polyhedron as a plane, and move those planes from their starting locations to the spots where they just barely enclose the ending polyhedron. At the same time, move the planes defining the ending polyhedron from their locations just outside the starting shape to their resting spots.

The result is that the original shape seems to get larger while the

Figure 8.8

Two views of the morphs of Figure 8.7 stacked on top of each other.

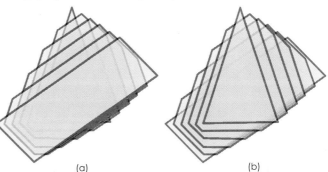

(a) (b)

193

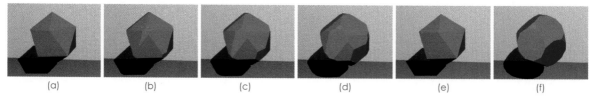

(a)   (b)   (c)   (d)   (e)   (f)

Figure 8.9

Six steps in a three-dimensional morph from an icsoahedron to a truncated dodecahedron.

(a)   (b)   (c)   (d)   (e)   (f)

Figure 8.10

Six steps in a three-dimensional morph from a small rhombicuboctahedron to the dual of a great rhombicosidodecahedron.

(a)   (b)   (c)   (d)   (e)   (f)

Figure 8.11

Six steps in a three-dimensional morph from a small rhombicosidodecahedron to the dual of a twisted pentagonal prism.

(a)   (b)   (c)   (d)   (e)   (f)

Figure 8.12

Six steps in a three-dimensional morph from a great rhombicuboctahedron to the dual of a truncated dodecahedron.

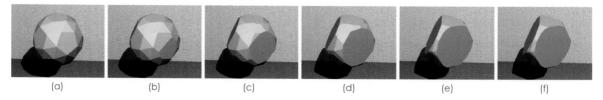

(a)   (b)   (c)   (d)   (e)   (f)

Figure 8.13

Six steps in a three-dimensional morph from a snub dodecahedron to a truncated tetrahedron.

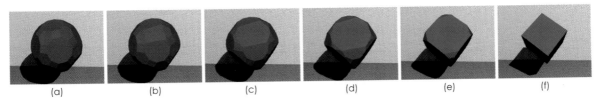

Figure 8.14

Six steps in a three-dimensional morph from a great rhombicosidodecahedron to a cube.

final shape is getting smaller, and the morph is that region of space where they overlap.

Figures 8.9 through 8.14 show a variety of three-dimensional morphs. To make a chain of more than two transformations, just string together a series of two-object morphs.

Note that the objects don't have to be in any specific position relative to each other. If you're morphing a lemon at one end of a table into an orange at the other end, the intermediate shapes will be nice blends of the two shapes and will appear on the table moving from one location to the other.

Of course, you could extend this algorithm easily to handle three or more shapes, which you can blend together to any degree you wish.

The algorithm is nice because it doesn't require anything except the two objects, and they don't have to have any specific properties except that they're both convex.

PROGRAMMING

I implemented an early version of this idea many years ago in the Cedar programming environment at Xerox PARC. I had to write my own code to create the models, find the planes, clip polygons, fill holes, do planar CSG (Constructive Solid Geometry), and more. Some of these steps are very tricky, because there are special cases that can wreak havoc on the integrity of your models, and this algorithm invites some of those special cases.

For example, suppose you're in the process of constructing a morph. You have a three-dimensional polyhedron, and a plane, and you want to cut away those parts of the polyhedron that are in back of the plane. Easy enough, except when one or more vertices are just touching the plane. Then numerical precision becomes very important. Just as important is numerical consistency: if the vertex is considered to be just barely in front of the plane for one polygon, it needs to be evaluated the same way for the next polygon. This becomes an even more critical problem when a polygon lies just about in the plane itself.

One must be very careful to classify all the vertices the same way, and do it consistently.

You can get all of these details right, but it's hard work. Life is much better when you can get someone else to do the hard work!

To that end, the code I wrote for this algorithm is actually in three pieces, each in its own language.

1. VRML to Text via Perl

I wanted to test the algorithm with a bunch of complex but interesting models. Many cool convex polyhedra are available for free on the web in the VRML format. I decided they would serve as my test objects.

I chose to make my life easy by using text-only VRML files that contain a single object in point-polygon format.

I simply read up the whole file, and then search it for the pieces I need using a little script written in Perl. To get the vertices, I look for a list of numbers in square brackets that are preceded by the keyword "Coordinate." To find the polygons, I similarly look for a list of numbers in square brackets preceded by the keyword "CoordIndex." In both cases I simply pull out the numbers in brackets, apply a little reformatting to them, and then print them out to a new text file.

2. Text to MAXScript via C#

The next stage of the system takes that text file and creates a new text file in the MAXScript language, used by Discreet's 3ds max 5.

This program is written in C#. I read in the text files for the two objects I want to morph, and for each one I compute the planes that make up the object.

To find the plane for each polygon, I just take the first three points of the polygon (if they're colinear, I keep moving the three-point window forward until I find three points that aren't colinear). Let's call these points v_0, v_1, and v_2. I find the vectors $\mathbf{A} = v_1 - v_0$ and $\mathbf{B} = v_1 - v_2$, and find their cross product $\mathbf{C} = \mathbf{A} \times \mathbf{B}$. I normalize $\mathbf{C}$ by scaling it to a length of 1, giving me the plane normal $\mathbf{N}$. Any point $\mathbf{P}$ on the plane satisfies the plane equation $\mathbf{N} \cdot \mathbf{P} + d = 0$, so I plug in v_0 for $\mathbf{P}$ and solve for d. Together, $\mathbf{N}$ and d tell me how this plane is oriented in space, and how far it is from the origin.

Once I have all of the planes for both objects, it's time to find their starting and ending positions. Since the planes don't rotate, all I need to find is the values of d that specify these two extremes; I call them d_0

and d_1. Each plane moves during a morph from d_0 at the start to d_1 at the end. This is why I call the algorithm *DMorph*.

Let's start with the first object, S_0. Since its planes begin where they were computed, I set $d_0 = d$ for each plane. To start the process of finding d_1 for this plane, I grab the first vertex of S_1, and move the plane so it includes that vertex. Then I test every remaining vertex S_1 one by one, and if it is on the negative side of the plane, I move the plane by computing a new value of d so that it includes the vertex. When I'm done, the final value of d for that plane is saved as d_1. I repeat this process for all the planes in S_0.

The planes for S_1 are handled the same way, but in reverse: each plane is moved when needed so that all the vertices of S_0 are on its positive side, its original value is saved in d_0, and the computed value is saved in d_1.

Next I merge the two lists of planes together. From now on, the fact that they originally belonged to two different objects is lost. All I need to have around now is this one combined list of planes.

Now I open up a new text file and start writing MAXScript into it. Let's suppose that I've told the program to create an animation that takes n steps to go from the start shape to the ending shape. For each frame f from $[0, n)$ the process is the same.

I first create a very large box, centered at the origin (I call this box "the marble," like the slab of marble a sculptor starts with before he starts cutting away at it). Then I compute $\alpha = f/(n - 1)$, which gives me a floating point number from 0 to 1 telling me where I am in the animation. For each plane in the combined list, I compute the value of d at this time as $d_f = d_0 + \alpha(d_1 - d_0)$. To cut the box using this plane, I use a technique provided by 3ds max called a *slice modifier*. This is a plane that can be set up to simply cut the model and remove everything that is behind it.

I create a new slice modifier for each plane. Using the plane's normal and this value of d_f, I build up matrices to rotate and position the slicer so that it's sitting where the plane is located. I then tell 3ds max to cap any holes produced by the slicing (using a *cap_holes* modifier), and then I collapse the modifier stack so that I'm back to just a single, simple object. Then I cut it again with the next plane, and so on again and again until I've processed every plane. The last step is to tell the program that this cut-up box is visible at frame f, but invisible at all frames before and after.

Now I deselect the box, increment the frame counter f, and start over again with a new piece of marble.

3. MAXScript to Image via 3ds max

This is the easy part! I just open up 3ds max and tell MAXScript to evaluate the text file produced by the previous step. After a little chugging away, the result is an animation of the first shape turning into the other, ready for rendering.

Because I can rely on 3ds max to handle all the delicate work of numerical accuracy and stability in the clipping phase, I save myself a ton of hard work. This is a really satisfying way to do geometry!

WRAPPING UP

Like any algorithm, DMorph has pros and cons.

On the pro side, it's satisfyingly simple and robust, and easy to program. It doesn't place any constraints on the two objects being interpolated except that they're convex. One object can be a 200-sided cone where 200 polygons all share a single vertex, and the other object a 37-sided baseball, and the algorithm doesn't care. There's no feature matching, automatic or otherwise. The transformations are smooth, and the blending looks very nice.

On the con side, the program is limited to convex objects. If you look around, you'll probably see very few convex objects in the environment around you. Umbrellas, trees, and paper clips are all concave. So are pianos, people, and giraffes. DMorph doesn't help us with these objects, much less any really wacky transformations that we might want to do, such as turning a paper clip into the Golden Gate Bridge.

That's okay, though. It just means we have another interesting problem around to think about!

FURTHER READING

You can read about Sederberg's blending algorithm in "2D Shape Blending: An Intrinsic Solution to the Vertex Path Problem," by Thomas W. Sederberg, Peisheng Gao, Guojin Wang, Hong Mu (*Proceedings of SIGGRAPH* 93, pp. 15–18, 1993).

A great VRML library of polyhedra in WRL format is at the kaleido website, http://www.math.technion.ac.il/~rl/kaleido/. The Geometry Center, as always, provides a great resource at http://www.geom.uiuc.edu/software/weboogl/zoo/polyhedra.wrl.html. The sculptor George Hart provides a huge number of polyhedra, including many obscure ones, at his site http://www.georgehart.com/virtual-polyhedra/vp.html.

Everyday Computer Graphics

9

People today are using augmented reality to analyze complex molecular geometry, perform surgery, and figure out how the weather works. Some groups are also experimenting with augmented reality in more everyday settings. Today's technology is frequently pretty awkward, heavy, and obtrusive. But soon enough we'll reach the day when we all can pop on a pair of glasses with little computer displays embedded within them, and they'll be in wireless contact with a fancy portable computer in our pocket or backpack, or even sewn into our belt. The glasses will also have cameras on them, so the computer can see what we're seeing.

Our pocket computers will know everything we're seeing and hearing; they'll know where we are, thanks to built-in GPS (Global Positioning System) receivers; and they'll know all about our personal history and preferences (because, after all, these are truly personal computers). I certainly hope that a strong security system will keep all of this information utterly private.

If augmented reality were everywhere, then we could use it for casual, small things that would simply make our daily lives a bit easier. Of course, I'm hardly the first person to think about using augmented reality for everyday tasks. You can catch up with the current state of the art by checking out the Further Reading section. There are even entire conferences devoted to wearable computers, where people frequently talk about some of these issues.

Here I'll suggest some of the applications that I'd like to have available for personal or individual use on an everyday basis. Their

(a)

(b)

(c)

Figure 9.1

Finding a place to park. (a) Where can I park in this slushy, filled lot? (b) This map is helpful. (c) Even better, an open space is marked in red.

common thread is that there's almost no text involved; rather, graphics do all the work.

ON THE ROAD

There's nothing quite like the joy of driving around a parking lot looking for a space. You crawl along, looking for spots, avoiding the occasional pedestrian, and then always seeing a space open up where you were a moment ago just in time for someone else to grab it. When you're driving around inside a garage, you get the added pleasure of inhaling the exhaust fumes of the people in front of and behind you, who are also trolling for spaces.

Figure 9.1(a) shows a parking lot I needed to park in a few years ago. One big help would be a picture of the lot itself, as in Figure 9.1(b), so we can at least see where it is we're going. But even better, we can indicate which spaces are open, as in Figure 9.1(c). Just go to one of the red spots and park.

How will the signboard know which spaces are free? If the day is clear, it can use satellite imagery. Alternatively, little magnetic sensors under each space could report back to the signboard whether or not there's a car over them. Such sensors are showing up all over and are used today for everything from counting how many cars get onto a ferry to enforcing the speed limit on some highways.

Figure 9.2

(a) If the sign of Figure 9.1 is obscured by weather, parking's still a hassle. (b) Unless you can open a dynamic map inside. (c) A close-up of the map.

(a)

(b)

(c)

If the weather is awful, it might be hard to make out the signboard. Then we could put the signboard into the car. Into the dashboard of Figure 9.2(a) let's install a little pull-out drawer, as in Figure 9.2(b). It's got a small display that can receive a signal from the signboard; a close-up is in Figure 9.2(c). Of course, if the car has any other internal displays, like an on-board map readout, that display could be used temporarily for parking information as well.

Figure 9.3

(a) Where did I park?
(b) Oh, right over there.

GETTING HOME

The remote-control door opener is the modern dowsing rod. Once you've parked your car somewhere and spent the day, you have to remember where you parked in order to get home again. I spend too much time hunting for my car. Other people have the same problem, and I'm

(a)

(b)

increasingly hearing cars honk and beep as their owners walk around a garage, pushing the lock and unlock buttons on their remotes in hopes of hearing a familiar sound they can follow to its source. When you get a few people walking around a concrete parking garage like this, in the midst of a cacophony of empty cars honking and blinking their lights, calling to their owners, everyone's individual search gets more difficult, and the whole scene becomes surreal and somewhat deafening.

But if the computer in your pocket can determine when the computer in your car turns off, then it knows where you parked your car. Then anytime you return to that endless parking lot, as in Figure 9.3(a), you can just ask the system where your car was when you left it and get an immediate and precise answer, as in Figure 9.3(b). You won't have to play a game of Hotter-and-Colder with your car horn anymore.

Figure 9.4

(a) Where was I sitting?
(b) Oh, right over there.

LOST AND FOUND

As Lady Bracknell said in Oscar Wilde's *The Importance of Being Earnest*, "To lose one parent, Mr. Worthing, may be regarded as a misfortune; to lose both looks like carelessness." How much worse than losing your car, then, is it to lose your friends.

(a)

(b)

At any big outdoor concert, like the one at the Seattle Zoo in Figure 9.4(a), there are going to be lots of people. If you need to leave your friends for some reason, getting back to them can be difficult. If people are sitting close together, walking around and looking for your friends becomes a tough proposition. But since your pocket computer has a built-in GPS receiver, you can just ask it where you were a few minutes ago, and it can point the way immediately, as in Figure 9.4(b).

Figure 9.5

(a) I'm in time for the big 4th of July fireworks, but my friends got there before me. Where are they? (b) Oh, right over there.

(a)   (b)

Sometimes you show up a little late to an event, and your friends are already there. Even if you climb up to the top of a hill, as in Figure 9.5(a), it's tough to find your friends. Even binoculars many not help. But if your pocket computer can talk to theirs, the two machines can compare their locations, and you can go right to them, as in Figure 9.5(b).

Figure 9.6

I've been to this building in Seattle, but I'm still not sure what its street address is.

Sometimes you just want to know where it is you actually are. What's the street address of the office building in Figure 9.6? I hope the postman knows; you certainly can't tell from the numbers.

There are times when it's not enough to just know where to go, but you also need a little help figuring out the best route to get there. Road atlas programs work hard to find the fastest or most convenient routes using the highway and road systems. But what if you're in a more natural environment, like that of Figure 9.7(a), and you want to find your campsite? There may be significant topographical information that's relevant to you (you might not want to climb up too steep a hill or have to jump across a deep ravine). Your pocket computer can combine your location, your goal, and knowledge of the intervening topography to suggest the course of Figure 9.7(b).

Figure 9.7

(a) Where is my campsite? (b) Ah, it's that way.

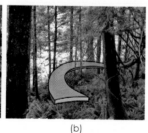

(a)   (b)

This kind of information is also useful in man-made environments. Figure 9.8(a) shows a photo of the Los Angeles Convention Center during SIGGRAPH a few years ago. I arrived early in the morning to prepare for a course, and needed to find the right room. Although

SIGGRAPH has unusually good signage for a conference, you can still get lost or confused in the caverns of the Convention Center. But if you follow the Pac-Man dots in Figure 9.8(b), it's easy to navigate the maze from here to there.

(a)　　　　　　　　　　(b)

Shopping

Snack-food manufacturers just love it when we go the grocery store hungry. We're tempted to grab some of their richly-flavored and richly-textured wares, temporarily unconcerned with the nutritional choices they represent. And of course, those little nutritional labels reveal not just the empty calories, but also a brew of polysyllabic chemicals that is enough to make many of us swear (for a moment, anyway) to eat nothing but tree bark and lettuce for the rest of our lives.

Figure 9.8

(a) Where is the room for my session? (b) Ah, upstairs and to the right.

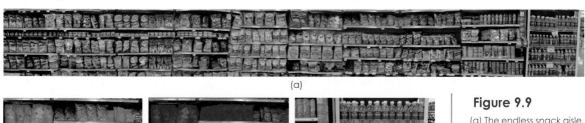

(a)

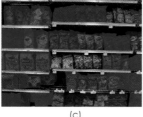

(b)　　　　　　(c)　　　　　　(d)

Figure 9.9

(a) The endless snack aisle. (b) Which ones have a lot of salt? The less obscured, the saltier. (c) Which ones have a lot of fat? (d) Show me calories. (Note that these examples don't represent a real nutritional analysis).

But augmented reality can help us out when we wander down a snack-food aisle like that of Figure 9.9(a). If we're in the mood for something really salty, we could ask the system to rank the foods by how much salt they contain. In Figure 9.9(b) the snacks that have a lot of salt are more visible than those that are less salty. If we're feeling just a little bit health-conscious, we could ask the system to show us how much fat is in one bag relative to another, as in Figure 9.9(c). Finally, we might ask how many calories we're going to snarf down by eating one bag relative to another. I don't know why stores stock shelves the way they do, but Figure 9.9(d) shows us the caloric value of some of the elements at the end of the aisle.

As I discussed in Chapter 1, you can make greeting cards using techniques from origami to pop-up devices. But sometimes a store-

(a)   (b)

Figure 9.10

(a) Do they have any cards with a photo on the front and no message inside? (b) Ah, these two.

(a)   (b)

Figure 9.11

(a) Are there any Granny Smith apples of the size and ripeness I like? (b) Ah, right over here.

bought card is a good choice. One problem with buying a card in the store is that there are often hundreds of cards, and you can only see a little strip along the top of each one. Faced with a display like Figure 9.10(a), how can you find the kind of cards you like?

Many card manufacturers make their catalogs available online. Our pocket computer can scan the display, match the visible bit of each card with the catalogs, and guess at what the cards are. Then we can ask for, say, a picture of a moose, or maybe a card without a prewritten message inside. The system can match those criteria against the catalogs and the visible cards, and point us to just the ones we like, as in Figure 9.10(b).

Buying fruit is a common activity: if we're going to eat it right away, we want something ripe, but if it's going to sit around for a while, we might want something that has a few days to go. It's easy to tell how ripe a banana is just by looking at it, but other fruits are best estimated by feeling them. Some fruits go through subtle visual changes as they ripen. These changes might be too small for us to spot, but a good sensor might be able to pick up on them. If we're looking for a Granny Smith apple that's just right for eating for our tastes from the display of Figure 9.11(a), a pocket computer could spot the best one, as in Figure 9.11(b).

HOME IMPROVEMENT

Keeping track of lots of little things can be hard, even if you try to be careful. Suppose you're visiting a friend, and you take down a CD from his collection in Figure 9.12(a). You're in a mood for New Orleans jazz, so you choose a fine CD called *Dr. John Plays Mac Rebennack*. When you go to put it back, you realize the records are shelved in alphabetical order. Where does this go? Under "D" for Doctor, or "J" for John? Or maybe it should go under "R" for Rebennack, because after all, Dr. John and Mac Rebennack are two names used by the same guy. Where should you put the CD?

Your pocket computer can easily remind you just where you took the CD from, as in Figure 9.12(b), and help you put it right back in its place.

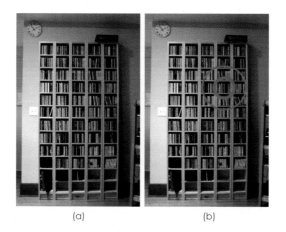

(a) (b)

Figure 9.12

(a) Where does that Dr. John CD go back on the shelf? (b) Ah, right there.

(a) (b)

Figure 9.13

(a) Where is that biography of Thomas Jefferson? (b) Ah, right there.

The same problem goes for books. Let's suppose this time that you're searching for a particular book, but because your shelves are in disarray and look something like Figure 9.13(a), you're not sure where to find it. You can simply tell the system what you want (perhaps as easily as by saying the book's name), and the book you want gets highlighted as in Figure 9.13(b).

How many times have you opened up the refrigerator looking for something to eat? Each time you open the door, of course you let the cold air out and that burns up some energy. To the normal eye, most home refrigerators look like a bulletin board, like the one in Figure 9.14(a). If you had X-ray vision (courtesy of your pocket computer and augmented-reality glasses) you could see just what was inside, as in Figure 9.14(b). If you were planning a trip to the store, you could even ask the system to show you just how much is left inside various containers, as in Figure 9.14(c).

(a)   (b)   (c)

Figure 9.14

(a) I'd like to see what's in the fridge without opening it up and wasting energy. (b) Easily done. But how much milk is left? (c) How much milk, water, and lime juice is still there.

(a)

(b)

Figure 9.15

(a) Where did I pack those items? (b) Ah, in those boxes.

Moving a household is no fun. It's inevitable that you'll lose track of something in one of the dozens of the boxes that seem to accompany even the smallest or most local of moves. Suppose you've moved and you're now unpacking, but you can't find your plates and silverware, or some other specific items you want to lay your hands on. Figure 9.15(a) shows a typical pile of moving boxes; even those with printed information on the box rarely contain what they originally did. But because your pocket computer and glasses were active during the whole packing process, you can simply ask the system where some of your items are located, and, as in Figure 9.15(b), it can immediately show you where to find them.

Telephones are a big part of everyday life. Many people now have a service called Caller ID to help them separate wanted calls from unwanted ones. A Caller ID box usually has a little text display on the front, and when the phone rings, the box shows the number of the phone originating the call, and sometimes the name of the person that owns that phone (or that you've told it to associate with that number).

Even better would be to literally see who's calling. If the phone of Figure 9.16(a) rings, we can tell if it's the doctor, a friend, or the

Figure 9.16

(a) The phone's ringing—who is it? (b) Oh, the doctor. (c) It's a friend. (d) It's the vet.

(a)

(b)

(c)

(d)

(a)   (b)   (c)

(d)   (e)   (f)

vet (Figures 9.16(b) through (d)) just by looking over and seeing who's placed the call. This strikes me as a lot more natural than trying to remember a number, or even reading a name.

Let's take a slight detour from using just augmented-reality glasses, and suppose that we can put displays in the environment. Many companies are pursuing technologies that will ultimately give us flexible displays. Think of these as wallpaper displays: you have a flexible sheet of stuff, you put it up on the wall, and voilà, it's a computer display!

Home offices are a great place to get work done, and you might even have a nice view, like that out the windows of Figure 9.17(a). If we put up some display wallpaper on the windows, as in Figure 9.17(b), then we can change the view to anything we fancy, from a still image or a movie, to a synthetic animation or the live video coming out of a remote camera or webcam. Figures 17(c) through (f) show just a few possibilities.

AVOIDING PRESSURE

Many of us check the weather report before we go out of the house in the morning, but perhaps we could get some value from a report before we come back in again at the end of the day.

Returning to the house of Figure 9.18(a), you might think that everything's just fine and you're in for a warm welcome and a relaxing

Figure 9.17

(a) It would be nice to have another view. (b) Coating the windows with display sheeting. (c) An exciting fire-dancing display. (d) On photo safari. (e) Underwater. (f) Over a lush forest.

Figure 9.18

(a) I wonder what the emotional weather is like inside? (b) Oh. I probably should avoid the kitchen right now.

(a)

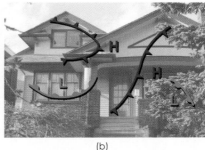
(b)

evening. But of course there's no way of knowing what sort of day the other people inside have had, and they might be feeling a lot of pressure right now. Your dog might have eaten someone's favorite book, and that person might have a pretty frosty expression on his or her face right now.

Enter the pocket computer emotional weather map. Figure 9.18(b) shows us where the high and low pressure zones are in the house right now. Perhaps forgetting someone's birthday is responsible for things looking a little chilly over in the kitchen. Maybe on the basis of this information, we'll decide that it's a good idea to avoid the kitchen for a little while, and just go hide out in the living room until the pressure front moves through.

WRAPPING UP

With a pocket computer and a nice head-mounted display, lots of little everyday tasks can become a lot easier. None of these is anywhere nearly as important as helping surgeons perform operations or analyzing the safety of a nuclear power plant, but if the technology is around, we may find that its everyday, casual uses are just as desirable.

FURTHER READING

There are lots of great papers out there that discussion virtual reality and augmented reality. Some good places to start are "Interface with angels: The future of VR and AR interfaces" by Wolfgang Broll, Leonie Schäfer, Tobias Höllerer, and Doug Bowman (*IEEE Computer Graphics & Applications*, 21(6), November/December 2001, pp. 14–17), and "Exploring MARS: Developing Indoor and Outdoor User Interfaces to a Mobile Augmented Reality System" by T. Höllerer, S. Feiner, T. Terauchi, G. Rashid, and D. Hallaway (*Computers and Graphics*, 23(6), Dec. 1999, pp. 779–785).

Wearable computers are becoming an important research topic. You can read about them in "Embedding Multimedia Presentations in the Real World" by T. Höllerer, S. Feiner, J. Pavlik, Situated Documentaries: (*Proceedings ISWC '99* (Third Int. Symp.on Wearable Computers), October 18–19, 1999, pp. 79–86) "A Wearable Computer System with Augmented Reality to Support Terrestrial Navigation" by B. Thomas, V. Demczuk, W. Piekarski, D. Hepworth, and B. Gunther. (*Proceedings of the Second Int. Symp.on Wearable Computers*, Pittsburgh, PA, October 1998, pp. 168–171), and "Wearable Computing: A First Step Toward Personal Imaging" by S. Mann (*IEEE Computer*, 30(2), February 1997).

Devices that know where they are in the world are capable of acting on that information, as discussed in "Location Aware Mobile Computing" by H. Beadle, B. Harper, G. Maguire Jr., and J. Judge (*Proceedings ICT '97* (IEEE/IEE Int. Conf. on Telecomm.), Melbourne, Australia, 1997) and "WorldBoard—What Comes After the WWW?" by J. Spohrer, 1997 (available at http://www.worldboard.org/pub/spohrer/wbconcept/default.html).

A real-time example of combining the virtual and real worlds with a sense of fun and play is described in "Mixed Reality and the Interactive Imagination" by Christopher Stapleton, Charlie Hughes, and Michael Moshell (*Proceedings of The First Swedish-American Workshop on Modeling and Simulation* (SAWMAS–2002), 2002).

If you're in the mood for some really terrific jazz piano and you're okay with some ambiguity about where to file it on the shelf, I heartily recommend "Dr. John Plays Mac Rebennack: The Legendary Sessions, Vol. 1." The emotional weather map was inspired by the Tom Waits song "Emotional Weather Report" on the album *Nighthawks at the Diner*.

About
Face

10

I love letters. From the squiggly *g* to the stately *m*, our modern alphabet offers a wealth of beautiful shapes.

One of the great benefits of the revolution in desktop publishing is that it's opened up the doors of typeface design to anyone with a computer and patience. Talent and a sense of aesthetics aren't required to create a valid typeface, but they don't hurt.

There are dozens of websites that offer visitors thousands of free typefaces (see the Further Reading section). Most of these free fonts are the work of inspired amateurs who had an idea for a typeface, created it using commercial design tools, and then released their work into the world. You can also buy collections of free typefaces on CD compilations, saving you the trouble of downloading them one by one. And of course commercial foundries offer many professional typefaces created by skilled and trained designers.

I love browsing new typefaces and collecting the ones I like. This collecting pays off when a graphic-design job requires me to pick just the right typefaces to go with the artwork, text, and overall feel of the piece.

I'm pretty discriminating in what I choose to save from the public-domain sites. But when I find one that I like enough to think that it might be useful one day, I'll download it and add it to my collection. The quality of the typographical information provided with a free font varies tremendously: very few include technical information for important details like kerning and hinting, and most are missing at least a few characters like ampersands or semicolons. But if you're willing to live with these limitations, there are some great designs out there.

Between the free typefaces that I've saved from the web, those that I've gotten with magazine CDs and in packages I've purchased, and the commercial typefaces that I've bought for specific jobs, I've now got over 9,000 typefaces on my computer.

Of course, they're not all installed. Every typeface that's installed in an operating system consumes system resources and slows down everyday tasks. Happily, there are several programs out there that let you browse through all the font files on your computer, both those that are installed and those that aren't, and temporarily install the ones you want at a given time.

But 9,000 typefaces is a lot to look through; in practical terms, it's way too many. I recently designed a logo for a company, so I had to look for a good typeface for the company name. Using a commercial font browser, I set the name of the company in the preview window, and then stepped through every typeface on my disk so I could see how the name looked in that font. Since I had to visually consider each one, my top speed was about two fonts per second. A little math shows that if I ground through without a single break, I could have theoretically looked them all over in about an hour and a quarter. In reality, my eyes glaze over after just a couple of minutes of this kind of thing, and it took about four hours to consider the whole collection. When I'd finally finished looking through everything, I knew I never wanted to go through that again.

Categories

Nobody wants to sort through 9,000 typefaces every time they start a new project. Commercial foundries often label their work in a wide variety of categories to make them easier to find. For example, Apple uses 28 different categories such as Blackletter, Cyrillic, Glyphic, Monospaced, Opticals, Ornamentals, and Swash. Planet Typography has a very different set of categories, but they're just as useful.

Searching through categories is great when you have a general feeling for what you want and all of your fonts have been given useful and accurate labels. Unfortunately, almost none of the free fonts have been categorized. In my collection, I have only a few hundred commercial typefaces, and the rest are nothing more than a family name and, if I'm lucky, indication if the font is regular, bold, or italic.

I thought about sitting down and going through all my typefaces and assigning categories to them. This wouldn't be difficult, but it

Figure 10.1

Serifs for the letter F. The top row goes from a letter with clear serifs on the left to a sans-serif letter on the right. On the lower row, you could argue about whether these have serifs at all, or not. Top row: Amery, Freeman Condensed, Antique, Loose Cruse, Castle, Architect, Adams. Bottom row: Cowboy, Epic, Cocoa, Adorable, Freedom 9, Amaze, Banner Light.

would be colossally boring and time-consuming. I could get a head start by using the same categories as one of the commercial catalogs, but still, assigning them one by one to each face would take forever. Even if I wrote a program to help me out, I figured it would take at least a whole day to go through everything. And even then, a huge number of the public-domain typefaces are so oddball that they would end up in the Miscellaneous or Novelty categories, which would defeat the whole point of the exercise.

My next thought was to write a program to do this categorization for me. Happily, I threw that idea out almost immediately. The categories for many of these typefaces are very subjective, and even the most common ones can be unclear. For example, consider the letters in Figure 10.1, and ask yourself which ones should be labeled as serif fonts, and which are sans-serif (broadly speaking, the serif is the little flare at the ends of lines, like the "foot" at the bottom of the letter F in the upper left of Figure 10.1). Reasonable people can hold different opinions on which of these letters have serifs and which don't, and there's no way a computer is going to settle any disputes. Writing a program to reliably detect serifs in even the easiest cases still seems pretty hard to me.

METRICS

If deciding whether or not a character has serifs or not is hard, imagine how much tougher it would be to determine if a typeface should be categorized as "Handwritten" or "Brushstroke." These kinds of quality distinctions would be just about impossible. Yet I wanted some kind of procedural way to help me sort through my collection of fonts. So rather than try to automatically assign qualitative descriptions and labels, I decided to see how far I could get with simple numerical measures.

Of course, other people have looked into developing numerical measures, or metrics, for typefaces. The Panose system specifies about 65 different measurements to help describe a font and distinguish it

About Face

from others. A Panose description of a Latin Text face is made up of ten numbers, one each for the type of family, serif style, weight, proportion, contrast, stroke variation, arm style, letterform, midline, and X-height. To each of these categories you can assign a number drawn from a list of standardized values. For example, "family kind" is set to 2 for Latin Text, and "serif style" is set to 5 if the serifs are of the form the Panose documentation calls "obtuse square cove." If you're looking for a particular typeface, you can figure out what its Panose code would be and then use that code in a directory of fonts to see a sample and identify its name.

Another approach to identifying a particular font is to use a tool that tries to work backwards from one or more characters you already have, to help you find out what typeface they came from. The *Identifont* website leads you through a series of questions about the shape and style of different characters. Using a process of elimination, the site eventually identifies the typeface by name and foundry. If you're just browsing for something interesting, you can answer the questions according to your intuition or how you think your desired font would look, and see what it gives you.

If you have a sample in-hand, you can submit it to the *What The Font?!* site. You simply upload to the site an image of a type sample you have, and it will look through its database to name the font for you.

Neither of these approaches is quite as nice as hunting through a wide variety of typefaces all at once and choosing among them, like flipping through the pages of a font catalog. I wanted to try creating a system that would let me characterize my intentions in some general, high-level way and browse through the typefaces that match those goals, yet not require me to hand-annotate every typeface in my collection with one or more descriptive labels.

I decided to cook up a bunch of different metrics that seemed easy to measure and had a chance of being meaningful, and then write a tool that let me browse through my collection according to how well they met a weighted collection of those metrics.

About Face

Figure 10.2 shows a screenshot of my program, *About Face*, in action. The interface all happens in three windows. I call the top window the *preview window*, the lower left the *control panel*, and the lower right the *font browser*.

Let's start with the control panel in the lower left. The gray section at the top lets us pick which characters are displayed in the font browser, and the text and point size of the sample shown in the preview window.

Below that are six pairs of sliders. Each pair of sliders lets you specify the value for a particular metric, and how much that value should matter. For example, the top metric is *density*, which can take on a value from 0 to 1. To measure density, I typeset the character entered in the *Measure* box (in the top left of the control panel), find its bounding box, and then compute the average density of the character. White is 0, black is 1, and gray values are intermediate. I add up the density of all the pixels and divide by the total number of pixels in the bounding box to get a measure for the density of that character. You can move the *Level* slider from 0 at the left to 1 at the right, describing the density you'd like. Then you adjust the *Weight* slider, again from 0 at the left to 1 at the right. This slider describes how much the density value should factor into the system's choice of font.

There is a pair of sliders for each of the other four metrics, which I'll describe below.

When you press the *Update* button, the system goes through all the fonts in the program's directory and scores the *Measure* character of each font with regard to the metrics. The sorted results are shown in the font browser window in the bottom right. The best result is in the upper left, and descending scores run left-to-right, top-down.

You can click on any font in the font browser window, and the preview window will show you the preview text using that typeface. The name of the window changes to identify the face that's currently displayed.

It's fun to think about what constitutes good preview text. Obviously if you're setting something in particular, like a company name, you'll want to see that text. If you're going to use the typeface in a more general way, you want to get a feeling for its general appearance. One approach is to use a short fragment of text from the copy you're going to set. Another approach is to use a *pangram*, which is a sentence that contains all the letters of the alphabet. The best-known pangram is "The quick brown fox jumps over a lazy dog." Some people enjoy constructing ever-shorter pangrams. The shortest one that I know of that reads like a real sentence, and doesn't use odd abbreviations, is "Sphinx of black quartz, judge my vow." I tend to change the preview text several times as I'm considering a typeface, just to look at different combinations of letters and see how the text feels overall.

In Figure 10.3(a) I've set the desired density to 0, cranked the weight for density all the way up, and set all the other weights to zero. Thus the fonts are sorted so that the lightest (or whitest) is first,

(a)

(b)

Figure 10.3

Looking at the effect of the density metric. The weights for all other metrics are set to 0. (a) Density = 0. (b) Density = 1.

Figure 10.4

Looking at the effect of the aspect ratio metric. The weights for all other metrics are set to 0. (a) Aspect Ratio = 0. (b) Aspect Ratio = 3.

with increasingly darker faces following. In Figure 10.3(b) I moved the desired density to 1, and the darkest letters bubble to the top. If I want to sort on some other letter, I just enter it into the *Measure* box and press *Update* again.

MAKING NEW METRICS

Finding good metrics is the key to making this approach work. I wanted metrics that I could easily compute and that wouldn't require any kind of shape analysis. I thought about many of the standard morphographic measures, but they didn't seem like they'd be of much value in finding fonts.

I eventually settled on a set of five measures. We've already covered density, so let's look at the others.

(a)

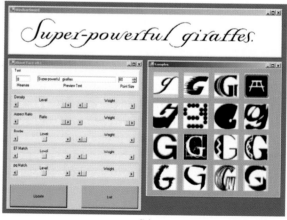

(b)

The *Aspect Ratio* is simply the value of dividing the width of the character's bounding box by its height. Figure 10.4 shows this value set to its minimum and maximum values, with the weights for the other metrics set to 0.

To compute *Border* I run through all the pixels in the character's bounding box and try to determine which are on the character's edge. I do this by thresholding the bitmap of the character to 0 and 1 (I put the breakpoint at 0.5) and looking for black pixels that have at least one eight-connected white neighbor. The number of such pixels, divided by the total number of pixels in the bounding box, gives me an estimate for the length of that character's border. Figure 10.5 shows this value set to its minimum and maximum values, with the weights for the other metrics set to 0.

Figure 10.5

Looking at the effect of the border metric. The weights for all other metrics are set to 0. (a) Border = 0. (b) Border = 1.

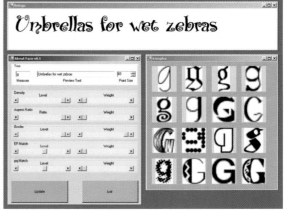

(a)　　　　　　　　　　　　　　　　　(b)

The last two metrics ignore the letter in the *Measure* box and instead check two specific characters in the typeface. The first is the *EF Match*. My thinking is that this match tells me something about the regularity of a typeface. Traditional typefaces, plus many others that have a traditional feeling, tend to have a capital *F* that looks a lot like their capital *E*. Figure 10.6(a) shows a few examples of this. On the other hand, more irregular and free-form typefaces, and those drawn by hand, will have a much weaker match between these letters, as shown in Figure 10.6(b). To measure the similarity between these two letters, I typeset them, align their bounding boxes, and then count the number of pixels that are different in the two bitmaps. I divide this count by the number of pixels in the bounding box, and subtract this ratio from 1, resulting in a value from 0 to 1 telling me how much the *E* and *F* match one another.

About Face

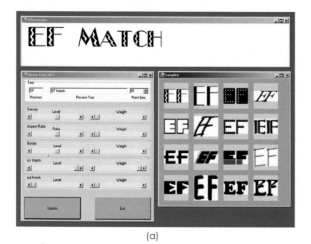 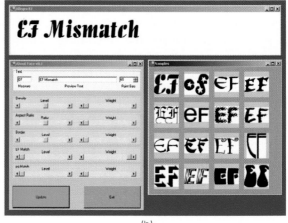

Figure 10.6

Looking at the effect of the *EF Match* metric. The weights for all other metrics are set to 0. (a) *EF Match* = 1 (b) *EF Match* = 0 (this gives higher scores to fonts where the *E* and *F* are as dissimilar as possible).

We've all heard the phrase "mind your p's and q's," which urges us to pay attention to details. This phrase started out as advice to typesetters, who set metal type in frames to create words. These metal letters were shaped backwards so that the text would appear correct when the letters were inked and pressed up against paper. Because the lower-case letters p and q usually looked similar, it was easy to mix them up (the same thing applies to the lower-case b and d, but I don't remember hearing any specific advice regarding those). This aphorism seemed to me a good metric, like the *EF Match* metric, so that's what the last sliders control. I measure this just like the *EF Match*, but I mirror-reverse the q before computing the measure. Figure 10.7(a) shows some p-q pairs that are good matches, and Figure 10.7(b) shows some poor matches.

Figure 10.8 shows the program in action. I played with the sliders for a bit, adjusting the values and the weights, and I was able to follow my instincts to find the kind of letter forms I was after.

EFFICIENCY

As I said earlier, I have thousands of typefaces on my disk. If I had to measure all of these characteristics each time I changed a value, the program would be far too slow to use.

Instead, I precompute all of these metrics for each character in each typeface and save the results in a file (the *EF Match* and *pq Match* metrics are saved only once per face, of course). When I enter a new character into the *Measure* box, I read through the file and pull into memory the values for that character from all the faces. Then each time I move the sliders, it's a simple matter to compute the score.

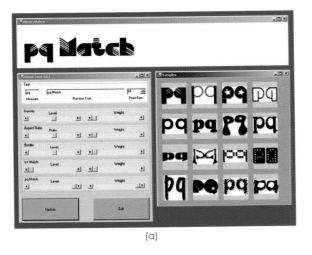

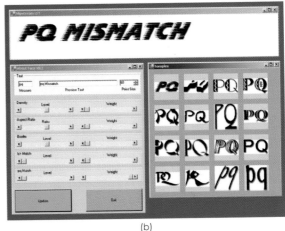

(a)   (b)

To compute a score, let's say that the value for slider i is v_i, and its weight is w_i. In my current system, that means *density* is v_0, *aspect ratio* is v_1, and so on. All of the values, and all of the weights, are between 0 and 1 (the only exception is the value of the desired aspect ratio, which ranges from 0 to 3). I score each font one at a time. I start by looking up the metrics for the character in the *Measure* box. Let's call them p, so the density of that character is p_0, its aspect ratio is p_1, and so on. The highest-scoring character will be the one whose values exactly match the desired values on the sliders; that is, each $p_i - v_i = 0$. Of course, most of the time these values will be different, so we weight the absolute value of the difference by the corresponding weight for that metric, and then add everything up. In symbols, we compute the score S by

$$S = \sum_{i=0}^{5} w_i |v_i - p_i|$$

I could normalize by the sum of the weights, but there's no need since they're the same for all the typefaces, and we only care about the relative scores, not their actual values.

I wrote this program in C# using Microsoft's .NET development environment. This made it easy to create little bitmaps with typeset characters in them. I didn't have to learn how to read or parse the font files themselves, or figure out how to use them to render text. Instead, I just gave the system the font, the text to be set, and a bitmap, and it did the rest.

Figure 10.7

Looking at the effect of the *pq* match metric. The weights for all other metrics are set to 0. (a) *pq* match = 0 (this gives higher scores to fonts where the *p* and *q* are as dissimilar as possible). (b) *pq* match = 1.

Figure 10.8

A snapshot of *About Face* in use.

Each time I press the *Update* button and create a new sorted list of typefaces, I read them into memory one by one, typeset the given character, scale it down if necessary, and then copy it into the browser window. I do this until the browser's filled up.

Then any time I get a mouse click in the browser, I find which box it's in, look up that typeface, and update the preview window accordingly.

It can take a few seconds to measure all the metrics for all the characters in a given font, including all of its variant faces (e.g., bold, italic, condensed, etc.). But once that information is saved away, it's fast to read in and use for updating. I can get new sorted lists almost instantly for databases of a few thousand fonts.

WRAPPING UP

As I mentioned before, the big trick here is figuring out the right set of metrics that make it possible to search through a huge number of fonts efficiently and pleasantly. I approached this system as a testbed: it's pretty easy to add new metrics and try them out, and toss them overboard if they don't measure up.

I probably went through a few dozen metrics before settling on this set of five. They seem pretty reliable at measuring what they're supposed to, and I find that often when I'm searching for some kind of typeface, these let me get in the ballpark. Unfortunately, with so many fonts on my disk, the ballpark is pretty huge. I show the top 36 candidates for each search in the browser window, but I often find myself wishing for more (I wanted to make sure that the characters in the browser window would be legible when printed, so for these figures I temporarily set the browser window to show a 4-by-4 grid of fonts rather than the 6-by-6 grid I use in practice).

I'd like to add a few things to this program. One is a *Next* button, so for example I can see the second-best set of 36 candidates, or the third-best, and so on. I'd also like to add a *More Like This* button, so I can select a typeface and quickly get others that match up with it closely. This can be on the basis of just the selected character in the *Measure* box, or of an overall score for the whole typeface.

On the whole, I'd say that the program is a qualified success and a good start. I can sometimes find good typefaces pretty quickly, and I'm sometimes pleasantly surprised by what I discover. On the other hand, when I have something fairly specific in mind, I've found that these metrics don't let me hone in on my preconceived ideas very closely.

More work on the metrics and the user interface (which is admittedly very crude and just for proof of concept) would definitely pay off in a more pleasant-to-use and robust tool for finding typefaces.

FURTHER READING

All of the fonts in this chapter's figures are from *ClickArt Fonts 2*, published by Broderbund, and the *2000 Font Collection*, published by Greenstreet. Many of the fonts on these CDs are also available for free on the web, but I've found it still worth buying the packages. It's more convenient than downloading them all one by one, of course, but these companies seem to spend some time cleaning up the font files. Many of the free fonts available online have corrupted or badly-formed descriptors in the file, which means that some programs will be able to use a given typeface, but others won't. Of course, you only encounter the failures when you're trying to finish a project mere moments before a deadline. I've had no problem reading any of the fonts on these compilation CDs, which makes them worth the purchase price to me. But be aware that the quality of the fonts in these collections tends to vary considerably.

You can read about the type metrics saved in Adobe fonts in the document "Adobe Font Metrics Format Specification File" by Adobe Systems. Version 4.1 is available online at http://partners.adobe.com/asn/developer/pdfs/tn/5004.AFM_Spec.pdf.

The Panose specification are laid out in the "Panose 2.0 White Paper" by Michael S. De Laurentis. It's available at http://www.w3.org/Fonts/Panose/pan2.html. Another source for Panose data is the "Panose Classification Metrics Guide" available online from AGFA Monotype at http://www.panose.com/printer/pan1.asp.

There are many great tools available for browsing fonts on your computer. On my PC I use *Printer's Apprentice* (http://www.loseyourmind.com). Other popular tools are *Typograph* for the PC (http://www.neuber.com/typograph), and *Font Book* for the Mac (http://www.apple.com/macosx/features/fontbook).

You can see the type classifications used by Apple at http://www.adobe.com/type/browser/classifications.html, and those used by Planet Typography at http://www.planet-typography.com/manual/families.html.

If you're looking for the name of a particular typeface, there are two great web sites to check out. *Indentifont* asks you a series of questions based on the qualities of the typeface you're looking at (http://www.identifont.com). *What The Font?!* lets you upload an image of a few characters and responds with the name of the typeface (http://www.myfonts.com/WhatTheFont).

About Face

If you enjoy the thrill of the hunt and discovering new amateur typefaces as they're developed, there are lots of sites online that collect these typefaces together, often providing version in both PC and Macintosh formats. DaFont (http://www.dafont.com/en) and Abstract Fonts (http://www.abstractfonts.com/fonts) as both sort the typefaces by category. Other sites I periodically check are High Fonts (http://www.highfonts.com) and 1001 Fonts (http://www.1001fonts.com). Once you've browsed the collections at these sites, most let you sort by date, so you can quickly catch up on what's been added since the last time you stopped by. There are also many other smaller sites that specialize in different varieties of typefaces.

And of course don't forget professional, commercial fonts. You must pay for these, but your money buys you a high-quality typeface with sophisticated kerning and hinting information, ligatures, and other professional details that will make your typeset work look professional and polished. The Adobe Type Library provides a wide variety of high-quality typefaces (http://www.adobe.com/type/main.jhtml). A good consolidated source of fonts offered by many different foundries is MyFonts (http://www.myfonts.com).

A nice general resource for typefaces is at http://jeff.cs.mcgill.ca/~luc/classify.html.

A nice collection of pangrams can be found at http://rinkworks.com/words/pangrams.shtml.

Rolling
Your
Own

11

eleven

Everybody loves making pictures with Spirograph. This wonderful toy was introduced in 1966 by Kenner Products and is now manufactured and sold by Hasbro.

The basic idea is simplicity itself. The box contains a collection of plastic gears of different sizes. Each gear has several holes drilled into it, each big enough to accommodate a pen tip. The box also contains some rings that have gear teeth on both their inner and outer edges. To make a picture, select a gear and set it snugly against one of the rings (either inside or outside) so that the teeth are engaged. Put a pen into one of the holes, and start going around and around. The result is a pretty, swirly design, like the pictures in Figure 11.1.

I got to thinking about this toy recently and wondered what might happen if we used other shapes for the pieces, rather than circles. I wrote a program that produces Spirograph-like patterns using shapes built out of Bézier curves. I'll describe that later on, but let's start by looking at traditional Spirograph patterns.

ROULETTES

Spirograph produces planar curves that are known as *roulettes*. A roulette is defined by J. Dennis Lawrence this way: "If a curve C_1 rolls, without slipping, along another fixed curve C_2, any fixed point P attached to C_1 describes a *roulette* " (see the Further Reading section for this and other references). The word "trochoid" is a synonym for

Rolling
Your Own

Figure 11.1

Several Spirograph-style roulettes.

Figure 11.2

Three cycloids. In this figure, the wheel radius $r = 1$, and the pen is at a distance h from the wheel's center. (a) $h = 0.5$. (b) $h = 1.0$. (c) $h = 1.5$.

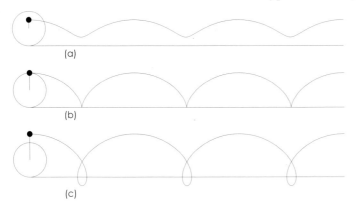

(a)

(b)

(c)

roulette. From here on, I'll refer to C_1 as the "wheel" and C_2 as the "frame," even when the shapes aren't circular.

The simplest way to create a roulette is probably to use a circle for the wheel and a straight line for the frame. This results in a figure that has the special name *cycloid*. Where we choose to put our pen tip results in three different types of curves, as we can see from Figure 11.2.

Spirograph is limited to the curves of the type in Figure 11.1 and Figure 11.2(a), where the pen is inside the wheel. To make the other types of curves, it may be useful to think of attaching a rigid arm to the center of the disk. As the disk rotates, the arm spins with it.

Determining whether the pen tip is inside the rolling wheel, right on its edge, or outside of it is a useful tool for distinguishing among the different types of roulettes. Figure 11.3 shows the mathematical names for the different types of roulettes. The first distinction is whether the wheel is inside or outside of the frame. If it's outside, we call it an *epitrochoid*; otherwise it's a *hypotrochoid*. If the pen is right on the edge of the wheel, then it's an *epicycloid* or *hypocycloid*. If the pen is not on the

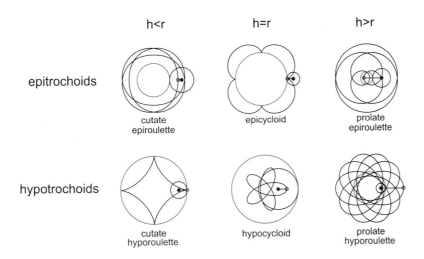

Figure 11.3

Distinguishing among the roulettes. The upper row are epitrochoids, because the wheel is outside of the frame. The lower row are hypotrochoids. The wheel has radius b and the pen is a distance h from its center.

edge, then the curve is an *epiroulette* or *hyporoulette*. There are two forms of each of these. If the pen is inside the wheel, then we have a *cutate* epiroulette or hyporoulette; otherwise it's a *prolate* epiroulette or hyporoulette.

There are some special cases of these curves that mathematicians have studied over the years. I'll mention these briefly, without going into detail. In each of these special cases, both the wheel and the frame are circles. I'll call the frame circle C_f with radius r_f, and the wheel C_w with radius r_w. The distance of the pen tip from the center of C_w is h.

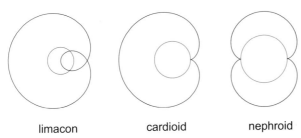

limacon   cardioid   nephroid

Figure 11.4

Three special epitrochoids: A *limaçon* ($r_f = r_w$), a *cardioid* (an epicycloid with $r_f = r_w$), and a *nephroid* (an epicycloid with $r_f = 2\,r_w$).

Figure 11.4 shows three special epitrochoids. A *limaçon* is created when $r_f = r_w$. The *cardioid* is the epicycloid case of the limaçon, created when $h = r_w$ and $r_f = r_w$. The *nephroid* is another epicycloid, resulting from $r_f = 2r_w$.

Figure 11.5 shows five special hypotrochoids. You get an *ellipse* when $r_f = 2r_w$. The other examples are all hypocycloids, so $h = r_w$. The *Tusi couple* is what you get when drawing an ellipse with $r_f = 2r_w$: it's a straight line. The three-pointed star called the *deltoid* appears when $r_f = 3r_w$, and the four-pointed star called the *astroid* is created when $r_f = 4r_w$. You probably get the general idea that you can make

Figure 11.5

Special hypotrochoids. In the upper left is an ellipse ($r_f = 2r_w$). The other figures are all hypocycloids (so $h = r_w$). A *Tusi couple* ($r_f = 2r_w$), a *deltoid* ($r_f = 3r_w$), an *astroid* ($r_f = 4r_w$), and a 10-pointed star with no special name.

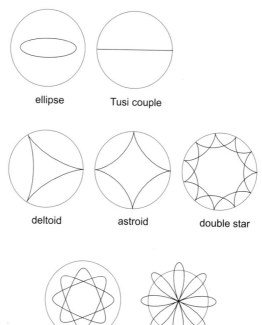

ellipse   Tusi couple

deltoid   astroid   double star

Figure 11.6

Rosettes are hypocycloids ($h = r_w$) generated by the formula given in the text. The four curves here are generated with $n = 4$, using different values of h. From left to right, $h = 0.3$, $h = 1$, $h = 2$, $h = 5$.

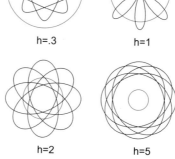

h=.3   h=1

h=2   h=5

an n-pointed star with $r_f = nr_w$, and that's correct; I've included a ten-pointed star in the figure as well.

Figure 11.6 (b) shows a special hypocycloid called a *rose* or *rosette*, sometimes also called *rhodonea*. These are hypocycloids where the center of the flower passes through the center of the frame. You can generate rosettes with different numbers of petals with these formulae:

$$ r_f = \frac{2nh}{n+1} \qquad r_w = \frac{(n-1)h}{n+1} $$

The flower in the figure uses $n = 4$, and a variety of values of h.

Now that we've looked at a bunch of particularly special epitrochoids and hypotrochoids, let's gather up the families for some group portraits and see what they look like together. Figure 11.7 shows the epitrochoids,

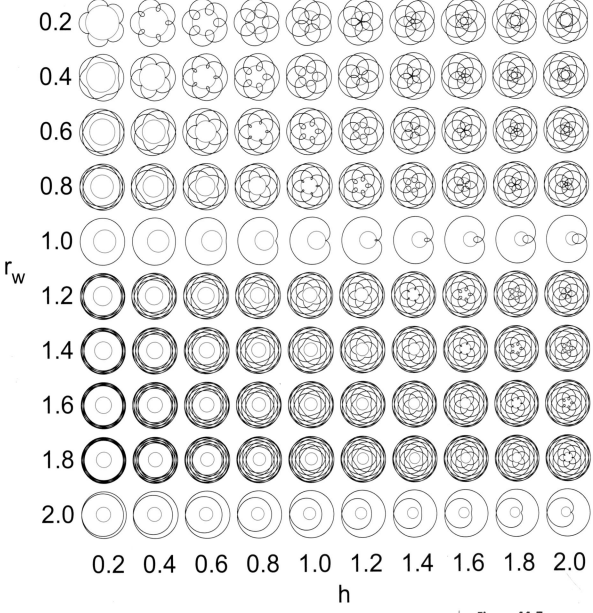

r_w

0.2 0.4 0.6 0.8 1.0 1.2 1.4 1.6 1.8 2.0

h

Figure 11.7

A grid of epitrochoids. The horizontal axis shows different values of h, the vertical axis r_w. Throughout, $r_f = 1$.

and Figure 11.8 shows the hypotrochoids. Using Spirograph we can make all the curves in Figure 11.7 and in the upper-left quadrant of Figure 11.8. On the right side of Figure 11.8, we'd need an extension arm to get the pen tip outside of the inner gear, and on the bottom, the gear is too big for the inner ring and would need to pass through it.

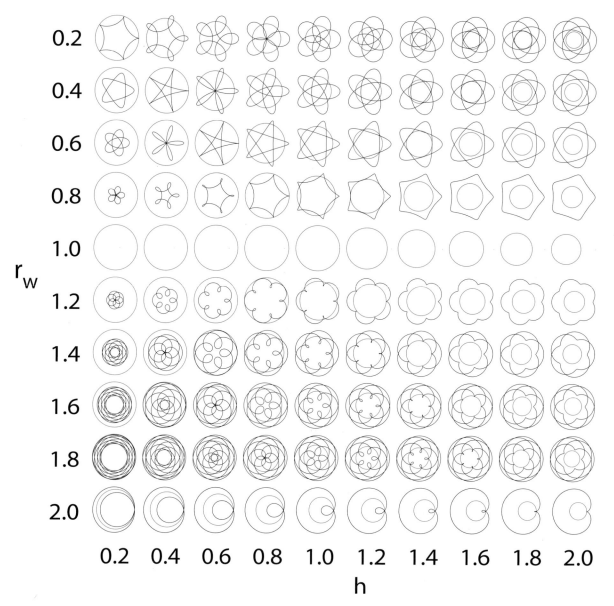

Figure 11.8

A grid of hypotrochoids. The horizontal axis shows different values of h, the vertical axis r_w. Throughout, $r_f = 1$.

THE GEOMETRY

I certainly didn't draw Figure 11.7 and Figure 11.8 by hand! It turns out that it's easy to derive a simple formula for the two different types of roulettes. Implementing these formulae is easy in just about any modern programming language.

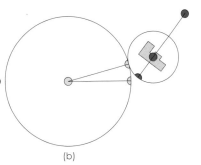

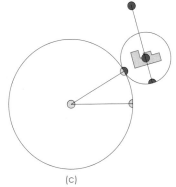

(a)

(b)

(c)

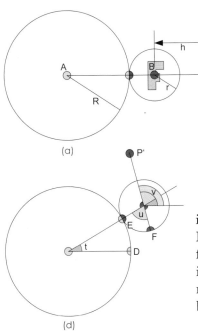

(d)

The easiest way to set up the geometry is as in Figure 11.9. For the illustrations, I'll use a wheel that's smaller than the frame. I'll never use that relationship in the math, so the geometry works no matter what the relative sizes are between the wheel and frame.

Figure 11.9

The geometry for the epitrochoids. (a) The starting position, where the wheel is sitting outside of the frame. (b) The wheel starts to rotate. (c) The wheel rotates more. (d) Labels on the geometry of part (c).

We'll put the larger circle (the frame), with radius R, at the origin (which I'm calling point A), and the smaller circle (the wheel), with radius r, on the X axis to the right of the origin, just touching the frame. So the center of the wheel is $B = (R + r, 0)$. The point P representing the pen tip is at a distance h to the right of B: $P = (R + r + h, 0)$. At the start, $P_0 = B_0 + h$.

The parameter t rotates the wheel around the frame counterclockwise by t radians. So for any given value of t, the center of the wheel is at $B_t = (R + r)(\cos(t), \sin(t))$. As the wheel rolls around the frame, it too rotates counter-clockwise, as shown in Figure 11.9(b) and (c). If we can find out how much the wheel has rotated for a given value of t, we can rotate P about B_t by that amount, and we'll have our pen tip location P_t.

Let's label everything as in Figure 11.9(d). The angle we've rotated by is t, shown at the center of both the frame circle and the wheel. The wheel has rotated by an angle v. From the drawing, we can see $v = u + t$, so now we need to find the angle u.

The trick to finding u is to remember that since the wheel is not slipping as it rotates, the arc EF around its perimeter has the same length as the arc DE around the perimeter of the frame. Writing $|EF|$ for the length of arc EF, we know that $|EF| = ur$, and similarly, $|DE| = tR$. So $|DE| = |EF|$ means $tR = ur$, which tells us $u = t(R/r)$. Now we can plug this back into our expression for $v = u + t = t + [t(R/r)] = t[1 + (R/r)]$. Let's write this as $v = ct$ where $c = (R + r)/r$.

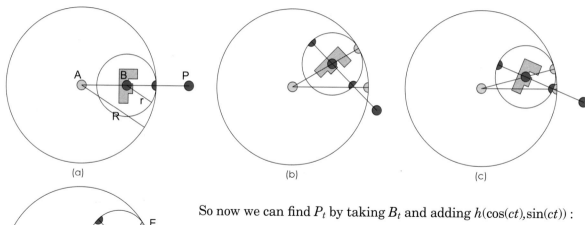

(a)   (b)   (c)

(d)

Figure 11.10

The geometry for the hypotrochoids. (a) The starting position, where the wheel is sitting outside of the frame. (b) The wheel starts to rotate. (c) The wheel rotates more. (d) Labels on the geometry of part (c).

So now we can find P_t by taking B_t and adding $h(\cos(ct),\sin(ct))$:

$$P_t = (R + r)(\cos(t),\ \sin(t)) + h(\cos(ct),\sin(ct)),$$

where $c = (R + r)/r$.

The explicit parametric form of the epicycloid is thus

$$x_e(t) = (R + r)\cos(t) + h\ \cos(ct),$$
$$y_e(t) = (R + r)\sin(t) + h\ \sin(ct).$$

The hypocycloid follows the same reasoning. As shown in Figure 11.10, we put the wheel inside the frame this time. As shown in Figure 11.10(b) and (c), as the wheel rotates it turns clockwise.

From the figure we see that $|DE| = |EF|$, or $tR = vr$, giving us $v = t(R/r)$. Observing that $v = t + u$, we isolate $u = v - t = t(R/r) - t = t[(R/r) - 1]$, or $u = dt$, where $d = (R - r)/r$. We want to rotate P not by u but by $-u$, because the wheel is turning clockwise. Write this out as

$$P_t = (R - r)(\cos(t),\ \sin(t)) + h(\cos(-dt),\ \sin(-dt))$$
$$= (R - r)(\cos(t),\ \sin(t)) + h(\cos(dt),\ -\sin(dt)),$$

where $d = (R - r)/r$, and we noted that $\cos(-x) = \cos(x)$ and $\sin(-x) = -\sin(x)$ for any x.

The explicit parametric form of the hypocycloid is thus

$$x_h(t) = (R - r)\cos(t) + h\cos(dt),$$
$$y_h(t) = (R - r)\sin(t) - h\sin(dt).$$

FROM CIRCLES TO BÉZIERS

To write a more general curve-based Spirograph program, I decided to use Bézier curves. There are many curve representations out there, but Béziers are very simple to program, numerically stable, and easily controllable. Maintaining smooth continuity across Bézier segments is also easy. For a little project like this, they're just about perfect.

Figure 11.11 shows the basic idea using screenshots from my system. I have two curves: the wheel (in red) and the frame (in blue). I can toggle on and off the display of control points for each curve independently. When the knots are displayed, I can simply click in them and drag them where I want.

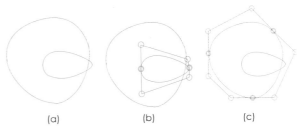

Once I've got the curves shaped the way I like them, I need to assign what I call *zero points*. These are the initial points of contact between the two curves. I have a slider in the interface that lets me pick the zero point anywhere on each curve, as shown in Figure 11.12. Once I've identified the zero point on each curve, I snap them together. The wheel moves to the frame so that the zero points are coincident, and then it rotates so that its local tangent is parallel to the tangent of the frame.

Figure 11.11

Creating shapes with Bézier curves. (a) The curves. (b) The Bézier polygon for the wheel. (c) The Bézier polygon for the frame.

It's important to specify whether the wheel is inside or outside the frame. Figure 11.13 shows the same curves, but starting inside and outside. Figure 11.13 (c) shows the outside version after a few steps have been taken. You can start to see the trail left behind by the pen tip. Figure 11.13 (d) shows the result after many more steps. Figure 11.14 shows the curve resulting from this pair of shapes.

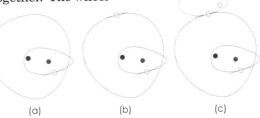

Figure 11.12

Setting the starting points. (a) Choosing a pair of zero points. The solid dots show the center of curve, the diamond on the curve is the zero point, and the local tangent is also drawn. (b) A different pair of points. (c) The wheel translated and rotated into position, shown in green.

PROGRAMMING

Figure 11.15 shows a picture of my system in action. The control panel is on the left, and the design window is on the right. I'll discuss some of the programming ideas as we walk through the controls.

At the top of the control panel is a cluster of controls in a pale yellow box. These relate to the wheel. Using the checkboxes, you can enable or disable the display of the curve itself, its Bézier polygon, and the zero point. The upper horizontal scrollbar lets you specify where the zero point is: if the Zero checkbox is on, then as you move this scrollbar from the left to the right, you see the zero point make a full orbit around the wheel. The lower scrollbar lets you rotate the curve into any orientation.

When you move the upper scrollbar to set the zero point, the system asks the wheel for its arclength, s. Then the value of the scrollbar is used to select a point in the interval $[0, s]$, and the zero point is moved there. So the first job is to compute the arclength of the wheel. I do this

Figure 11.13

Starting off a drawing. The green version of the wheel is the moving copy. (a) Starting the wheel inside the frame. (b) Starting the wheel outside the frame. (c) Part (b) after a few steps; the wheel has rotated as it moved around the frame. (d) After many more steps.

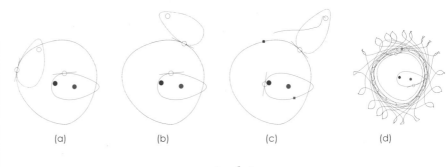

(a)　　　　　(b)　　　　　(c)　　　　　(d)

Figure 11.14

The curve created by the starting setup in Figure 11.13(b).

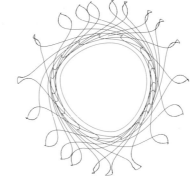

Figure 11.15

My Bézier roulette program in action. The control panel is on the left, and the graphical design window is on the right.

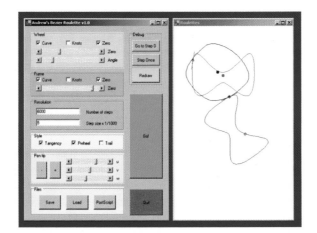

by summing up the arclengths of each Bézier segment. These I find by a simple numerical evaluation. Bézier curves are parameterized by a single value that sweeps along their length. So I simply take many tiny steps and add up the length of each step. Since my design window initially represents a unit square, most of my curves have a length of around two or three units. A little experimenting with these curves showed that 3,000 steps was way more than necessary to find an accurate arclength, but it was quick to compute and gave me lots of headroom for accurately computing the lengths of larger curves, so I left it there. Thus the parameter u along each Bézier runs from 0 to 1 in steps of 1/3000. I save the length of each Bézier curve along with that segment. To find the arclength of the total curve, I ask each segment for its length and simply sum them up. I then save that total with the curve. Any further requests for the curve's length, or the length of any Bézier segment, are easily served just by returning the saved value. If at any time I add or delete a Bézier segment, or move any of the control points, I invalidate all of the arc lengths associated with that curve, so the next request triggers a recomputation. That new result is saved again so further requests are once again nice and quick.

Armed with these arclengths, I can find the point at arclength s by basically going the other way around. I step through the segments of the curve until I find the one that holds this value, and then I step through that segment, again in steps of 1/3000, until I reach that arclength, or have a couple of steps that contain it. In the former case I simply return that point, and in the latter case I interpolate between the two points.

I also compute the tangent vector at the point at arclength s by finding the points at arclength $s - \delta$ and $s + \delta$, using a technique I'll describe below.

Each time I move the slider, I find the point corresponding to the arclength at that value of the slider, and save both the arclength and the position of the point. If the Zero checkbox is turned on, I draw a little diamond at that point, and a short line to indicate the tangent vector.

The pale blue box just beneath the wheel controls holds an identical set for the frame.

Beneath this is a purple box that controls the resolution of the roulette that's generated by the wheel and frame. To see what these numbers do, let's look at how the roulette gets generated.

To create the roulette, I march along the perimeter of the wheel, rolling it along the frame. I find a point on the wheel, move it to the frame, rotate the wheel so that it's tangent to the frame, compute the location of the pen tip, and draw a little line to that point from the last pen tip. Then I do it again. Let's see this in more detail.

To start the process, I first find the arclength of the zero point on the wheel. For reasons that will become clear, let's call this arclength c_w. I can use this value to find the corresponding point on the wheel, $W(c_w)$. Of course, at the start of the process that's just the wheel's zero point.

I now want to find the tangent at this point. I find two points that surround the current point: $T_0 = W(c_w - t)$ and $T_1 = W(c_w + t)$. The value of t tells me how far ahead and back to move along the curve.

237

To match my arclength computation above, I use an initial value of 1/3000. This gives me the vector $\mathbf{T}_w = T_1 - T_0$, which is the local approximation to the tangent. Just in case I'm at a part of the curve where the parameter is changing slowly, I compute the length of the vector $\mathbf{T}_w$. If it's smaller than some threshold (I use 4/3000), then I double the value of t and compute T_0 and T_1 again. I repeat this until $\mathbf{T}_w$ becomes large enough or I've repeated it ten times (in practice, one or two loops is all that's usually needed). I normalize the vector $\mathbf{T}_w$ and save it with the wheel.

I then repeat the whole process for the frame. I find the arclength c_f for the zero point of the frame and save the point $F(c_f)$. I compute the tangent $\mathbf{T}_f$ and save it.

Now I move the wheel by the vector $W(c_w) - F(c_f)$, so that the two curves come into contact at their respective points (the letter c in the arclength values c_w and c_f stands for contact). I compute the angles θ_w and θ_f corresponding to the tangent vectors for the two curves. I then find the smallest rotation that I can apply to the wheel's most recent orientation so that the tangent vectors are parallel. When we're starting, the wheel's current orientation is whatever I set it to by using the rotation scrollbar in the interface.

Now that I've got the wheel in the right position and orientation, it's time to locate the pen tip. The pen tip is represented by five numbers: the Bézier curve number b, the first-knot number k, and three weights u, v, w. The idea is illustrated in Figure 11.16. I imagine a triangle from the center of the wheel (this is just the average of all the vertices in the Bézier polygon) to one edge of the Bézier polygon. The Bézier curve number b tells me which Bézier curve to use, and the first-knot number k tells me which knot forms one vertex of the triangle; the next knot forms the next vertex. So if $b = 2$ and $k = 1$, as in the figure, then I know the triangle is made up of the wheel's center (call that point C), and the second and third control points in the third Bézier curve (call these K_0 and K_1). I compute the center of this triangle, called point T, by averaging these three points together. Using these four points, I use the weights u, v, w to compute the pen tip P this way:

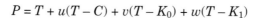

$$P = T + u(T - C) + v(T - K_0) + w(T - K_1)$$

I let the weights u,v,w range from about -5 to 5, which lets me move the point pretty far from the wheel if I want. Figure 11.17 shows the triangle used for determining the pen tip during the drawing process.

Once I have the pen tip, I check to see if this is the first point of the roulette. If it's not, I draw a line from the last pen tip location to the current one. Then I save this location for use in the next line.

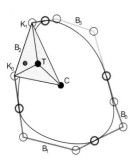

Figure 11.16

The geometry for finding the pen tip.

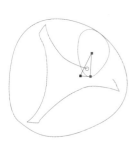

Figure 11.17

Showing the pen tip calculation in action.

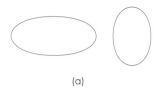

(a)

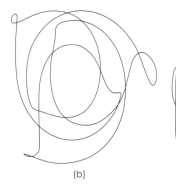

(b)

(c)

To generate the next point on the roulette, I need to first move the wheel. I retreive the contact arclength c_w and bump it to get the new contact arclength: $c_w' = c_w + \Delta_s$ (Δ_s is derived from one of the numbers you can set from the interface). From this, I get a new point on the wheel $W(c_w')$, and of course a new tangent as well. I do the same thing with the frame, getting a new contact arclength c_f', a new contact point $F(c_f')$, and a new tangent.

It's worth a moment to consider an important subtlety: the increment along the two curves is the same because we're dealing with arclength, not with the intrinsic parameterization of the curve. Remember from our discussions of the geometry using Figures 11.9 and 11.10 that because the wheel doesn't slip, the arclengths along the wheel and the frame at each step are the same. So it's important that the distance $|F(c_f') - F(c_f)| = |W(c_w') - W(c_w)|$.

Now that I have new contact points, I move the wheel so that $W(c_w')$ sits on top of $F(c_f')$, and then rotate it by the smallest angle that I can so that it's tangent to the frame. I locate the pen tip, draw a little line to there from the last location, and then repeat the whole process.

Return to the purple box in the control panel. The first number determines how many of these steps I should take to make the roulette. If the roulette is closed and matches up with itself, taking too many steps will simply cause it to repeat on top of itself. But generally with these oddball shapes, the roulette doesn't close up, and so this becomes a matter of choosing an endpoint based on aesthetic and time considerations.

The other number controls the precision of each step. Recall that the arclengths are bumped by Δ_s. The number in the second purple box sets this in multiples of $1/1000$. So if the number is 5, then the

Figure 11.18

Generating roulettes with ellipses. (a) The wheel is in green, the frame in red. (b) A roulette generated by this pair. (c) Another roulette.

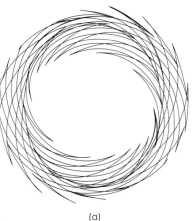

(a)

Figure 11.19

(a) The wheel is now an egg shape. (b) The roulette is quite different from Figure 11.18.

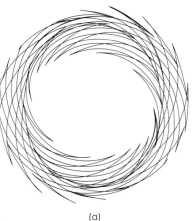

(a)

239

Rolling Your Own

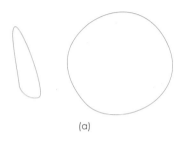

(a)

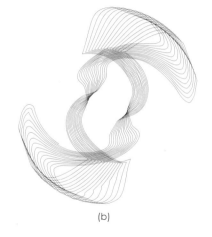

(b)

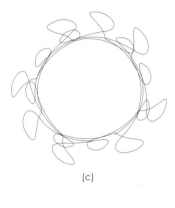

(c)

Figure 11.20

(a) The frame is roughly circular, but the wheel is a thin, bent egg. (b)–(c) A variety of roulettes generated by moving the pen tip, while the wheel rotates outside the frame. (d)–(e) The wheel is rotating inside the frame.

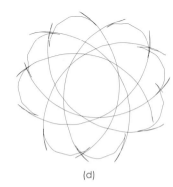

(d)

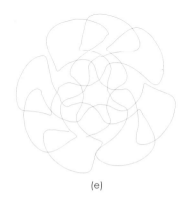

(e)

Figure 11.21

(a) The same frame as in Figure 11.20, but the wheel is more asymmetrical. (b) Rotating the wheel inside the frame. (c) Rotating the wheel outside the frame.

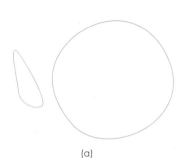

(a)

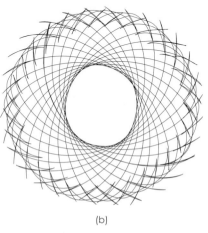

(b)

(c)

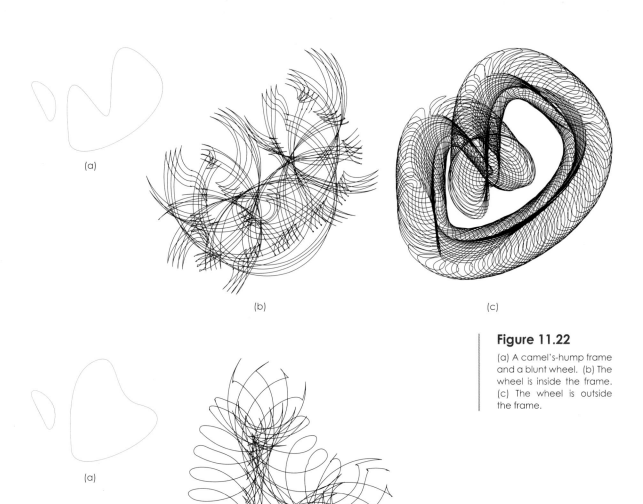

(a)

(b)

(c)

Figure 11.22

(a) A camel's-hump frame and a blunt wheel. (b) The wheel is inside the frame. (c) The wheel is outside the frame.

(a)

(b)

Figure 11.23

(a) The same wheel as in Figure 11.22, but a softened frame. (b) The roulette.

arclength is incremented by 5/1000 on each step. As I mentioned, I start with a drawing space in the unit square, so curves tend to have lengths of around two or three units. A smaller number in this box means that the steps are smaller, resulting in more precision at a cost of slower drawing time and a bigger output file.

The orange box contains three checkboxes. The first toggles on and off the tangency constraint. Just for fun, I thought I'd give myself the

Figure 11.24

(a) A bow-tie shaped wheel and a blobby frame. (b) The roulette.

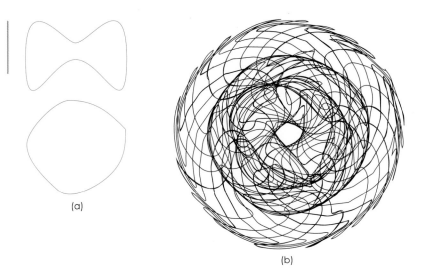

(a)

(b)

option of turning off the rotation at each step that causes the wheel to become tangent to the frame. If you turn off this box, the wheel still moves around the frame, and the point of contact still moves around the wheel, but it doesn't rotate. The other two boxes simply turn on and off the display of the transformed wheel as it moves, and the trail it leaves behind. Turning these off during the calculation, and then turning them on again when it's over, can save some time.

The next box down controls the location of the pen tip. The two buttons select which triangle is being used as the reference for the tip. Pressing the button with a minus sign in it moves backward along

Figure 11.25

(a) The same blobby frame as in Figure 11.20, but a kind of strange wheel. (b) The resulting roulette.

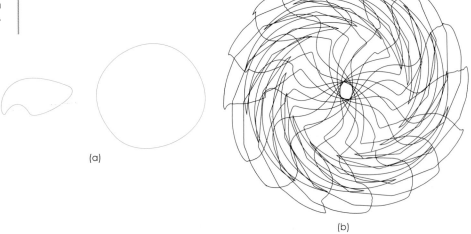

(a)

(b)

the curve by one knot, backing up to a previous curve if necessary. Similarly, the button with a plus sign moves forward one knot. For example, pressing the minus button would move the pen tip in Figure 11.16 into the triangle defined by C, the knot labeled K_0, and the knot just below it. The three scrollbars let you set the value of the three weights that set the location of the pen tip.

The bottommost set of buttons lets me save and load files that contain the curve coordinates and all the control settings. I can also save the current wheel and frame and the computed roulette to PostScript, which I used to save the examples in the next section.

The buttons in the upper right are for debugging. The big green button on the right starts the computation of the roulette. The button in the lower right causes the system to pack up and quit.

EXAMPLES

Let's look at some roulettes that I made with Bézier curves for the wheel and frame. Figure 11.18 through Figure 11.25 show a variety of roulettes generated by a bunch of different shapes. I don't show the location of the pen tip with the shapes, because for many of the most interesting roulettes, the pen was far away from the wheel, which would have meant leaving a lot of blank space on the page. If you're interested in reproducing these roulettes, fooling around with the shapes and the pen tip is enough fun to be worth the effort.

Because I calculate my roulettes by taking many small steps, the PostScript files that I generate tend to be huge. To trim these figures down to a sensible size, I opened my roulettes in *Adobe Illustrator* and used its built-in Simplify command to reduce the number of points in the curve. This had the side effect of eliminating some of the tiny jiggles in the curves due to the finite precision of my calculations. These mostly occurred in places where both the wheel and the frame were nearly flat, and the approximated tangent vector wiggled by a very small angle from one contact point to the next.

SOME HISTORY

Although Spirograph is a wonderful toy for exploring roulettes, mathematicians started studying them long before the 1960s.

In 200 B.C., the astronomer Apollonius of Perga described the motion of celestrial objects with combinations of circles. In 150 B.C., Hipparchos of Nicaea followed up on this idea and worked out the apparent motions of the planets and the sun using circles. Ptolemy popularized this model in 150 A.D., and his name became associated with the idea of solar system that had the Earth in the center, with everything else spinning around the Earth in orbits that were described by combinations of circles. As these planets rotated around the Earth, and themselves rotated, they traced out epicycloids.

In 1515, Albrecht Dürer wrote about epicycloids, calling them "spider lines" in his book *Instruction in Measurement with Compass and Straight Edge*. Since then, epicycloids have been studied by a host of famous mathematicians, including Desargues, Huygens, Leibniz, Newton, de L'Hôpital, Jakob Bernoulli, la Hire, Johann Bernoulli, Daniel Bernoulli, and Euler.

Many roulettes have special names, given to them by the mathematicians who studied their properties.

Among the epitrochoids, the *nephroid* was named in 1878 by R. A. Proctor in his book *The Geometry of Cycloids*. The full name of the *limaçon* is the Limaçon of Pascal (limaçon means "snail"). The Pascal here is not the famous Blaise Pascal, but his father, Etienne. The *cardioid* was named by De Castillon in a 1741 paper.

Among the hypotrochoids, the *ellipse* was probably first studied in 350 B.C. by Menaechmus and named in 200 B.C. by Apollonius. The *deltoid* (or *tricuspid*) was studied in 1745 by Euler. The *astroid* (or *tetracuspid*) was first studied in 1674 by Roemer. The name of the straight line called the *Tusi couple* comes from the Persian astronomer and mathematician Nasir al-Din al-Tusi, who studied this shape in the late thirteenth century.

FURTHER READING

I found a bit of history on Spirograph at the Kenner Toys website, http://www.kennertoys.com/history.html.

There's a ton of information on roulettes available on the web; just go to Google and type in "roulette." A great reference for all kinds of curves is the paperback book *A Catalog of Special Plane Curves* by J. Dennis Lawrence (Dover Publications, New York, NY, 1972).

You can find lots of the mathematical details behind epitrochoids at http://www.math.hmc.edu/faculty/gu/curves_and_surfaces/curves/epicycloid.html and similar information for hypotrochoids at http://www.math.hmc.edu/faculty/gu/curves_and_surfaces/curves/hypocycloid.html, as well as at http://mathworld.wolfram.com/Epitrochoid.html.

Two nice galleries of pretty roulettes are available at http://aleph0.
clarku.edu/~djoyce/roulettes/roulettes.html and http://www.xahlee.
org/SpecialPlaneCurves_dir/EpiHypocycloid_dir/epiHypocycloid.html.

My information on Nasir al-Din al-Tusi came from http://mathworld.
wolfram.com/TusiCouple.html.

Synthetic Cubism

Where would computer graphics be without cameras? To make a synthetic picture with computer graphics, we usually image a camera of some sort, taking a picture of a scene. Such cameras range from the simplest pinhole camera, to a sophisticated simulation of optics and shutters. Usually, though, our imaginary cameras are pretty close analogs to the real things.

If we're willing to move away from the idea of simulating a real camera, we can start to explore some interesting, alternative imaging models, like digital Cubism. If we're thoughtful, we'll be able to harness their new possibilities for communicating ideas and story points in new and expressive ways. Let's look at some basic camera models, then consider how we can extend them.

PINHOLE CAMERAS

You can see the traditional pinhole camera in Figure 12.1. It's probably the simplest form of a working camera, and it does indeed work. See the Further Reading section for pointers to some websites of wonderful images made with pinhole cameras and advice for building your own.

Figure 12.1

(a) A simple pinhole camera can be made out of any light-tight box. (b) The film is taped to the inside back wall of the box, and a tiny hole is poked in the front.

(a)

(b)

Synthetic Cubism

You can literally make a working pinhole camera out of almost any light-tight enclosure. A humble shoebox works very well. In a shoebox camera, you typically mount the film on the inside bottom of the box and poke a tiny hole in the top cover. The hole is covered by an opaque shield, typically made of black paper or metal. To make an exposure, set the camera on the ground or a wall or some other steady surface, point the pinhole towards whatever you want to take a picture of, move the shield away from the pinhole so that light can reach the film, and wait a while. Then cover up the pinhole again. That's it for the exposure; now take your negative to a darkroom and develop it like any other photograph.

The optics of a pinhole camera are easy to diagram, as shown in Figure 12.2. If we think of the pinhole as an ideal point, then for every point on the film, there's exactly one ray of light that can pass from the scene, through the pinhole, and onto that point on the film. This observation is what made the early forms of ray-tracing practical. Ray tracing systems create *eye rays* (also called *screen rays*), which correspond to points on the film. Reasoning that any light striking a given point must have arrived along the ray associated with it, the system follows that path of the ray into the environment, looking for objects and volumes that can send light back to the pixel along the ray.

The simple geometry of the pinhole model can get very complicated when we start incorporating ideas like lenses and shutters. The basic idea remains the same, though: rays of light in the scene strike the front of the camera and pass into some selecting and routing mechanism, which directs specific rays towards specific locations on the film.

But just as we've seen nonphotorealistic rendering methods in the last few years, we can also imagine nonmechanical camera models.

Perhaps the simplest variant on the shoebox pinhole camera is the sideways oatmeal-box pinhole camera, shown in Figure 12.3. Here

the film is no longer sitting against a flat wall, but it's bent around the inside of the cylinder. Of course, the light that's entering the camera through the pinhole is unaffected by the shape of the film. As before, rays of light pass from the scene, through the pinhole, and strike the film. And as before, we can work out a specific

(a)

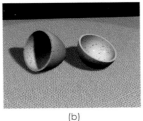
(b)

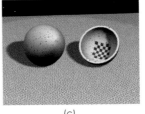
(c)

(d)

Figure 12.4

(a) A Silly Putty egg. (b) Splitting the egg along its equator. (c) Making a pinhole camera out of the egg by poking a hole in the tip of the narrow end, and placing film in the inside of the thick end. (d) A ray of light entering the egg pinhole camera. I've made the top part transparent for this illustration.

one-to-one mapping from points on this cylindrical film to the rays that carry light to those points.

Bending a piece of film around the inside of a cylinder is pretty easy, but other shapes can be harder. The popular squishy goop known as Silly Putty is sold in a plastic egg that separates down the middle, as shown in Figure 12.4(a). Although this egg is pretty small, there's no reason we couldn't drill a pinhole into the narrow end and press a piece of film into the blobby end, as shown in Figure 12.4(b). Getting the film to smooth down would prove a bit tricky, though, because a flat sheet would naturally bunch up and buckle as we tried to press it against the inner wall of the egg.

This is a place where the computer graphics version of something is easier to manage than its real-world counterpart. Since our film is simulated, we can easily direct the light onto film that's been shaped any way at all, as long as we can write the equations (or procedures) that tell us which rays of light illuminate which spots on the film. If we can follow this up with a nice two-dimensional mapping, or "unwrapping," of the film onto a plane, then we can show the image as usual, though it will be distorted by the unwrapping.

The technique of unwrapping a curved surface onto a planar surface was studied in depth by mapmakers during the era of ocean exploration with tall ships. They needed to find ways to take the distributions of land, sea, wind, currents, and other phenomena on and near the Earth's surface and draw them onto sheets of paper that enabled efficient navigation of a ship at sea. The Earth isn't a sphere, but it's definitely round, and you can't represent it on a flat piece of paper without distorting it in some way. Cartographers came up with a great many possibilities for this transformation, and each one had its own strengths and weaknesses, both geometrically and in terms of ease of use by navigators. The Further Reading section offer pointers into this fascinating topic.

Cameras typically take a picture from a single point of view. But what if we want to use multiple points of view in one image? The Cubist painters thought about that very question, almost 100 years ago.

Cubism

Cubism is the name given to a short-lived but highly influential style of art. Cubism developed between about 1907 and 1914, mostly through the work of Georges Braque and Pablo Picasso.

Cubist art threw away traditional ideas of perspective, chiaroscuro, and other standard painterly techniques used in representational art, instead emphasizing the flat plane of the canvas. An aspect of Cubism that's of value to us here is that Braque and Picasso often painted objects so they could be seen from multiples points of view at the same time, overlapping or fragmenting the different projections in the same painting.

The name Cubism derives from derogatory comments about Braque's 1908 painting "Houses at L'Estaque" (see the Further Reading section for pointers to online images of this and other paintings). Henri Matisse and Louis Vauxcelles dismissed the painting as nothing but a collection of cubes. It's easy to see why they said this: Braque's painting is made of simple geometric forms and flat coloring. Many historians point to Picasso's "Les Demoiselles d'Avignon" as the seminal work of what came to be called Analytical Cubism. In this painting, five female nudes have been reduced to angled, simply shaded forms. Analytical Cubism was characterized by the disassembly and simplification of forms, representing the subjects of the paintings and their environments with simple planes.

After about 1912, the painters produced works now referred to as Synthetic Cubism. The shapes were still simple, but they became rounder and less stark. Actual objects were pasted onto the canvas amidst the painted objects.

By 1918 both painters had moved on to other styles, bringing an end to Cubism as a movement. But the ideas of Cubism were very influential and affected a wide range of other schools and styles of painting including Futurism, Constructivism, and even Expressionism. Of course, I've barely scratched the surface of this subject; you can learn much more about Cubism and its related movements in almost any book on art history that includes the twentieth century.

As I mentioned earlier, the aspect of Cubism that is relevant to us here is its use of simultaneous, multiple points of view. Analytical Cubism asserted that there is no privileged point of view for an object, and that multiple views are appropriate, or perhaps even necessary, for understanding the structure of objects. That's an interesting idea for looking at, say, a guitar or mandolin, but can it do anything for visual storytelling using computer graphics? You bet it can.

Cameras are fascinating devices, and lots of people have used computer graphics to explore the possibilities of algorithmically-driven cameras that would be impractical or impossible in real life. Researchers and developers have studied and simulated complex real-world camera designs, even including the special optics of lenses like those used by Omnimax cameras and projectors. People have also studied entirely fanciful cameras like those that wrap the film around a torus (see the Further Reading section for references to these projects and others discussed below).

By far the most common camera model used in computer graphics today is based on a flat sheet of film that is sitting behind a simple lens, controlled by a simple shutter. The shutter opens, light passes through the lens and onto the film, and then the shutter closes, completing the process. Of course, nothing is wrong with this model at all; it's served us well for many millions of still and animated images.

But computer graphics can do things that no real camera could ever do. My original inspiration for this project came when I was thinking about how to shoot a film script that I had written that required showing numerous different events simultaneously. They were all in roughly the same area, but no single shot could have captured them all. I started to think about the different tools available to directors and cinematographers for addressing this problem.

Any time we talk about new visualization techniques for storytelling, it's important to keep in mind that filmmaking is a craft of artifice. Today's familiar grammar of film contains elements such as cuts, dissolves, and montages. The grammar of film is hardly static, though, and is constantly expanding as new technologies become available. Recent innovations include the "bullet time" effect featured in *The Matrix*, the overlapping narrative structure of *Run Lola Run*, and the parallel imagery of *Timecode*. These are all mainstream films, but similar innovation is ocurring in television, video, and animation.

What are our options when we want to show a scene with two or more simultaneous actions that are too far apart, or too detailed, to capture with a single camera? One way to show this action is to shoot the scene several times, with the camera in a different location for each take. Then the editor can cut the multiple pieces of footage so that the audience sees each one for a moment, and then another, and another, and so on. Audiences are accustomed to the idea of cutting among concurrent images, and it's now a part of everyday filmmaking grammar.

Synthetic Cubism

Several other ways exist to show simultaneous action. A split-screen effect divides the screen into regions, each showing the same action from a different point of view. Typically the regions are offset from one another by black lines or boxes. Perhaps the first example of the split-screen effect used in an artistic way to help tell a story is Abel Gance's classic film *Napoléon* (1927). More recently, it's used from start to finish in *Timecode*. The split-screen is a very powerful idea, but it is typically used sparingly. One of its problems is that the black lines between the image regions can be distracting. Perhaps more troublesome is that the audience can find it difficult to interpret the relationships between the different views of the scene.

Alternatively, the editor could choose to show the different takes of the same action consecutively. With this technique, we see one point of view and then another, but we're alerted through sound and visual cues that each shot is meant to occur at the same moment as the other shots. So the film presents multiple views of the same action, in effect rewinding and replaying the same segment of time over and over. We often see this kind of thing in horror movies, where some particularly gruesome event is shown from one person's point of view, and then again from another's, and so on, often in slow motion just to make things just that much gorier.

Note that none of these techniques is "realistic" in the sense that it captures real life. Camera lenses do not see the world the way the human eye does, and even everyday cuts and wipes have no corollaries to our normal visual experience. Audiences understand that film and video have languages of their own with their own rules, and as long as audiences are comfortable with those rules, they are willingly oblivious to the artifice of the technique.

My goal was to develop something like a split-screen technique that didn't have those annoying black bars. But what could possibly replace them? One good candidate seemed to be those parts of the visual field that would naturally fit between the different pieces of the image, if we were somehow able to see them. Then we'd have a very flexible imaging tool: the image would be smooth and continuous, and the regions could change fluidly over time. I call this new technique the *Multicamera Collage*, or MCC.

SOME FILM IDIOMS

The multicamera collage is related to several existing techniques in filmmaking and computer graphics.

The closest work in filmmaking is the previously mentioned *bullet time* effect, made famous in the 1999 film *The Matrix*. In this technique, a number of still cameras surround an environment, all looking inward at a central region. As the action takes place, all the cameras are fired simultaneously. By sequencing the resulting images, the director can create a single shot that travels around the central region. The effect is that we're moving around a three-dimensional tableau that appears to be frozen in time. We can use image registration and morphing techniques to smooth the transitions between frames. A straightforward but expensive variation of this technique uses film cameras rather than still cameras. The result is that we can freely manipulate time, running forward and backward at any speed, while the point of view moves around the scene.

Another way to capture spatially disjoint action "in-camera" (that is, without postproduction effects) uses a technique called *slit-scan imaging*, made famous by Douglas Trumbull in the 1968 movie *2001: A Space Odyssey* (Trumbull was a special photographic effects supervisor for the film). The idea is shown schematically in Figure 12.5. In this arrangement, the camera is pointed down, shooting a piece of artwork held on an animation stand. In front of the artwork is an opaque piece of material that has a thin slit cut into it.

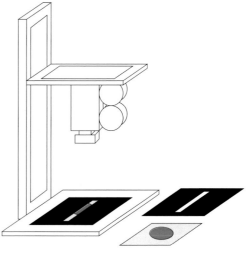

Figure 12.5

The basic setup for slit-scan photography. The camera is looking down on artwork that is sitting underneath an opaque sheet with a single slit cut into it.

To shoot a frame of film, turn off all the lights in the room except for those illuminating the artwork. Open the camera's shutter and leave it open as you slowly move the camera itself, the artwork, and the slit from one position to another. When the motion is finished, close the shutter. You've now completed the exposure for that frame. Advance the film in the camera; reset the positions of the camera, the artwork, and the slit, and start the next frame.

Of course, all of these elements can be generalized: the slit doesn't have to be linear; we don't have to use a single slit; and the motion of the slit(s), art, and camera can be very complex over the exposure's duration. We can of course change other imaging elements over time as well, for example by changing aperture or focus, or varying the illumination on the artwork.

This is a pretty complicated mechanical process: you could have three motors controlling the camera in as many directions, two motors controlling the motion of the animation stand, two more controlling the motion of the slit, and additional devices adjusting camera optics, lights, and so on. Everything has to be kept synchronized and calibrated over the course of a complete shot, which can involve hundreds of frames or more.

Synthetic Cubism

Computer graphics can simulate this entire process easily and with absolutely precise repeatability. In one sense it's a little sad to lose the charm of a complex mechanical system that one probably could grow to love, but it's also great to know that with software, nobody can accidentally bump the project and ruin two weeks' worth of work. Graphics also let us easily add effects that would be difficult to accomplish in a mechanical system, such as the imaging of three-dimensional objects (rather than an animation stand), motion blur, and even effects like lens flare.

The slit technique is also useful in other applications. Many panoramic imaging methods, such as those used for Quicktime VR, use a camera model that you can think of as a horizontally moving camera with a horizontally moving aperture made of a vertical slit.

We could also move the slit off of the animation stand and make it part of the camera. In 1889, J. Damoizeau patented a camera called the *cyclographe*, which he demonstrated in 1891 at a meeting of the Société Française de Photographie in Paris. The camera was specifically designed to take 360° panoramic photographs onto wide pieces of film that measured 8.5 by 80 cm. The camera had a built-in motor that you wound with a key and a thin vertical slit just in front of the film. Once the camera was wound up, you placed it on a tripod and released the motor. The motor spun the camera in one direction while it wound the film the other way, past the slit. We might say that the camera imaged one vertical slice of the negative at a time as it turned through a complete circle. Damoizeau later built a second version of the camera that used a pair of mechanisms to shoot stereoscopic images (see the Further Reading section for a pointer to a photograph of this remarkable camera).

Cameras used to digitize real objects, such as faces and three-dimensional works of art, often turn this idea inside out. Rather than rotate in place to collect the environment that surrounds them, they orbit the object under study to get an image of it from all sides.

One of the more unusual imaging models in computer graphics is the *multiperspective panorama*. The work was motivated by a desire to capture a technique that's used in animated films. To create what looks like three-dimensional motion of the camera, artists paint a large background image that smoothly blends among a number of different points of view. By panning a camera across the surface of this painting, the change in viewpoint can make it look like the camera is actually moving through space. It's a difficult trick to pull off, but skilled background painters have learned how to do it beautifully. The multiperspective panorama system, or MP, was designed to create those kinds of backgrounds from full three-dimensional models.

At a glance, the results of the MP system look like the results of the MCC, which I'll detail in the next section. But they're really very different tools that produce quite different results. The most obvious difference is that the audience isn't supposed to see MP images all at once. Indeed, it's the very fact that the camera moves over the image that creates the magic. On the other hand, MCC images exist to explicitly address the desire to show multiple perspectives at the same time. Another important distinction is that the MP technique is designed to simulate the motion of a single camera over a single path, while MCC is designed to blend together multiple cameras operating independently.

Despite these differences, the techniques can be compatible. In fact, some multicamera collage ideas nicely augment the multiperspective panorama, and vice-versa.

PUTTY CAMERAS

Let's imagine the most general geometry for finding the light falling on a piece of film. It would probably be simply an algorithm that took as input the (x, y) location we want to fill in and produced six real numbers: the three coordinates of a ray's starting point A, and the three coordinates of its direction vector $\mathbf{D}$. All of the cameras we've discussed so far can be written in terms of such an algorithm. In fact, many of them can be written as a straightforward mathematical formula.

But writing out algorithms and mathematical functions is hardly a good match to the start of mental states we're in when we're working on a storytelling project. Maybe things would be easier if we could find a physical analogy for our camera optics, rather than abstract mathematics and computer science.

I'll describe here my first approach to addressing this problem. It didn't work out in the long run, but it's a great conceptual tool and helps us visualize the kinds of cameras that we could find useful.

Earlier I mentioned the plastic egg that Silly Putty comes in. Let's open up the egg and think now about the putty itself. Suppose that instead of using a piece of photographic film for our camera, the film was made out of putty. Then we could stretch and bend the film into any shape we liked. Now let's imagine that we could do the same thing with the lens. Then we could take our camera and stretch and twist it into any shape we want.

Figure 12.6

Two people having a conversation outside their neighborhood café. (a) A view from the side. (b) A two-shot of the same scene.

(a)   (b)

Figure 12.7

Both characters in Figure 12.6 are photographed, from the front, and the two images are combined using a split-screen technique.

Figure 12.8

Inserting a sheet of putty film into Figure 12.6. The checkerboard texture is just to make the film sheet easier to see.

Figure 12.9

The rendered version of Figure 12.8 using the "porcupine's quills" model for the direction of light rays leaving the film.

For example, suppose we want to film a conversation between two people facing each other over a table at a local café as in Figure 12.6. Normally we would take a two-shot of the couple, and then some over-the-shoulder shots of each person, and later edit these all together into a conversation. But suppose that for our storytelling purposes, we wanted to show both people from the front at that same time. We could of course create a split-screen, as in Figure 12.7, but that has all the problems of split screens that I discussed earlier.

A putty camera would give us another option. Let's put a sheet of film putty into the scene as in Figure 12.8, and imagine that it's collecting light from rays that strike it perpendicular to its surface. In other words, think of the sheet of film as having a porcupine's quills sticking straight out of it at every point; those spikes are the direction of the light that strikes the film.

The image produced by this porcupine-putty camera is in Figure 12.9. Even this simple camera has the features that I'm after: the black line is gone, both characters are facing forward, and the space between them is imaged continuously and smoothly.

Of course, we might want to have some better control over the rays than just accepting whatever the porcupine's quills give us. Let's make another image with two flexible sheets instead of one. The first, called the "film," will be the one we already have. But we'll add another sheet which I'll call the "lens." These are both flexible sheets with a mathematical description that support a two-dimensional parameterization (such as Bézier surfaces, NURBS surfaces, or subdivision surfaces). As long as I can give the sheet a pair of (u, v) coordinates and get back a three-dimensional point on the surface, that's all I need.

Now to fill in a point on the film, I take its (u, v) coordinates to get the ray origin A, and use the same (u, v) values to find a point B on the lens surface. The ray heads off in the direction vector $\mathbf{D} = B - A$. Figure 12.10 shows these two surfaces in our scene, and Figure 12.11 shows a rendered image.

This technique is a good start, but it's got a few problems. First, positioning these sheets in three-dimensional space is difficult, even using modern production systems. Second, figuring out how the sheets interact to determine the ray directions is just about impossible. Moving around control points on the two surfaces to get the rays to point where you want them to is, in my experience, a never-ending task of endless tweaking: every change throws off all the others, and you can go around and around forever. It's hopeless to try making small or local changes.

The essential problem here is that we're trying to manipulate these three-dimensional sheets in order to achieve a two-dimensional result. Part of the problem in getting the surfaces to behave the way we want is that the mapping from three dimensions to two dimensions is hard to visualize and control.

I don't think this two-sheet approach has much of a future. It's a great way to think about the possibilities offered by this kind of camera model, but it's a lousy interface for actually specifying it. Let's look at something better.

THE OLD COLLAGE TRY

Since our goal is to produce a two-dimensional image, let's see if we can find a way of working that better matches the two-dimensional results we're after.

The general approach that I'll describe here uses conventional cameras to create pieces of the final picture, which you then use to build a collage. The computer fills in the empty spaces in the collage.

Figure 12.10

Adding a sheet of lens putty to Figure 12.6. The lens is the yellow-and-red checkerboard.

Figure 12.11

The rendered version of Figure 12.10. Compare this to Figure 12-9. Here we can see the front of the café. The windows and door are compressed, but visible.

Synthetic Cubism

(a)   (b)   (c)   (d)   (e)

Figure 12.12

An overview of the Multicamera Collage. (a–c) The three camera images. Note that there's something floating in her drink. (d) The collage built from these three images. (e) The re-rendered result.

The general idea is shown in Figure 12.12. The process is the same whether you're making a single still image or an animated sequence. Start off by rendering your scene from as many different points of view as you like, using your system's built-in cameras. Figure 12.12(a-c) shows the result for three different cameras. During this process, you tell the program to use a custom lens shader (which I call the *lens writer*). This shader has no visible effect on your rendering but creates a couple of files per frame. Follow this up by running the *camera tagger* program. It takes no arguments and has no user interface; just run it, and when it's finished, move on to the next step.

Now load up the images you created in the last section into any image-editing program that supports layers. Use a selection tool to cut away the parts of each image that you don't want in the final. Figure 12.12(d) shows such a collage using the images from Figure 12.12(a-c). Save the collage picture. Run another program, called the *lens builder*, and wait for it to finish.

Now open up your three-dimensional scene again, tell the renderer to include a different lens shader, which I call the *lens reader*, and render the image. This shader will create a new image that looks like your collage, but the black regions will be smoothly filled in with views of the scene, as in Figure 12.12(e).

If you're making an animated sequence, you'll probably want to make several collage files at different points in the sequence. The system will smoothly interpolate those collages along with everything else, producing a smooth animation with your changing cameras.

Note that there's no restriction on the types of cameras you use, how many you can use, or the shapes you pick from each one. You can pick one big blob from each camera, or a dozen tiny spots from each one.

This technique has at least three nice things going for it. First, we don't have to accomplish anything difficult in three dimensions; we just use the regular three-dimensional system with its built-in cameras, and make the images we want. Second, building the collage is an easy process in any two-dimensional image editing package that supports layers. Third, and maybe most important, the person using the system doesn't need to know anything about the underlying technical details. In the course of putting together a newly-rendered frame, the user runs a couple of programs that manipulate files, but there are no user interfaces on those programs, and no variables to be selected or controlled. The programs do their work silently and independently.

Let's look under the hood at the two shaders and the two programs, which are the essential software that makes this all work.

Taking Shade

Shaders were invented by Rob Cook to open up the traditional rendering pipeline. Shaders are little nuggets of programming that tell the rendering system what to do at various steps along the way of creating an image. The Multicamera Collage depends on a pair of custom (but easy to write) lens shaders.

Most ray-tracers let you plug a lens shader into the pipeline. Once the system has built the eye ray, but before it starts using it to find illumination from the environment, it calls your lens shader. This little piece of code can do anything at all: compute the square root of π, simulate the flow of wind over a wing, or, more commonly, adjust the ray parameters. In our case, we'll either simply save the ray into a file, or we'll adjust the ray origin and direction.

Once the lens shader is finished, the system uses the eye ray to find the color to be associated with the corresponding spot on the film. If the system wants to do anti-aliasing, motion blur, depth of field, or any other process that requires more eye rays, it simply makes them and traces them as usual, though the lens shader is always called just before the ray goes into the world.

Len shaders typically have two sections: the *initialization* routine, and the *shader* proper. The initialization procedure is usually called at the start of a new frame, and the shader itself once per ray.

The Multicamera collage uses two lens shaders.

The *lens writer* is used when you're rendering your initial views of the scene that get placed into the collage, as in Figure 12.12(a). The initialization routine creates a new text file, whose name is a combination of the camera number and the frame number. For example, if we're rendering frame five from camera three, the file is called "frame0005camera03.txt." It saves the name of this file internally and closes it.

From now on, each time the lens writer is called, it simply opens up the file, appends a plaintext line containing the ray's two-dimensional screen location, three-dimensional origin point, and three-dimensional

Synthetic Cubism

Figure 12.13

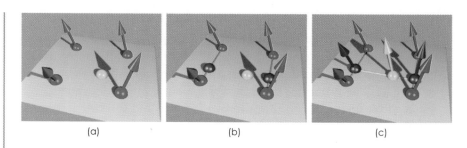

A schematic view of how camera rays are combined to create a new, interpolated ray for re-rendering. (a) The yellow dot is the location we want to sample, and the red dots show where we have rays, indicated by the red arrows. (b) First we interpolate the left and right pairs of values, finding the rays at the blue dots. (c) We interpolate the rays computed in the last step, shown by the blue arrows, to form the yellow ray.

direction vector to the end, and closes the file. Then it returns and lets the system follow the ray as usual.

For convenience in later processing, I tell the system to create exactly one ray per pixel while rendering these images. So if the image has dimensions of w by h pixels, there are wh lines in the text file.

When each frame has been created, the image is saved in TIFF format using the same base name as the text file. The frame rendered by camera three for frame five is "frame0005camera03.tif."

The *lens reader*, used at the end of the process to compute the interpolated image, carries out this process roughly in reverse. It assumes that the lens builder program has been run already. That program creates one file per frame, in the same format as that of the lens writer: one line per ray, containing the ray's screen location, origin, and direction.

When the lens reader is initialized, it opens the file for that frame (frame 51 is "frame0051.txt"). It reads in all of the ray descriptions and saves them in local memory, then closes the file.

From now on, each time the lens reader is called, it looks up the given ray's two-dimensional screen location. It then consults the database of rays that it read in, and uses the screen coordinates to interpolate the input rays, as shown in Figure 12.13. I blend the ray positions using linear interpolation, and the directions using multipoint direction interpolation, discussed later. I overwrite the input ray's origin point and direction vector with this computed ray, and then return it to the rendering system.

So although the renderer is generating eye rays and setting them up for rendering, the lens reader overwrites those rays before they head out into the environment. The renderer doesn't know that, of course, so it anti-aliases and does motion blur and everything else as usual. The result is a picture in which every ray has been independently placed and directed by the lens reader in order to create the smooth scene we desire.

Let's now look at the two programs that complete the system.

CAMERA TAGGER

The first program is run after you render the source images for the collage, but before you import the pictures into your favorite image editor.

The job of the *camera tagger* is very simple: it overwrites a few bits in every pixel with the number of the camera that created that image.

For example, suppose we open a rendered frame called "frame0013camera09.tif," which tells us that the image was rendered by camera nine. The camera tagger reads each pixel in the image one at a time and extracts the eight-bit values for red, green, and blue.

I think of the low-order two bits of each color as forming a single six-bit binary number. The two low-order bits of blue correspond to the two highest-order bits in the number, the two low-order bits of green are in the middle, and the two low-order bits of red make up the lowest-order bits of the number. In our example, camera nine corresponds to binary 001001. So I'd put 00 in the two low-order bits of the blue color, 10 in the two low-order bits of green, and 01 in the two low-order bits of red, and save the pixel. I do this for every pixel in the image.

Of course, this can introduce some visible artifacts into the image, such as color shifting and banding. But these modified pixels are only used in the collaging process and don't appear in the final image. As long as the image is still clear enough to be useful in making the collage, then no harm is done.

Since I'm using six bits, I can represent 63 cameras (as we'll see later, the number 0 is reserved for "no camera"). I've never wanted that many cameras in a single frame, but if you wanted more, you could just use more bits. Taking three bits per channel would let you encode 511 different cameras.

LENS REMAPPER

The collage file is an image that contains two types of pixels: those that are from the black background (that is, they have 0 in all three color channels), and those that are from a camera (so at least one of the lowest-two bits in at least one of the color channels is a one). Note that the background black is different than black from an image. For example, if camera six was looking at a pitch-black object and wrote (0,0,0) in the RGB channels for some pixels, those pixels would become (2,1,0) after the camera tagger went to work (red = 10, green = 01, blue = 00, which go together in the order 000110, forming the binary number 6). So pixels with the color (0,0,0) mean "no camera," and those are the ones we'll fill in.

Figure 12.14

The edge images from the
cameras of Figure 12.12.

The job of the lens remapper is to create a new input file for the lens reader, giving it the location and direction of one ray in the center of each pixel. The lens reader (remember that's our lens shader in the final step) will interpolate these rays as necessary for screen rays generated by the renderer.

The lens remapper takes the approach that the pixels in the collage that have a camera number associated with them are pixels you want to see in the final image. So if a given pixel in the collage is labeled with camera five, then in the output file the ray for that pixel will come from the text file stored with camera five, which gives the exact origin and direction of the ray that was used for that pixel by that camera.

On the other hand, pixels that have no camera have a ray computed for them. The computation is designed so that the rays sample the visual field smoothly over the entire image. I do this by finding the nearest pixel from each camera, and coming up with a weight for those pixels, so that the nearer ones make more of a contribution than those far away. Then I go to the text files for each camera, weight the rays associated with those pixels by the given amount, and then add them all up. The key is to remember that the text files let us retrieve the ray information associated with every camera and every pixel.

The first step in the process is to find the edges for each camera, as shown in Figure 12.14.

The edge-finder is pretty straightforward. It marches through the collage image, and calls a routine that returns true or false, identifying whether the pixel is to be considered on an edge or not.

The identifying routine begins by extracting the pixel's camera number. If the camera is 0 (that is, the pixel is from the black background), the routine returns false. Continuing on, if the pixel is on the outermost border of the collage, the routine returns true. Otherwise, the routine compares the pixel's camera number to the camera number of its eight neighbors. If the camera number associated with any of those eight cameras is different than the camera number for the pixel we're processing, the routine returns true; otherwise, it returns false. Figure 12.15 shows these tests visually.

When I find an edge pixel, I add it to a list of edge pixels for its associated camera. So later on, when I want to look through all the edge pixels for any camera, I can easily access them all without any additional processing.

With the edge lists completed, I now start computing weights. Let's say that $A_i(x, y)$ is the ray origin saved at pixel (x, y) for camera i, and $\mathbf{D}_i(x, y)$ is the ray direction saved at pixel (x, y) for camera i. Let's package this information together as a ray $R_i(x, y)$. The weighting process involves finding a set of scalar weights that I can apply to these points and vectors to create a new ray. For each camera i, I find a scalar weight α_i, and a particular pixel (x_i, y_i), so the new ray R drawn from C cameras in the collage is

$$R(x, y) = \sum_{i=1}^{C} \alpha_i R_i(x_i, y_i).$$

In words, to find the ray at (x, y), I find a pixel (x_i, y_i) for each camera i, get the ray information R_i for that pixel from the text file for that camera, weight it by α_i, and add it into the running total for the new ray. Just how the rays are scaled and added up requires a little discussion, which I'll get back to below. For now, let's concentrate on the problems of finding the pixel we want for each camera, and then the right weight for it.

I compute all of this information across the whole picture before I actually build the new rays, because I process the weights after they've all been calculated.

One way to think of this is that if the input image has dimensions $w \times h$, then I build C two-dimensional data structures, each $w \times h$, one for each camera. Each element of these data structures contains a floating-point number (the weight α) and two integers (identifying the pixel (x, y) that should be used from that camera to contribute to the pixel where it's located).

Let's process a single pixel P from the collage, located at (x_p, y_p).

I retrieve the pixel and look for its camera tag. If it has one (that is, the camera number encoded in those low bits is nonzero), then I know I want that pixel to have exactly the same ray as the one used by its camera. Let's say it was made by camera c. Then I set $\alpha_c = 1$ and all the other α_i to 0. I also set the pixel coordinates in all data structures for all the cameras to (x_p, y_p). The result is that when I go to build the

Figure 12.15

Finding the edges. If a pixel is in the background, it is not on an edge (the red dot). If a pixel is in a camera but on the border, it is an edge (the blue dot). If a pixel is on the border of a camera region and black, it is an edge (the yellow dot). If a pixel is on the border of two camera regions, it is an edge (the green dot).

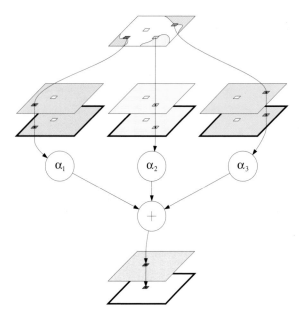

Figure 12.16

A schematic of the weighting process. At the top we show the pixel we want to find values for, and the nearest pixel in each of the three camera regions. In the middle, we see using the location of that pixel to look at the data stored with those cameras to find the ray origin and direction for that camera at that pixel. These values are scaled and summed together, creating a final origin and direction for the ray at that pixel, shown at the bottom.

ray for this pixel later, the ray used by camera c at this pixel will be what I compute. Figure 12.16 shows this idea. Then I move on to the next pixel.

On the other hand, if the pixel has no camera, then I need to work harder. First, I scan through the edge list for each camera and locate the edge pixel that is nearest to P. The coordinates of that pixel get written into the data structure for each camera.

Now I need to compute the weights. For this, I use the multipoint weighting technique I described in my March 2001 column, "Tricks of the Trade" (see the Further Reading section for pointers to book versions of this and other columns). To summarize this idea quickly, let's call each camera pixel c_i for $i = [1, C]$. I start by finding the distance from P to each of these pixels:

$$d_i = |P - c_i|.$$

Now I normalize these so that they sum to 1. I call the normalized distances g_i:

$$D = \sum_{i=1}^{C} d_i$$

$$g_i = d_i/D .$$

Now I find a strength v_i that tells me how much each of the pixels is affecting P:

$$v_i = (1 - g_i) \prod_{\substack{j = 1 \\ j \neq i}}^{C} g_j .$$

To get our weights w_i, we just normalize the v_i:

$$V = \sum_{i=1}^{C} v_i$$

$$w_i = v_i/V .$$

Although the weights produced by this method are continuous across the image, they're not continuous in the first derivative. Figure 12.17 shows an example of the weight applied to a camera as we move from a

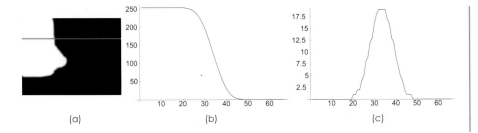

Figure 12.17

(a) The red scanline starts within a camera region and moves into the background. (b) The weight associated with this camera across this scanline is continuous. (c) The first derivative of the weight is not continuous.

region where that camera is present into the black zone next to it. The sharp edge in the weight will affect the later steps in the process and the final image: it will seem to have a crease along that edge.

To smooth things out, I apply a little bit of filtering. Each filter runs on the weights for each camera independently. It's important to double-buffer these filters, which means that I process all of the weights and compute new values for the entire camera before I write them back.

First I blur the weights using a box filter of radius 4. This just means that for each black pixel P, I add up all of the weights applied to the 9-by-9 block of pixels centered around P, divide by 81, and use that for the new value at P (for boundary pixels, I divide only by the number of pixels that are actually in the image and get added to the average).

Then I apply an ease curve to the weights. This is simply an S-shaped curve that smoothes the edges a bit more. Returning again to my March 2001 column, I use the ease curve described there with a premapped control value of 0.75, shown in Figure 12.18.

After this I blur with another box filter of radius 3, which smoothes out any remaining rough edges.

I then pass through each pixel one at a time, and re-normalize the weights so that they sum up to one again. To do this, I just add up the weights, and divide each one by that sum.

Now that I have everything I need, I just run through the pixels and apply the formula we saw at the start of this section, weighting and combining the camera rays at each pixel to create a single new ray. I said that I'd return to how that's done later, and now the time has come.

Weighting and adding up the ray's origins is a snap: I just scale the three coordinates by the weight and add them up, just like interpolating any real numbers. Since the weights sum to 1, no further normalization is needed:

$$A(x, y) = \sum_{i=1}^{C} A_i(x_i, y_i) .$$

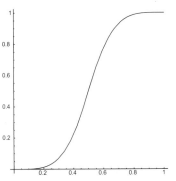

Figure 12.18

The ease curve that I apply to the weights.

The direction vectors are a little trickier. As I discussed in my March 1997 column, "Situation Normal," if we simply interpolate the vector coordinates independently and then renormalize the result (à la Phong shading), we don't quite get circular interpolation. In this situation, we'd end up with visible creases. What we want is to interpolate the direction vectors as vectors, not points. In that column I gave a formula for interpolating two unit vectors $\mathbf{P}$ and $\mathbf{R}$:

$$\mathbf{Q}(\alpha) = \frac{\sin(\theta - \psi)}{\sin \theta}\mathbf{P} + \frac{\sin \psi}{\sin \theta}\mathbf{R}$$

where α is our interpolating variable that sweeps from 0 to 1, $\psi = \alpha\theta$, and θ is the angle between the two vectors: $\theta = \cos^{-1}(\mathbf{P} \cdot \mathbf{R})$. That's fine when there are only two vectors, but here we need to combine c vectors, which will usually be 3 or more.

The solution comes yet again from the March 2001 column, where I presented a method called *burp*, for bilinear uniform interpolation. I'll summarize the essential details here. We want to find a linear sum P as

$$P = \sum_{i=0}^{n-1} \alpha_i p_i \quad \text{where} \quad \sum_{i=0}^{n-1} \alpha_i = 1$$

using a series of two-point interpolations. We can decompose this result into several small pieces. We want to find $P = r_0$:

$$r_0 = \sum_{i=0}^{n-1} \alpha_i p_i \quad \text{where} \quad \sum_{i=0}^{2} \alpha_i = 1 \ .$$

We'll start by computing r_{n-1} and then work our way back up to r_0:

$$
\begin{aligned}
r_{n-1} &= p_{n-1} \\
r_k &= \frac{\alpha_k}{\beta_k} p_k + \frac{\beta_k - \alpha_k}{\beta_k} r_{k+1} \\
\beta_k &= \sum_{j=k}^{n-1} \alpha_j \ .
\end{aligned}
$$

For more details, and a worked example, consult the references in the Further Reading section. Now that I have both the origin and direction of a ray for this pixel, I simply write these six numbers out to a plain-text output file. The file has one line per ray, and one ray per pixel. This is the file that's read in by the lens reader shader to make the final image.

REGIONS

The above algorithm does a pretty good job on some images, but it makes terrible mistakes on others. The essential problem is that the algorithm finds the new ray by combining a ray from every camera. But there are times when we don't want all of the cameras to contribute to a pixel.

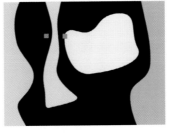

Figure 12.19

This is a schematic collage, where the camera regions are shown as solid blobs of different colors. In this collage, the pixel marked in red should probably not be influenced by the pixel marked in green, belonging to camera number four, associated with the yellow blob.

For example, consider Figure 12.19, where I've shown a collage made from four cameras and a current pixel P, marked in red. The nearest pixel from the yellow blob, marked in green, isn't very many pixels away, so it's going to have a strong influence on P. But we can see from the picture that we'd rather that the yellow camera didn't contribute to P at all.

To control this influence, you can draw a *region image* when you make the collage image. A typical region image is shown in Figure 12.20. It's just a bunch of areas of arbitrary shapes, each filled with a different color.

When there's a region image available in the same directory as the collage image, I use it to guide the selection of pixels from each camera. When I start processing a pixel P, I first check to see what region it's in (I just use the color of that pixel in the region image). Now when I run through the list of edge pixels for each camera, I

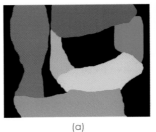

(a)　　　　　　　　(b)

Figure 12.20

(a) A hand-drawn regions image to control which cameras contribute to which pixels in Figure 12.19. (b) The region map laid over the collage of Figure 12.19.

retrieve the region for each pixel, and if it's not the same as the region for P, I skip it. If I get to the end of the list and I haven't found any pixels from that camera in the same region as P, I just mark that camera as a nonparticipant for that pixel. If there's no region image, then implicitly every pixel in the picture is in the same region.

The shapes in the region image can have any shape or size, they can be filled with any color, and there can be any number of them. Just draw them as you like, but use a drawing tool that doesn't anti-alias your selection (otherwise those blended pixels will each be its own one-pixel-large region!).

Regions aren't a perfect solution, though, because they can introduce visible discontinuities in the final image. Figure 12.21 shows the boundary between two different regions. In one region, we're interpolating cameras one and two, and in the next, cameras one and three. I don't have a very good solution for this problem; the way I handle it now is to try to use my eye when I draw regions, and to

Figure 12.21

A possible problem with regions. (a) A schematic collage of three cameras. (b) Adding regions, shown here in light blue and green. The upper and lower edges of this boundary, shown by the red and yellow pixels, would probably display a crease if the weights weren't smoothed.

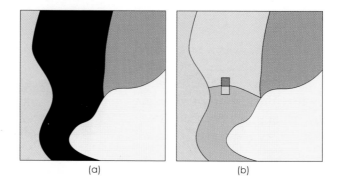

(a) (b)

try to avoid creating sharp edges like this. The filtering and blurring steps that I apply to the weights help smooth out this crease, but I'd prefer to have never created it in the first place.

The multicamera collage technique raises some interesting artistic and technical ideas.

Suppose we have a collage where the top half is one rendering, and a small blob appears somewhere on the bottom edge, as in Figure 12.22(a). What should happen in the lower corners? The general problem is that outside the convex hull of the renderings, we don't have data to interpolate. One reasonable solution might be to use some kind of extrapolation. An alternative would use an iterative approach that "grows" extrapolated data beyond the interpolated convex hull using incremental techniques. My general solution to this is to always render images slightly larger than I need, so that I can always include a "frame" of in-camera pixels along the outermost border of my collages, as in Figure 12.22(b). After my new frames are computed, I crop them and discard the border.

Figure 12.22

(a) The blob problem. How do we find weights for the pixels in the lower right corner? (b) My solution is to always include a frame of camera pixels in the collage.

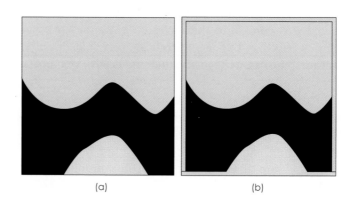

(a) (b)

DETAILS

I implemented this system using 3ds max 6 and the mental ray 4.3 rendering system that ships with it. Mental ray is very good at taking advantage of parallelism and will make use of as many processors as it can find. On my home computer, I have two Pentium processors.

This combination caused me endless headaches while I was trying to get my lens writer shader to work, because different but parallel copies of the shader were trying to write to the same file at the same time. Once I realized what was happening, I took the easy way out and put the little bit of code that writes to the file inside a locked region, which means that only one instance can be running at a time. The locked region opens the text file, appends a ray, then closes the file. It's inefficient and you can definitely see a slowdown, but because I'm only firing one ray per pixel, and this is just a testbed, this quick-and-dirty solution was okay.

It did mean that I had to precede each line with the (x, y) coordinates of the pixel being written, since they could arrive in any sequence. The lens remapper uses those coordinates to make sure the right data goes into the right pixel.

Similarly, the lens reader initialization routine is locked, because I want to make sure that it completes its reading-in of the data before any rendering occurs. After that, there's no locking, since the reader is only looking up data from its database of per-pixel ray information, which remains constant.

It's important when building the collage and region images to use selection tools that don't anti-alias. The reason is that such tools typically blend nearby pixels to create a smooth edge. In the collage, such blending will mess up the camera tags that we've written to our pixels, which will both create extraneous cameras and misidentify pixels on the edge. In the region image, anti-aliased pixels will end up becoming tiny one-pixel-large regions, each of its own color. The collage and region boundaries should be hard edged and very likely will show ugly jaggies. As with the other image artifacts produced during the collaging process, this has no effect on the final image.

EXAMPLES

Figures 12.23, 12.24, and 12.25 show three scenes rendered with the multicamera collage technique. Notice that the same scene can be shot, composed, and collaged in many different ways.

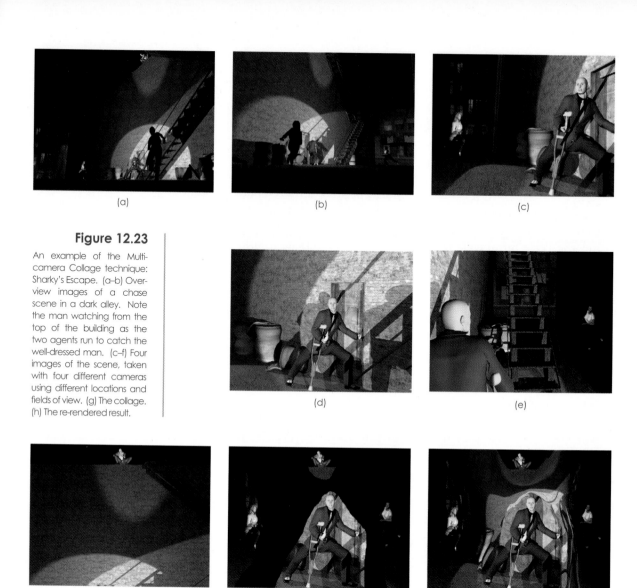

Figure 12.23

An example of the Multi-camera Collage technique: Sharky's Escape. (a–b) Over-view images of a chase scene in a dark alley. Note the man watching from the top of the building as the two agents run to catch the well-dressed man. (c–f) Four images of the scene, taken with four different cameras using different locations and fields of view. (g) The collage. (h) The re-rendered result.

One of the most interesting effects comes from reversed versions of scene elements that appear between camera regions. If we're seeing the same character from the back in two adjacent places on the screen, then the camera is moving over their body from left to right. So in the space between these regions the camera naturally has to move right to left, filling in the smooth scene and creating a reversed version of the character.

(a)

(b)

(c)

Figure 12.24

Another example of the *Multicamera Collage* technique: A Bad Night at Big Light. (a) An overview image of the scene. Skippy is hanging on for dear life from the top of the lighthouse, above the skeleton waiting to grab him when he falls. Sarah, whose ankle is broken, watches from the side while her dogs attack the skeleton. (b–e) Four different *Multicamera Collages* of the scene.

(d)

(e)

Synthetic
Cubism

(a)

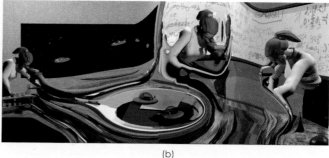

(b)

(c)

Figure 12.25

Another example of the Multicamera Collage technique: Revenge of the Bugs. (a) An overview of the scene. A scientist is working alone late at night. (b–c) Two different Muticamera Collages of the scene.

ANIMATION

This algorithm is frame-based, which makes it very easy to use for animation.

Suppose that you want to create a 500-frame animated sequence using three cameras. You might render all the cameras at frames 0, 200, 350, and 500, for a total of 15 images. From these, you would create four different collages, one from each set. You could also create a region image for each collage if you like.

Run each of these files through the standard MCC process, creating a new file that would be appropriate for re-rendering with the lens reader. In fact, you can go ahead and render those images and confirm that the interpolation is to your liking. If not, you can go back and tweak the cameras and the collages until everything looks just right.

Now think of those four files as the equivalent of keyframes. For each pixel, for each of these four frames, we have a screen position, a ray origin, and a ray direction. A small program, which again has no user interface, looks in the directory where these files are located and fills in the missing files. For example, if we're shooting a picnic scene we might have named our four keyframes *picnic0000.dat, picnic0200.dat, picnic0350.dat,* and *picnic0500.dat.* The *frame interpolator* program creates all the missing files, from *picnic0001.dat* to *picnic499.dat*. Each of these files is structurally identical to the four key files produced directly by the MCC pipeline.

The frame interpolator makes all the new frames in parallel. First I note which frames already exist (in this case, 0, 200, 350, and 500). Next I create each of the necessary intermediate files, and save the image resolution (width and height) at the start of each one.

Now I'm ready to process rays. I read the first ray from each of the four key files, and I build six interpolating cubic splines, one each for the three ray origin coordinates and the three ray directions. In this case the first spline would be built from the four pairs $(0,FX_0)$, $(200,FX_{200})$, $(350,FX_{350})$, and $(400,FX_{400})$, where FX_f is the x coordinate for the ray origin at frame f. To find the value for the ray x coordinate at any other frame, I just evaluate this spline using the frame number.

When I've built all six splines, I produce a new ray for each new frame. In this example, I'd first plug in frame 1 and get back six values, three for the ray origin point and three for the direction vector. I normalize the direction vector, and then I write this ray's screen-space location, origin, and direction into *picnic001.dat*. Then I evaluate the splines for frame 2, write the ray into *picnic002.dat*, and so on, until I finish with *picnic0499.dat*.

Then I return to the input files and get the next four rays, corresponding to the key values for the second ray at the four key times. I build new splines, evaluate them for each intermediate frame, and append the new rays to the end of each intermediate file. In this way, I build up the interpolated files in parallel, each of them growing by a single ray on each pass.

The result is that the directory now holds 501 complete files, one each from 0 to 500. When I render an animated sequence, the lens reader simply opens the file corresponding to the frame number it's currently working on.

This technique uses a lot of disk space, since I have to build a complete file for each frame. But remember that thanks to the lens reader's interpolation procedure, these frames don't have to be the full resolution of the output frames. In fact, I usually build my MCC frames at one-quarter of my final output resolution, so these files are one-sixteenth the size that they would have been at the final resolution.

I used six different splines for interpolation because it was easy to program. For interpolating the ray direction, I'd get nicer results if I used the angle-based vector interpolation process that I use in the lens reader code. The artifacts that come from interpolating vector components, and then re-normalizing, are exactly those of Phong shading, except that they show up in motion rather than brightness or color. This shortcut hasn't produced any artifacts that I've seen so far, but I plan to replace it with the proper vector interpolation scheme.

Figures 12.26 and 12.27 show two examples of keys and interpolated frames.

If you're concerned with motion blur, you can easily adapt the lens shader so that it reads in not just the data for the present frame, but for the next frame as well, and then use the ray's time value to interpolate between the two sets of data.

(a)

(b)

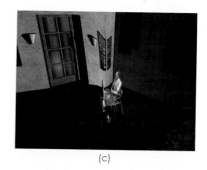

(c)

Figure 12.26

The Multicamera Collage used for animation. (a–b) Two key frames for the café scene, at frames 0 and 90. (c–g) Interpolated frames 15, 30, 45, 60, and 75.

(d)

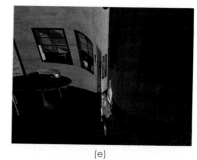

(e)

(f)

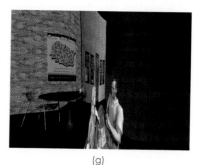

(g)

(a)

(b)

(c)

(d)

(e)

(f)

(g)

(h)

(i)

(j)

(k)

(l)

(m)

Figure 12.27

Another example of the Multicamera Collage for animation. In this shot from Sharky's Escape, the two agents are closing in on Sharky. (a–e) Key frames at times 0, 200, 400, 600, and 800. (f–m) Interpolated frames 50, 100, 150, 250, 300, 350, 500, and 700.

Synthetic Cubism

Discussion

An important quality of the multicamera collage is that it adds almost nothing to the cost of rendering a frame. The lens reader has to open the data file containing the ray information and read it into memory, which can take a few seconds. From then on, the only work done by the lens reader is the interpolation of those input rays to produce a desired eye ray. Compared to the typical work required to render an image, or a frame of animation, this small calculation is negligible.

Another nice aspect is that you can do all of the processing and collage work at a resolution significantly below that of your final rendering. As I mentioned earlier, I often work with images that have a width and height one-quarter of the final image. This makes all of the calculations faster and all of the data files one-sixteenth the size that they would be if I was working at final resolution. It also reduces the amount of time required to read the ray information at the start of each frame. I only work at the final render resolution when I need very local control of the camera selections, or when there are sharp edges between selections that I want to preserve.

I've thought about making a painting interface on top of the rendering system. Imagine starting with a blank image, selecting a camera, and then painting over the image. Where paint is placed, the camera is rendered and immediately displayed. The director can work with these image regions like camera viewports in the rendering system: they can be moved around, cut, pasted, and changed in shape. The director can select controls like those in the rendering interface and directly change the camera's location, direction, field of view, etc. The system could produce low-resolution interpolation results in as close to real time as possible; when the director ceases to paint for a moment, the system takes the idle time to compute an ever-denser smattering of interpolated pixels, giving an ever-better impression of the final result. The director could then respond immediately and adjust the cameras and renderings as desired. This might be more convenient than building a collage from prerendered images.

The MCC approach computes the pixels missing in the collage by ray-tracing a synthetic environment. An alternative approach would use image-based rendering (IBR) to retrieve environment data from images of the scene. The director could start the process with rendered images built from the IBR data, or with real photographs taken on a set, while another program takes the camera calibration information and writes the ray data that corresponds to the camera's image. If during the interpolation phase the MMC algorithm needs pixels that aren't available from the IBR data set, it could tell the user where to place and direct a camera in order to gather the missing imagery. I think we could integrate both IBR data and synthetic three-dimensional renderings in the same scene, either mixing them seamlessly for a single continuous image, or deliberately making it clear which is which for artistic reasons.

FURTHER READING

Pinhole cameras are great fun. You can find information on building them from Kodak at http://www.kodak.com/global/en/consumer/education/lessonPlans/pinholeCamera/, or from the Exploratorium at http://www.exploratorium.edu/light_walk/camera_todo.html. Wonderful galleries of pinhole photography, along with advice and other resources, are available online at http://www.pinhole.org, http://www.photo.net/pinhole/pinhole, and http://www.pinholeresource.com. A fascinating pinhole camera was printed in the Czech technical magazine *ABC* mladých techniků a přírodovědců, (*An ABC of Young Technicians and Natural Scientists*) in 1979. One needed only cut the heavy pages out of magazine and fold them up to make a camera, called the Dirkon, that looked like a 35mm camera, but was actually a working pinhole camera, complete with a winding mechanism! You can download the plans for the Dirkon in PDF format from http://www.pinhole.cz/en/pinholecameras/dirkon_01.html. You can find instructions for building an oatmeal-box camera, along with lots of photos, at http://users.rcn.com/stewoody/.

The geometry of a pinhole camera is pretty simple. You can see the details in my article "A Simple Viewing Geometry" by Andrew Glassner (in *Graphics Gems II*, edited by Jim Arvo, Academic Press, San Diego, 1991, pp. 179–180).

You can read up on the fascinating subject of maps and map projections, and see dozens of different projections, in *An Introduction to the Study of Map Projections* by J. A. Steers (University of London Press, London, 1965). You can find a more compact description aimed at the computer graphics audience in "Digital Cartography for Computer Graphics" by Alan W. Paeth (*Graphics Gems*, Academic Press, 1990 pp. 307–320).

Panoramic cameras have a long and colorful history, full of idiosyncratic inventors and rival patent wars. You can see a summary of the history of the subject at http://www.panoramicphoto.com/timeline.htm. I described Damoizeau's panoramic camera called the *cyclographe*; you can see a photo of it at http://www.geh.org/fm/cromer-tech/htmlsrc/mD16300002_ful.html. There's a brief but very clear discussion of slit-scan techniques in http://www.underview.com/2001/how/slitscan.html. Panoramic cameras are an important part of the virtual panorama viewing environments, like the Quicktime VR system described in "Quicktime VR—An Image-Based Approach to Virtual Environment Navigation" by Shenchang Eric Chen (*Proceedings of SIGGRAPH 95*, pp. 29–38, August 1995).

In my discussion of Cubism I referred to some well-known works. You can see Braque's "Houses at L'Estaque" online at http://www.artchive.com/artchive/B/braque/housesle.jpg.html, and Picasso's "Les Demoiselles d'Avognon" at http://moma.org/collection/depts/paint_sculpt/blowups/paint_sculpt_006.html. An excellent book on Cubism is *Picasso and Braque: A Symposium* (Museum of Modern Arts, New York, 1992), but any book on twentieth-century art history will have something interesting to say on the subject.

If you want to think about putting real optics in front of your simulated cameras, there are lots of places to find guidance. Check out "Synthetic Image Generation with a Lens and Aperture Camera Model" by M. Potmesil and I. Chakravarty (*ACM Transactions on Graphics*, 1(2), pp. 85–108, April 1982; "Simulation of Photographics Lenses and Filters for Realistic Image Synthesis" by Jorge Alberto Diz, George Nelson Marques de Moraes, and Leo Pini Magalhaes (*COMPUGRAPHICS '91*, I, pp. 197–205, 1991), and "A Realistic Camera Model for Computer Graphics" by Craig Kolb, Pat Hanrahan, and Don Mitchell (*SIGGRAPH 95*, pp. 317–324, August 1995).

Special-purpose real lenses have received their own special study, particularly those used by OMNIMAX cameras and projectors. See "Computer Graphics Distortion for IMAX and OMNIMAX Projection" by Nelson L. Max (*Nicograph '83 Proceedings*, December 1983, pp. 137–159), and "Creating Raster Omnimax Images From Multiple Perspective Views Using the Elliptical Weighted Average Filter" by Ned Greene and Paul S. Heckbert (*IEEE Computer Graphics & Applications*, 6(6), June 1986, pp. 21–27). Unusual projections are used now all the time for environment mapping; the seminal paper on that subject is "Environment Mapping and Other Applications of World Projections" by Ned Greene (*IEEE Computer Graphics & Applications*, 6(11), pp. 21–29, November 1986).

I've referred in the text to a number of my previous columns. My discussion of vector interpolation and the formula for computing circular interpolation appears in "Situation Normal" (*IEEE Computer Graphics & Applications*, 17(2), March 1997). My discussion of camera shutters appears in my May 1999 "An Open and Shut Case" (*IEEE*

Computer Graphics & Applications, 19(3), pp. 82–92, May 1999). Multipoint interpolation and the *burp* algorithm both appear in "Tricks of the Trade" (*IEEE Computer Graphics & Applications*, 21(2), March 2001). These columns are now all available in book form, where they have been revised and expanded. "Situation Normal" is Chapter 5 of *Andrew Glassner's Notebook* (Morgan-Kaufmann, San Francisco, 1999), and the other two columns are Chapter 1 and Chapter 8, repsectively, in *Andrew Glassner's Other Notebook* (A K Peters, Natick, MA, 2002).

Perhaps the richest camera is the one that's defined by nothing more than some geometric equations or procedures. If you want make an image with your film wrapped around a torus, for example, ray tracing is a great way to go, as discussed and demonstrated in "Optical Models" by G. Wyvill and C. McNaughton (*Proceedings of CG International '90: Computer Graphics Around the World*, pp. 83–93, 1990).

Film grammar is evolving quickly. The basics, discussed in *Grammar of the Film Language* by Daniel Arijon (Silman-James Press, Los Angeles, 1976), are expanding with every new technology. The "bullet time" effect was used to great effect in *The Matrix* (written and directed by Andy Wachowski and Larry Wachowski, 1999). For some of the details on the technique, see "Jacking into the Matrix" by Kevin H. Martin (*Cinefex*, October 1999, pp. 66–89). Split-screen was used as a storytelling tool in *Napoléon* (written and directed by Abel Gance, 1927) and more recently was the central gimmick in *Timecode* (written and directed by Mike Figgis, 2000). Rewinding narratives are also becoming more common, exemplified by *Run Lola Run* (written and directed by Tom Tykwer, 1998).

Shaders are a very important subject and the focus of many software and hardware designs. The seminal paper on shaders is "Shade Trees" by Robert L. Cook (*SIGGRAPH 84*, 18(3), pp. 223–231, 1984).

The multiperspective camera technique is described in "Multiperspective Panoramas for Cel Animation" by Daniel N. Wood, Adam Finkelstein, John F. Hughes, Craig E. Thayer, and David H. Salesin (*SIGGRAPH 97*, pp. 243–250, August 1997).

I wrote this implementation of the MultiCollage Camera with a variety of software tools. All of the complicated processing is done with a couple of standalone programs that I wrote in C# using Microsoft's .NET programming environment. To make the images, I used discreet's 3ds max 6 production system. I wrote my lens shaders for mental ray 4.3, which I used to create the rendered images. I created the collages in Photoshop CS.

I've been thinking about these ideas for a long time. I wrote my first implementation in 2000 when I worked at Microsoft Research. A

Synthetic Cubism

summary of my work at that time is available in "Cubism and Cameras: Free-Form Optics for Computer Graphics" by Andrew S. Glassner (*MSR-TR-2000-05*, January 2000, available online at http://research. microsoft.com/research/pubs/view.aspx?msr_tr_id=MSR-TR-2000-05).

Thanks to Steven Drucker, Ned Greene, Tom McClure, and Claude Robillard for discussions, ideas, and help.

Crop
Art

What's the coolest display medium for computer graphics that you've ever seen? We're all used to beautiful CRT and LCD screens. Graphics look great on film of many sizes, from 35mm and 70mm to IMAX. There are also the computer-controlled lasers used in planetariums and rock concerts, and we've seen graphics on surfaces as diverse as sheets of fog and curtains of water, big pieces of stone, birthday cakes, and even the sides of buildings.

There's another medium out there that people don't often think about: a field of crops. The medium is very high-resolution and capable of displaying very large images, dozens of yards or meters on a side. That's the good news. On the other hand, it's got very limited color fidelity; in fact, there are only two colors available, and you don't even get to pick them. Making an image requires either hours of exhaustive effort with a small team, or the cooperation of friendly space aliens with UFOs and other technology.

Not any field of crops will do: thanks to how easy they are to bend, and their willingness to stay bent, canola, wheat, barley, and oats are your best choices for efficient construction and crisp presentation. The general idea is to create a two-color design by flattening down some of the crop, as shown in Figure 13.1. The parts that are flattened will appear a different color than the parts that are left standing. Using some form of technology (simple, complex, or extraterrestrial), you flatten the crops according to a pattern, and you've created your output!

Figure 13.1

Two photographs of crop circles. Note that there are only two colors available in the design. (Images copyright Colin Andrews, http://www.CropCircleInfo. com, used by permission.)

These types of patterns are often called "crop circles" because the earliest examples were indeed simply circles, or small collections of circles. Today, crop art has moved far beyond simple circles, as Figure 13.1 shows. Sometimes crop designs are called pictograms or formations.

The subject of crop circles is fascinating in two ways. First, there are interesting geometric challenges posed by the very limited number of tools that one can typically use when creating such a design in the field, typically under the cover of darkness. Second, the social phenomena surrounding these designs is a rich mixture of people who create them, those who study them, and those who vigorously debate a wide variety of conflicting theories regarding their creation and meaning.

A BALANCED BREAKFAST

There's no way to know exactly when or where the crop circle phenomenon started. It certainly goes back to at least August 15, 1980, when the British paper the *Wiltshire Times* published an account of three circular shapes in the oat fields of England. Over the next few years, circles began to appear in other English fields, and local papers would run stories along with a photograph or two. Nobody really knew what to make of the circles, although there was widespread speculation that they were somehow associated with, or even created by, space aliens. Groups of researchers started to form, dedicated to studying each new formation as it was discovered.

On September 9, 1991, the British tabloid *Today* published an article titled "The Men Who Conned the World." According to the article, two landscape artists named Doug Bower and Dave Chorley announced that they had been behind many of the crop circles that had been observed in the previous decade. The next day the two men, respectively 67 and 62 years old, demonstrated their technique at a live press conference in Chilgrove in Sussex. Using a couple of boards with ropes, they created a pair of dumbbell-shaped crop formations for a group of reporters, who filmed the entire demonstration.

Anyone who thought that this demonstration would put an end to the theories that the circles were of extraterrestrial origin would have been surprised by the reaction. Although a few people doubtlessly accepted this explanation, many of the crop circle groups rejected both the claims and the demonstration as "fakes." It's an interesting point of view: two men who came forward as the perpetrators of a hoax were declaimed themselves to be hoaxsters of a higher order, since their claims to have created the hoax were seen as bogus!

This set the stage for what is now standard terminology used by those who study crop circles, called *cerealogists*. A "genuine" crop circle is one that was created by space aliens, using any of a wide variety of possible technologies, from radiation or controlled whirlwind fields, to ball lightning and undetectable manipulations of matter. On the other hand, formations that are created by people are termed "hoaxes," "frauds," and "fakes." The people who make such formations are considered "hoaxsters" and "frauds."

Cerealogists have developed a number of techniques that they use to determine whether a given crop formation was made by humans or left behind by space aliens. These tests include rubbing stalks of grain together and noticing towards which cardinal direction they seem to move, using dowsing rods on the area, and measuring for unusual levels of phenomena ranging from bacterial activity to radioactivity. Cerealogists also investigate the nature of the bent and broken crops themselves, reasoning that certain patterns of flattening, and specific types of damage to the stalks, are impossible for humans to create. Formations that demonstrate those patterns must therefore be genuine (that is, of extraterrestrial origin).

People who make crop circles, known as *circlemakers*, are of course motivated by a wide range of impulses. One of the most common of these is the desire to create very large and impermanent art. They share an aesthetic with the artists who build elaborate sand castles at the beach: the fun is in the process, and in the knowledge that the art itself is fleeting and will soon disappear.

The sociology of crop circle creators, investigators, and adherents of each theory is a fascinating symbiosis: the investigators wouldn't exist without the formations to look into, the theorists couldn't hypothesize without some kinds of measurements to refer to, and it's likely that many of the artists wouldn't bother to make the works if there wasn't such an attentive and appreciative audience out there to receive them. The fact that most circlemakers work anonymously is probably due to the legacy of "Doug and Dave," who set the tone for overnight, stealth construction.

Today, crop circles are the subject of a large number of books and websites. Organizations exist to create crop circles, study them, and promote and debunk every kind of theory of construction. You can find pointers to some websites in the Further Reading section.

In this chapter, I'll look first at some of the interesting geometry behind crop circles and related formations. Then I'll talk about a language I've developed to help make it easier to design and construct crop circles. Finally, I'll discuss some of the practical aspects of making crop circles, illustrated with my experience of actually making a formation.

BASIC CONSTRUCTION

Let's suppose we've decided that we would like to make a crop circle design. If we're to go about it in the traditional way, we have a few constraints to obey.

The most important limitations are that we need to make our construction under the cover of darkness, over the course of a single evening. To avoid detection, we can't use flashlights, lasers, or any other large, light-emitting devices. We want to leave behind as little evidence of our presence as possible, so that means not only no trash, but no accidentally-crushed stalks, no chalk lines or other marks, and no holes left over from posts and stakes pushed into the ground. Traditionally, we'll go out with nothing but some surveyor's tape, string, a plan, and a *stomper*. A stomper is a tool for flattening grain.

Like many elegant tools, the stomper is simplicity itself. It was originally shown by Doug and Dave in their famous 1991 demonstration.

A typical stomper is shown in Figure 13.2. It's just a single board, usually about three feet wide, with a six-foot length of rope knotted or tied near the ends of the board. To flatten a chunk of crop, you hold the rope handle in your hands, put your leading foot on the stomper, and press down. Then you bring your trailing foot up to just behind the stomper, and take another step with your leading foot, flattening another swatch of grain. And that's all there is to it. Just stomp, step, stomp, step, stomp, until your design is complete.

So how do you use a stomper to make a design? Generally crop formations are made up out of straight lines, circles, and arcs. A pattern usually begins by establishing one or more construction marks to guide your later stomping. For example, to make a circle

Figure 13.2

A stomper for flattening crops.

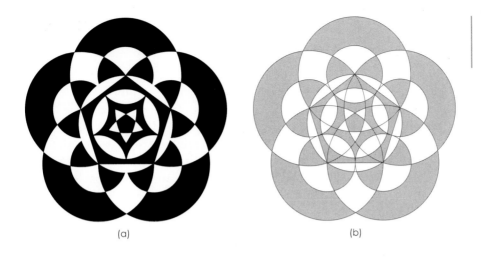

Figure 13.3

(a) An original crop formation. (b) The schematic behind the formation.

(a) (b)

you'd have a friend stand at the center of the circle, holding one end of a piece of string. Facing your friend, you'd pull the string taut and then step sideways, keeping the string pulled tight. You'd push down the stalks under your feet as you walk, eventually creating a thin ring. You could then use the stomper to flatten down the interior of the ring.

Depending on how you choose to flatten the crops inside the circle, the lay of the flattened grain can form concentric circles, a spiral, a woven thatch, or any other pattern you like.

Most designs are made out of very simple geometric elements. A final formation like Figure 13.3(a) can be described by the schematic of Figure 13.3(b). Once all of the construction lines have been laid down, you just stomp down the interiors of the regions that you want filled in.

There's an important caveat here, which affects this technique in practice: *there is no eraser*. You cannot remove your construction lines after you're done. This means it's important to create designs where all of the construction lines are eventually incorporated into the design itself. Any stray or leftover construction lines will show up in the field. Of course, if you like them and feel that they're part of the pattern,

Figure 13.4

(a) We'd like to make these three equal circles. Their centers lie on a straight line. (b) We can make the center circle anywhere. (c) To find the center of circle **A**, simply pull a string of radius 2r from the center of **B** to any point. (d) To find the center of circle **C**, hold one end of a string of length 4r at the center of **A**. Have a friend stand at the center of **B** to make sure it passes through that point. The other end of the taut string is the center of **C**.

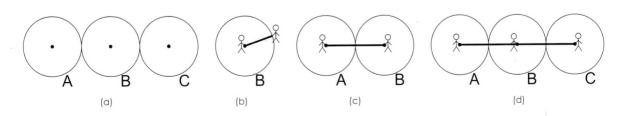

(a) (b) (c) (d)

that's fine, but one traditional mark of a quality construction is that it's "clean," or has no visible artifacts of its construction.

Suppose you want to make a trio of three equal circles in a row, as in Figure 13.4(a). How might you do this? Here's one way. You could create one of the circles just about anywhere, as in Figure 13.4(b). This will be the center circle, marked **B** in the figure. Let's say it has radius r. To make circle **A**, one person stands in the center of **B** holding the surveyor's tape, and another person walks away, keeping the tape taut, until he reaches a distance $2r$. That's the center of circle **A**, as in Figure 13.4(c). To find the center of circle **C**, one person holds one end of the tape standing in the middle of **A**, another person holds it loosely at the center of **B**, and a third person pulls it taut to a distance of $4r$. That's the center of **C**, as shown in Figure 13.4(d).

If you were working on your own, or with just one friend, you could tie down one end of the tape with a post or stake, but you'd want to remember to come back later, not only to retrieve the post, but also to fill in the hole you created. Remember, leave no stray marks.

When the designs get more complicated, developing a precise construction plan becomes critical to successfully making the design without error, particularly given the usual constraints of darkness, not enough time, and not enough people. Finding key points for the centers and ends of arcs and lines has to be efficient and accurate.

The limitations of working in the field create some interesting limits on our designs. In the next section, I'll focus strictly on the pencil-and-paper stage of crop circle design, when we're still indoors, dry, and warm. What makes the process interesting is that we need to always keep in mind our very limited capabilities when we're actually out in the field.

HAWKINS' FIVE THEOREMS

Let's look at some of the design problems related to the geometry of traditional crop formations.

Since photographs of crop circles first started appearing in newspapers and magazines in 1980, people have been assembling archives in their homes, in books, and most recently on the Web. Several of the sites in the Further Reading section offer huge galleries of gorgeous photographs of crop circle formations.

One person who was fascinated by the geometric regularity of many crop circles was Gerald Hawkins. Hawkins was a professor of physics and astronomy at Boston University in Massachusetts, publishing a steady stream of technical papers in research journals. In 1961, he traveled with a group of students to Salisbury Plain in England, the site of Stonehenge. Together, they measured every stone, rock, pit, and formation at the site. Upon returning home, Hawkins used an IBM 704 computer to help him analyze the data and look for patterns.

He concluded that Stonehenge was an observatory, designed to predict eclipses, solstices, and other celestial phenomena. He published his argument in a 1963 paper in *Nature* (see the Further Reading section for full citations). The paper created a wave of public interest and made him a famous popular figure. But the paper was met with an almost immediate backlash of objections from archaeologists and astronomers, who rejected both his methodology and his conclusions, claiming he had inflated a few accurate observations of sunrises and sunsets with many hypothetical and unfounded extrapolations. Despite this professional criticism, his ideas resonated with the general public, and today many people still think of Stonehenge as a celestial observatory.

In the late 1980s Hawkins found himself fascinated by crop circle formations. Working from published photos, he measured the radii of the circles, the distances between them, the lengths and angles of the lines, and everything else that seemed measurable. As he did with Stonehenge, he then hunted through the data, looking for patterns.

Of course, he must have known that there were plenty of patterns to be found, because simply by looking at most of the formations of the day, it's clear that they are based on regular polygons. But he had a hunch that there was something more profound to be discovered.

After several months of measuring and searching, he started to find some of the relationships he was looking for. Abstracting the formations into their underlying geometry, he found nice whole-number ratios between various measures. This excited him because these ratios (such as 2:1 and 4:3) are also the ratios between notes in a well-tempered major musical scale. Feeling that he was onto something, Hawkins organized his observations as five "theorems."

I'll present these theorems in detail below, but the story behind them is very interesting, so I'll stick with the narrative for now.

After Hawkins finished describing the geometry of several formations to his satisfaction, but before he shared his ideas with anyone, two strange things started to happen.

The first is that Hawkins started suggesting that at least some of the people who were making new designs had knowledge of his theorems and were using them actively to design their formations. The implication seemed to be that they must have independently discovered his theorems, because otherwise they would have been

Figure 13.5

The schematic of a formation in Guildford, England, which Hawkins asserted proved knowledge of his first theorem (after an image in "Geometry in English Wheat Fields").

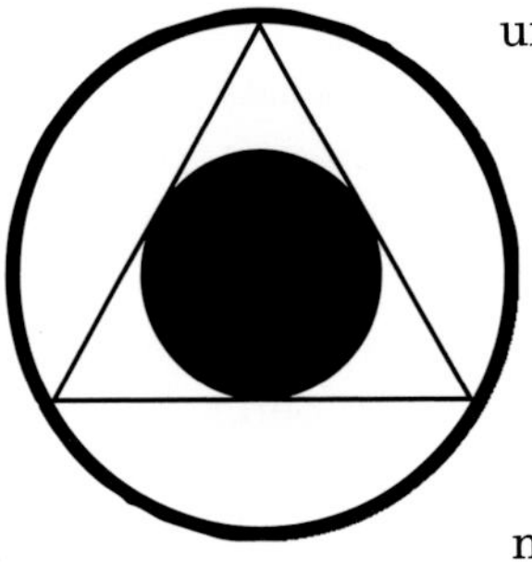

unable to produce those particular formations. As a prime example he pointed to a formation in Guildford, England (shown in Figure 13.5). The strange thing is that Hawkins claimed that these formations actually *proved* that the designers knew about his theorems and were using them actively.

Of course, the pattern in Figure 13.5 proves nothing. Anyone could draw this design simply by drawing an equilateral triangle, and then setting the size of a compass by eye to draw inscribed and circumscribed circles. If you chose to actually compute the radii of those circles, you could easily do it with standard first-year trigonometry. The design of Figure 13.5 could indeed have been made with Hawkins' First Theorem, as he asserted, but it could just as easily have been designed with a computer-aided drafting program, a ruler and a compass, or a beer mug, a silver dollar, and the side of a square coaster. Despite this, Hawkins asserted in a 1992 article in *Science News* that the people who made this design "had to know a tremendous lot of old-fashioned geometry."

The second strange thing took the form of a public challenge. That same 1992 article described his first four theorems and alluded to a fifth. The article said that Hawkins was "inviting anyone interested to come up with the theorem itself before trying to prove it." We'll discuss the "Fifth Theorem" below, but there's nowhere near enough information in the article to have any idea what that fifth theorem could be. Asking people to come up with the theorem is like an author challenging his audience to discover the plot of his next novel, and then summarize it; there's just not enough information available to get started on the problem.

Nevertheless, the mysterious "Fifth Theorem" started to take on a life of its own among cerealogists, where it began to be seen as a piece of secret information communicated to Hawkins by extraterrestrials. Hawkins couldn't publish the theorem, the story went, because it was either too complex for people to understand, or because the information was too dangerous for humans to know at our current stage of evolution. Hawkins was keeping it a secret for the good of mankind, holding it back until our species was ready for it.

The fires of this story were fanned when the *Mathematics Teacher* published a one-page article on Hawkins' theorems. The article was only six paragraphs long, with an equal number of references, but it offered a summary of his Five Theorems. Theorems I–IV are pretty straightforward, and we'll see them below. But as with the *Science News* account, the article only said that Theorem V was a generalization of Theorems II, III, and IV, without adding any more details. It concluded by saying, "If you create theorem V and prove it by Euclidean methods, send two copies to the *Mathematics Teacher*." Again, there was little chance of that happening given the information in the article.

The longer these two challenges remained unanswered, the larger the myth of "Theorem V" became. All sorts of improbable ideas began to get associated with the power of this presumably vital geometric relationship. Perhaps, some speculated, it held the clues for world peace, nuclear fusion, or even time travel.

Fifth Theorem fever got another boost in 1996, when *Science News* ran a follow-up article on Hawkins' Theorems. This article contained a couple of figures that were described as relating to the now-legendary Theorem V. The article also presented a photograph of a formation found in the field that led Hawkins to assert, "the crop-circle makers . . . showed knowledge of this fifth theorem." The implication was that someone had answered his challenge and presented their proof to him by creating the formation. Figure 13.6 shows this design. Once again, this formation doesn't prove or "show knowledge" of anything; it's simply a nice pattern that could be produced by anyone handy with a compass and ruler.

Figure 13.6

A formation which Hawkins asserted proved knowledge of his fifth theorem (after an image in "Crop Circles: Theorems in Wheat Fields").

In 1998, a company identified as Boston University Research took out a quarter-page advertisement in the *Mathematics Teacher*. The advertisement, which didn't name an author (but which was presumably written by Hawkins), reiterated the challenge and contained the following cryptic remark: "This 'Fifth Theorem' is of unusual interest in mathematics teaching because of its changing shape, which can be shown by computer graphics." I found the reference to "computer graphics" intriguing, but I couldn't figure out what the "changing shape" might be. The article provided a schematic drawing labeled "V," but again, provided no information describing the fabled "Fifth Theorem."

Hawkins died at the age of 75 on May 26, 2003. As far as I could tell after exhaustive searching online, and extensive help from a University of Washington research librarian, Hawkins never published his Fifth Theorem. However, we found an old copy of an unattributed homework handout on the web (which has since disappeared) that mentioned Hawkins' Fifth Theorem in passing, but in enough context that it became easy to see what it was all about. Once you know what it is, it seems that Hawkins was playing a game with his audience,

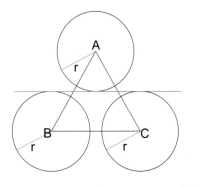

Figure 13.7

The setup for Hawkins' First Theorem. Three circles of radius r are centered on the vertices of an equilateral triangle $\triangle ABC$. Their radius r is chosen so that all three circles share a common horizontal tangent, shown in blue.

Figure 13.8

The geometry of Hawkins' First Theorem. (a) The 30-60-90 triangle formed by the right side of the equilateral triangle. (b) The 30-60-90 triangle in the lower right of the equilateral triangle. The circumcircle **H** has radius $2h/3 = 4r/3$. (c) The circle **G** drawn from the center of one vertex of the triangle through the other two vertices has radius $2h/\sqrt{3} = 4r/\sqrt{3}$.

giving them just enough information to let their speculation run unchecked, while withholding enough information to make sure that nobody could answer his challenge.

Now that we know the history behind Hawkins' five theorems, let's actually look at them. It won't surprise you that given their storied past, each time these theorems appeared in print, they were described in a different way, sometimes with typographic or other errors. They also have been illustrated with different figures, some of which are utterly at odds with each other. For such simple geometrical statements, this confusing wealth of contradictory and incomplete detail is maddening.

For the sake of clarity, I'll present them here with a single consistent form. I also won't try to prove them as rigorous "theorems," since I think they fit much more in the class of "observations." I'll provide proofs that are only as rigorous as necessary to be convincing.

Hawkins Theorem I

Theorem I: *Place three circles of equal radii at the corners of an equilateral triangle, and choose their radius r so that they share a common tangent. Draw a circle **G** centered on a vertex of the triangle and passing through the other two vertices. (a) The radius of the circumcircle **H** of the equilateral triangle is $4r/3$. (b) The radius of circle **G** is $4r/\sqrt{3}$.*

Let's start with the drawing in Figure 13.7. Each of the three circles has radius r, they sit on the corners of an equilateral triangle $\triangle ABC$, and they share a common horizontal tangent. The height of the triangle is thus $2r$.

To prove part (a), in Figure 13.8(a) I've extracted the right side of the equilateral triangle, which is a 30-60-90 triangle with a long leg of length $h = 2r$; thus the short leg of the triangle is $h/\sqrt{3}$, and the

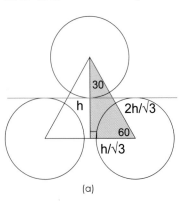

(a)

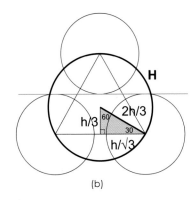

(b)

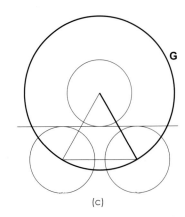

(c)

hypotenuse is $2h/\sqrt{3}$. In Figure 13.8(b) I've drawn another 30-60-90 triangle, finding that the distance from the triangle's center to one vertex is $2h/3 = 4r/3$. That proves part (a).

To prove part (b), in Figure 13.8(c) I've drawn the required circle **G**. We know that its radius is the length of one side of the triangle, which we know from the last step is $2h/\sqrt{3} = 4r/\sqrt{3}$, as claimed.

We can generalize this idea and find the radius r of the little circles that share a common tangent for any regular polygon of n sides, which for convenience in the rest of this chapter I'll simply call a regular n-gon, or just an n-gon. Figure 13.9(a) shows three sequential vertices of a regular n-gon, along with the circles and their common tangent. Figure 13.9(b) shows this triangle for several different values of n.

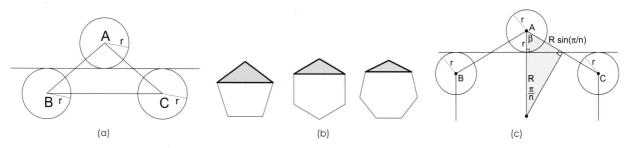

(a)   (b)   (c)

To find the radius r, look at Figure 13.9(c). We'll say the n-gon has a radius R from the center to any vertex. I've drawn a right triangle from the center to a vertex and the midpoint of a side. The angle of the triangle at the polygon's center is $2\pi/2n = \pi/n$. Thus $\beta = \pi - (\pi/2) - (\pi/n) = \pi(n - 2)/2n$, and the short leg of the triangle is $R\sin(\pi/n)$. If we now consider the top part of the gold triangle, we can build another little right triangle, from which we can see $r = R\sin(\pi/n)\cos(\beta)$. To find the value of r for any n-gon, we only need to plug a value for n into this formula. For example, when $n = 3$, $r = 3R/4$; when $n = 4$, $r = R/2$; and when $n = 6$, $r = R/4$.

Hawkins Theorem II

Before we get to Theorem II, let's find a useful relationship. Take any regular n-gon, and draw the smallest circle that encloses it (the circumcircle) and the biggest circle that fits inside (the incircle), as shown in Figure 13.10. What's the ratio of the areas of these two circles?

Figure 13.11(a) shows the general idea. The circumcircle is centered at the center of the polygon and passes through all of its vertices.

Figure 13.9

Generalizing Hawkins' First Theorem for a regular n-gon. (a) Three points of the n-gon with three equal circles that share a common horizontal tangent. (b) That triangle for three different n-gons. (c) The geometry for finding the radius r of the small circles.

Figure 13.10

The circumcircle (red) and the incircle (blue) for a triangle, pentagon, and octagon.

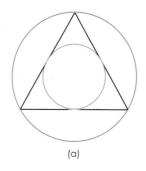

(a)

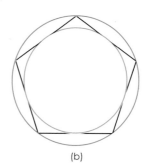

(b)

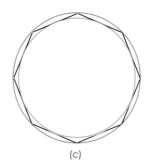

(c)

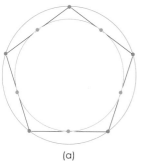

(a)

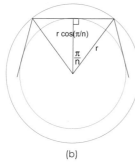

(b)

Figure 13.11

(a) In a regular n-gon, the circumcircle passes through the vertices, while the incircle passes through the midpoints of the edges. (b) The distance from the center of the n-gon to the center of an edge is $r\cos(\pi/n)$.

The incircle is also centered at the center of the polygon, but it passes through the midpoints of the edges.

Figure 13.11(b) shows the triangles formed by one side of the n-gon and the center. Since the n-gon spans 2π radians and it has n sides, each side spans $2\pi/n$ radians. Half of that, as shown in the figure, is π/n. This gives us the triangle as shown, showing that the distance to the center of the midpoint is $r\cos(\pi/n)$.

So the radius of the circumcircle is just r, and the radius of the incircle is $r\cos(\pi/n)$. The ratio of their areas is thus

$$\frac{\pi r^2}{\pi[r\cos(\pi/n)]^2} = \frac{\pi r^2}{\pi r^2[\cos(\pi/n)]^2} = \frac{1}{\cos^2(\pi/n)}.$$

Okay, we're now set to dig into Theorem II:

Theorem II: *The ratio of the area of the circumcircle and incircle of an equilateral triangle is 4.*

This is easy enough; just plug $n = 3$ into our formula:

$$\frac{1}{\cos^2(\pi/3)} = \frac{1}{(1/2)^2} = 4.$$

Hawkins Theorem III

Theorem III: *The ratio of the area of the circumcircle and incircleof a square is 2.*

Plug $n = 4$ into our formula:

$$\frac{1}{\cos^2(\pi/3)} = \frac{1}{(1/2)^2} = 4.$$

Hawkins Theorem IV

Theorem IV: *The ratio of the area of the circumcircle and incircle of a regular hexagon is 4/3.*

You know the drill:

$$\frac{1}{\cos^2(\pi/6)} = \frac{1}{(\sqrt{3}/2)^2} = 4/3 \ .$$

Hawkins Theorem V

And now (drumroll, please), the legendary fifth theorem!

Theorem V: *Given any triangle inscribed in a circle of radius r, the perpendicular distance from the circle's center to any side of the triangle is $r\,|\cos(\theta)|$, where θ is the angle opposite the side.*

The geometry here is shown in Figure 13.12(a). We have a triangle $\triangle UVW$ inscribed in a circle with center C and radius r (the point W is chosen so that it does not lie on the minor, or shorter, arc connecting U and V). I've placed point M at the intersection of UV and the line perpendicular to UV that passes through C. As instructed, I've labeled the angle opposite side UV at point W with θ. I've marked the distance $d = |CM|$. The theorem says $d = r\cos(\theta)$. Let's prove it.

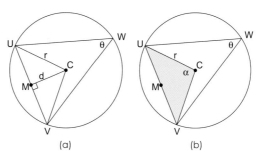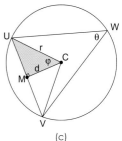

(a)   (b)   (c)

This is really easy if we remember the Inscribed Angle Theorem from basic geometry. It says that in a circle, any inscribed angle is half of the corresponding central angle. Figure 13.13 shows this for a circle with center C, and three points U, V, and W, where W is not on the minor arc between U and V. The central angle formed by the arc UV is angle $\alpha = UCV$, while the inscribed angle is $\theta = UWV$. For any points U, V, and W chosen in this way, angle UCV will always be double that of UWV. You can find proofs of the Inscribed Angle Theorem in any basic geometry text, as well as on many websites.

Figure 13.12

(a) The setup for Hawkins' Fifth Theorem. The points U and V sit on a circle centered at C with radius r. Point W is also on the circle, but not on the minor arc between U and V. The angle at W is θ. Point M is at the intersection of UV and the line perpendicular to it that passes through C. The distance $d = |CM|$. (b) The central angle $\alpha = UCV$. (c) The angle α is twice the angle $\varphi = UCM$.

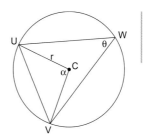

Figure 13.13

The Inscribed Angle Theorem. Angle $\theta = UWV$ is half of $\alpha = UCV$.

Crop Art

With this in our pocket, we can draw Figure 13.12(b) and (c). In part (b), I'll mark angle UCV as α, and in part (c), I'll mark the angle UCM as φ.

Now that we've got everything labeled, we can prove this theorem just by looking at the picture! The Inscribed Angle Theorem tells us that angle $\alpha = UCV = 2\theta$, so $\alpha/2 = \theta$. From symmetry, we see $\varphi = \alpha/2 = \theta$, so $d = r\cos(\varphi) = r\cos(\theta)$, as claimed.

Figure 13.14

A pentagon and a non-agon in black, and their stellations shown in color.

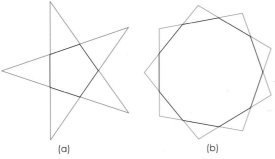

(a)   (b)

You'll notice that the theorem uses an absolute-value sign around $\cos(\theta)$. You can see the reason for that if you draw the triangle so that $\theta > \pi/2$; the absolute-value sign is just a way to save us from having to write the theorem in two cases.

OTHER USEFUL GEOMETRY

The interesting Hawkins Theorems are the first and the last ones. They can actually help us design interesting structures to flatten with our stompers.

Following in that spirit, I'd like to offer a few more useful design relationships of my own.

Stellate

Figure 13.15

The geometry for stellating a regular n-gon.

Suppose you have a regular n-gon and you'd like to put points on each side, as in Figure 13.14. The points are found by extending neighboring pairs of sides until they meet.

To find the point at the tip of each star, look at Figure 13.15. Here I've drawn a regular n-gon with $n = 5$ and radius R. From the green triangle, we can simply read off $s = R\sin(\pi/n)$. The third angle in the green triangle is β, which is what's left from the π radians in every triangle after we remove the right angle and the angle of π/n at the origin: $\beta = \pi - (\pi/2) - (\pi/n) = \pi(n - 2)/2n$.

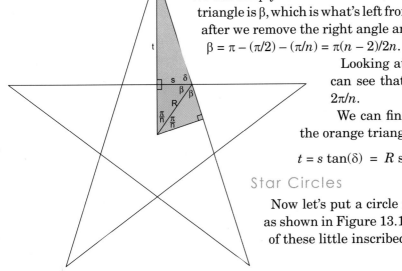

Looking at all three colored triangles, we can see that $\beta + \beta + \delta = \pi$, so $\delta = \pi - 2\beta = 2\pi/n$.

We can find the length of the long side of the orange triangle from $\tan(\delta) = t/s$, so

$$t = s\tan(\delta) = R\sin(\pi/n)\tan(2\pi/n).$$

Star Circles

Now let's put a circle into each point of Figure 13.14, as shown in Figure 13.16. Our goal is to find the radius of these little inscribed circles.

Figure 13.17 shows the geometry. Let's start with the green triangle. As before, $\beta = \pi(n-2)/2n$. Moving to the pink triangle, we can see that this also has a right angle and an angle of π/n, like the green triangle, so the remaining angle (the one touching the center of the circle) must also be β. We can see that $\tan(\pi/n) = h/R$, so $h = R\tan(\pi/n)$.

We're almost there. From all three triangles, we see that $\alpha = \pi - (\pi/2) - \beta = \pi/n$. Thus

$$r = h\sin(\alpha) = R\tan(\pi/n)\sin(\pi/n).$$

Finding the center of the circle only requires following a line from the center of the n-gon through the midpoint of its edge, and then moving a distance r beyond that point.

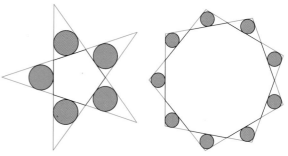

Figure 13.16

Star circles for a pentagon and a nonagon.

Figure 13.17

The geometry for star circles.

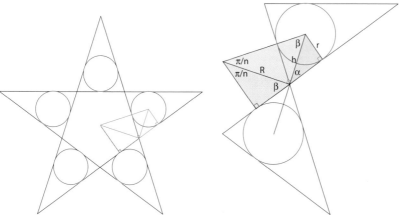

Twist Circles

Let's come up with another pattern from circles and regular n-gons. Suppose we take an n-gon, copy it, and give it a twist and a scale so that the midpoints of the new version are lined up with the vertices of the old one? Figure 13.18 shows the idea. Then we can put little circles into the newly-formed triangles. What's their radius?

Figure 13.19(a) shows the two polygons, and a couple of right triangles that will be useful to us. The radius R is the distance from the common center of the polygons to any vertex of the inner polygon. As before, the angle from the center to a vertex and a neighboring midpoint is π/n.

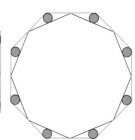
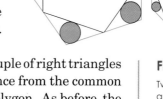

Figure 13.18

Twist circles for a pentagon and a nonagon.

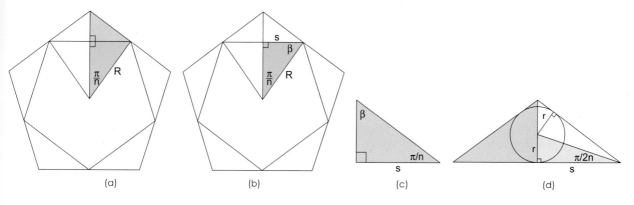

| (a) | (b) | (c) | (d) |

Figure 13.19

The geometry for twist circles. (a) Two triangles formed by the center of a pentagon, the midpoint of one edge, and one vertex. (b) The triangle from part (a) corresponding to the inscribed pentagon. (c) The upper triangle from (a). (d) The triangle at the top of (a), with its inscribed circle.

Let's look first at the lower triangle, isolated in Figure 13.19(b). We can see that half the length of a side of the inner polygon is $s = R \sin(\pi/n)$. And as before, we know that the third angle is $\beta = \pi(n - 2)/2n$. Let's now look at the upper triangle, isolated in Figure 13.19(c). We know that the interior angle of a regular n-gon is $\pi(n - 2)/n$, so the angle at the top of this triangle is half of that, or $\pi(n - 2)/2n$, which is β. Since the other angle is a right angle, the remaining angle must be π/n. The blue and gold triangles are similar!

In Figure 13.19(d) I've placed two of these gold triangles back-to-back, so they fill in the gap between the two polygons in part (a). I've drawn in the circle that we want to inscribe in this triangle, and labeled its radius r. You can see that the line from one of the lower vertices of the triangle to the center of the circle creates two identical triangles. Since the angle π/n is bisected, the angle at the narrow tip of the triangle is $\pi/2n$. From the yellow triangle we can read off the relationship $\tan(\pi/2n) = r/s$. Solving for r, we find

$$r = s \tan(\pi/2n) = R \sin(\pi/n) \tan(\pi/2n).$$

Whew! But now it's easy to draw the circle: we just walk along a line from the center to the midpoint of any edge of the inner polygon, continue for a distance r, and then draw a circle of radius r.

Figure 13.20

To draw an ellipse, put down two pegs and tie a piece of string to them. Pull the string taut and move your pen.

ELLIPSES

Today's crop formations are mostly composed of straight lines and circular arcs. This makes good sense: these shapes are easy to make with string and posts.

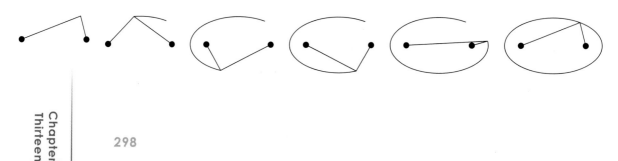

Figure 13.21

(a) The angle θ gives us the rotation of the ellipse. (b) The geometry of an ellipse. (c) The geometry for converting between the circlemaker's description and the geometer's description.

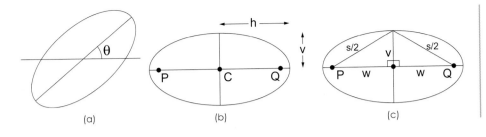

But there's at least one other shape that's almost as easy to make, yet I've rarely seen any in the hundreds of photos of crop circles that I looked at while working on this project: the ellipse.

You may recall that you can draw an ellipse with two pegs and a piece of string (now doesn't that sound appealing for crop circles?). Just put down the pegs, tie the string to each one, pull it taut, put the pen at the tip of the of the pulled string, and start to move it around the pegs, as in Figure 13.20. By the time you get back to the starting point, you'll have drawn an ellipse.

This is just about a perfect crop circle technique. The two pegs, or foci, can be either posts in the ground or friends holding ends of a piece of string. Facing them, and keeping the line taut, you simply walk sideways until you've made a complete circuit, creating the outline of the ellipse as you go.

There are two popular ways to describe the shape of a given ellipse. The form we've just seen, which I call the *circlemaker's ellipse*, can be written (P, Q, s), specifying the locations of the pegs at points P and Q, and the length of string s. The other form of the ellipse, which I'll call the *geometer's ellipse*, is written (h, v, C, θ), where h and v refer to the half-width and half-height of the ellipse, C is the center point, and θ is the counter-clockwise angle by which the ellipse is rotated. These parameters are shown in Figure 13.21.

How do we convert from one to the other?

Here's how to go from the circlemaker's parameters to the geometer's parameters:

1. Find $\theta = \text{atan2}(Q_y - P_y, Q_x - P_x)$.
2. Find $C = (P + Q)/2$.
3. Find $w = |P - Q|/2$. This is the distance $|CP| = |CQ|$.
4. Find h. The following steps don't depend on orientation, so for convenience I'll use the ellipse aligned with the axes in Figure 13.21(b). If we draw the string of length s taut along

Figure 13.22

An original design based on ellipses.

Crop Art

the +X-axis, then it will extend $(h - w)$ to the right of Q and $w + h$ to the right of P. Point $Q = (w, 0)$ and $P = (-w, 0)$. So adding these together, $(h - w) + (h + w) = 2h$.
Thus $s = 2h$, or $h = s/2$.

5. In Figure 13.21(c), when the string is taut at $+Y$, we have two equal triangles. From either one, and using $h = s/2$,
$v = \sqrt{(h^2 - w^2)}$.

6. Our ellipse is (h, v, C, θ).

In Step 1, I used the function atan2(y, x), which is the standard math library function for computing the arctangent of y/x in the correct quadrant (that is, making sure the result has the right sign). To go the other way, we use this procedure:

1. From above, $s = 2h$.
2. Also from above, $w = \sqrt{(h^2 - v^2)}$.
3. Compute vector $\mathbf{M} = w(\cos(\theta), \sin(\theta))$.
4. Find $P = C - \mathbf{M}$, $Q = C + \mathbf{M}$.
5. Our ellipse is (P, Q, s).

Figure 13.22 shows a formation that I'd like to make that's based on a simple arrangement of ellipses.

Another beautiful formation could be based on the five mutually intersecting ellipses discovered by Branko Grünbaum for representing a five-element Venn diagram, as discussed in Chapter 7. Figure 13.23 shows a potential crop formation based on that pattern.

RECONSTRUCTION

Now that we've looked at some of the basic geometric tools behind crop circles, let's think about designing formations that we can actually build in the field.

As I discussed earlier, the challenge is to find designs that are amenable to construction in a field of grain, in the dark of night, with only primitive tools. The old ruler-and-compass constructions of the ancient Greeks are a good starting point. You can mine catalogs of constructions (like the book in the Further Reading section) for tons of ideas and ready-made geometric constructions to realize them.

As I discussed before, in the field you can't erase your construction marks. So if you cook up a design that requires you to draw a bunch of

Figure 13.23

An ellipse-based design inspired by the five-Venn elliptical diagram by Branko Grünbaum.

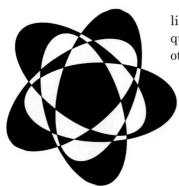

Figure 13.24

We're given a circle center A and radius A_r, and asked to draw another circle with center B and a radius that makes it tangent to the far edge of the circle at A. Determining the radius of this circle is easy on paper, but hard in the field.

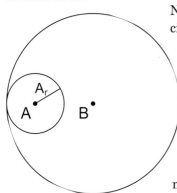

lines and arcs in order to simply locate a point to be used later, you're going to be in trouble because those lines and arcs will be visible in the final image. I find that if I draw my constructions in ink (rather than pencil), it gives me a good idea of what marks I've made so far, and how to incorporate them into the final design.

There are some other compass-and-ruler techniques that are harder to carry out in the field than on paper. For example, we might have a diagram like Figure 13.24, where we have a circle centered at point A and a nearby point B, and we want to create a new circle that is centered at B but is tangent to the far side of the circle centered at point A. Using hand tools on a paper design, we can easily adjust our compass to the right radius by eye and then draw the new circle. But this would be very difficult to do in the field, because when you're out there in the grain, it can be hard to know just where to stand to find that point of tangency. And as you walked around to locate that point, you would certainly leave marks behind.

If you have a design that calls for this kind of step during the paper construction, it's important to work out an efficient, alternative method with which to locate the key points in the field.

One nice aspect of working out the design on paper first is that you can find quantitative measures for all sorts of things and then use those measures in the field. For example, if we want to make a design that incorporates the twist circles of Figure 13.18, we can work out the geometry beforehand and march into the field armed with knowledge of the radius r already computed and in our plans.

Of course, one of the best ways to learn how to do something is to reverse-engineer high-quality examples that other people have created. Zef Damen has created dozens of careful ruler-and-compass style constructions based on actual formations in the field. He starts with photographs, measures them, and then ultimately checks his reconstruction by overlaying it on the original photo (see the Further Reading section for a pointer to his site).

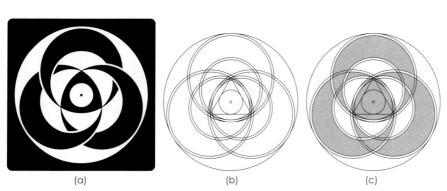

(a)   (b)   (c)

Figure 13.25

(a) The "Folly Barn 2001" formation. (b) The schematic of the formation. (c) The schematic and formation overlaid.

Crop Art

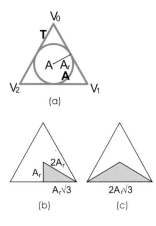

Figure 13.26

Step 1 in the "Folly Barn 2001" construction. (a) Draw circle **A** and its circumscribed triangle **T**. (b) The geometry of the 30-60-90 triangle in the lower-right corner of the triangle **T**. It has radius $2A_r$. (c) The geometry of the bottom of the triangle **T**; it has a side length of $2A_r\sqrt{3}$.

To get the flavor for how large formations get created, let's work through a reconstruction. I've chosen the "Folly Barn 2001" construction, shown in Figure 13.25(a), because I think it's beautiful, elegant, and about the right level of complexity for us here (crop circles are typically named for the location and year in which they're found). Of course, we can find simpler formations on the crop circle sites, as well as many that are far more complex. I'll paraphrase Mr. Damen's analysis here, changing it a bit to make it simpler and easier to follow.

Our goal is to build the schematic diagram of Figure 13.25(b), which contains all the edges of the darkened regions that we'll flatten with our stompers, as well as the equilateral triangle that's at the heart of the pattern.

We're going to draw a lot of circles in this section. I'll refer to circles in boldface. A circle named **G** will have a center at point G and a radius G_r. Many of the steps involve drawing three similar circles. For convenience, I'll refer to individual circles with a subscript, such as $\mathbf{G}_0$ and $\mathbf{G}_1$, which are centered at points G_0 and G_1 respectively. They both have the same radius, G_r. If I want to refer to all of the **G** circles at once, I'll use the subscript i, so G_i refers to the group of all of the **G**-type circles. I'll also write the triangle **T** in boldface, but there will only be that one triangle in the discussion.

1. We'll start with a circle **A** of radius A_r centered at the origin (so $A = (0, 0)$) and circumscribe an equilateral triangle **T** around it, as in Figure 13.26(a). We can see from the triangles in Figure 13.26(b) and (c) that the distance from the center of the circle to any vertex of the triangle is $2A_r$ and the length of a side of the triangle is $2A_r\sqrt{3}$.

2. Draw circles $\mathbf{B}_0$, $\mathbf{B}_1$ and $\mathbf{B}_2$, each from one vertex of **T** through the other two, as in Figure 13.27. Notice that we're starting out with a construction similar to Hawkins' Theorem I. Since we know the length of the side of the triangle from Step 1, $B_r = 2A_r\sqrt{3}$.

Figure 13.27

Step 2 in the "Folly Barn 2001" construction. (a) The circle $\mathbf{B}_0$ is centered at vertex V_0 and passes through the other two vertices. (b) Circles $\mathbf{B}_1$ and $\mathbf{B}_2$. (c) The diagram after Step 2 is complete.

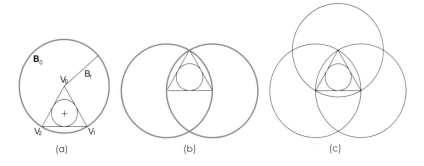

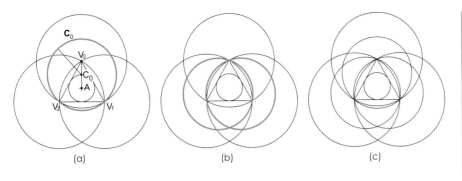

(a) (b) (c)

Figure 13.28

Step 3 in the "Folly Barn 2001" construction. (a) Circle C_0 is centered at the point of intersection of circle **A** and the line from the center of circle **A** to vertex V_0. The circle's radius is set so that it passes through the farther two vertices. (b) Circles C_1 and C_2. (c) The diagram after Step 3 is complete.

3. Locate point C_0 at the top of circle **A**, as in Figure 13.28(a). You can find this point by drawing a line from the center of circle **A** to vertex V_0 of triangle **T** and noting where it crosses circle **A**. The coordinates of this point are $C_0 = (0, A_r)$. We want to draw a circle C_0 centered at point C_0 that passes through each of the other vertices of the triangle **T**. Consider the vertex V_1 in the bottom-right. As we know from Figure 13.26(b), its coordinates are $V_1 = (A_r\sqrt{3}, -A_r)$. Therefore the distance between these two points is

$$
\begin{aligned}
|C_0 V_0| &= \sqrt{[(0 - A_r\sqrt{3})^2 + (A_r - (-A_r))^2]} \\
&= \sqrt{(3A_r^2 + 4A_r^2)} = \sqrt{(7A_r^2)} \\
&= A_r\sqrt{7}.
\end{aligned}
$$

Figure 13.29

Step 4 in the "Folly Barn 2001" construction. (a) Circle D_0 is centered at V_0 and has a radius so that it's tangent to the bottom of C_0. (b) The point W is the point of common tangency of D_0 and C_0. (c) Circles D_1 and D_2. (d) The diagram after Step 4 is complete.

So our new circle C_0 has center C_0 and radius $A_r\sqrt{7}$. Now repeat this for the other two vertices, creating circles C_1 and C_2 by drawing a line from the point A to each vertex, locating where it crosses circle **A**, and drawing a circle of radius $A_r\sqrt{7}$, as in Figure 13.28(b). We have found that $C_r = A_r\sqrt{7}$.

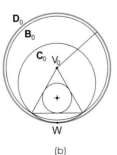
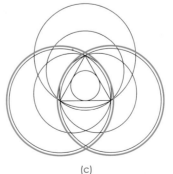
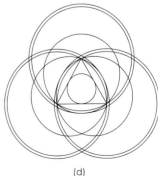

(a) (b) (c) (d)

4. We'll now draw three new circles $\mathbf{D}_0, \mathbf{D}_1$, and $\mathbf{D}_2$ on the same centers as the circles $\mathbf{B}_i$, but with a radius so that they're tangent to the circles $\mathbf{C}_i$ that we drew in Step 3, as in Figure 13.29(a). To find the radius of these circles, consider Figure 13.29(b), where I'm showing circles $\mathbf{B}_0$ and $\mathbf{C}_0$ involved in constructing $\mathbf{D}_0$. Circle $\mathbf{B}_0$ is centered at vertex $V_0 = \mathbf{B}_0 \, (0, 2A_r)$. The point at the bottom of the circle $\mathbf{C}_0$ is labeled W.

Since C_0 is centered at $C_0 = (0, A_r)$ and has radius C_r, to find W we start at the origin, move up A_r units, and then move down C_r units; so, $W = (0, A_r - C_r) = (0, A_r \, (1 - \sqrt{7}))$. Thus the distance between W and B_0 is

$$
\begin{aligned}
|WB_0| &= \sqrt{[(0-0)^2 + (2A_r - A_r(1 - \sqrt{7}))^2]} \\
&= 2A_r - A_r + A_r\sqrt{7} = A_r(1 + \sqrt{7}).
\end{aligned}
$$

So our three circles $\mathbf{D}_i$, shown in Figure 13.29(d), are centered at the vertices of triangle $\mathbf{T}$ (just like circles $\mathbf{B}_i$) and have a radius $D_r = A_r(1 + \sqrt{7})$.

This step shows an example of the sort of process I mentioned before, where what's easy on paper is hard in the field. Imagine carrying out this step during construction. It's two o'clock in the morning, you're tired and thirsty, you're in a dark field, and your pants are soaked from the dew that has rubbed off the grain. Your legs ache from stomping, and you're walking around in the dark, trying to find the point of tangency with the circle you made in Step 2. Once you think you've found it, your friend moves to the center of the circle from Step 3 (here's hoping you remembered to mark it with something that hasn't moved or gotten lost or knocked over), you measure off the tape, your friend moves to point B_0, and then you draw the circle. Life is so very much easier when you can simply move to point B_0, grab the tape at the right length (which we just computed above), and march away.

5. Now we'll draw a circle $\mathbf{E}$ from the center of the formation with a radius that makes it tangent to the circles we drew in Step 4. Again, finding the radius of this circle now will save time in the field. As we can see from Figure 13.30, the radius is

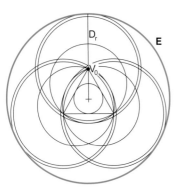

Figure 13.30

Step 5 in the "Folly Barn 2001" construction. The circle **E** is centered at the center of circle **A**, and is tangent to the outer edge of circle **D**$_0$.

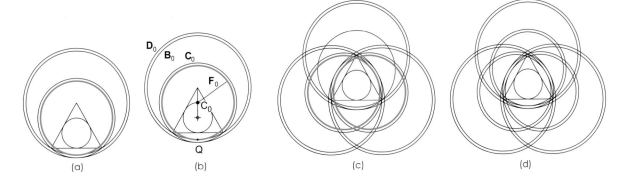

simply the distance from the center to vertex V_0, which we know is $2A_r$, plus the radius of circle D_0, which we know is

$D_r = A_r(1 + \sqrt{7})$.

Thus $E_r = 2A_r + D_r = A_r(3 + \sqrt{7})$.

6. It's time to draw our last set of three circles! These circles, which I'll call F_i, will be centered on the same points as the circles C_i, but will have a slightly smaller radius. Figure 13.31(a) shows the idea. As shown in Figure 13.31(b), we want to find the radius of a circle centered at point $C_0 = (0, A_r)$ that is tangent to circle B_0. Recall that $B_0 = (0, 2A_r)$. The point Q that we want to just touch is found by going up to the center of B_0, and then down by the radius B_r, so $Q = (0, 2A_r - B_r)$. The distance between them is

$$
\begin{aligned}
|C_0Q| &= \sqrt{[(0 - 0)^2 + (A_r - (2A_r - B_r))^2]} \\
&= A_r - (2A_r - B_r) = B_r - A_r \\
&= 2A_r\sqrt{3} - A_r = A_r(2\sqrt{3} - 1).
\end{aligned}
$$

As shown in Figure 13.31(c), we can simply move to the centers of circles C and draw circles with radius

$F_r = |C_0 Q| = A_r(2\sqrt{3} - 1)$

7. We're just about done, but we need to account for the little circle G that's at the center. Its diameter is equal to the gap between circles from the last step, so its radius is half that: $G_r = (C_r - F_r)/2$. Figure 13.32 shows this final circle added in.

Figure 13.31

Step 6 in the "Folly Barn 2001" construction. (a) The circle F_0. (b) F_0 is centered at C_0, and has a radius that makes it tangent to the bottom of circle B_0 at the point Q. (c) Circles F_1 and F_2. (d) The diagram after Step 6 is complete.

Figure 13.32

Step 7 in the "Folly Barn 2001" construction. The little circle G in the center.

Figure 13.33

If we lay down all the marks of Figure 13.32 in the field, we'll end up cutting through regions that should be left untouched.

We're finished! Our construction in Figure 13.32 matches the schematic in Figure 13.25. If we wanted to go out and make this figure, we'd pick a value for A_r, and then we would write down numerical lengths for every radius involved.

In this process I followed Zef Damen's philosophy of determining everything using strictly geometric information. But we could have taken a number of shortcuts if we weren't feeling so pure. For example, several steps involved computing concentric circles of slightly different radii, like circles C_0 and F_0. We could have simply said at the outset that the gap between these two circles should be, say, two feet. Then when we'd found the larger circle in the field, we could just shorten up the tape by two feet and draw the next one. It would also make our calculations easier on paper.

Notice that although I've been talking about marking out complete circles, in this case you wouldn't want to do that. If you stepped through all of the circles we created here in the field, you'd end up cutting extraneous circular arcs through areas that you'd rather were left as solid pieces, as Figure 13.33 shows. While working in the field, you need to keep in mind where you need to stop marking your construction lines and err on the conservative side. When the basic pieces of the design are in place, you can return to incomplete arcs and finish them off, since you'll now know where to stop.

CROP

If you look at a lot of crop circle formations, you'll see many of the same underlying geometric ideas appearing over and over. This isn't surprising, because as we've seen, many crop circles can be built with string-and-peg techniques.

Many formations are built on the skeleton of a regular polygon, just as Figure 13.32 was built on an equilateral triangle. Circles are defined by a center and a radius, which are often derived, as we saw above, from the distances between two points. Similarly, straight lines in a formation are of course simply drawn between two known points.

After looking at a large number of crop circle photographs and working through many of Zef Damen's excellent reconstructions, I started to think about creating a symbolic shorthand notation that could capture these lengthy geometric constructions.

Such a notation would have three advantages. First, it would be compact and easy to read, which in itself would be helpful for understanding the structure of these formations. Second, it would make it easier to design new patterns. Third, the notation could be

Figure 13.34

The *Crop* version of the "Folly Barn 2001" formation shown in Figure 13.25.

```
[ V0 < 3.46 3.64 > circle ] # 3 2 ngonloop
[ V0 < 2.46 2.64 > circle ] # 3 1 ngonloop
# < 1 5.64 0.09 > circle
```

parsed to create diagrams, as well as specific, step-by-step instructions for forming the figure in the field.

We're all used to online map sites that print out directions. Obviously they haven't been programmed with explicit information for how to travel from every point on the map to every other point. Instead, they use their general knowledge of the streets to create a route, and then print out turn-by-turn instructions for getting from your starting point to your destination.

Similarly, a parsable crop circle notation could be used to create step-by-step instructions for creating the formation.

To achieve these goals, I've come up with a language that I call *Crop*. The design of *Crop* is simple, and its goals are modest: to represent crop circle formations efficiently in a form that can be parsed into construction steps. It is most certainly not a general-purpose programming language!

To give you the basic idea, Figure 13.34 gives the *Crop* code for the "Folly Barn 2001" formation shown in Figure 13.25. Although this is very short, it captures the entire geometry we just spent so long building! When I hand this little snippet of text to my *Crop* interpreter, it produces the PostScript drawing of Figure 13.25 (though I don't include the triangle). It can also produce the step-by-step instructions for creating the formation in the field.

Crop uses a postfix syntax, like my *AWL* language described in Chapter 5. If you're unfamiliar with postfix (also called reverse Polish notation), you may want to review the discussion there. To quickly summarize, consider the traditional infix expression (3+5)*2. Here the 3, 5, and 2 are *operands*, and the + and * are *operators*. We write this in postfix by naming the operands first, and then the operators, as either 3 5 + 2 * or 2 3 5 + *. Both of these versions compute the same thing as the infix version. Postfix languages often make use of an idea called the *stack*: operands are pushed onto the stack when they're named and popped off by operators.

You can define variables within *Crop*, just as in any other language. The collection of all the variables that exist at any given time, along with their values, is called the *dictionary*. Initially the dictionary starts off empty, but there are a few special variables that get computed for you on the fly when you need them, as I'll discuss later.

There are three distinct types of objects in *Crop*: *scalars* (floating-point or integer numbers), *points* (represented by pairs of numbers), and *objects* (circles, ellipses, and polygons). In the following discussion, I'll identify variables using the letters s, p, or o to designate their type (I'll also use i to refer to scalars that must be integers). I'll usually include something after the type letter (a number or another letter) to distinguish it from the others or to suggest its meaning (e.g., I'll usually write sr for a scalar that defines a radius). After each example operation, I'll show an arrow and then the type of the result pushed back onto the stack. If nothing gets pushed back, I'll mark that with a ∅.

Crop is written in plaintext, with tokens separated by white space. Any string of characters bounded by white space that doesn't have a predefined meaning is simply pushed on the stack as that string of characters. Anywhere a single space would do, you can insert as many spaces, tabs, carriage returns, or other white space that you want in order to improve legibility.

The language is case-insensitive for all commands (so, for example, makepoint, makePoint, and MAKEPOINT all do the same thing), but it's case sensitive for variable names (so bob, BoB, and Bob are all distinct variables).

Let's start with the basic mathematical operations for calculating with scalars:

> s1 s2 + → s
> Push the sum s1+s2 onto the stack.

> s1 s2 - → s
> Push the difference s1-s2 onto the stack.

> s1 s2 * → s
> Push the product s1*s2 onto the stack.

> s1 s2 / → s
> Push the ratio s1/s2 onto the stack.

Points are obviously important for describing formations. We create a point by naming two scalars and then bundling them together with makePoint:

> s1 s2 makePoint → p
> Create the point (s1, s2) and push it onto the stack.

There's a shortcut for the special point (0, 0), called the *origin*. You can use the symbol # any time to represent the origin (this is meant to remind us of the center of a coordinate system; I'd have used the plus sign, but that was taken!).

We can add and subtract points, and multiply and divide them by scalars:

    p1 p2 p+ → p
Add the components together and push the new point onto the stack.

    p1 p2 p- → p
Subtract the components and push the difference onto the stack.

    s1 p1 p* → p
Scale the components and push the scaled point onto the stack.

    s1 p1 p/ → p
Divide the components and push the scaled point onto the stack.

Note that the operators here are all prefixed with the letter p, giving us for example p+ instead of simply +. In computer science terms, the + operator is not overloaded (that is, built so that it works differently for different types of operands). If you try to add two points with +, rather than p+, you'll get an error. I think that for this little language, there's value to explicitly distinguishing these operators.

We can also find the distance between two points:

    p1 p2 distance → s
This pushes the distance |p1-p2| onto the stack.

To name an object so we can use it later, we use the name command. This takes whatever object is on top of the stack (a scalar, point, or object) and assigns it to the given name. You can redefine a name any time by just assigning a new value to it.

    pso varname name

For example, you might say 3.14 pi name to create a scalar value for pi, or p1 p2 p+ 2 / midpoint name to set the variable midpoint to the point between p1 and p2. This makes it easy to refer to the same thing multiple times in your formation without creating it anew each time. You don't need to declare your variables, and they can even change type over the course of the program. Variables take on the value and type of the object they're assigned to, and if they're re-assigned, they adopt the new type as well as the new value.

Okay, that finishes up the foundation. Let's make some geometry! Our three stars of the geometry world are line, circle, and ellipse:

```
< p0 p1 p2 ... pn > line → ∅
```
Draws a line from p0 to p1, then to p2, and so on, to pn. Requires a minimum of two points.

```
p < s1 s2 ... sn > circle → ∅
```
Draws concentric circles centered at p, with radii s1, s2, and so on. Requires at least one radius.

```
pp pq ss ellipse → ∅
```
Draws an ellipse using the points pp and pq as foci, and a string of length ss.

The `line` and `circle` commands use *lists*. A list is just a sequence of values between angle brackets. The angle brackets are necessary, even if the list has just one or two elements. Lists cannot be empty (or else you'd be drawing nothing).

Points are useful objects. *Crop* also supports circles, ellipses, and two types of regular polygons, or *n*-gons. Here are the commands that create circles, ellipses, and polygon objects. Each one creates its associated object and pushes it onto the stack:

```
pc sr makeCircle → o
pp ps ss makeEllipse → o
pc in sr makeNgon → o
pc in sr makeSgon → o
```

A circle is defined by a center and a radius. An ellipse is defined by two points and a length. A polygon is defined by a center, the number of sides, and a radius; the radius is the distance from the center to the first vertex. In an Ngon, the first vertex is located on the X-axis. In an Sgon, the shape is rotated clockwise by π/in radians, so that the midpoint of the last edge lies on the X-axis. Figure 13.35 shows these two shapes.

The next command we'll look at is `trope`, which takes four arguments: two points and two scalars. The name is a contraction of "triangle-rope," which is a way to think of locating points in the field. Suppose that you have two points *A* and *B* and you know you want to find a new point that is a distance *a* and *b* from each point, respectively. You could make this point easy to find in the field by tying the two ends of a rope together. In addition to that, mark two more points (for example, by wrapping a piece of tape around that spot on the

Figure 13.35

(a) The command `# 5 1 makengon` creates an n-sided polygon. The vertices are labeled A–E. The first vertex, A, is on the +X-axis. (b) The command `# 5 1 makesgon` creates a similar polygon, but it's been rotated so that the midpoint of the last edge (EA) is on the +X-axis.

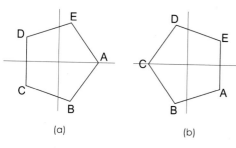

(a)   (b)

rope). Put one mark (call it M_a) a units away from the knot, and put the other mark (call it M_b) b units away from the knot, going in the other direction around the rope.

Now to locate your new point, have one person stand at point A holding the rope at M_a, and have another person stand at B holding the rope at M_b. Now grab the knot and walk away from your friends until the rope is taut, creating a triangle. You've now found your point! There are two possible such points, one on either side of the line AB. You'll want to make sure as you're walking around in the field that you're standing on the correct side of the line for the point you're trying to locate. I call this loop a triangle-rope, so the command that emulates it is trope:

```
pa pb sa sb trope → p
```

Let's see the command in action. Internally, *Crop* draws a circle of radius sa around point pa, and a circle of radius sb around point pb, and tries to intersect them. The result could be that there are no points of intersection, just one (if they happen to be tangent), or two distinct points, as shown in Figure 13.36. If there are no points of intersection between the two circles, the system reports an error and returns the origin point $(0, 0)$. If there's just one point, the system returns that. Otherwise, it imagines a line from pa to pb, and it returns the point that's on the left side of that line, as shown in Figure 13.36(c).

Finding the point of intersection of two circles is straightforward. Figure 13.37 shows the geometry. We can see from the figure that $a^2 = p^2 + h^2$ and $b^2 = q^2 + h^2$. Rewriting these for h^2, we get $h^2 = a^2 - p^2$ and $h^2 = b^2 - q^2$. Since these are both h^2, we have $a^2 - p^2 = b^2 - q^2$. Since $d = p + q$, then $q = d - p$. Substituting this value for q into the last expression and simplifying gives us:

$$
\begin{aligned}
a^2 - p^2 &= b^2 - q^2 \\
&= b^2 - (d - p)^2 \\
&= b^2 - d^2 + 2dp - p^2.
\end{aligned}
$$

Removing p^2 from both sides and solving for p, we find

$$p = (a^2 - b^2 + d^2)/(2d).$$

We can now find the point Q as $Q = A + (p/d)(B - A)$.

To find J, we first compute $h = \sqrt{(a^2 - p^2)}$. Now we make the vector **S** that's perpendicular to AB, so $\mathbf{S} = (-(B_y - A_y), B_x - A_x)$. Normalize **S** to unit length (call it $\hat{\mathbf{S}}$), and now find $J = Q + h\hat{\mathbf{S}}$.

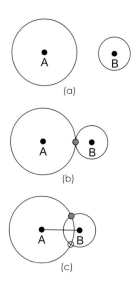

Figure 13.36

(a) No intersections between circles. (b) One intersection between circles. (c) Two intersections between circles. The system returns the point on the left side of the line from A to B.

Another way to find a point with respect to other points is with the pwalk command:

```
o1 p1 sd pwalk → p
```

This command takes an object o1, a starting point p1, and a distance sd to walk clockwise around the perimeter of that object, and returns a new point. Note that the distance is not the straight line between the starting point and the ending point, but instead is the distance as measured along the object itself. If the object is a circle or ellipse, then the point is found by walking along the curve. If the object is a polygon, then we walk along the polygon's edges until we've covered the necessary distance.

As a convenience, before pwalk begins it looks at the starting point, and if it's not already on the perimeter of the object, it moves the starting point temporarily to its closest point on the perimeter of the object. This adjustment does not count towards the distance by which we move the point.

Related to pwalk is pspin:

```
o1 p1 sd pspin → p
```

This command takes an object o1, a starting point p1, and an angle sd about which to rotate that point around the center of the object. This command will move the rotated point to the nearest point on the perimeter of o1 if it's not already on there before pushing it onto the stack.

Many crop formations are built on a structure defined by one or more regular polygons. We've seen above how to define a polygon. Now we'll see how to use a polygon to drive the formation of a structure. In many ways, the next two commands are the heart of *Crop*:

```
[ commands ] pc in sr ngonloop
[ commands ] pc in sr sgonloop
```

Like makeNgon, the values pc in sr define a regular polygon with a center at pc, with in sides, where sr is the distance from the center to each vertex. If you use ngonloop, the first vertex is on the X-axis. If you use sgonloop, the whole shape is rotated so that the last edge midpoint is on the X-axis.

The stuff between the square brackets gets executed in times, once for each vertex in the polygon (remember that a regular polygon of in sides also has exactly in vertices). What makes this loop special is that while a loop is executing, variables beginning with the letter V take on a special meaning: they refer to the vertices of the polygon defined by the command. The system takes the rest of the name of the variable and interprets it as a number (if you use variables in the loop that begin with V but aren't immediately followed by an integer, you'll get an error).

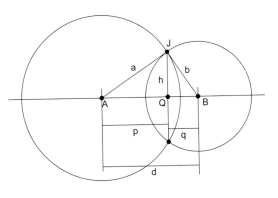

Figure 13.37

The geometry of trope. Circle **A** has center A and radius a. Circle **B** has center B and radius b. The distance between them is d, and they meet at point J. The line perpendicular to AB through J meets the line AB at Q.

The variable V0 has the value of the current vertex (that is, it's a point). The variable V1 is the next vertex clockwise around the polygon, V2 is the one after that, and so on. Variable V-1 is the vertex preceding the current vertex (that is, counter-clockwise from V0), V-2 is the one counter-clockwise from that one, and so on. Note that V-2 is a variable name, not an arithmetic expression (both because *Crop* is not an infix language, and because V-2 has no spaces).

For example, let's suppose that we have the command [...] # 5 1 ngonloop, which creates a pentagon of radius 1, centered at the origin. For this discussion, let's label the vertices *A* through *E*, as in Figure 13.36(a). We'll execute the commands between the brackets five times.

The first time through, any time the variable V0 is encountered, the system treats it as a point with the coordinates of vertex *A*. Similarly, V1 will have the coordinates of vertex *B*, V2 will be vertex *C*, and so on. Even though there are only five vertices, the system supports any vertex number and finds the corresponding vertex using modulo arithmetic. So the first time through the loop, V6 will also have the coordinates of vertex *A*, V-1 will be vertex *E*, V-2 will be *D*, etc. The second time through the loop, everything moves forward one vertex: V0 will have the value of vertex *B*, V1 will be *C*, V-1 will be *A*, and so on. The fifth and last time we execute the loop V0 will have the coordinates of vertex *E*.

Before each pass through the loop begins, the system saves the current stack. When each pass through the loop is finished, the stack is reset to its saved condition.

You can nest loops if you want, for example by putting one ngonloop inside another. The variables V0, V1, V-1, and so on, always refer to the vertices of the polygon defined by the innermost loop in which they appear. If you want to refer to the vertices of the polygon in an outer, or enclosing, loop, append a prime to the variable name. Thus V0′ refers to the polygon one loop up and has the value of the current vertex in that polygon; V1′ takes on the coordinates of the vertex one step clockwise from V0′, and V-1′ refers to the vertex one step counter-clockwise from V0′. If there's yet another loop outside that one, then from the innermost loop we can refer to those outermost vertices as V0′′, V1′′, and so on. You can use as many primes as you need, but if you try to reach upward beyond the outermost loop you'll get an error.

Each nested polygon loop can of course have a unique center, radius, and number of vertices. In fact, a common idiom using nesting is to create smaller polygons at the vertices of a larger polygon. For example, suppose we want to place a small pentagon on each vertex of a big triangle and draw a line from each vertex of each pentagon to the vertex of the triangle it's centered upon. We could write:

```
[[ < V0 V0' > line ] V0 5 1 ngonloop ] # 3 6 ngonloop
```

In the innermost loop, V0 refers to the current vertex of the pentagon, and V0' refers to the current vertex of the triangle.

That's it for the body of the language. There are a few miscellaneous housekeeping commands that are common to most postfix languages:

pop

This command takes no arguments; it just pops the top element off the stack and discards it.

printDictionary

This command takes no arguments; it prints the complete current dictionary to the output.

printStack

This command takes no arguments; it prints the current stack to the output.

// comment

Anything after a pair of double slashes is considered a comment until the end of the line.

Figure 13.38 shows a summary of all of the commands in *Crop*.

The *Crop* description of the "Folly Barn 2001" formation in Figure 13.34 is a lot more compact than the very detailed and lengthy geometric construction we saw in the last section.

Let's walk through the code quickly. The first line defines a loop, so the commands aren't executed immediately. Let's jump to the end of the loop and the polygon command that controls it. That's at the end of the line and reads # 3 2 ngonloop. This tells *Crop* to create a polygon centered at the origin, with three sides (that is, a triangle) and a distance of 2 from the origin to each vertex. For each of these three vertices, we'll execute the commands between the preceding square brackets.

Those commands are actually just one command: V0 < 3.46 3.64 > circle. So *Crop* will draw two concentric circles, with these two

Command	Usage summary	Action
+	s1 s2 + → s	add two scalars
-	s1 s2 - → s	subtract two scalars
*	s1 s2 * → s	multiply two scalars
/	s1 s2 / → s	divide two scalars
makePoint	s1 s2 makepoint → p	create a point object
makeCircle	pc sr makeCircle → o	create a circle object
makeEllise	pp ps ss makeEllipse → o	create an ellipse object
makeNgon	pc in sr makeNgon → o	create an *n*-gon object
makeSgon	pc in sr makeSgon → o	create a *p*-gon object
p+	p1 p2 p+ → p	add two points
p-	p1 p2 p- → p	subtract two points
p*	s1 p1 p* → p	scale a point
p/	s1 p1 p/ → p	divide a point by a scalar
distance	p1 p2 distance → s	compute distance between points
varname	pso varname name	assign variable name to object
line	< p0 p1 p2 ... pn > line → ∅	draw a chain of lines
circle	p < r1 r2 ... rn > circle → ∅	draw concentric circles
ellipse	pp pq ss ellipse → ∅	draw an ellipse
trope	pa pb sa sb trope → p	find a point defined by triangle
pwalk	o1 p1 sd pwalk → p	perimeter walk around object
pspin	o1 p1 sd pspin → p	spin a point and move to object
ngonloop	[commands] pc in sr ngonloop	repeat the commands for each vertex in the polygon, substituting variables starting with V for current vertex
sgonloop	[commands] pc in sr sgonloop	like ngonloop but for a rotated polygon
pop	pop	pop and discard the top of the stack
printDictionary	printDictionary	print the dictionary (for debugging)
printStack	printStack	print the stack (for debugging)
//	// comment	comment to end of line
V	V0, V1, V-1...	coordinates of vertices in closest loop
V'	V0', V1', V-1' ...	vertices in enclosing loops

Figure 13.38

A summary of commands in the *Crop* language.

slightly different radii, both centered at the current vertex of the triangle. The result of this loop is that we've drawn two concentric circles at each vertex.

Line 2 has the same structure, only the triangle has a radius of 1, and the circles are both smaller than those in the last loop.

The third line draws three concentric circles centered at the origin, and that completes this formation.

This wraps up the *Crop* language as it stands today. *Crop* is a completely phenomenological language, designed to match the

(a)

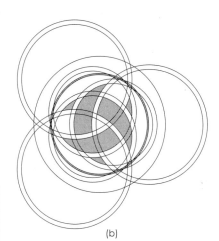

(b)

(d)

Figure 13.39

(a) The "Barbury Castle 1999" formation. (b) The schematic. (c) The *Crop* code. (d) A constructed formation.

```
[ V0 < 2.89 3.21 > circle ] # 3 1 ngonloop
[ V0 < 3.89 4.21 > circle ] # 3 3.6 ngonloop
# < 3.5 3.6 4.8 > circle
```

(c)

(a)

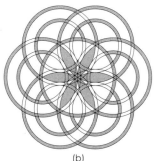

(b)

(d)

Figure 13.40

(a) The "Tegdown Hill 2003" formation. (b) The schematic. (c) The *Crop* code. (d) A constructed formation.

```
1.0 Ar name
1.08565 Br name
0.732051 Cr name
0.646402 Dr name
[ V0 < Ar Br Cr Dr > circle ] # 6 Ar ngonloop
# < Ar Br > circle
```

(c)

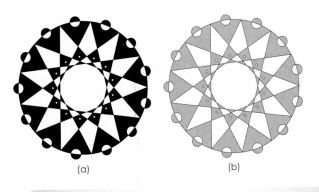

(a)

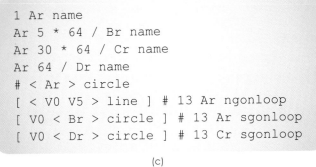

(b)

(d)

```
1 Ar name
Ar 5 * 64 / Br name
Ar 30 * 64 / Cr name
Ar 64 / Dr name
# < Ar > circle
[ < V0 V5 > line ] # 13 Ar ngonloop
[ V0 < Br > circle ] # 13 Ar sgonloop
[ V0 < Dr > circle ] # 13 Cr sgonloop
```

(c)

Figure 13.41

(a) The "West Stowell 2003" formation. (b) The schematic. (c) The *Crop* code. (d) A constructed formation.

(a)

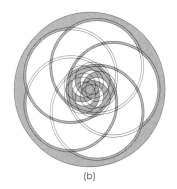

(b)

(d)

```
# < 10.3 > circle
[ V0 < 1.6 > circle ] # 5 1 ngonloop
[ V0 < 2.4 > circle ] # 5 1.3 ngonloop
[ V0 < 6.1 6.4 > circle ] # 5 3.2 ngonloop
```

(c)

Figure 13.42

(a) The "Windmill Hill 2003" formation. (b) The schematic. (c) The *Crop* code. (d) A constructed formation.

Crop Art

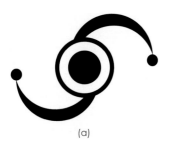

(a)

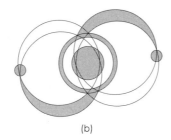

(b)

(d)

Figure 13.43

(a) The "Sompting 2002" formation. (b) The schematic. (c) The *Crop* code. (d) A constructed formation.

```
1.414 Dr name
# < 1 0.866 0.555 > circle
# 1 makecircle CAr name
[
  V0 < Dr > circle
  CAr V0 0.383 pwalk J name
  J < Dr > circle
  J V0 Dr Dr trope P name
  P # distance Pr name
  # Pr makecircle CPr name
  CPr P 0.195 pwalk K name
  K < 0.195 > circle
]
# 2 1 ngonloop
```

(c)

formations that I've looked at and tried to replicate compactly. I've tried hard to keep it as simple and small as possible, while also remaining legible and easy to understand. I encourage readers to extend the language if they think of other commands that are as simple and useful as the ones above.

CROP EXAMPLES

Let's look at some examples of the *Crop* language as applied to formations actually found in the field.

Figures 13.39 through 13.44 show some images of actual crop formations and the *Crop* code that describes them. In several of these

(a)

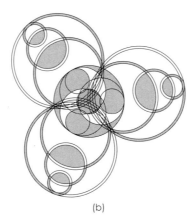

(b)

(d)

```
0.348 r5 name
0.652 r6 name
# < r5 > circle
[
  V0 < r5 > circle
  # V0 38 39 / 13 39 / trope < 73 78 / 78 78 / > circle
  # V0 73 39 / 48 39 / trope < 42 78 / 47 78 / > circle
  # V0 94 39 / 69 39 / trope < 22 78 / 27 78 / > circle
  # V0 56 39 / 31 39 / trope < 98 78 / 103 78 / > circle
]
# 3 r6 ngonloop
[ V0 < r6 > circle ] # 3 r5 ngonloop
# < 1 > circle
```

(c)

Figure 13.44

(a) The "Ivinghoe Beacon 2002" formation. (b) The schematic. (c) The *Crop* code. (d) A constructed formation.

examples, Ar is the radius of the *n*-gon that is at the heart of the design, and the other radii are derived from that either by measuring the observed pattern or by making a small geometric calculation.

These examples are based on formations that were actually created in the field, but they are not photographs of those formations. The many photographs of crop circles that are on the web and in books are all copyrighted works that are owned by their respective photographers, who are naturally protective of their work. The underlying patterns, though, are in the public domain (indeed, they are anonymous!). So for these figures I've used Photoshop to create simulations of these formations. Since I could, and since I thought it would be fun, I used a variety of different media in which to form the patterns.

It's interesting to ponder what these Photoshopped images should be called. Crop formations made by people are described as "fakes," but these aren't even real fakes! Are these images fake fakes?

CASE STUDY

There's an old aphorism that says, "In theory, there's no difference between theory and practice. But in practice, there is. " I decided to put theory into practice and actually create a crop circle.

There was a small problem of timing and location to be overcome first: when I started this project, it was the middle of winter. There simply aren't many crops of mature wheat to stomp down near Seattle in the winter. A friend and I considered a number of possible alternative canvasses, including a flat beach at low tide and a snow-covered frozen lake. Creating a formation in either of these locations in the middle of winter would have been very unpleasant from a creature-comfort point of view.

Of course, we could just find a big flat area somewhere and practice, but I wanted to build a formation using tools and techniques as close as possible to those used in a field of crops.

Then my friend had a brainstorm: he managed a parking structure that needed to be cleaned. A couple of years of grime and dirt had accumulated on the top floor, and it needed to be pressure washed. The high-velocity water that shoots out of the nozzle of the pressure washer would dislodge the dirt, revealing the lighter-colored, clean concrete underneath. We realized that this was a great opportunity: we could create our art and give him a head start on the cleaning of the parking deck.

We scouted the site, walking and measuring. There were several concrete planters that broke up the space, and they each contained trees that blocked the visibility of the parking desk itself. I eventually selected a big area between the planters that was mostly visible from an upper floor of a nearby building.

The next step was to create the design. Three of us would be working on the formation, but we had only one pressure washer, so only one person could actually be blasting away the dirt (our analogy to flattening crops) at a time. We also wanted to get the project done between about 9:00 in the morning and 1:00 in the afternoon. I needed to find a design that would give me good experience with this process, yet not take too much time or precision to create. I decided to make a three-part design. We'd build it in stages and stop when we ran out of time.

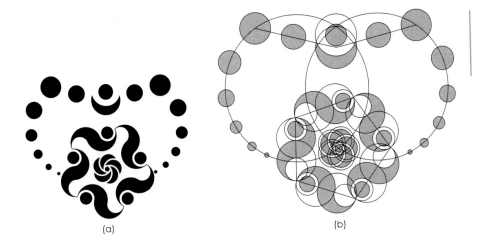

Figure 13.45

(a) The design for my "Seatle 2003" formation. (b) The schematic of the design.

(a)   (b)

```
// make central core of crescents
[ V0 < 25.290 30.708 > circle ]
# 5 18 ngonloop
// make outer swirls
25.108 d1 name
44.251 d2 name
17.576 d3 name
# 5 118 makengon N1 name
[
   N1 V0 d1 pwalk < d1 > circle
   N1 V0 d2 pwalk < d2 > circle
   V0 V1 distance edgelen name
   N1 V0 edgelen d1 - pwalk < d1 > circle
   N1 V0 edgelen d2 - pwalk < d2 > circle
   N1 V0 edgelen d3 - pwalk < d3 > circle
]
# 5 118 ngonloop
```

Figure 13.46

The *Crop* code for the main part of my formation in Figure 13.45.

Figure 13.45(a) shows the three-part design: a ring of nested crescents, surrounded by waves, hung on a necklace of circles. Figure 13.45(b) shows the underlying schematic. Figure 13.46 provides the *Crop* code for this design. I've left off the code for the circles on the necklace because there's nothing interesting about those specifications: it's just a list of `trope` and `circle` commands that locate one circle after another.

Figure 13.47

The One Dot. Our first circle, and the unwashed "canvas" behind it. This is the large circle in the upper left of Figure 13.45. The pressure washer is sitting to the right of the dot.

I made a handout for each of the team members that boiled down the essential geometry and the steps we'd take to create each element of the design.

The day before we were to make the design, we put together our essential supplies: chalk for marking circles and key points (since we didn't have any crops to flatten), cloth surveyor's tape (much easier to manipulate than metal tapes), earplugs (pressure washers are loud!), pens and paper, and miscellaneous additional items (extension cords, drinking water, snacks, etc.).

When we gathered at the site to start working, we were met with a parking lot wet from the previous night, but at least it wasn't raining now. We first made a single test circle (the large circle in the upper left of the necklace) to make sure that the contrast between the washed and unwashed regions would be enough. In the process of clearing the circle, we found that (of course) this was going to take much longer than we had thought. First, the pressure washer's nozzle was only about four inches wide, so each pass of the pressure washer could only clear a stripe of that width. Second, really getting rid of the grime required two and sometimes even three passes with the washer. And finally, getting a nice, sharp edge around the circle meant going very slowly, because the pressure washer was difficult to control with all that water shooting out of it. But we eventually cleared the circle, and looking down on it we felt there was enough contrast that the project was a go. Figure 13.47 shows our view of the one big dot and the unwashed parking deck behind it where our design was going to go.

We returned to the parking deck, broke out the tape and chalk, and started to measure out the skeleton pentagon at the heart of the design.

Drawing the circles turned out to be far more difficult than I had anticipated. One person held the surveyor's tape at the center of the circle, and the other person crawled on hands and knees, holding the chalk tight against the tape, keeping the tape taut, drawing the circle on the ground. Crawling around on concrete is no fun, and we didn't have kneepads or other gear to make it more palatable. Not only is it a surprisingly slow way to work, but it's physically painful on your back to be bent in half and crawling over what quickly start to feel like very large distances.

Necessity gave birth to invention: the chalk-on-a-stick. We simply taped a piece of chalk to one end of a broom handle, and taped the surveyor's tape next to it. Then we were able to simply walk around the circle, pulling against the tape and leaving a line behind. We realized once we'd made this device that surveyors have a tool just like this, complete with a little wheel on the bottom and a self-feeding chalk mechanism. But the jury-rigged version worked great, and we were marking circles much more quickly and with less pain than before.

We marked out all five of the larger circles in the inner part of the design and then started marking the smaller ones. Once we had a couple of these drawn on the ground, it was time to start pressure washing.

Figure 13.48

The author pressure washing the parking deck. Note the very small width of the spray coming out of the nozzle. Because of the glare and the reflections off of the puddles in this image, it's hard to see where the ground has been washed and where it hasn't.

Looking at the maze of lines on the ground of course was confusing, and since there was no opportunity to erase (just like in a field, once we'd washed clean a part of the deck, it was going to stay clean), it was critical that we knew which regions of these overlapping marks should be cleaned and which should be left alone. I took a deep breath and chalked a big squiggle inside each segment that should be cleaned. We fired up the pressure washer, and while one of us slowly blasted away the grime, the other two measured circles. Figure 13.48 shows the job in progress.

Then it started to rain.

Happily, we were all locals, and so we had our rain gear ready. The rain didn't do much to slow down the pressure washing, but it was nearly a showstopper for marking our circles: the rain was washing away many of our chalk marks almost as soon as we drew them. We found that by pressing hard with the chalk, some little bits would get caught in the concrete and would stay where the rain couldn't get at them, leaving just enough visible to see the line. But unfortunately, pressing that hard with our chalk-on-a-stick caused the already soaking-wet tape to lose its grip even faster, and we had to stop and reattach the chalk and the tape every few feet, each time ending up with a slightly more precarious and fragile bond. Our backs and knees were okay, but our layout progress slowed to a crawl.

Another problem with the chalking process was that the pressure washer removed not only the grime it was pointed at, and any chalk immediately under it, but the spray from the washer also eroded nearby chalk marks which were needed for later sections. So whatever chalk had managed not to be washed away by the rain was getting blown away by the pressure washer. We found that we often had to go back and touch up the circles, staying just a few minutes ahead of the person working the pressure washer. We usually tried to blast away

Figure 13.49

A photograph of the completed "Seattle 2003" formation.

the edges of each segment of the design first, and then we could more quickly clear away the dirt inside the regions.

We had intended to stop at about 1:00 P.M., but we had just started on the outer pattern of swirls at that point, and everyone agreed that we wanted to continue. Another friend came to visit us, and as two people went off to retrieve lunch, the other two kept chalking and washing.

Then it started to rain harder.

Now we were trying to make chalk marks on regions of the parking deck that were literally underwater. Sections of the parking deck formed little depressions, or bowls, without drainage, so we were trying to make chalk marks on the bottoms of puddles two or three inches deep. Of course, the chalk simply washed away as soon as it scraped against the ground, and all we achieved was tinting the puddle a delicate shade of yellow. Back on hands and knees, we ground the chalk hard into the concrete just to get a faint smudge of color. This had the side effect of wearing away our chalk supply almost instantly, so what had originally seemed like an embarrassing oversupply of chalk was quickly reduced to a handful of little pebble-sized pieces that we treated like nuggets of precious metals, as we ground them into the concrete with numb fingertips.

Around 4:30 the sun was starting to set, but the rain stopped. We started working ever faster with the pressure washer, now trying to simply get all of the design at least clean enough to be visible. About twenty minutes after sunset, we finally got the last of the swirls completed. Visibility was dropping fast, so we packed up quickly. When we were done, it was too dark to even see the design, so we left the site with no idea of what our work looked like.

A few days later, my friend and I returned to the site with our cameras, and I took the picture in Figure 13.49 as he posed. You can see a region near the back where unevaporated water is still covering up much of one of the white circles; this was completely underwater when we worked on it. Nevertheless, I'm very happy with the result. We managed to make the design I'd drawn without significant errors, it fit in the space, and we all remained friends throughout the process and afterwards. That's a pretty good record for a piece of collaborative art!

In this chapter I've only scratched the surface of the subject of crop circles. Almost every aspect of this phenomenon, from the cultural and social to the practical and geometric, gets more interesting the more you look into it.

And if, like me, you find yourself drawn into making crop art (or something like it) of your own, then it becomes an expressive medium in its own right.

FURTHER READING

There are lots of books available on crop circles if you'd like to investigate the subject further. Virtually all of them contain dozens or even hundreds of color pictures of beautiful crop circle formations. Most advocate some particular point of view on their origin and meaning, and many of these theories are in direct contradiction with each other. If you search for crop circle books, you'll have no trouble turning up a large number of them. I've not read many of them myself, so I'll refrain from recommending any over the others.

I did use two books while working on this project. Some of my historical overview of crop circles was drawn from *Crop Circles* by Werner Anderhub and Hans Peter Roth (Lark Books, New York, 2000). This book also contains a wealth of nice images.

For more practical matters, I learned from the small pamphlet, *A Beginner's Guide to Crop Circle Making*, by Rob Irving, John Lundberg, and Rod Dickinson (Circlemaker's Press, London, 2004).

The story of Gerald Hawkins and his five theorems is a fascinating one, and I gave only the general outlines of it here. You can easily follow up on it and learn more. Hawkins' original paper on Stonehenge that got the ball rolling was "Stonehenge Decoded" by Gerald Hawkins (*Nature*, Vol. 200, 1963, pp. 306–308). His later books on the subject included *Stonehenge Decoded* (Dell Publishing, New York, September 1988) and *Beyond Stonehenge* (HarperRow, New York, 1989). His public connections to crop circles probably started in the 1992 feature article "Off the Beat: Euclids's Crop Circles" by Ivars Peterson (*Science News* 141, February 1992, pp. 76–77 (available online at http://www.gaiaguys.net/Science_News_2.92.htm)). A slightly revised version appeared as "Theorems in English Wheat Fields" by Ivars Peterson (*Science News* 163(26), June 28 2003 (available at http://www.sciencenews.org/articles/20030628/mathtrek.asp)). Follow-up articles were "Geometry in English Wheat Fields" (unattributed, possibly by

H. B. Tunis) (*Mathematics Teacher* 88(9), December 1995, p. 802) and "From Euclid to Ptolemy in English Crop Circles" by Gerald S. Hawkins (*Bulletin of the American Astronomical Society*, Vol. 23, No. 5, p. 1263, 1997). The unattributed advertisement I mentioned in the text is frequently referenced in crop circle literature as a formal publication, but it's clearly labeled "Advertisement." It appears with the title "New Geometry in English Crop Circles" (*Mathematics Teacher*, 91(5), May 1998, p. 441). Another follow-up article was "Crop Circles: Theorems in Wheat Fields" by Ivars Peterson (*Science News*, October 12, 1996 (available online at http://www.gaiaguys.net/ffgeom.htm)). The obituary for Gerald Hawkins published by *The Guardian* is available online at http://www.guardian.co.uk/obituaries/story/0,3604,1004737,00.html.

There are dozens of websites devoted to crop circles. Many of them contain extensive libraries of beautiful color photographs of formations found in the field, as well as discussions of different theories of construction and interpretation. Most sites provide a wealth of links to other sites, so once you get started, it's easy to spend a long time browsing. Some good sites to get a running start into the subject include (in alphabetical order) http://www.bltresearch. com, http://www.circlemakers.org, http://www.cropcircleconnector.com/anasazi/connect.html, http://www.fgk.org, http://www.invisiblecircle. org, http://www.kornkreise.ch, http://www.lovely.clara.net, and http://www.swirlednews.com.

Zef Damen has published many geometric reconstructions of actual formations on his website. He holds to a purist's aesthetic, constructing everything geometrically using a compass and unmarked ruler. His presentations are clear and easy to follow, and I learned a lot by studying them. You can find pointers to many of his reconstructions at http://home.wanadoo.nl/zefdamen/en/Crop_circles_en.htm.

A nice source for some esoteric constructions is the book *Geometric Constructions* by George E. Martin (Springer-Verlag, 1998).

index